Macedonia under the Argead Kings

Macedonia under the Argead Kings

The Rise and Fall of an Ancient Superpower

IAN WORTHINGTON

OXFORD
UNIVERSITY PRESS

OXFORD
UNIVERSITY PRESS

Oxford University Press is a department of the University of Oxford. It furthers the University's objective of excellence in research, scholarship, and education by publishing worldwide. Oxford is a registered trade mark of Oxford University Press in the UK and in certain other countries.

Published in the United States of America by Oxford University Press
198 Madison Avenue, New York, NY 10016, United States of America.

Library of Congress Cataloging-in-Publication Data
Names: Worthington, Ian author
Title: Macedonia under the Argead kings : the rise and fall of an ancient superpower / Ian Worthington.
Description: New York, NY : Oxford University Press, [2026] |
Includes bibliographical references.
Identifiers: LCCN 2025049513 | ISBN 9780197667972 hardback |
ISBN 9780197667996 epub
Subjects: LCSH: Macedonia—History—To 168 B.C. | Macedonia—Kings and rulers |
Greece—History—Macedonian Expansion, 359-323 B.C.
Classification: LCC DF261.M2 W67 2026 | DDC 938/.1—dc23/eng/20260330
LC record available at https://lccn.loc.gov/2025049513

DOI: 10.1093/9780197668009.001.0001

Printed by Marquis Book Printing, Canada

The manufacturer's authorized representative in the EU for product safety is Oxford University Press España S.A. of Parque Empresarial San Fernando de Henares, Avenida de Castilla, 2 – 28830 Madrid (www.oup.es/en or product.safety@oup.com). OUP España S.A. also acts as importer into Spain of products made by the manufacturer.

FSC
www.fsc.org
MIX
Paper | Supporting responsible forestry
FSC® C103567

Contents

Preface

This book is a history of ancient Macedonia under the Argead dynasty, from the mid-seventh century to the late fourth century, and its remarkable rise from a small tribal area at that time to a fourth-century imperial power under Philip II and especially Alexander the Great and then its dramatic collapse following Alexander's death. It is not surprising that Philip and Alexander are credited with making Macedonia one of the more remarkable success stories of antiquity and that what happened before and after them is often sidelined by their center-stage position in Macedonian history. But how did the kingdom come into being? How did previous kings serve Macedonia and deal with the various hostile peoples on its borders, the Greeks to its south and even the Persians to its east, and overcome internal disunity and frequent dynastic upheaval?

The reigns of the Argead kings before Philip and Alexander vary between success and failure, with several victims of assassination. All too often this earlier period is regarded as weak and uninspiring. That is wrong. We need to consider is Macedonia's continuous history even into the Hellenistic period (323–30) rather than dividing it into three, as is often the case: before Philip and Alexander; Philip and Alexander; from Alexander to the Roman conquest in the first century. When we do, as is the thesis of this book, we see that Macedonia's earlier history was not a continuum of decline but rather a series of rises and falls, with a steep rise under Philip and Alexander and then a final fall, bringing with it the end of the Argead dynasty in 310. Moreover, analogies to the rises and falls of the succeeding dynasty, the Antigonid, throughout the Hellenistic era also play a role in our evaluation of the Argead kings.

The result is a re-examination of one of the most important kingdoms of the ancient world to show that there is much more to Macedonia than just Philip II and Alexander the Great.

I have several people to thank for their help and support in the writing of this book: First and foremost, all the staff at Oxford University Press and especially—and always—Stefan Vranka for his interest in the proposal and comments, patience, and advice throughout.

I am also indebted to several friends and colleagues who read drafts of the book and improved it in countless ways: Carol King, Joseph Roisman, and Miroslav Vasilev. Also, Vasiliki Saripanidi was a godsend, especially for the second chapter, in which I could mention her in virtually every note: I hope my thanks here are enough. Of course, any remaining blunders are my own.

My thanks go also to the publisher's anonymous referee for his sharp suggestions and for liking much of what he or she read.

I am also grateful to Sarah Plant for compiling the index in her usual exemplary manner and putting up with me again.

Finally, I must extend the customary appreciation to my family, Tracy, Oliver, and Rosie, who do their own things and leave me be to do mine until they need something. I was made redundant along with several respected and influential colleagues at the end of 2025 so my family may see more of me now.

Ian Worthington

Macquarie University
December 2025

Figures

Abbreviations

BNJ	*Brill's New Jacoby* (*Jacoby Online*), numerous ancient writers prepared by modern scholars, editor-in-chief Ian Worthington (Leiden: 2003–)
IG	*Inscriptiones Graecae*, many volumes with various editors (Berlin: 1873–)
Liddel	P. Liddel, *Decrees of Fourth-Century Athens (403/2–322/1 BC)*, 2 vols. (Cambridge: 2020)
Meiggs-Lewis	R. Meiggs and D.M. Lewis (eds.), *A Selection of Greek Historical Inscriptions*[2] (Oxford: 1988)
Rhodes-Osborne	P.J. Rhodes and R. Osborne (eds.), *Greek Historical Inscriptions, 404–323 BC* (Oxford: 2003)
SEG	*Supplementum Epigraphicum Graecum*, many volumes with various editors (Leiden: 1923–)
SIG[3]	W. Dittenberger (ed.), *Sylloge Inscriptionum Graecarum*, 4 vols. (Leipizg: 1915–24)
Tod	M.N. Tod (ed.), *A Selection of Greek Historical Inscriptions*, 2 vols. (Oxford: 1946–48)

Maps

Map 1 Macedonia, Greece, and the Balkans
Source: Worthington 2016, map 2.

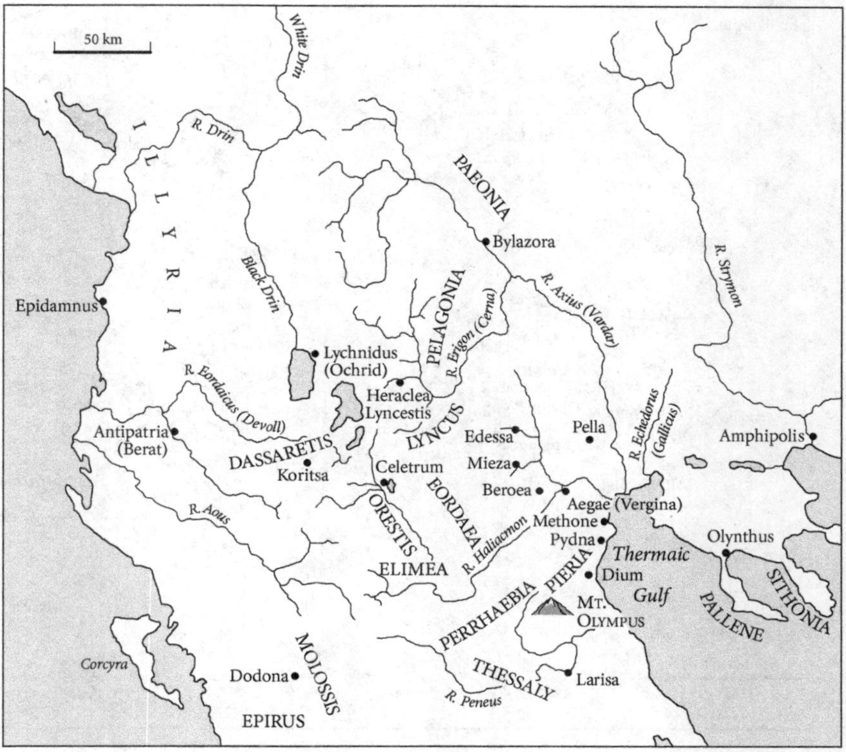

Map 2 Macedonia and neighbors
Source: Worthington 2021, map 2.

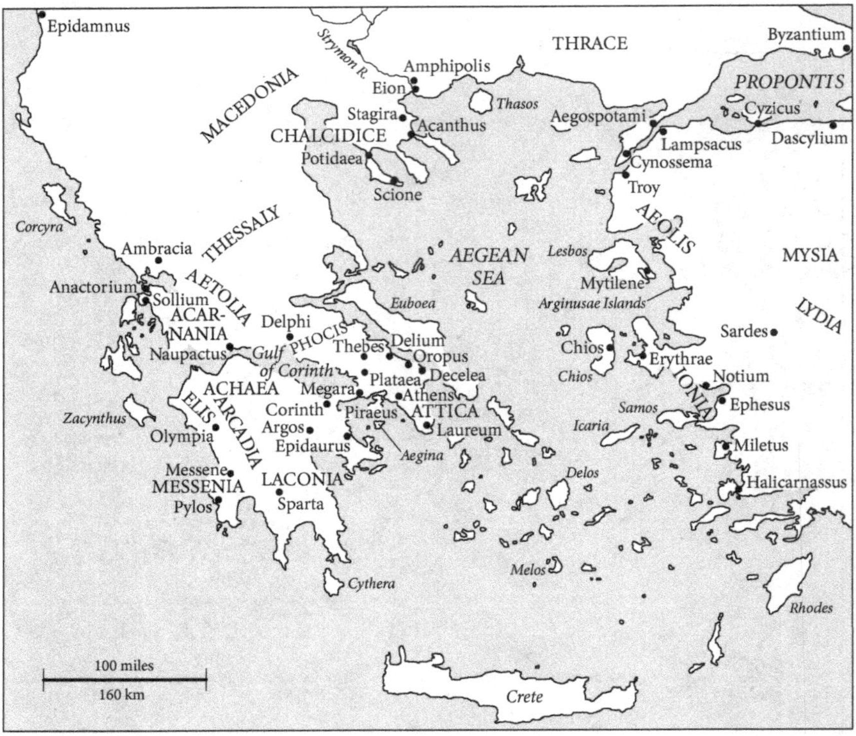

Map 3 Greece and the Aegean

Source: Worthington 2021, map 5.

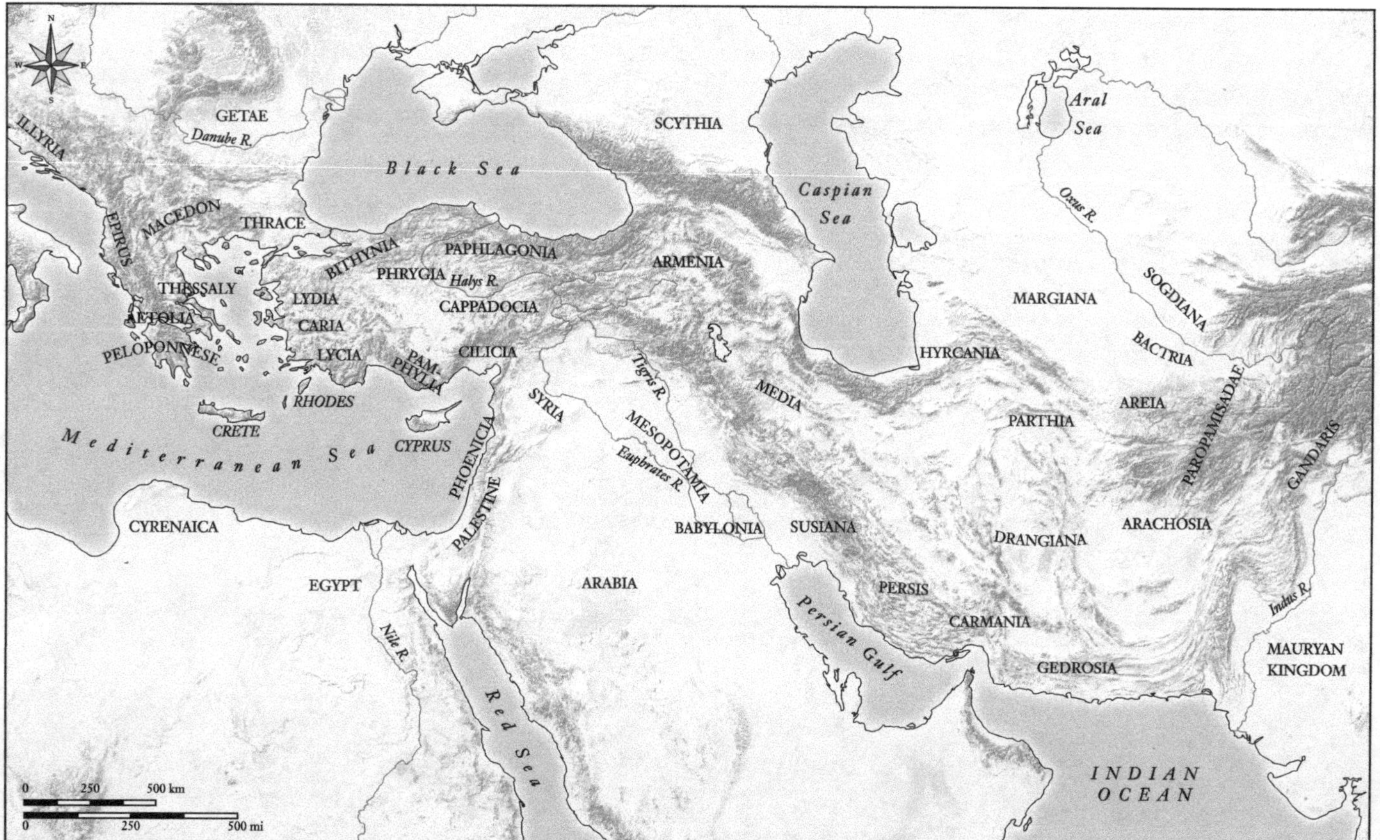

Map 4 Alexander the Great's empire

Source: Worthington 2016, map 1.

Introduction

More Than Just Alexander the Great

Ancient Macedonia is often synonymous with Alexander the Great (r. 336–323). His spectacular conquests in Asia, from toppling the Persian Empire in hard-fought battles and sieges to sailing down the Indus River, brought about a Macedonian Empire stretching for thousands of miles that for a time was without equal in antiquity. Even more astonishing was that he was only 20 when he became king and not quite 33 when he died in Babylon in 323. He was a legend in his own time, and he is still a force with which to be reckoned in modern popular culture as interest in him shows no sign of waning.

Coming in a close second to Alexander's fame is his father, Philip II (r. 359–336). He raised Macedonia to superpower status in the ancient world, imposing his kingdom's hegemony over Greece and the eastern Balkans, fashioning a professional army that was the most successful and feared before the rise of Rome, and devising plans for invading the Persian Empire, which Alexander inherited on his father's assassination. Philip's legacy enabled Alexander to do what he did.

It is therefore not surprising that Philip and Alexander are the "center of gravity" of ancient Macedonia, as one scholar remarks in a recent book on Macedonia.[1] But what was Macedonia like before Philip and Alexander, and how did previous kings serve and expand their kingdoms and influence their successors? If Philip and Alexander represent the heyday of Macedonian power, how did the kingdom come into being and deal with the various peoples on its borders, the Greeks to its south, and even the Persians to its east, and eventually boast an empire from Greece to India?

The answers to these questions are not easy. The kingdom was often plagued by internal disunity, frequent dynastic upheaval, regicide, incursions by enemy peoples including the Greeks, and what seems to have been a second-rate army. This gloomy picture is perhaps aptly summed up by

[1] Hatzopoulos 2020 and see the review by Arnhold 2021.

one scholar's remark: "The history of Macedonia from the death of Alexander I in about 454 to the death of Perdiccas III in 360/59 is a story of decline, blurred by the poor quality of the evidence."[2]

This is certainly true of the literary evidence, of which only some is contemporaneous with the reigns of certain kings and the rest is much later (and, as with the case of Alexander the Great, for example, drawing on works now lost to us). All in all it is often sporadic, one-sided, opaque, hostile, and even mythical, not to mention biased against the Macedonians because their authors are Greeks who have different perspectives on what the Macedonians were like.[3]

Some writers, like Herodotus and Thucydides, our principal sources for earlier Argead history, are contemporaneous—Herodotus with Alexander I and Thucydides with Perdiccas II—and both historians may have visited Macedonia. Alexander I may have personally told Herodotus about the dynasty's Greek origins or even of his participation in the Olympic Games, knowing Herodotus would broadcast that news.[4] But Herodotus was less concerned with other kings or events in Macedonia once we move past Alexander I, and what he does tell us is always from the Greek perspective.

Thucydides followed Herodotus in many respects when it came to the lineage of the earlier kings but focuses almost entirely on Perdiccas II with scattered mentions about Archelaus, and his account is also suspect.[5] The historian provides a lengthy—and controversial—account of the various stages by which the Macedonian state came into being, but whether it is in geographical or chronological order is disputed.[6] Thus, Herodotus and Thucydides had the means and opportunity to provide detailed narratives of Macedonia up to their time, but they leave us in the dark as they were interested in other things.

Then we have non-historical writers like Plato, whose dialogue *Gorgias* has a truly damning attack on Archelaus' character and the bloodthirsty way he took the throne.[7] Yet the philosophical nature of the work as well as chronological issues make us question what Plato has to say about this king.

[2] Roisman 2010, p. 145.

[3] On this, see for example, Asirvatham 2008; Asirvatham 2010a; Asirvatham 2017. On sources see, for example, Müller 2016, pp. 41–84; cf. Lane Fox 2011b, pp. 210–215 (390s to 360s).

[4] Origins: Herodotus 8.137–139; games: Herodotus 5.22. Alexander and Herodotus: Hammond and Griffith 1979, pp. 98–99; contra Scaife 1989; Badian 1994.

[5] Origins: Thucydides 2.99.3; Perdiccas II: 2.95–101; Archelaus: 2.100.2. See Badian 1993 for a critique.

[6] Thucydides 2.99.2–6.

[7] Plato, *Gorgias* 471d.

Several of our literary authors were at work in the Hellenistic and Roman eras, so centuries after the events in question.[8] Prominent among these are Diodorus Siculus (of Sicily), who in late republican Rome wrote a *Universal History* from mythical times to Caesar's campaigns in Gaul of 54. He used several earlier sources but is not always reliable when it comes to chronology and telescoping events, and there seems to be a doublet in his account of Amyntas III's reign that misrepresents the kingdom's stability and security.[9]

Another issue is that as the Roman era continued, a literary trend developed known as the "Second Sophistic," from the mid-first century to the mid-third century AD. One of its principal writers was the second-century AD biographer Plutarch of Chaeronea, who wrote a collection of "'parallel lives" of influential Greeks and Romans to the end of the Roman Republic. Plutarch was a biographer; hence factual accuracy or unromantic details were not as important to him as sensationalism, gossip, and the morality of his subjects. Moreover, in the Roman period there was a dwindling interest in the Argead kings before Alexander the Great, including Philip II, which also contributed to making earlier periods a dark age.[10]

The literary evidence for Philip II and Alexander the Great is more plentiful because of their roles in the establishment of a Macedonian Empire and control of Greece, even though all narrative writers lived centuries after their reigns. A note about sources on them may be found at the start of chapter 9 on Philip and chapter 11 on Alexander.

The literary sources we have raise more questions than they answer. For example, was the first king really a Greek named Perdiccas (I) who traveled from Argos in the Peloponnese to Macedonia (hence the dynasty was named the Argead) and founded the first capital, Aegae? When Persian envoys demanded King Amyntas I bow to Persian rule, did his young son Alexander (I) pack his father off to bed and dress up men as courtesans to murder the drunken Persians at a banquet? Did Alexander I compete at the Olympic Games—at which only Greeks could participate—when the other competitors called him a "barbarian"? Several kings who we know of were polygamists, but what problems did sons from different mothers cause for succession? Why did regicide become common after Archelaus, and how

[8] See Hammond and Griffith 1979, pp. 31–39, on Hellenistic authors and Asirvatham 2017 for Romans. On Diodorus generally, cf. Stylianou 1998, pp. 1–25.

[9] Diodorus 14.92.3–4 and 15.19.2–3. This is discussed in chapter 7, including views that the two passages are distinct ones.

[10] Cf. Asirvatham 2010b on Philip.

did he rescue Macedonia from some sort of oblivion, if we believe Thucydides' laudatory comments about him?[11] And within 40 years of his death Macedonia was in crisis, with threats to its border security, a devastated army, and an economic slump. What had gone wrong?

Fortunately, frustrations with the paucity of literary sources are tempered by more plentiful archaeological evidence. Excavations of settlements and especially cemeteries with their grave goods of varying quality and expense show changes in wealth, social standing, gender roles, religious beliefs, and even the sociopolitical structures of the kingdom, as we shall see throughout this book.[12] Coinage of various kings and inscriptions such as treaties also feature throughout the book, although the former does not start until Alexander I and the latter are not plentiful. They provide us with a valuable insight into a ruler's monetary policy and the economic state of his kingdom as well as his interstate affairs.[13] Although such evidence often cannot tell us what happened or why, archaeological finds enable us to make reasonably informed deductions, and without them we would be in the dark about many aspects of Macedonian society, religion, culture, and daily life.

The point quoted above, about earlier Argead Macedonia being a kingdom in decline, is shared by most historians. But this view is more questionable because of archaeological evidence, especially grave goods as mentioned above, which counters a view of economic decline in the early fifth century and even suggests the introduction of a narrower, richer elite. True, the reigns of the earlier Argead kings vary between success and dismal failure; several were victims of assassination, and the kingdom was often faced with dynastic and security crises. But what we need to consider is Macedonia's continuous history even into the Hellenistic period (323–30) rather than simply dividing it into three, as is often the case: before Philip and Alexander; Philip and Alexander; from Alexander to Rome. When we do consider it, we see that Macedonia's earlier history was not a continuum of decline but rather a more subtle rise and fall, then greater rise and fall, an even greater rise until

[11] Thucydides 2.100.2.

[12] A good starting point for archaeological evidence is the chapters on individual sites in Lane Fox 2011a; Palagia 2017; cf. Saatsoglou-Paliadeli 1999. More exhaustive, though at times controversial, are the analyses of grave goods (especially vases and funerary kits from 20 sites and what they tell us about society) by Saripanidi 2017; Saripanidi 2019a; Salminem 2023—for gender roles, see also Saripanidi 2020; Salminem 2023; cf. Kottaridi 2011a.

[13] Likewise, good starting points for the numismatic evidence are the valuable discussions of Raymond 1953; Poulios 1993; Price 1974; Greenwalt 1994b; Dahmen 2010; Kremydi 2011; Heinrichs 2017; cf. Hammond and Griffith 1979, pp. 69–91 and 104–115.

Philip and Alexander, and then a final fall, bringing with it the end of the Argead dynasty with the murder of Alexander IV in 310.

Moreover, the rises and falls of the succeeding dynasty, the Antigonid, throughout the Hellenistic era until the Roman conquest in the first century play a role in our evaluation of the Argead kings. While this book is concerned with the Macedonia's first ruling dynasty, the Argead, we will survey the Antigonid kings in the final chapter's conclusion. Those kings are often part of the story of Rome's rise in the Mediterranean and the Near East, but that does not do them justice. As I argued in a previous book, when we divorce them from the shadow of Roman expansion and consider them on their own merits, we see that they generally benefited Macedonia and strove to protect the kingdom no matter the odds.[14] Likewise, the Argead kings are often subsumed within outside factors, such as the Persian and Peloponnesian Wars, or their interactions with the Greeks or neighboring tribes like the Illyrians and Thracians. When brought out from these shadows, as is the aim of this book, we see their importance in the kingdom's development and their influence on one another.

Macedonia's history should not be set into the three blocks of before Philip II, Philip and Alexander, and after Alexander, but considered from start to finish. Its rise from a small tribal area to a fourth-century imperial power is one of the more remarkable success stories of antiquity—as indeed is the story of its later military defiance of the juggernaut that was Rome.

All translations are from Loeb Classical Library editions except where indicated.

All dates and references to centuries are BC except where indicated.

Macedonia under the Argead Kings: The Rise and Fall of an Ancient Superpower. Ian Worthington, Oxford University Press. © Oxford University Press 2026. DOI: 10.1093/9780197668009.003.0001

14 See Worthington 2023.

1
Macedonia

Macedonia in the time of Philip II (r. 359–336) and Alexander the Great (r. 336–323) was a formidable power in the Greek world and, under Alexander, Asia—a far cry from its humble beginnings as a small city in roughly the mid-seventh century. This chapter discusses the kingdom, its neighbors, and its people and their customs with an emphasis on its "heyday" under Philip and Alexander. Doing so now allows us to appreciate even more the remarkable history and achievements of the Argead kings in transforming Macedonia and how they benefited Philip as he turned the kingdom into one of antiquity's superpowers, as the following chapters demonstrate.

The Argead dynasty

The royal dynasty is usually referred to as the Argead because of Alexander I's claim that its first king, Perdiccas, came from Argos in the Peloponnese, although that name is not a foregone conclusion.[1] The dynasty's name may have originated in the time of epic heroes, as an Argeas is mentioned in Homer's *Iliad*.[2] Yet Appian, a later Roman writer, says the dynasty's name originated from the city of Argos in Orestis in Upper Macedonia, though that claim is commonly rejected.[3] To complicate matters further, the Byzantine lexicographer Stephanus of Byzantium believed the dynasty was called Argead after the mythical Argeas, son of Macedon, while Justin claimed that a mythical king named Caranus changed the name of the supposed first capital Edessa to Aegae and so called its citizens Aegeads.[4]

[1] Cf. Hammond and Griffith 1979, pp. 27–29, and especially Mallios 2011.

[2] Athenaeus 14.659; Homer, *Iliad* 16.417. See Rosen 1978, pp. 9–10; Hammond and Griffith 1979, pp. 27–29; cf. Sprawski 2010, p. 130.

[3] Appian 9.2, with the arguments of Dascalakis 1965, pp. 110–113; Hammond 1972a, pp. 80 and 110–116; Rosen 1978, pp. 1–27; Xydopoulos 2012a, pp. 527–529; Hatzopoulos 2020, pp. 11–15 and 60–63.

[4] Stephanus of Byzantium, s.v. Argeou; Justin 7.1.10.

There is also a view that Argeadae was not a family name but a tribal name, just as Thucydides, for example, calls the inhabitants of Lyncestis "Lyncestian Macedones," and neither Herodotus nor Thucydides uses the name Argead for the dynasty. Since they claim the earlier kings were descendants of Temenus of Argos, there is a view that the dynasty should therefore be that of the Temenidae or Temenids, especially as Diodorus cites a Delphic prophecy given to Perdiccas that "the noble Temenidae have royal rule over a wealth-producing land."[5] Moreover, the term "Argeads" is found only in later literary and even epigraphical sources.[6] The argument has been that since the name starts to appear only in the Hellenistic era, the dynasty before then must have been called the Temenid.[7] Nonetheless, I use the name Argead for the dynasty as it is still the commonly accepted one.

What we can say with certainty is that the dynasty had a long life ending with the execution of Alexander IV in 310.[8]

The kingdom and its neighbors

Macedonia was a mountainous region, split in effect by the Varnous, Vermio, and Pierian mountains into Upper (or western) and Lower Macedonia.[9] Herodotus says Upper Macedonia was located somewhere in the mountains north of Olympus.[10] It was a mountainous plateau and comprised the semiautonomous kingdoms of Elimea in the south, Orestis to the west, and Lyncestis to the northwest, by Lake Lychnitis, along with cantons such as Tymphaea, Eordaea, Lyncus, Pelagonia, and Derriopus.[11] Lower Macedonia stretched to the Thermaic Gulf and the Strymon River and was less mountainous. It consisted of the districts of Olympus, Pieria, Emathia, and Bottiaea,

[5] Thucydides 2.99.3; Diodorus 7.16, with Hammond and Griffith 1979, pp. 27–29.

[6] Strabo 7.11; Pausanias 7.8.9 ("Argive kings"); Appian 11.63 ("Argeadae Macedones"); cf. the Hellenistic inscription from Xanthus referring to "the Argead kings who descend from Heracles": Bousquet 1988; Hatzopoulos 1996, vol. 1, p. 105; Hatzopoulos 2003, p. 216.

[7] See Mallios 2011, pp. 253–267; Sarakinski and Panovski 2023—I thank Vasiliki Saripanidi for these references.

[8] Argeads: Cloché 1960; Hammond 1972a; Hammond and Griffith 1979; Borza 1990; Müller 2016; Müller et al. 2017; see too Errington 1990; Hammond 1992a; King 2018; Roisman and Worthington 2010; Sawada 2022 is in Japanese, so regretfully I was unable to read it.

[9] Hammond 1972a, pp. 3–211; Hammond and Griffith 1979, pp. 102–123; Borza 1990, pp. 23–57; Hatzopoulos 1996, vol. 1, pp. 167–216; Thomas 2010; Hatzopoulos 2011a; Hatzopoulos 2020, pp. 4–48.

[10] Herodotus speaks of *ano*, or Upper Macedonia (7.128.1, 8.137.1), and of *kato*, or Lower Macedonia (7.173.1); cf. Thucydides 2.99.6.

[11] Xydopoulos 2012a; cf. Rosen 1978, pp. 12–13; Hatzopoulos 2003, pp. 207–213.

along with Amphaxitis, Crestonia, Mygdonia, Bisaltia, Crousis, and Anthemus, though the borders of these areas were fluid.[12]

Upper Macedonia had a harsh climate, causing herdsmen to move their flocks into the more temperate Lower Macedonia in the winters.[13] The latter's climate and rich soil enabled its people to grow cereal crops, vegetables, grapes, and fruits, as well as graze their sheep, goats, cattle, and horses, and its fertility and timber reserves were praised by ancient writers.[14] But Lower Macedonia was not without its problems. In its midst lay the marshland of the swampy Emathian (or central) plain, which seasonally flooded thanks to the rivers Haliacmon, Loudias, and Axius.[15] It was also a breeding ground for mosquitoes, which may have led to bouts of malaria.[16]

Disunity and instability between Upper and Lower Macedonia were a source of weakness for Macedonian kings.[17] But the kingdom also faced hostile tribal peoples surrounding it in the time before Philip II, such as the Thracians to the east; the Paeonians to the north; and—particularly dangerous for much of Macedonia's earlier history—the Illyrian tribes of the Dardanians, Taulantians, and Grabaei to the north and west, often collectively called the Illyrians.[18]

The Illyrians were a warrior race living in the upper cantons of Macedonia as well as west of the Pindus to the coast and became prosperous thanks to their region's rich mineral resources. Archaeological finds have shown there were major urban settlements, especially at Aiani in Elimiotis, where the remains of large public buildings and grave goods in several tombs indicate a high standard of living.[19] Philip II defeated their energetic king Bardylis in 358, which allowed him to unite Upper and Lower Macedonia for the first time in the kingdom's history. Yet the Illyrians continued to give him trouble, forcing him in the mid-350s to build a series of military outposts along his northwest frontier for protection.

[12] Amphaxatis, Crestonia, Mygdonia, Crousis, Anthemus: Hammond 1972a, pp. 176–191. Bisaltia: Hammond 1972a, pp. 192–199. Pieria: Hammond 1972a, pp. 123–139.

[13] Borza 1990, pp. 25–28.

[14] Xenophon, *Hellenica* 5.2.16. Resources and economy: Millett 2010; Ruffing 2017; cf. Borza 1982a, especially pp. 12–15, on agriculture. Timber: Borza 1987; Karathanasis 2019.

[15] Hammond 1972a, pp. 142–175.

[16] Borza 1979.

[17] Hammond 1992a, pp. 71–99.

[18] On the various tribes, see Hammond 1966, pp. 239–245; Papazoglou 1978, importantly modified in areas such as territorial extent by Mihajlovic 2014; Hammond and Griffith 1979, pp. 22–31; Wilkes 1995, pp. 13–25 and 94–104; Müller 2016, pp. 19–22. Thrace: Casson 1926; Hoddinott 1981; Archibald 1998; Delev 2007; cf. Bouzek 1986; Archibald 2010. Paeonia: Merker 1965. Illyria: Casson 1926; cf. Papazoglou 1965; Hammond 1966; Dell 1970; Cabanes 1993; Wilkes 1995; Greenwalt 2010.

[19] Implications of finds for political, social, and cultural life: Karamitrou-Mentessidi 2011, citing bibliography; cf. Paspalas 2011, p. 180.

The Paeonians of the Axius Valley bordered on Illyria and Thrace and wielded much influence until their defeat by the Persians in the fifth century. Even so, they posed a danger to Macedonia if they decided to march south, and they were not conquered until 358 by Philip II.[20] Further east the Thracians, "the biggest nation in the world next to the Indians," were considered the most formidable and invincible of all Balkan peoples.[21] They controlled the rich metal resources of the lower Strymon Valley and had taken advantage of disruptions caused by the Illyrians' raids to dominate the territory east of the Strymon and push westward toward the Axius. It was only in the 340s, again thanks to Philip II, that Thrace was absorbed into Macedonia's growing empire.

There was also a danger from the Chalcidice.[22] Thanks to Perdiccas II in the fifth century, a powerful Chalcidian League was formed, with relations between it and the Macedonian kings strained until Philip II conquered the region in 348 and disbanded the league. Then to Macedonia's southwest was the wealthy and largely independent kingdom of Epirus, which fluctuated in its relations with Macedonia before Philip installed a puppet ruler on the throne in 340, Alexander, who remained loyal to the king.[23]

Finally, south of Mount Olympus lay Greece, where cities like Athens and Thebes had a history of often hostile dealings with Argead kings. But directly bordering on Macedonia, hence allowing access from the south into the southernmost cantons, was Thessaly. Always a concern for Macedonia's border security, the kings were especially careful to maintain good relations with the state.[24]

All these areas fell to Philip by the 340s, who went on to conquer Greece in 338, thus doubling the kingdom's size and population to as many as 500,000. In addition, his unification of Macedonia allowed him to exploit its natural resources on a greater scale. Mines and timber were the major revenue generators, especially timber, which was coveted throughout the Greek world.[25] The western mountains were covered with thick forests, and the Athenians especially needed the region's fir, pine, and cedar for shipbuilding;

[20] Merker 1965, pp. 41–45; Hammond 1972a, pp. 78–84; Hammond and Griffith 1979, pp. 55–57.

[21] See Herodotus 5.3.1.

[22] West 1918; especially Zahrnt 1971, with pp. 12–27, on origins, and Psoma 2001; cf. Tsigarida 2011; Psoma 2011.

[23] Hammond 1967 is still the standard work on Epirus; cf. Cabanes 1993; Greenwalt 2010.

[24] Westlake 1993; Graninger 2010.

[25] Borza 1982a; Borza 1987; Borza 1990, pp. 50–57; Hammond 1992a, pp. 177–187; Hammond 1988, pp. 383–391; Karathanasis 2019; Boufalis 2022. See too on resources and the economy Millett 2010; Ruffing 2017, pp. 125–135. Standard book on timber in the ancient world: Meiggs 1982.

hence demand for Macedonian timber was high and often dictated politics as oil does today.[26] Previous kings had taken advantage of their timber supplies in dealings with Greek cities, but it was Philip who really transformed the economy.

The people

By the time of Philip II, the people lived in cities, which were the military and economic nuclei of the kingdom.[27] As archaeology has shown, these cities were of varying sizes, carefully laid out, often located on overland routes (such as Dium and Pella), and well defended with fortification walls.[28] Indeed, many Upper Macedonian cities were new foundations with a mix of Macedonians and non-Macedonians and played a role in security and the economy, stimulating agriculture and trade as well as reinforcing defenses. The agoras or marketplaces of cities were of varying sizes, giving us a glimpse of a busy and flourishing city life.

Macedonian society was a tough one. Thus, for example, boys, including those of the royal family, were subjected to the same training regimen from an early age of fighting, riding, and hunting, which continued even in adulthood. For example, a soldier had to wear a rope or sash around his waist until he had killed his first man in battle. Also, no man could recline at a banquet until he had killed a ferocious wild boar without using a net to trap it—even at age 35 Cassander, who ruled Macedonia at the end of the fourth century and early third, had to sit because he had not killed a boar even though he was "a brave and a good hunter."[29]

But our knowledge of these customs comes from later Greek sources, whose prejudices may have distorted their accounts.[30] We may well see this in the case of symposia, which appear to be rowdy affairs as wine was said to have been consumed neat (*akratos*) rather than watered down, as was the Greek habit; hence attendees were drunk "while they were still being served the

[26] King 2018, p. 34.

[27] Hatzopoulos 1996, vol. 1, pp. 51–123, 129–165, and pp. 464–486, on locations, populations, nature, political and civic institutions; Kahrstedt 1953; especially Papazoglou 1988; Hatzopoulos 2015; Hatzopoulos 2020; and the chapters in Roisman and Worthington 2010 as well as those on individual cities in Lane Fox 2011a; cf. the succinct discussion of Hammond and Griffith 1979, pp. 197–199.

[28] Papazoglou 1988; Hatzopoulos, 1996, vol. 1, pp. 51–104.

[29] Rope: Aristotle, *Politics* 1324b. Boar: Athenaeus 1.18a (from Hegesander), who also tells us about Cassander.

[30] See Xydopoulos 2006; cf. Errington 1983.

first course" and were prone to fighting.[31] But this habit may be untrue and the product of Greek writers bent on denigrating the Macedonians—the hostile Demosthenes, for example, accused Philip II of being interested only in "a life of drunkenness, debauchery and indecent dancing," which was hardly the case, as we will see in chapters 9–10.[32] Archaeological evidence, however, counters the critical literary presentation of wine-drinking. Among the grave goods in both wealthier and poorer graves from the sixth century onward are clay kraters and bronze cauldrons, the latter used for cooking but likely for mixing wine, indicating the Macedonians did mix their wine with water.[33]

Another feature of court life was same-sex homoerotic relationships among men, which in any case were common in the ancient world, though the Greeks had no notion of homosexuality or bisexuality, as in our society. If males happened to be married, their wives accepted their husbands' dalliances with other men. Macedonian kings were no exception—perhaps most famous is Alexander the Great's likely relationship with his boyhood friend and confidant Hephaestion. Such liaisons could be dangerous—as we shall see, Archelaus and Philip II were assassinated by former male lovers.

Little is known about Macedonian women from our literary sources, but archaeological evidence, especially grave goods from various cemeteries across Macedonia, sheds light on women of noble and non-noble status. Thus, since military equipment in graves is male only, we can say that women did not fight or go to war. The funerary evidence indicates noble women performed important religious roles such as priestesses and even enjoyed some equality with men, while those who were members of royal families could play a role in court and public life.[34] The graves of non-noble women were poorer, as is to be expected, and they perhaps had less personal freedom than elite women. The common view that women of all socioeconomic groups did not attend symposia has been challenged thanks to funerary evidence, at least for the sixth century: since women went to the theater and festivals with their husbands, they may have attended symposia as well.[35]

[31] Ephippus, *BNJ* 126 F 1 (= Athenaeus 3.120e). Symposia: Tomlinson 1970; Sawada 2010; Carney 2015.

[32] Demosthenes 2.18–19. Querying the sources: Murray 1996, p. 18; Müller 2016, pp. 64–68, on a topos of "drunkenness."

[33] They became less common in the earlier classical period, but there is an increase in finds from Philip II's time: See Saripanidi 2019a, pp. 387–388, 393–398, and 406; Saripanidi 2019b.

[34] Carney 1995; Carney 2000, pp. 3–37; LeBohec 2006; Carney 2010; cf. Kottaridi 2011a; Saripanidi 2020; see too Saripanidi 2017; Saripanidi 2019a; Saripanidi 2019b; Mirón Pérez 2000 discusses powerful royal women, with an emphasis on Olympias.

[35] Carney 2015 on women and symposia; Saripanidi 2020.

Macedonian kings at least were polygamous, not divorcing a wife before marrying another; hence there could have been several queens at the same time—Amyntas III had at least two wives and Philip II seven. Queens appear to have had equal status and eventually lived with the king in the palace at Pella; if one had influence over the others, it may have depended on factors such as lineage or the sons they produced.[36] Philip II's fourth wife, Olympias, may have had more authority because she was the daughter of the deceased king of Epirus, niece of the current king, and mother of the heir Alexander, but there is no evidence to say so.

Whether the queens all got along with each other is unknown. Plutarch speaks of "quarrels which took place in the women's apartments" between Philip's multiple wives, and Athenaeus tells us that the king's marriage to his seventh wife, Cleopatra, "threw the entire course of his life into utter confusion," though whether this disruption affected relations with his wives is not clear.[37] It has been argued based on modern sociological studies of polygamous marriages in Africa that the reverse was true, especially with Philip's wives, because they were foreign and hence homesick and lonely, which drew them together: "A generally harmonious picture interspersed with occasional rows seems far more likely that the conditions of endless upheaval painted by Plutarch."[38] But just because something happens in the modern world does not mean it can be successfully applied to the past—or should be.[39]

The Greeks called the Macedonians "barbarians," which has caused immense controversy. For example, Herodotus calls Alexander I a barbarian, and Thrasymachus of Chalcedon uses the term of Archelaus: "Shall we, who are Greeks, be slaves to the barbarian Archelaus?" (chapter 6).[40] However, "barbarian" was not so much about a perception of Macedonians lacking in culture but a term the Greeks used of people speaking a different language.[41] It has been argued that the Macedonians were not Greek, and certainly

[36] Carney 2000, pp. 23–27; cf. Greenwalt 1989, pp. 39–40, echoed mostly by Mortensen 1999; see too Mirón Pérez 2000. On women in Alexander's court with an overview of those before that king, see Carney 2003b.

[37] Plutarch, *Alexander* 9.5–6; Athenaeus 13.557d; cf. 13.560c ("entire household overthrown").

[38] Mortensen 1999, p. 805.

[39] The same may be said for the analogies with polygamist Merovingian dynasts in Greenwalt 1989, pp. 32–34.

[40] Herodotus 5.22.2; Thrasymachus, F 85 B2 in Diels and Kranz 1952, with Dascalakis 1965, pp. 228–236; and see Xydopoulos 2006, in detail. As late as 341 we find Demosthenes (9.31) describing Philip II as "not Greek."

[41] Dascalakis 1965, pp. 225–276, has an excellent discussion of "barbarism" in ancient writers and the odium attached to the Macedonians; see too Vlassopoulos 2013; cf. Hatzopoulos 2020, pp. 121–123, on perceptions.

their social customs, beliefs, and political systems made them seem worlds apart from the Greeks south of Olympus and elsewhere, as even the early Greek sources stress.[42] There is no compelling answer to his problem; however, their original ethnicity was surely Greek, and they were Greek speaking, even though over time, as Macedonia expanded, interactions with peoples in different areas and intermarriage made for a multiethnic and thus multilingual population.[43]

Among other things, we are told the supposed origins of the Argead dynasty in Alexander I's account of his descent from the Temenids of Argos in the Peloponnese that convinced officials to allow him to compete in the Olympic Games, open only to Greeks (chapter 4). Further, Macedonian proper names are Greek ones, and archaeological evidence such as inscriptions and coins is all in Greek.[44] In 360 festival envoys from Epidaurus traveled to Greek cities to invite people to their city celebrations—including a visit to Perdiccas III, which shows they considered the Macedonians Greeks and could attend their festival.[45] Equally telling is the similarity between Macedonian and Greek religion: the Macedonians were polytheistic, having many of the same gods in their pantheon as the Greeks, in particular Zeus, Dionysus, and Heracles.[46] Zeus was honored by Archelaus with a major festival at Dium and Dionysus at Pella. Asclepius was also revered, with a priest of the god in every city.[47] And excavations at Aegae, Pella, Dium, and other cities reveal statues and epigraphs attesting to cults to Greek female deities such as the Mother of the Gods, Aphrodite, Demeter, and Kore, evidence of a similar belief in the afterlife.[48]

Greek was also the language of communication. We never hear of interpreters needed when Macedonians met Greeks, and in 480 Alexander I, then in league with the Persians, allegedly warned the Greek troops at Tempe about Persian forces and in 479 secretly visited Athenian generals before the battle of Plataea: such interactions would have been fruitless unless he

[42] See, for example, Badian 1982a.

[43] Dascalakis 1965; Hammond and Griffith 1979, pp. 39–54; Kalléris 1988; Hammond 1992a, pp. 12–15; Hatzopoulos 1996, vol. 1, pp. 167–209; Engels, J. 2010; Hatzopoulos 2011a; Hatzopoulos 2011b; Hatzopoulos 2020, pp. 49–124; cf. Borza 1991; Saatsoglou-Paliadeli 1999, pp. 364–366; Müller 2016, pp. 41–48.

[44] Cf. Kalléris 1988, pp. 76–77.

[45] Hatzopoulos 1996, vol. 1, p. 473; Lane Fox 2011b, pp. 268–269.

[46] Kalléris 1988, pp. 532–572; Christesen and Murray 2010; Mari 2011a; see too Hatzopoulos 1994a; Voutiras 2006; Hatzopoulos 2020, pp. 79–88. On Greek religion, see, for example, Mikalson 2005.

[47] Hatzopoulos 2020, pp. 82–83, citing sources.

[48] Hatzopoulos 2020, pp. 83–88, citing sources; see especially Kottaridi 2020.

spoke Greek.[49] Elsewhere, the orator Aeschines was said to have described Philip II as "a Greek of the Greeks," and Alexander the Great trained Persian youths in Macedonian tactics and ordered them to learn Greek, not "Macedonian"—in the midst of battle we should not expect orders to be given in both Macedonian and Greek![50]

Most likely, then, is that the various peoples on Macedonia's borders such as the Thracians and Illyrians impacted how the people spoke, just as there were carryovers in material culture between the Macedonians and bordering peoples.[51] Hence, Upper Macedonians may have kept their own speech after being overrun by Alexander I, but a Macedonian dialect may have arisen that *seemed* like another language that Greeks could not understand.[52] In Curtius' account of the trial of the cavalry commander Philotas in 330, we are told that "Macedonian" was spoken, which non-Macedonians could not understand.[53] But if this was a northern Greek dialect, for example, so different from central and southern Greek dialects that Greeks found it foreign, they may well have called it a different language.[54] A modern instance may support this view—of the many dialects throughout the Korean peninsula, that of Jeju Island is so different that it is deemed a separate language, called "Jeju speech" (제주말).[55]

The Greeks and others clearly had their own views of the Macedonians, which were often warped and a product of different periods.[56] Indeed, the Macedonians' artistic output shows them to be sophisticated in their tastes. Their craftsmen produced artworks of stunningly beautiful quality—gold, silver, and bronze, tomb paintings, jewelry, and especially mosaics.[57] Banquets were splendid affairs to judge from the valuable gold and silver vessels discovered in tombs.[58] The nobility at least were educated in Greek culture, and kings like Archelaus were clearly intellectuals who were keen for themselves and their court to be perceived in this way.[59] Thus, Perdiccas III

[49] Daskalakis 1965, pp. 78–79—one of his "arguments from silence" for Greek-speaking Macedonians, and see pp. 79–81 for other arguments.

[50] Philip: Demosthenes 19.308; cf. Mari 2011b, p. 82. Alexander: Plutarch, *Alexander* 47.3.

[51] Archibald 2010, pp. 330–338, citing bibliography.

[52] Dascalakis 1965, pp. 60–66; Kalléris 1988, pp. 488–503; especially Hatzopoulos 2017; cf. Hatzopoulos 2020, pp. 63–69.

[53] Curtius 6.9.34–36, "native tongue" (*patrio sermone*). On the episode, see chapter 11.

[54] The anonymous referee makes the analogy of British English to Scottish English and the poetry of Robert Burns, which is hard to understand.

[55] See Yeon 2012.

[56] On this, see for example, Asirvatham 2008; Asirvatham 2010a; Asirvatham 2017.

[57] Touratsoglou 1983; Hardiman 2010; Kousser 2010; Paspalas 2011; Palagia 2011.

[58] Saatsoglou- Paliadeli 2011, pp. 272–273; see too Saripanidi 2019a.

[59] Cf. Badian 1982a.

was a patron of Plato's Academy, Archelaus invited, among others, Socrates and the Athenian tragic playwrights Agathon and Euripides to Pella, and Philip II enjoyed intellectual exchanges with the Athenian orator Isocrates and Speusippus (Plato's successor at the Academy), as well as famously hiring Aristotle to tutor his son Alexander, who in turn took a retinue of intellectuals and surveyors with him to Asia.[60]

Kingship and organization

The earlier Macedonian monarchs may not have exercised the same power as later ones, arguably from the time of Alexander I (c. 498–454).[61] While subject to some checks, they eventually became to all intents and purposes autocrats; they oversaw all domestic and foreign policy, had the right to make treaties and declare war, during which time they commanded the army, and were chief priests, sacrificing daily to the gods to ensure the state's safety, good harvests, and success in warfare.[62] There is also a belief that kings were worshiped after death or even in their lifetime, perhaps as part of a ruler cult, though that is controversial.[63] Along with their political, military, and religious authority, over time—as well as through conquest—kings also came to own all their kingdom's natural resources, from timber to mines.

It appears that kings were polygamists who married for political and military reasons when it suited them.[64] As mentioned previously, Amyntas III had two wives at the same time, while Philip II married seven times without ever divorcing a wife and was said to have "made war by marriage."[65] But polygamy brought with it great risk: multiple wives opened the door to

[60] Tutoring: Worthington 2014a, pp. 95–97. Retinue: Badian 1991; Tritle 2009. On education, see Carney 2003a.

[61] See Saripanidi 2019a, for example, pp. 400–404, on Alexander using Persian dominance to overcome the influence of powerful families in local areas and centralizing his kingship. Alexander I is discussed in chapter 4.

[62] Hammond and Griffith 1979, pp. 152–158; cf. pp. 383–404; Kalléris 1988, pp. 576–623; Errington 1990, pp. 218–229; Hammond 1992a, pp. 21–24, 60–70, 166–170, and 391–395; Müller 2016, pp. 24–27; cf. Errington 1978. Against the autocratic power of the king: Anson 1985a; Anson 1991; Hatzopoulos 1996, vol. 1, pp. 219–260 and 487–496; King 2010; Hatzopoulos 2015; cf. Hatzopoulos 2020, pp. 103–116. See too Roisman 2012a (later Classical and Hellenistic, but relevant to earlier Argeads). See also Hatzopoulos 1996, vol. 2, nos. 23–35 (cf. nos. 64–81 for dedications by city and other officials, sometimes linking king to a god).

[63] Mari 2008; Mari 2011a, p. 458.

[64] Polygamy: Greenwalt 1989; Carney 2017; cf. Heckel 2017, pp. 68–69; Müller 2016, pp. 62–64.

[65] Satyrus in Athenaeus 13.557b–d. See Carney 2000, pp. 51–81; Hatzopoulos 2020, pp. 138–142, for royal wives of Philip.

multiple sons vying for the throne, especially if they had the support of influential court factions, even if a king had made his successor clear.[66] As we shall see, regicide was common, often throwing the succession and even the kingdom into chaos.

It has often been assumed that an Assembly of male citizens existed that could make decisions and advise the king, though its existence has been doubted by many scholars.[67] What little we know of this body concerns only its ability to hear treason cases (in which the king was the final judge), to decide on a regent if the heir was a minor, and to acclaim the next king.[68] Hence a body might meet for these reasons but not play any political role in advising the king or sharing in his rule. The monarch did apparently rely on a group of nobles known as the companions, who he may have selected and who also served as cavalrymen and enjoyed a privileged place next to him at banquets.[69] Such preferential favor would be much sought after and clearly was dependent on keeping in the king's good graces. Likewise, there were also powerful factions at the court, but these too depended on the king's goodwill.[70]

The king and his subjects enjoyed a close social relationship, coming together at religious festivals, symposia, and even hunting, when these events turned into quasi-political ones because of his presence.[71] But at the end of the day it was the king who led his kingdom: referred to simply by name and not title. he identified with his people, but he was not their friend.[72] In many respects he personified the state, as his successes and failures directly impacted the state, whose fortunes rose and fell with the king, as we shall see in the following chapters.

Social, religious, and cultural life

The scant literary evidence tells us little about the daily lives of the Macedonians at least before Philip II, which emphasizes even more the value

[66] Carney 1983; Carney 2017; cf. Muller 2016, pp. 27–30, on factions. Polygamy: Greenwalt 1989; Heckel 2003a, especially pp. 200–205.

[67] Anson 1985a; Anson 1991.

[68] Hatzopoulos 1996, vol. 1, pp. 260–322; see too Hammond and Griffith 1979, pp. 160–162; Hammond 1992a, pp. 60–64; Hatzopoulos 2020, pp. 103–116. Judicial: Anson 2008a; cf. Roisman 2012a. Regency and age: Hatzopoulos 1986, but see LeBohec 1993a that the age for kings was 20.

[69] Hammond and Griffith 1979, pp. 395–404.

[70] Heckel 2003a, especially pp. 200–205; cf. Weber 2009.

[71] Hammond and Griffith 1979, pp. 383–392; Hammond 1992a, pp. 64–70; Carney 2002; Müller 2016, pp. 36–37.

[72] On nomenclature see Errington 1974.

of archaeological finds for Macedonian society.[73] Excavations of cities, especially the capitals of Aegae and Pella, reveal among other things impressive theaters, large and luxurious palaces, bustling market areas, houses of varying sizes, workshops, and other shops.[74] Of particular importance are cemeteries, which from numerous sites across Macedonia have yielded an array of funerary goods ranging from clay vases to high-quality gold and silver vessels and jewelry as well as arms and armor, informing us about people of all socioeconomic groups and their lives.[75] From about 570 there was an increase in the wealth of grave goods and in particular the introduction of funerary kits including vases, jewelry (usually for women and often made of gold and silver), figurines, and military equipment for males.[76]

It has been suggested that the increase in more expensive grave goods and the appearance of funerary kits reflect changes in society and even gender roles at key points, such as following the reign of Alexander I, with the emergence of a narrower and wealthier elite.[77] Yet the funerary goods, as has been vigorously argued, cast light on the lives of the lower social stratum as well. Though they may be fewer and of lesser quality, as to be expected, they show similarities in textile and pottery manufacture and even dress, allowing us an insight into the relationship of rich to poor in society.[78]

Yet the funerary goods found in all graves at least show us that regardless of the different regions of the kingdom, the people as a whole shared the same religious beliefs.[79] Excavations at Sindos and Archontiko, for example, have given us an abundance of gold and silver goods, including death masks, jewelry, weapons, and containers for food, perfume, and ointment (the most common grave good and part of the funerary kit), indicating the people thought these needed to be taken with them into the next life, hence a belief in an afterlife.[80]

[73] Cf., for example, Hatzopoulos 2020, pp. 19–33. For the most up-to-date finding and discussion see the volumes from the annual conference *The Archaeological Work in Macedonia and Thrace*, published annually from 1987 by the Hellenic Ministry of Culture, Aristotle University Thessaloniki.

[74] Aegae: Saatsoglou-Paliadeli 2011; Kottaridi 2011b (palace); especially Kottaridi 2020. Pella: Akamatis 2011, all citing bibliography.

[75] On these finds and their implications for all socioeconomic groups, see especially Saripanidi 2017; Saripanidi 2019a; Saripanidi 2020.

[76] Saripanidi 2017; Saripanidi 2019a.

[77] Saripanidi 2017, for example, pp. 93–123; Saripanidi 2019a, for example, pp. 398–400; gender: Saripanidi 2020.

[78] See Saripanidi's articles cited in the preceding note. Attempting to shine the spotlight on non-noble Macedonians is Salminen 2023, though many observations are general.

[79] Salminen 2023, pp. 209–262, on regional differences.

[80] Religion: Hatzopoulos 1994a; Christesen and Murray 2010, pp. 431–433; Mari 2011a, pp. 456–458; cf. Hatzopoulos 2006. Finds and interpretations: Saatsoglou-Paliadeli 2011, pp. 288–290;

To worship and celebrate their gods the Macedonians opted for festivals (as did Greeks) and smaller sanctuaries. At Pella excavators discovered a sanctuary to Aphrodite and the Mother of the Gods as well as to a local healing god named Darron, with the first inscriptional evidence of this god coming from there.[81] At Aegae a sanctuary of the goddess Eucleia ("good repute") boasts a long royal interest in it since we have a dedicatory inscription by Eurydice, wife of Amyntas III (r. 393/2–369/8), and one by Laodice (the name is partially restored), wife of Perseus, the last legitimate king of the succeeding Antigonid dynasty (r. 179–16).[82]

The Macedonians usually did not cremate their dead but buried them by inhumation.[83] Simple cist tombs grew into a more common rectangular barrel vault with one or two burial chambers, perhaps drawing on eastern practices in the later fourth century.[84] One feature of the tombs of royal and wealthy families was a façade painted to look like the front of a Doric or Ionic building, often in bright colors, behind which was the barrel vault with one or two burial chambers.[85] This illusory façade was developed by the Macedonian artists, influenced by Greek architecture, and may perhaps have been intended to make the final resting place more of a home for the deceased than merely a repository.

Of the large and elaborate tombs excavated to date, the most famous is the complex of three tombs at Aegae with a *heroon* or altar for worshiping the deceased—presumably one of the occupants.[86] Tomb I, which was plundered, was a cist tomb and had in it only some bones of an adult man, woman, and child. Tomb II, probably that of Philip II, was of barrel vault construction with a larger main chamber and smaller antechamber. In each one was a sarcophagus containing skeletal remains as well as various grave

and see especially the exhaustive treatments of Saripanidi 2017, especially pp. 99–114, on afterlife; Saripanidi 2019a; Saripanidi 2020. For types and functions of objects: Saripanidi 2019a, pp. 384–398; Saripanidi 2020, pp. 75–90. On Sindos, see especially Gimatzidis 2010; Despoini 2016.

[81] Akamatis 2011, pp. 404–405.

[82] Saatsoglou-Paliadeli 2000; cf. Saatsoglou-Paliadeli 1999, pp. 361–362; on the excavations at the site see Saatsoglou-Paliadeli 2011 (pp. 277–278 for Eucleia).

[83] Saatsoglou-Paliadeli 1999, p. 363, with sources, though see Kottaridi 2020, pp. 89–104. Rare instances of cremation: Saripanidi 2017, p. 112.

[84] Eastern influence: Saatsoglou-Paliadeli 1999, pp. 357–359; Saatsoglou-Paliadeli 2011, p. 289, citing bibliography.

[85] Borza 1990, pp. 271–274; Saatsoglou-Paliadeli 1999, pp. 367–359, on the façade and barrel vaunt construction, citing bibliography. On painted decorations, see Brecoulaki 2006.

[86] Andronikos 1980, pp. 188–231; Andronikos 2004; cf. Kottaridi 2020, pp. 27–55; Hatzopoulos 2020, pp. 21–22.

goods. Tomb III, which may be that of the last Argead king, Alexander IV, contained the remains of a teenage male.[87] We will revisit the identity of the occupants in chapter 10.

Cities were carefully constructed. Pella, for example, was a strongly fortified city, built to a strict urban grid plan, with regular-sized building plots and roadways (figures 1a and 1b).[88] There was also a water supply, with wells, fountains, a reservoir, baths, and a drainage system. The agora was also built to a grid plan in the city center and was surrounded by large stoas with various administrative offices, shops, and workshops in them. The palace was built on the middle hill of three hills north of the city, away from the noise and bustle, and was in effect a compound with five complexes linked to each other by corridors and stairs. Each had living quarters, storerooms, rooms for entertaining, and guardrooms, and there were even a swimming pool and a training/exercise yard.

The large agora at Pella is Hellenistic, but perhaps its size was not much smaller in Philip's time and so testifies to a bustling and lively city life. So too do theaters. That at Aegae, for example, excavated in 1981, has the largest orchestra found in Greece so far, though the seating area is by comparison limited.[89] The size discrepancy is probably because theaters were also used as meeting places and for processions—it was in the one at Aegae that Philip II was assassinated in 336 (chapter 11).

Expensive grave goods in different metals, the development of illusory façades, tomb paintings, and sculptures show that there were expert Macedonian craftsmen and artists who produced artworks of the highest quality in bronze, silver, and gold, not to mention marble sculptures (although marble had to be imported). Even more spectacular were paintings in many tombs and mosaics in richer households and palaces.[90] At Aegae, a magnificent painting of Hades abducting Persephone adorns the north wall of Tomb I (figure 1.2)—chthonic deities such as Hades, Demeter, and Persephone reflect

[87] The identification of these kings has been challenged often with little new to say; for detailed arguments in favor of them, see Lane Fox 2011c, citing bibliography. But note Palagia 2017, pp. 157–160, for continued skepticism.

[88] See Akamatis 2011.

[89] Andronikos 2004, pp. 46–49; cf. Borza 1990, pp. 255–256; Saatsoglou-Paliadeli 1999, p. 360.

[90] Andronikos 1980; Andronikos 2004; Hardiman 2010; Paspalas 2011; Saatsoglou-Paliadeli 2011; see too Hatzopoulos 1994b, pp. 116–219, with many lavish illustrations, for example, mosaics: pp. 116–136; pottery: pp. 138–143; tombs: pp. 145–191 (at Vergina, pp. 154–177); dedications outside Macedonia: pp. 193–219.

Figure 1.1a and b Pella

Source: Photos by Ian Worthington.

Figure 1.2 Hades abducting Persephone (Vergina)
Source: Wikimedia Commons.

Figure 1.3 Mosaic of stag hunt
Source: Danvis Collection/Alamy Stock Photo.

the Macedonians' belief in the afterlife.[91] And there is a splendid frieze of what is a royal hunt (sadly in poor condition) across the façade of Tomb II.[92]

Mosaics had had a long life in Macedonia. Archelaus patronized the fresco painter Zeuxis to move from Italy and install mosaic floors in his new

[91] Hardiman 2010, pp. 511–514; Paspalas 2011, pp. 192–197; Saatsoglou-Paliadeli 2011, pp. 285–286; cf. Saatsoglou-Paliadeli 1999, pp. 362–363, all citing sources.

[92] Hardiman, 2010, pp. 511–512; Saatsoglou-Paliadeli 2011, pp. 282–285. Painting: Hardiman 2010, pp. 511–514; Paspalas 2011, pp. 192–197.

palace—presumably the one at Pella.[93] In doing so the king probably inaugurated a school that pioneered mosaic painting. The superb mosaics include ones from wealthier households of the early Hellenistic period, such as a lion hunt involving a young Alexander and one of his friends from Building I, or a stag hunt from Building II, shown in figure 1.3.

Macedonia in its "heyday" was powerful and impressive, though few would have predicted that when the first Argead kings began to take over nearby territories. We can now begin our study of how Macedonia rose from obscure and small beginnings to an imperial power.

Macedonia under the Argead Kings: The Rise and Fall of an Ancient Superpower. Ian Worthington, Oxford University Press. © Oxford University Press 2026. DOI: 10.1093/9780197668009.003.0002

[93] Aelian, *Varia Historia* 14.17 tells us about Zeuxis but does not specify whether Pella or Aegae is meant.

2
Founding and Forming Macedonia

Our knowledge of the kingdom's early history and the foundation of the Argead dynasty has many gaps thanks to the paucity of sources. What little literary evidence we have is more mythological than historical, but fortunately the rich archaeological discoveries shed more light on early Macedonia.[1] Supposedly the five earliest kings were Perdiccas, Argaeus, Philip, Aeropus, and Alcetas. However, it is not until the next one, Amyntas I, who ruled from about 547 to 498, and especially his successor Alexander I, who was king until 454, that we start to know what was happening in the kingdom. If we accept the regnal dates of Amyntas and Alexander and assume an average reign of 25–30 years for each of their predecessors, as is often thought, then Perdiccas—Macedonia's first king—ruled from the middle to the later seventh century.[2] But as we shall see, Perdiccas' role as founder of the Argead dynasty is suspect, and even the stages of Macedonian expansion are controversial.

Perdiccas I and the origins of the Argead dynasty

Herodotus, who wrote a history of the Persian Wars in about the middle of the fifth century, is our principal source for the origins of the dynasty. He tells the story of three brothers who traveled from Argos in the Peloponnese and made a home in Macedonia:[3]

> Three brothers descended from Temenus came as banished men from Argos to Illyria, Gauanes and Aeropus and Perdiccas; and from Illyria they crossed

[1] Good summary at Hatzopoulos 2020, pp. 19–33; see too Hammond and Griffith 1979, pp. 1–22. Sources: Rosen 1978, pp. 1–2; Zahrnt 1984, pp. 326–330.

[2] Hammond and Griffith 1979, pp. 3–5 (30 years); Errington 1990, p. 2; cf. Borza 1990, p. 98; Sprawski 2010, p. 130; Mari 2011b, p. 81; Hatzopoulos 2020, p. 12.

[3] Herodotus 8.137–138 (modified by Worthington). See Zahrnt 1984, pp. 345–348 and Rosen 1978, pp. 6–11, on the brothers, and passim for both on the development of Macedonia. Most detailed analysis of this and all myths: Mallios 2011.

> over into the highlands of Macedonia until they came to the town of Lebaea. There they served for wages as servants in the king's household, one tending horses and another oxen, and Perdiccas, who was the youngest, the lesser flocks. Now the king's wife cooked their food for them; for in old times the ruling houses among men, and not only the ordinary people, lacked wealth. Whenever she baked bread, the loaf of the servant Perdiccas grew double in size. Seeing that was always the case, she told her husband; and when he heard it, it seemed to him that this was an omen signifying something important. He sent for three brothers and ordered them to leave his territory. They said it was only right that they should have their wages before they departed; whereupon the king, when they spoke of wages, acted foolishly, and said, "That is the wage you merit, and it is that I give you," pointing to the sunlight that shone down the smoke-vent into the house. Gauanes and Aeropus, who were the elders, stood astonished when they heard that; but Perdiccas said, "We accept what you give, O king," and with that he took a knife that he had upon him and drew a line with it on the floor of the house around the sunlight. After that he gathered up the sunlight into the fold of his garment three times and left with his companions. They departed, but a bystander saw a hidden meaning to what the boy had done and said to the king how he had accepted the gift for a deliberate purpose. When the king heard this, he grew angry and sent riders after them to kill them. But there is in that land a river, where the descendants of these men from Argos sacrifice as their deliverer, for when the sons of Temenus had crossed the river it rose in such a flood that the pursuers could not follow. The brothers came to another part of Macedonia and settled near the place called the garden of Midas, son of Gordius, where wild roses grew, each bearing sixty blossoms and of amazing fragrance. It was here according to the Macedonians that [the satyr] Silenus was taken captive. Above it rises the mountain called Vermion, which none can ascend for the wintry cold. Then they went forth when they had won the country and presently subdued the rest of Macedonia.

Herodotus follows this story with a genealogy of the first kings, starting with Perdiccas and then Argaeus, Philip, Aeropus, Alcetas, Amyntas (I), and Amyntas' son Alexander (I).[4] Perdiccas, thanks to his divine ancestry from

[4] On these kings see Dascalakis 1965, pp. 114–127; Kalléris 1988, pp. 503–531; Borza 1982b; Dascalakis 1970; Müller 2016, pp. 85–104.

Zeus, as kings and their families were believed to enjoy the gods' favor, was thus the founder of the Argead dynasty.[5] His account is mirrored a generation or so later by Thucydides, writing in the reign of Perdiccas II, who tells us that:[6]

> the country by the sea which is now called Macedonia was first acquired and made their kingdom by Alexander [I], the father of Perdiccas [II], and his forefathers, who were originally Temenidae from Argos. They defeated and expelled from Pieria the Pierians, who afterwards took up their abode in Phagres and other places at the foot of Mount Pangaeum beyond the Strymon.

Thus, we also have Greek descendants of Perdiccas from Peloponnesian Argos, who first settled around Mount Vermion, expelled the people from Pieria, and then expanded their territory.[7] We return to the full Thucydides passage below.

Herodotus provides the earliest and most detailed information for the Argive origins of the Macedonian royal house, but is what he tells us "a piece of antique folklore or, conversely, of late propaganda without any historical value, or does it preserve, albeit in mythical form, a unique record of early Macedonian history"?[8] He was a contemporary of Alexander I, who may have told him this story if he had visited Macedonia.[9] That does not mean the tale was not circulating before Alexander's time, of course, and Herodotus may have heard it from another local source. However, Alexander had a particular reason for claiming Greek ancestry as he had sided with the Persians in the Persian Wars and after their defeat worked to ingratiate himself with

[5] For the questionable suggestion that Perdiccas is the invented ancestor of Perdiccas II, see Ogden 2011, p. 65.

[6] Thucydides 2.99.3.

[7] But Borza 1990, p. 82, suggests no settlement around Mount Vermion despite Herodotus, but the first settlement in coastal Pieria

[8] Hatzopoulos 2003, p. 204, citing bibliography, and see further pp. 203–218. On early history see Dascalakis 1965, pp. 25–30 and 97–105; Dascalakis 1970, p. 156; Edson 1970; Hammond and Griffith 1979, pp. 3 and 10–11; Badian 1982a; Borza 1982b; Greenwalt 1986; Rosen 1987, pp. 28–32; Sprawski 2010, pp. 127–128; Ogden 2011, pp. 62–65; Mari 2002, pp. 19–28; Vasilev 2012; Müller 2016, pp. 85–91; Müller 2017a, especially pp. 184–192; Molinero 2024. Herodotus as a source: Rosen 1987, with Borza, 1990, pp. 80–84, for a skeptical view.

[9] Not everyone accepts Alexander's influence, or even that the two met: Scaife 1989. The story as the product of Perdiccas I: Greenwalt 1997, p. 130 n. 37. Herodotus' time in Macedonia: Vasilev 2016. See now Sprawski 2021, questioning that it was Alexander I who put out the story of his Argive heritage but the product of Greek writers, and that the king was more obsessed with Trojan mythology.

the Greeks and take part in the Olympic Games—open only to Greeks—as we discuss in chapter 4.[10] Hence, he could have made up a story of Argive lineage.[11]

Yet certain details in Herodotus' account suggest it is not all fanciful. For example, in referencing Illyria and *ano* (Upper) Macedonia, he is the first to use the term "Macedonia," and is followed by Thucydides (in the quoted passage above).[12] The river he speaks of was likely the Haliacmon, which has a strong current and in winter becomes a torrent and hard to cross.[13] Moreover, the Gardens of Midas were likely the lush region around Mieza in the foothills of Mount Vermion, where in mythological times Midas' shepherds captured Silenus, a satyr and companion of the god Dionysus.[14]

We also hear about aspects of early Macedonian life that are evident in the kingdom's later history, such as the simplicity of domestic life for even central figures like a king and queen.[15] The occupations of the three brothers calls to mind the pastoralism of those living in Upper Macedonia, and highlights what many Balkan tribes practiced even beyond antiquity.[16] In addition, sunlight calls to mind the influence of Thracian religion on a Macedonian kingship anchored in a divine bond.[17] Indeed, the symbol of Macedonian sovereignty is often called a starburst, but sunlight is more fitting.

The geographical elements show that the story has a kernel of truth to it and play a role in determining the kingdom's expansion, which we discuss below. Lebaea is probably the village of Alebea mentioned in manumission inscriptions from the sanctuary of the Mother of the Gods at Leukopetra under Mount Vermion. They refer to several places and call Lebaea a "village of Elimea" in Upper Macedonia to the west of Pieria.[18]

[10] Especially argued by Rosen 1978, pp. 6–12. See too King 2018, p. 15; cf. Mari 2011b, p. 81.

[11] But see Sprawski 2021.

[12] Herodotus is the first as far as we know to speak of *ano* or Upper Macedonia (7.128.1, 8.137.1) and of *kato* or Lower Macedonia (7.173.1); cf. Thucydides 2.99.6, with Edson 1970, pp. 22 and 28–29; Borza 1990, pp. 99–100; cf. Vasilev 2011a, p. 99; but see Xydopoulos 2012a, pp. 24–31.

[13] Rosen 1978, p. 13.

[14] Herodotus 8.138.3, with Mallios 2011, pp. 233–253, for the myth; cf. Müller 2017a, especially pp. 187–188.

[15] King 2018, p. 16.

[16] Pastoralism: Hammond 1972a, pp. 415–416 and 439; Hammond 1992a, pp. 5–7 and 54; Hammond and Griffith 1979, p. 28; cf. Hatzopoulos 1996, vol. 1, pp. 105, 479; Hatzopoulos 2011a, p. 47; but see Archibald 2010, pp. 329–330, citing bibliography.

[17] Greenwalt 1994a; with Rosen 1978, pp. 11–15; Greenwalt 1986, pp. 120–121; contra Mallios 2011, p. 209 n. 704.

[18] The name from the Thracian tribe, the Pieres, that controlled the area until displaced by the Argeads, who established their own authority: Hammond 1972a, pp. 416–418; on Pieria see too Hammond 1972a, pp. 123–139; cf. Edson 1970, pp. 19–21. Leukopetra: Hatzopoulos 2003, p. 206 and especially pp. 207–212 with references; Zahrnt 1984, p. 347.

Thus, we may well have three Greek-speaking brothers who overthrew an existing ruler (or several rulers) in Pieria and introduced a new Macedonian dynasty.[19] Just because these early kings are unknown to us does not mean they were ahistorical, for Macedonia was still developing in the seventh and early sixth centuries, and the king and his wife are said to be poor. If the increasing wealth and sophistication of later kings' burials are anything to go by, especially after the reign of Alexander I, these early rulers may not have held the same privileged position in society as later, and hence less is known about them.[20] Moreover, in this earlier period the Macedonians had next to no role in Greek politics, so Greek authors did not bother with them.[21] After all, while Thucydides may have followed Herodotus' genealogy, it is significant that he says nothing about Alexander I's predecessors, which may show skepticism or simply an inability to write about them because of lack of evidence.[22]

One question that has never been properly addressed and which plays an important role in the early foundation story is why Alexander I said the brothers were expelled from Argos and not another Greek city, like Corinth or Athens. The answer plausibly lies in the "tyranny," or rule by a single family, that overthrew aristocratic ruling families in many cities, especially in the Peloponnese, in the seventh century. These tyrant rulers were not despots—their policies benefited their cities economically and socially as well as ensured their own regime—but many of the noble families were exiled or chose to leave.[23]

Argos suffered a tyranny in roughly the mid-seventh century when a man named Pheidon seized power.[24] That gives us a plausible context for Perdiccas and his brothers leaving Argos either because they were exiled or decided not to live under a tyrant.[25] Since they likely enjoyed influence at home, it made sense that they would attempt to regain it in whatever region they settled; hence they expelled the Pierians to set up their own rule. The chronology also fits: if Amyntas I came to the throne in about 547 and each of

[19] Rosen 1978, pp. 11–15; cf. Greenwalt 1985a.

[20] Sprawski 2010, p. 131. On the increasing wealth of funerary goods and its implications for society after Macedonian expanded across the Axius, see especially Saripanidi 2017; Saripanidi 2019a, e.g., pp. 382–384.

[21] In a comment on my draft, for which I thank her.

[22] Greenwalt 1985a, pp. 43–44 with n. 3; Borza 1982b; cf. Vassileva 2007, pp. 773–774.

[23] On the tyrannies, see Andrewes 1956.

[24] Koiv 2001, and see Andrewes 1956, pp. 31–42, on Pheidon.

[25] Rosen 1978, p. 8, suggest the brothers were part of a colonizing movement, as many Greek cities from the mid-eighth century sent out colonies, but their departure seems forced rather than voluntary.

Perdiccas' five predecessors reigned for anything from 15 to 25 or so years, then Perdiccas would have become king in the middle of the seventh century.

Other cities such as Corinth and Sicyon suffered tyrannies in the mid-seventh century, but Alexander did not name any one of these. Nor did he have the brothers setting off from Athens, which by his time was an influential city. That was because its tyranny was only established after a third attempt by Pisistratus in 545, by which time Amyntas I would have been ruling Macedonia. The singling out of Argos is important, and the fact that Heracles, who was an important deity to the Macedonians, was worshiped there lends credence to Alexander's story.

So too does Hesiod's story of the two sons of Zeus and Thyia (Deucalion's daughter), Magnes and Macedon, who lived in Pieria around Mount Olympus.[26] Hesiod claims that Macedon gave his name to the Macedonians and Magnes to the Magnesians (east of Thessaly but eventually part of that state) and that the homeland of the Macedonians was Pieria and that of the Magnesians was Olympus. Hesiod has thus inserted a new name, Macedon, into the Macedonian pantheon, but the fragment containing this information—the first written reference we have of Macedonians and dating likely to the sixth century—probably refers to the time of Perdiccas I and shows a Greek ancestry.[27] On balance, then, we should accept that the Argead dynasty originated in Argos in the Peloponnese.

Variants and newcomers

Herodotus' list of early kings was not set in stone, for several variants appeared over time.[28] In the late fifth century the Athenian tragedian Euripides went to Pella at the invitation of King Archelaus, where he wrote the *Bacchae*, possibly a *Temenus* or *Temenidae*, and the (lost) *Archelaus*. This last play replaced Perdiccas with a certain Archelaus (not the then king) as the founder of the Argead royal house, who had escaped from his evil brothers in Argos and gone to Macedonia, which he saved it from hostile neighbors, married

[26] Hesiod's *Catalogue of Women* F 7 M-W, quoted by Hatzopoulos 2003, pp. 214–215.

[27] Dating: Rosen 1978, pp. 2–3 (700); Zahrnt 1984, pp. 349–352 (later); cf. Hammond 1972a, p. 430; King 2018, pp. 17–19. On the different traditions: Mallios 2011, pp. 105–134.

[28] Conveniently discussed by Harder 1985, pp. 131–137; Mallios 2011, pp. 179–198; see too Molinero 2024.

the daughter of a local king, and on the orders of Apollo founded the capital at Aegae.[29]

We can dismiss Euripides' tampering as a literary flattering of his host, and it may even have been at the behest of that king himself. But a more widespread variant was introduced in probably the early fourth century when a certain Caranus was said to have established the royal house.[30] In Greek, Caranus (*karanos*) means chief or lord; hence the name is meant to show a leader.[31] He apparently lived three generations before Perdiccas and was said to have traveled with followers from Argos to Macedonia on the advice of the Oracle of Apollo at Delphi, which told him to settle where he saw grazing goats.[32] Thus, when Caranus saw such goats at a town named Edessa, he seized it, changed its name to Aegae, expelled Midas and "other local kings," and founded the Macedonian kingdom.[33] He ruled there for 30 years and was succeeded, according to another source, by two kings named Coenus and Tirimmus, before Perdiccas I too the throne.[34]

Caranus, Coenus, and Tirimmus are not found in Herodotus, Thucydides, or Euripides, so when and why did they make their appearance in the foundation myth? It has been argued that Caranus was the oldest tradition and that it was Perdiccas II who was responsible for making Perdiccas I the founder of the royal house.[35] But more plausibly Caranus was fabricated after Archelaus' death in 399 when there were several kings in quick succession, each of them a descendant of a different son of Alexander I, as we shall see in chapter 7. Hence, rivalry between these branches of the Argead family led to the introduction of Caranus as a forefather to support claims to the throne.[36] Why Coenus and Tirimmus were included is unknown other than to relegate Perdiccas in the list, though he was not discarded from it.[37]

[29] Summary of the play: Hyginus, *Fabulae* 219. See also Dascalakis 1965, pp. 105–110; Hammond and Griffith 1979, pp. 5–12, citing references; Müller 2016, pp. 97–100; especially Xanthakis-Karamanos 2012, pp. 108–126; cf. Ogden 2011, pp. 67–70.

[30] Theopompus, *BNJ* 115 F 393; Justin 7.1.7–12; cf. Marsyas, *BNJ* 135–136 F 14, which is even found as late as Plutarch, *Alexander* 2.1; cf. Dascalakis 1970, pp. 156–158; Hammond and Griffith 1979, pp. 31–39; Ogden 2011, pp. 58–62; Müller 2016, pp. 100–104. See further Greenwalt 1985a; Vasilev 2012; Mladenovska-Ristovska 2017; Tiverios 2019 (Caranus earlier than Perdiccas I).

[31] Greenwalt 1985a, p. 45 n. 7, on the word to show authority. Ogden 2011, pp. 61–62, on the word associated with goat; cf. Sprawski 2010, p. 128.

[32] Diodorus 7.16; cf. Justin 7.1.7–10; Eusebius, *Chronicle* 1.227; cf. Clement of Alexandria, *Protrepticus* 2.11, with Hammond and Griffith 1979, pp. 7–11 and 13–14.

[33] On Caranus' exploits and the oracles, see Hammond and Griffith 1979, pp. 7–14 and 31–39; Greenwalt 1985a.

[34] Satyrus, *BNJ* 631 F 1.

[35] Tiverios 2019 (my thanks to V. Saripanidi for this reference).

[36] Greenwalt 1985a, especially pp. 47–49; Ogden 2011, pp. 57–71; cf. Hammond and Griffith 1979, pp. 6–12 (between 407 and 400); Borza 1990, p. 83; Sprawski 2010, p. 129.

[37] Greenwalt 1985a, p. 49; Sprawski 2010, pp. 128–129.

There is also an issue with the oracle. Caranus was supposed to establish his capital where he saw grazing goats, whereas Perdiccas, who also consulted the Delphic oracle, was told to settle where he saw sleeping goats:[38]

> Illustrious Temenidae have royal rule over wealth-producing land; for it is the gift of Zeus, bearer of the goatskin shield. But you [Perdiccas], go to the Bouteid land of many flocks, and where you see shiny-horned snow-white goats recumbent in their sleep, make sacrifice to the blessed gods and found the city of your state on the level ground of that land.

In both cases the capital is named Aegae, the "place of the goats," since *aix* is Greek for goat, although other theories associate the name with water.[39] But that is where the similarity ends. Caranus' oracle must be fiction; otherwise Herodotus, who delighted in oracles, would surely have mentioned it, as would Alexander I to help confirm his Greek lineage.[40]

The inclusion of Midas in some variants needs explanation.[41] His father was Gordius, who was said to have traveled from Macedonia to Gordium in Phrygia, where he became king. Some texts speak of Midas bringing Lydians and Phrygians to populate Edessa, and of Caranus expelling Midas from Edessa—the location of this town, as we discuss below, is less important for this story. Midas was popular in Greek mythology and associated with wealth and fertility, hence Midas of the "golden touch"—the linkage to the Gardens of Midas shows that Perdiccas (accepting Herodotus) chose the best place to establish the dynasty and provide for his people.[42]

One final theory on the dynasty's genesis is based on an onomastic study of names of rulers and argues that there was a dual origin from an Illyrian (Epirote) line and an eastern Thracian-Phrygian line.[43] Various Illyrian and Thracian tribes moved across the areas north of the Haliacmon River, perhaps for trade, and into Pieria, whose neighbors were called Makedones, or "highlanders."[44] The Pierian king attempted to oppose the newcomers but was defeated. Hence the names of the three brothers—Gauanes, Aeropus, and Perdiccas—gave rise to three related branches of the Macedonians:

[38] Diodorus 7.16; cf. Justin 7.1.7–8; Eusebius, *Chronicle* 1.108; Plutarch, *Alexander* 2.1. See Greenwalt 1985a, pp. 43–49; cf. Hammond and Griffith 1979, p. 5. Translation: Hammond 1992a, p. 4.

[39] Casson 1926, p. 50; Fowler 1988.

[40] Borza 1982b, p. 12; Greenwalt 1985a, pp. 45–46.

[41] Vassileva 2007; see too Hammond 1972a, pp. 407–414; Roller 1983; cf. Ogden 2011, pp. 65–67; Müller 2017a, pp. 187–188.

[42] Müller 2017a, especially p. 188.

[43] Rosen 1978, pp. 15–27, though see Zahrnt 1984, pp. 365–367.

[44] Dascalakis 1965, pp. 11–13; cf. Hammond 1995a, but on the name see Anson 1984.

Gauanes in Elimea, Aeropus in Lyncestis, and Perdiccas in Macedonia. These areas Thucydides also specifies: "The Macedonians also include the Lyncestians, Elimiotae, and other tribes of the upper region who are allies of the Lower Macedonians and subject to them yet have kings of their own." But then Alexander I's championing of Perdiccas and his Argive roots caused the lines of his brothers to be disregarded.[45] This theory, however, seems to complicate an already complicated issue.[46]

The veracity of the foundation myths is impossible to gauge, though on balance Herodotus' account, followed to an extent by Thucydides, is the most credible.[47] That means the Argead dynasty began with Perdiccas I, who came from Argos in the Peloponnese in the middle of the seventh century. What is important to recognize is that Macedonian kings starting at least with Alexander I wanted an Argive origin of the royal house made known to their subjects and the Greeks.[48] In doing so they proclaimed a Greek heritage and by extension an appreciation of, and even identification with, Greek culture.

Aegae: The first capital

The first steps of expansion appear to have been from Elimea along the valley of the Haliacmon to Pieria.[49] There Perdiccas is credited with founding what would be the first capital of the dynasty at Aegae in the northern foothills of Pieria, halfway between Mieza and coastal Pieria.[50] From this city—though really it was no more than a town in those days—Macedonia spread to encompass most of the Greek world and the Persian Empire thanks to Alexander the Great in the third quarter of the fourth century. Aegae's foundation was said to have been due to the Delphic oracle's fixation on goats, which we mentioned above. It came to be called the hearth of the kingdom, perhaps going back to the foundation story of the king's wife baking bread in the hearth of what for that time was the center of his power: their home.[51]

45 Borza 1990, p. 84; but see Rosen 1978, pp. 3–15.

46 Also against a Doric descent: Dascalakis 1970, pp. 160–161; Hammond 1972a, p. 63; Rosen 1978, pp. 3–6; Mallios 2011, pp. 115–122.

47 See now Molinero 2024.

48 Borza 1990, pp. 83–84; see in depth Rosen 1987; Hatzopoulos 2003; cf. Badian 1982a; Borza 1982b.

49 Though see Borza 1990, p. 82.

50 Diodorus 7.16; Justin 7.1.10 (Caranus); Eusebius, *Chronicle* 1.227; cf. Clement of Alexandria, *Protrepticus* 2.11, with Hammond and Griffith 1979, pp. 7–9 and 13–14; Sprawski 2010, p. 128, on location.

51 Hearth: Diodorus 22.12.1, with Greenwalt 1986, p. 121.

Aegae was strategically located close to major east–west and north–south routes, near the crossing of the Haliacmon River, and on the edge of the Emathian plain with an uninterrupted view over it. The town was originally and wrongly identified as Edessa, thanks to Caranus' oracle, but is in fact a town at Palatitsia-Vergina on the northern slope of the Pierian mountains, which Herodotus calls *Makedonis*.[52] There, a palace complex, theater, and necropolis of chamber tombs along with other graves have been located by the villages of Vergina and Palatitsa (figure 2.1).[53]

Aegae grew into a large city with a splendid palace until it was eclipsed as the administrative and military capital by Pella by Archelaus at the start of the fourth century. Even then Aegae remained an important city and was the venue for royal marriages and burials, perhaps going back to Perdiccas' order that his son Argaeus establish a burial site for his father's bones and

Figure 2.1 Aegae palace
Source: Michael Runkel / robertharding / Getty Images.

[52] Herodotus 7.127.1, with Hammond 1972a, pp. 53–67; cf. Zahrnt 1984, pp. 355–357; Hatzopoulos 1996, vol. 1, pp. 105–106; Hatzopoulos 2020, pp. 8–11 and 14, with further references. Edessa: Papazoglou 1988, pp. 111–112.

[53] Identification: Hammond 1972a, pp. 156–158; Hammond and Griffith 1979, pp. 13–14; Hammond 1997a rebutting Faklaris 1994 on not identifying Vergina with Aegae. See further on Aegae and its palace: Saatsoglou-Paliadeli 1999; Kottaridi 2002 (on p. 76 she says that even in the Early Iron Age it was rich and populous); Drougou and Saatsoglou-Paliadeli 2004; Drougou 2011; Kottaridi 2011b; Kottaridi 2020.

those of all succeeding kings—as far as we know, all Argead kings apart from Alexander the Great were buried there.[54]

Forming Macedonia

Hatzopoulos has said that Herodotus' foundation story preserves "a unique record concerning the origins of the Macedonian people and kingdom as well as the first stages of their territorial expansion."[55] By the late fifth century the small tribal area established by Perdiccas I had grown into a kingdom reaching as far as the Thermaic Gulf.[56] The stages by which this took place are hard to determine because our literary sources, principally Herodotus and Thucydides, are later and controversial.[57]

After Perdiccas and his brothers fled from Lebaea, they took control of "another part of Macedonia" and then "the rest of Macedonia," according to Herodotus in the excerpt above.[58] What were these places, and how did the brothers get there?[59] From Lebaea they likely crossed the Haliacmon River perhaps near Euia (Polymylos) and then over Mount Vermion through the Kastania pass and Leukopetra to the Gardens of Midas.[60] They seized what became Aegae and its area—*Makedonis*—which was either south of the Loudias and Haliacmon Rivers in the northern part of Pieria or within the plain enclosed between the courses of these rivers and Mount Vermion.[61] Hence the Haliacmon and the Axius (Vardar) Rivers became the boundaries of the original heart of the kingdom.[62] Archaeological finds support that the

[54] Justin 7.2.2–3; cf. Hammond 1992a, p. 24, Vasilev 2011a, p. 95 n. 10.

[55] Hatzopoulos 2003, p. 218. Contra Saripanidi 2017; Saripanidi 2019a; and Saripanidi 2020, on different stages and time periods.

[56] For the earlier Bronze and Iron Age eras, and what excavations have revealed about intra-Balkan connections rather than a Greek-Aegean one, see, for example, Borza 1990, pp. 58–74; Rosen 1978; especially Hammond 1972a, pp. 214–419; Mari 2011b, pp. 79–80, and bibliography on excavations quoted in n. 2.

[57] Edson 1970, especially pp. 19–30; Hammond 1972a, pp. 430–440; Sprawski 2010, pp. 127–134; Mari 2011b, pp. 79–81; King 2018, pp. 17–19; Hatzopoulos 2020, pp. 11–18 and 60–63; cf. Dascalakis 1965, pp. 25–30 and 97–105; Errington 1990, pp. 2–3. See also the detailed discussions of Dascalakis 1970; Rosen 1978; Zahrnt 1984; Chrysostomou 2018. On the limitations of the sources cf. Zahrnt 1984, pp. 326–330.

[58] Herodotus 8.138.2–3.

[59] Route: Hatzopoulos 2003, pp. 206–213; cf. Hammond 1972a, pp. 433–436; Rosen 1978, pp. 22–27; Hammond and Griffith 1979, pp. 6–8; Hatzopoulos 2020, pp. 11–15 and 61–62.

[60] Rosen 1978, pp. 12–13 (southern slopes); Zahrnt 1984, pp. 346–347 and 354 (eastern slopes), but Hatzopoulos 2003, pp. 206–207 and 212, places them near Beroia.

[61] Herodotus 7.131, 8.138.2–3. Northern Pieria: Edson 1970, p. 21 n. 16; Hammond 1972a, pp. 146–147. Plain: Zahrnt 1984, pp. 352–355; Hatzopoulos 1996, vol. 1, p. 171 n. 3.

[62] For example, Thomas 2010, pp. 68–70, on the rivers; see too Borza 1990, pp. 33–35.

first lands ruled by Macedonian kings were on both sides of the lower Haliacmon around Aegae and the foot of Mount Vermion because the main towns of Aegae, Beroia, Mieza, Edessa, and Dium in Pieria were founded at this time.[63]

From there the Macedonians went to conquer Pieria, then peopled by a Thracian tribe, and Bottiaea. After this conquest, early Macedonia comprised the Haliacmon Valley between the Loudias and the northern part of the Pierian mountains, as well as the foothills of Mount Vermion west of the upper Loudias River. The early presence of Macedonians in this area is also attested by Hesiod, who as noted above speaks of Zeus' two sons Magnes and Macedon living around Mount Olympus, which included the Pierian mountains.

But Herodotus' account of these expansion phases is contradicted by Thucydides in an aside during his narrative of the invasion of Macedonia by Sitalces of Thrace in 429, which we deal with in chapter 5. There Thucydides speaks of the Argive origins of the royal house, as we saw above, but goes on to describe Macedonia's hard-fought rise with several phases to it:[64]

> [Alexander the father of Perdiccas, and his forefathers, who were originally Temenidae from Argos, acquired and expanded Macedonia]. They defeated and expelled from Pieria the Pierians, who afterwards took up their abode in Phagres and other places at the foot of Mount Pangaeus beyond the Strymon (and even to this day the district at the foot of Mount Pangaeus toward the sea is called the Pierian Valley), and also, from the country called Bottia, the Bottiaeans, who now dwell on the borders of the Chalcidians; they acquired, further, a narrow strip of Paeonia extending along the river Axius from the interior to Pella and the sea; and beyond the Axius they possess the district as far as the Strymon which is called Mygdonia, having driven out the Edonians. Moreover, they expelled from the district now called Eordaea the Eordians, most of them were destroyed, but a small portion is settled in the neighborhood of Physca; and also from Almopia the Almopians. These Macedonians also made themselves

[63] Hatzopoulos 1996, vol. 1, p. 171; Sprawski 2010, pp. 132–134. See the chapters on individual cities in Lane Fox 2011a for archaeological finds; cf. Hammond 1972b.

[64] Thucydides 2.99.3–6, with Dascalakis 1965, pp. 29–34; Edson 1970, p. 27; Hammond 1972a, pp. 435–439; Rosen 1978, pp. 6–15; Hammond and Griffith 1979, pp. 435–438; Zahrnt 1984, especially pp. 330–341 (referencing others and their interpretation of the chronology on pp. 332–333); Borza 1990, pp. 85–87; Hammond 1992a, pp. 51–52; Hatzopoulos 2020, pp. 13–15; and in particular Vasilev 2011a, whose views I often follow.

masters of certain places, which they still hold, belonging to the other tribes, namely, of Anthemus, Crestonia, Bisaltia, as well as a large part of Macedonia proper. But the whole is now called Macedonia, and Perdiccas [II] son of Alexander was king when Sitalces made his invasion.

Thucydides speaks of Macedonia in his own time, during the rule of Alexander I's son Perdiccas II (?435–413). His description of the conquest of neighboring regions could be in chronological or geographical order, and the scholarly consensus is the latter.[65] But issues remain. For example, why would Eordaea and Almopia, the westernmost conquests of the Argeads, be mentioned after the expulsion of Bottiaeans (who went to parts of the Chacidice) as well as Lower Paeonia and Mygdonia?[66] In addition, the "migrationist" approach of Herodotus and Thucydides to the kingdom's expansion gives no idea of chronology for the various phases. Another hindrance is that the geographical landscape has changed considerably over the centuries, especially around the Thermaic Gulf and the courses of the Axius, Haliacmon, and Loudias Rivers—the Axius, for example, flowed over 20 kms further north than today.[67]

To make sense of Thucydides' order is Hatzopoulos' valid suggestion that he did not decide beforehand whether he would follow a chronological or geographical one.[68] He simply started his account of the expansion from Pieria as it was closest to Aegae, said to have been the first place captured, and then continued with regions that fanned out from there: Bottiaea, Lower Paeonia, and Mygdonia as far as the Strymon River. Then he realized he had failed to include the earlier, western conquests of Eordaea and Almopia so added them by using the expression "moreover, they expelled," before finishing with the most recent and most easterly and southerly conquests of Mygdonia, Crestonia, Bisaltia, and Anthemus by Alexander I. If we accept this argument, then the following reconstruction is plausible.[69]

[65] Edson 1970, pp. 20–29; Hammond 1972a, pp. 432–440, Rosen 1987, pp. 35–36; Hatzopoulos 2020, pp. 12–15; cf. Sprawski 2010, p. 132; see too Zahrnt 1984; Vasilev 2011a.

[66] Hatzopoulos 2020, pp. 13–14. Bottiaeans: Flensted-Jensen 1995, pp. 105–108 (inner and western part beginning south of Mygdonia).

[67] Hammond and Griffith 1979, pp. 3–14; cf. Thomas 2010, pp. 74–76; but against this view, see Hatzopoulos 2003, pp. 203–218; see too Mari 2011b, pp. 82–87, citing bibliography. On topography see Zahrnt 1984, pp. 334–341 and especially .

[68] Hatzopoulos 2020, pp. 12–13, on which this and the following paragraphs are based.

[69] Hammond and Griffith 1979, pp. 53–58 and 436–439, followed by Borza 1990, pp. 86–89; Hatzopoulos 2020, pp. 14–15; see too Edson 1970 (different stages); Rosen 1978; Zahrnt 1984; Mari 2011b; Vasilev 2011a. Archaeological evidence supporting slightly different stages: Saripanidi 2017; Saripanidi 2019a.

The stages of expansion (?)

There were perhaps six stages of expansion. The first one came when Perdiccas moved from the Gardens of Midas on the foothills of Mount Vermion into the lower Haliacmon Valley to capture Aegae in the area Herodotus calls *Makedonis*.[70]

The second stage was the conquest of Pieria and Bottiaea—obviously with more followers by then. The objective of the expansion was probably to gain more fertile land and natural resources as well as protect borders. The conquest of these areas was followed by the deportation of local peoples, with many perhaps moving to Mount Pangaeum near the Strymon in Thrace because there were Thracians already there.[71] Thus, Macedonia now comprised the Haliacmon Valley between the Loudias and the northern Pierian mountains along with the foothills of Mount Vermion.[72]

Control of Pieria provided a valuable frontier to the south as well as to the western Thermaic Gulf. Here the Macedonians would have encountered the Greek cities of Methone and Pydna, which may even have influenced them in founding their own settlements with administrative and social structures rather than just villages.[73] Further, their move into the fertile and equally strategic Bottiaea meant more land for growing crops, while the king acquired the region's natural resources.

Probably the third phase was when the Macedonians took over the nearby narrow strip of Paeonian land along the Axius River from the interior down to Pella.[74] Whether this was an actual new phase or was part of the Almopian campaign that came next is hard to tell; since it was to a different area, we may call it the third phase.

The fourth phase of expansion began after the mid-sixth century and was more wide-reaching. The kingdom's borders were almost all protected by natural barriers: west was Mount Vermion, south was the Pierian mountains, and to the north/northeast was the common riverbed of the Loudias and Haliacmon.[75] Eordaea to the west of Bottiaea and Almopia to its north were different matters as there was no natural obstacle; hence it made strategic sense to secure them

[70] Herodotus 7.127.1.

[71] Hammond 1972a, pp. 440–441; Vasilev 2011a, p. 95; cf. Borza 1990, p. 86.

[72] Zahrnt 1984, pp. 348–352; Hatzopoulos 2020, p. 14.

[73] Hatzopoulos 1996, vol. 1, pp. 106–109 (saying the same about Sindos and Therme, though perhaps any degree of influence is too much), and on cities and villages see pp. 109–123, and especially Papazoglou 1988.

[74] Thucydides 2.99.4, from Hecataeus, with Hammond 1972a, pp. 146–147 and 438–439; cf. Hatzopoulos 2020, pp. 14–15.

[75] Vasilev 2011a, p. 95.

next.[76] Moreover, Eordaea had considerable manpower and natural resources and was on several important routes within Upper Macedonia, including the only route from there to the Emathian plain and Thessaly beyond.[77]

Probably in about 520, during the reign of Amyntas I, came the move into Almopia and Eordaea.[78] In the capture of Eordaea, many of the "Eordi of Eordia," as Thucydides calls them, were killed and only a small number managed to flee to a remote part of Mygdonia, east of the Axius River. Macedonian colonists then settled onto the empty lands.[79] Likewise in the invasion of Almopia the Almopians were expelled and new cities founded, which had become part of a pattern when taking over land.[80] But we should be careful, as the belief that the Macedonians had crossed the Axius by the late sixth century thanks to Amyntas I is impacted by the contents of tombs datable to the sixth and the first half of the fifth century excavated throughout the region, especially Trebeniste, Aiani, Vergina, Pella-Archontiko, Sindos, Agia Paraskevia on the edge of the Anthemus Valley, Gavgelija in the north, and Amphipolis in the east.[81] Nevertheless, Macedonia now had secure frontiers in three directions: south, west, and north.

The fifth stage of expansion was into Mygdonia.[82] The native population was again expelled, with some fleeing east of the Strymon River and others south to the Athos peninsula.[83] Thanks to that campaign, the eastern border of Macedonia now reached as far as the Strymon River, perhaps even including the eastern part of Bisaltia, and the Argeads controlled a strategically important territory allowing them to play a role in the Chalcidice.[84]

[76] Hatzopoulos 2020, p. 15, is right to say chronological precision is impossible because Thucydides adds them as an "after-thought" after the conquest of Mygdonia. But they are likely to have taken place before then, so I follow others in putting them here. See further Edson 1970, pp. 20–27; Hammond 1972a, pp. 437–439; Hammond and Griffith 1979, pp. 28–31 and 62–64; Zahrnt 1984, pp. 332–334; Borza 1990, pp. 85–89 and 98 with n. 3; Errington 1990, pp. 5–7; Hammond 1992a, pp. 8–12 and 51–52; Sprawski 2010, pp. 131–134; Mari 2011b, pp. 83–84; King 2018, pp. 18–19; and in detail Hatzopoulos 2003; Vasilev 2011a.

[77] Hammond 1972a, pp. 106–110; Borza 1990, p. 87; cf. pp. 35–38, on the Bitola-Kozani corridor.

[78] Hammond and Griffith 1979, p. 62, based on Strabo 7.7.8, estimated that Eordaea was conquered between 520 and 510, which is followed by Borza 1990, pp. 87 and 292–293; cf. Vasilev 2011a, p. 97; contra Chrysostomou 2018 (Eordaea in the second quarter of the sixth century and Almopia in the middle of that century).

[79] The conquest of Eordaea did not lead to that of adjacent Lyncus and Elimea, at least not yet, probably due to the exhaustion for new acquisitions or strategic considerations: Vasilev 2011a, p. 97.

[80] Hammond 1972a, pp. 166–167 and 438.

[81] Borza 1990, pp. 88–89; Hatzopoulos 2020, pp. 15–16. See the summary of finds from various excavations at Hatzopoulos 2020, pp. 19–33. On the term *Makedones*, see Anson 1984.

[82] Vasilev 2011a, pp. 101–102; Hatzopoulos 2020, pp. 15–16.

[83] Hammond and Griffith 1979, pp. 61–62. But Thucydides may have erred here if Mygdonia was not taken over until later: Zahrnt 1984, pp. 341–342.

[84] Hammond and Griffith 1979, p. 102, suggest that Alexander I took advantage of the Persian withdrawal also to seize Ennea Hodoi ("Nine Ways"), where Amphipolis later stood, and that the king erected a golden statue at Delphi to mark this victory in 478–476/5. But Herodotus says

We thus move to what Thucydides has at the end of his list, the campaign against Anthemus in the Chalcidice, Crestonia along the upper reaches of the Echedorus River, and neighboring Bisaltia. The last was rich in silver mines, which was probably the motive for the incursion, as Herodotus says that Alexander I received one talent of silver per day from the Bisaltae mines.[85]

Herodotus makes it plain that Bisaltia and Crestonia were conquered after the retreat of the Persians from Greece in 479, during Alexander I's reign, since he says their people were then under the rule of their own king.[86] That information provides a context for the seizure of Anthemus, hence we may group these three places into a sixth phase of expansion. But against this is Herodotus' comment that Amyntas I offered Anthemus to Hippias, a member of the Pisistratid tyrant family that had controlled Athens until 510, which would indicate it was an Argead possession before the Persian invasion.[87]

Good arguments have been made against this earlier date of 510.[88] Thucydides, for example, and if we accept his chronological order, has Anthemus, Crestonia, and Bisaltia in the last stages of expansion. And Amyntas' offer might have been for a joint operation with Hippias to take over Anthemus, as it was located close to the mining region of Rhaecelus (in Crousis), which Hippias' family possessed. Hippias, however, declined the offer. Thus, we may put the capture of Anthemus by Alexander I after the campaign in Mygdonia.[89]

Macedonia had grown three or four times larger than the size of its original homeland by the end of the sixth century, but it had been a bloody expansion. Many of the local peoples had been killed or expelled; perhaps only a small number stayed in their homes, but everyone was subject to Argead rule, now part of the growing Macedonian kingdom, and were Makedones—Macedonians.

Macedonia under the Argead Kings: The Rise and Fall of an Ancient Superpower. Ian Worthington, Oxford University Press. © Oxford University Press 2026. DOI: 10.1093/9780197668009.003.0003

nothing of such a venture—while mentioning the gold statue of Alexander at 8.121.2–122.1—so for various reasons the view is untenable: Vasilev 2011a, p. 102, and see further Xydopoulos 2016.

[85] Herodotus 5.17.2, with Raymond 1953, p. 86.

[86] Herodotus 8.116.1; on dating, cf. Vasilev p. 103; Hammond and Griffith 1979, pp. 84 and 104–105. Cf. Edson 1970, p. 27 and n. 54, who believed that the conquest of Lower Paeonia, Mygdonia, and Anthemus was not before the Persian Wars, but see now Hatzopoulos 2020, pp. 16–17.

[87] Herodotus 5.94.1, with Xydopoulos 2012b.

[88] Hatzopoulos 2020, p. 17; cf. Vasilev 2011a, p. 99.

[89] Hammond and Griffith 1979, pp. 63–64, suppose that Alexander I conquered Upper Macedonia in 483–481, but their evidence is questionable: Vasilev 2011a, pp. 103–104.

3

Amyntas I and the Persian Alignment

Amyntas I's kingship takes us from myth to history and a rise in Macedonia's influence in the Balkans. Assuming Perdiccas was Macedonia's first king and ruled from the middle to the later seventh century, and that each of Amyntas' predecessors had a reign of 25–30 years, then Amyntas I was king from about 547 to 498 or 495, when he was succeeded by his son Alexander (chapter 4).[1] Unfortunately, Herodotus was not particularly concerned with Amyntas and devoted more time to Alexander I, while Thucydides does not mention Alexander's predecessors at all. Thus, what little we know of Amyntas' reign is set against the backdrop of Persian campaigns in the Balkans.

Amyntas and Persia

By 513 Darius I of Persia had set his sights on expanding his already vast empire into the Aegean and Greece.[2] In that year he sailed across the Hellespont to eastern Thrace, presumably intending to battle tribes such as the European Scythians and the Getae, the latter at the time the strongest tribe in northern Thrace, but he did not engage them.[3] Instead, he returned to Sardis, his empire's westernmost capital, leaving behind 80,000 men under the command of his general Megabazus.[4] In the following year and into 511 Megabazus took over several coastal cities, extended Persian power in Thrace, and campaigned against the powerful Paeonians, by then the dominant power in eastern

[1] Reign: Hammond and Griffith 1979, pp. 57–60; Borza 1990, pp. 98–103; Hammond 1992a, pp. 42–43; Sprawski 2010, pp. 134–136; Müller 2016, pp. 107–111.

[2] On the Persians and their empire see, for example, Dandamaev 1989; Allen 2005. Persian policy in Thrace and Macedonia: Vasilev 2015, especially chapter 1 on Darius' eastern advance.

[3] Scythian and Thracian campaigns: Vasilev 2015, pp. 45–83. See too Castritius 1972; Hammond 1980a; Balcer 1988; Archibald 1998, pp. 81–87; Stronk 1998–1999; Lerner 2017.

[4] Herodotus 4.143.1.

Macedonia.[5] They had expanded into the Strymon Valley perhaps as far as the coast at Mygdonia, occupying lands along with Thracians.[6]

But that expansion and the several cities the Paeonians founded obstructed the westward movement of the Persians. Hence in about 511 Megabazus ended the Paeonians' hegemony of the region. He deported them to Asia Minor, where on Darius' orders where they were resettled.[7] Perhaps, however, only the leading families were sent away, as many Paeonians continued to live around Lake Prasias and elsewhere.[8] In any case, Persian control of the Strymon Valley was "illusory" since some of the deported Paeonians returned home with the Persians unable to stop them.[9]

Amyntas had probably taken advantage of the reduction of Paeonian power in Thrace to expand beyond the Axius River and even to have taken over Amphaxitis.[10] But Persian expansion westward showed no signs of slowing down; hence if Amyntas were to continue adding to his realm, he may have countered Darius' plans, not to mention blocked his need for Macedonian timber for his fleet.[11] Perhaps against this background we have Herodotus' claim that Megabazus had subjugated "all the country as far as Thessaly" to the authority of the Persian king, though the extent of Megabazus' campaigns and what Persia came to control are controversial.[12] The issue of whether Macedonia submitted to Persian rule demands attention as it also affects Alexander I's relations with Persia, as we discuss in the next chapter.

Herodotus tells a lengthy story that after the defeat of the Paeonians Megabazus sent seven Persian envoys to Amyntas, presumably meeting the king at Aegae and following the same route that Xerxes later took in 481,

[5] Vasilev 2015, pp. 89–109; cf. Merker 1965, pp. 41–43. Megabazus' route: Zahrnt 1984, pp. 359–360.

[6] Paeonians: Merker 1965; for their ethnicity and location, see Merker 1965, pp. 39–41. Thracians also in Mygdonia: Delev 2005 (I owe this reference to V. Saripanidi).

[7] Possibly at Parsa (Persepolis): Herodotus 5.15.3, 17.1, with Balcer 1988, p. 9. But Herodotus 5.23.1 has Sardis and at 5.98.1 that they were then taken to Phrygia.

[8] Hammond 1980a, pp. 56–57; Delev 2005; cf. Sprawski 2010, p. 135; Vasilev 2015, p. 107.

[9] Archibald 1998, pp. 79–87, on "illusory;" see too Merker 1965, pp. 41–42; Hammond and Griffith 1979, pp. 56–57; Borza 1990, p. 104; Sprawski 2010, p. 135, drawing on Herodotus 5.98.3–4 (return of Paeonians).

[10] Hammond and Griffith 1979, pp. 57–59, though Borza 1990, pp. 87–88, expresses caution at the date, and Saripinidi 2019a that it was not long before 570. Amphaxitis: Hammond 1972a, pp. 176–179.

[11] Archibald 1998, pp. 81–82; Sprawski 2010, p. 134. Timber: Herodotus 5.23.3–4.

[12] Herodotus 7.108.2. Persian conquests in the Balkans: Hammond and Griffith 1979, pp. 55–60; Borza 1990, pp. 101–105; Briant 2002, pp. 141–146; Vasilev 2015, pp. 86–109; cf. Sprawski 2010, p. 134; Olbrycht 2010, pp. 343–344; and see too Moloney 2018.

who demanded earth and water—the customary tokens of submission.[13] After this demand, Herodotus says:[14]

> [Amyntas gave these tokens and invited them to be his guests.] He prepared a dinner of great splendor and received them hospitably. But after dinner the Persians said to Amyntas as they sat drinking together, "Macedonian, our host, it is our Persian custom after the giving of any great banquet to bring in also the concubines and wedded wives to sit by the men. Do you then (since you have received us heartily and are nobly entertaining us, and are giving Darius our king earth and water) follow our custom?" To this Amyntas replied, "Persians, we do not have the same custom as with us men and women sit apart; but seeing that you are our masters and would have this too, it shall be as you desire." With that, Amyntas sent for the women; they came at call and sat down opposite the Persians. Then the Persians, seeing the attractive women before them, spoke to Amyntas and said that there was no sense in what he had done; it would have been better (they said) if the women had never come at all than that they should come and not sit beside by the men, but sit opposite them, to torment their eyes. Amyntas, then, as needs must, bade the women sit beside them, which they did. At once the Persians, flushed as they were with too much wine, laid hands on their breasts and tried to kiss them. This Amyntas saw, but held his peace for all his anger, because he greatly feared the Persians. But his son Alexander, in his youth and fury at such bad behavior, could not bear it any longer. He angrily said to Amyntas, "Father, as befits your age, leave us and take your rest, and do not continue drinking; I will stay here and give our guests what they need." At this Amyntas saw that Alexander had some wild deed in mind, and said, "Son, you are angry, and if I guess your meaning rightly you want to send me away so that you may do some violent deed. For my part, then, I entreat you not to act rashly toward these men, lest you undo us, but endure the sight of what they are doing patiently. But if you would have me depart, I consent to that." Amyntas left and Alexander said to the Persians, "Sirs, you have

[13] Hammond and Griffith 1979, pp. 58–59; Borza 1990, pp. 101–103; Vasilev 2015, pp. 109–110. Xerxes' route: Herodotus 7.124, with Borza 1990, pp. 289–290; Vasilev 2015, pp. 109 and 113.

[14] Herodotus 5.18–21 (modified by Worthington); cf. Justin 7.3.3–9. See Kuhrt 1988 and Rung 2015 on the tokens, though Sprawski 2010, pp. 133, 135 with bibliography in n. 18, and pp. 137–138, argued that offering earth and water could signify something different from unconditional surrender to the Persian king and that there were other forms of submission.

> full freedom to deal with these women and may have sex with all or any of them. As to that, you will decide. But now, as the hour of your rest draws near, and I see that you are all well and truly drunk, allow these women to leave and freshen up, and then they have done so, wait for them to come back to you. The Persians agreed to this and after the women had left Alexander sent them to their apartments. He then took as many smooth-chinned men as there were women and dressed them in the women's clothing and gave them daggers. He brought them in and said to the Persians: "I think, men of Persia, you have feasted to your hearts' content; all that we had and all besides that we could find to give you has been set before you; now we make you a free gift of our best and most choice possessions, our own mothers and sisters. Know then that we honor you as you deserve and tell your king who sent you how his Greek viceroy of Macedonia has received you hospitably in board and bed." With that Alexander made his Macedonians sit next to each Persian, as though they were women. When the Persians began to grope them, the Macedonians killed them.... Not long after, the Persians sent out a search party for these men, but Alexander was cunning enough to put an end to it by giving a large sum of money and his sister Gygaea to Bubares, a Persian, the general of those who had searched for the slain men; by this gift he made an end to the search.

According to this account, a fearful Amyntas submitted to the Persians' demand and became a "viceroy" of Persia. He was also easily led by his young son Alexander and willingly left the banqueting hall suspecting that his son was intent on a dastardly deed, which indeed came about when he had the Persians murdered. Yet Amyntas must surely have expected Persian retaliation, and Herodotus tells us that the Persians sent out a search party led by Megabazus' son Bubares to find out what had happened to the envoys.[15] Again, according to Herodotus, it is Alexander who comes to the rescue by bribing Bubares with considerable money and marrying his sister Gygaea to him.[16]

Almost every aspect of Herodotus' tale has been dismissed as improbable.[17] Amyntas' quickness in making Macedonia subject to Persian rule, his meek

[15] Bubares as Megabazus' son: Herodotus 7.22.2, with Badian 1994, pp. 111–116; cf. Carney 2000, p. 16.

[16] Cf. Hammond and Griffith 1979, pp. 59–60; Borza 1990, pp. 102–103.

[17] Errington 1981; see too Dascalakis 1965, pp. 151–155; Hammond and Griffith 1979, pp. 98–99; Badian 1982a, p. 34; Scaife 1989, pp. 132–133; Borza 1990, pp. 102 and 104–105; Hammond 1992a,

role in the affair, and his willingness to bow to his son's dismissal hardly smacks of kingship. We also wonder how Alexander could have arranged for the male youths to don female disguises and arm themselves for action literally as events at the banquet unfolded as it is not certain he left the room, not to mention that the supposed conversation between himself and his father was in front of the Persians! And were the latter too drunk to notice the gender change or see the daggers? Perhaps—if their senses were incapacitated by alcohol. Then there is the fact that Herodotus tells us nothing about the Persian victims, not even their names, and as has been pointed out, seven is a questionably high number for an embassy of this sort.[18]

The timing of the marriage of Bubares and Gygaea is also suspect—they certainly married, as they had a son Amyntas (named after his grandfather), to whom the Great King gave the wealthy city of Alabanda in Caria.[19] But their marriage has been put anywhere between 510 and even 492.[20] It surely cannot be connected to the episode of the envoys as only kings arranged marriages of the royal family and Bubares would not have dealt with Alexander the heir on this matter.[21] In any case, it is beyond belief that Bubares suddenly lost interest in the fate of official envoys thanks to a bribe and a wedding. Likewise, an alternative account in Justin, that Bubares intended to punish the Macedonians but then fell in love with Gygaea and so made no moves against the kingdom after he married her, must also be rejected for its "romantic motive."[22] The marriage—incidentally that of the first "historical" Argead woman preserved in our sources—must be placed in Alexander I's reign, as we discuss in the next chapter.[23]

The spotlight in this whole account shines squarely on Alexander the protector defying the Persians. As we shall see, since he originally sided with Persia in the Persian Wars but then forged contacts with the Greeks, the episode of the envoys may be his own invention to turn bad into good and so promote his standing in Greece. If so, he circulated this story after the

pp. 42–43 and 99; Badian 1994, pp. 108–109; Karavites 1997, pp. 119–120; Fearn 2007a, pp. 98–127; Sprawski 2010, p. 136; Mari 2011b, p. 85; Vasilev 2015, pp. 109–110 and 228–229; King 2018, pp. 25–26, Müller 2016, pp. 115–116.

[18] Errington 1981, p. 142.

[19] Herodotus 8.136.1; cf. Badian 1994, pp. 115–116.

[20] 510: Hammond and Griffith 1979, p. 59. 511: Badian 1994, p. 112. During Amyntas' reign: Borza 1990, p. 103. After 498: Errington 1981, p. 141. 492 when Mardonius reached Macedonia: Rosen 1987, pp. 30 and 40 n. 43; Sprawski 2010, p. 137.

[21] Carney 2000, p. 16; Hammond and Griffith 1979, p. 59, assume that the king in question was Amyntas.

[22] Justin 7.3.9, with Sprawski 2010, pp. 136–137.

[23] Rosen 1987, pp. 30 and 40 n. 43; Carney 2000, p. 16; Kertész 2005, pp. 120–121; cf. Zahrnt 1992, p. 246.

Persians' defeat at Plataea in 479, as he would not have boasted in this manner before that battle in case the Persians won it and conquered Greece.[24]

We might also question whether there had been any demand of submission, for Herodotus speaks of the Persian Mardonius subjecting the Macedonians in 492, and Macedonia could not twice submit to Persia for the first time.[25] In addition, "Macedonians" are not found on Achaemenid royal inscriptions among the names of people conquered by the Persians. Then again, another name could have been used, such as *Yaunâ takabarâ*, which occurs in inscriptions, with *takabarâ* meaning "wearing a shield on the head," recalling the flat shape of the Macedonian hat (*kausia*).[26]

More likely is that Darius did demand submission from Amyntas but with a difference: despite Herodotus' silence on any special treatment, Macedonia may not have been conquered and garrisoned, as with the Paeonians or some Thracian cities, but enjoyed the privileged status of vassal state.[27] His successor, Alexander I, was described as *strategos* and *basileus*—"general and king"—of the Macedonians, and if Amyntas was known by this title, Macedonia may thus have been a Persian protectorate.[28] It may even have been included in the Thracian satrapy named "Skudra," though the existence of that locale has been doubted.[29]

Why did Herodotus include the anecdote of the envoys in his narrative, since it may be completely ahistorical? Perhaps he did so for literary reasons, using it as an example to show attitudes between the Greek world and the east.[30] Alternatively, if he had visited Macedonia and Alexander told him this story, perhaps to denigrate his father and show he was a better king, as we discuss in the following chapter, Herodotus may have been unable to resist what was after all a sensational tale.[31]

[24] King 2018, p. 25.
[25] Herodotus 7.108.2, with Errington 1981.
[26] Olbrycht 2010, pp. 243–244, with nn. 5–7; cf. Rosen 1978, pp. 6–7; Zahrnt 1992, p. 247; but note the caution of Vasilev 2015, pp. 114–117 and especially pp. 155–159.
[27] Edson 1970, p. 25; Rosen 1978, p. 6; Hammond 1980a, pp. 4–6; Zahrnt 1984, p. 361; Balcer 1988, p. 5; Zahrnt 1992, pp. 240–244; cf. pp. 250–253; Heinrichs and Müller 2008, pp. 289–290; Sprawski 2010, pp. 137–138; Olbrycht 2010, p. 343; Zahrnt 2011, p. 765; Vasilev 2011a, p. 100; Mari 2011b, p. 85; Xydopoulos 2012b, pp. 22–30; Vasilev 2015, pp. 112 and 115; cf. Hammond and Griffith 1979, pp. 58–59; Castritius 1972, pp. 2–3; Taceva 1992, pp. 60–61; Badian 1994, pp. 108–113; Karavites 1997, p. 119. See also Instinsky 1956.
[28] Herodotus 9.44.1, with Rosen 1987, pp. 28–29; Sprawski 2010, pp. 137–138.
[29] Hammond and Griffith 1979, pp. 59–60 and 64; Hammond 1980a, pp. 53–61; Balcer 1988, especially pp. 19–21, for such a satrapy. Doubted: Vasilev 2015, pp. 114–117, 120–121, 152–161, 228–230; Lerner 2017, especially pp. 13–21; cf. Müller 2016, pp. 112–118; see too Pjakowski 1983.
[30] Fearn 2007a, pp. 98–127, though perhaps reading too much into presentation and stretching interpretation at times.
[31] Hammond and Griffith 1979, pp. 98–99, though whether Alexander "charmed" Herodotus is unknown and the two may not even have met. See in detail on Alexander's influence and

Amyntas and Macedonia

Amyntas took advantage of Persian successes against the Paeonians and especially the Thracians to expand his kingdom. His territory already included the Emathian plain to the Thermaic Gulf, which gave him a strong defense against the various peoples of Upper Macedonia and the Molossian kings of Epirus to his west. But by the end of his reign, he had added considerably to Macedonia's territory, including Amphaxatis, Pella, and Ichnae, and incorporated local populations, except for the Paeonians into his kingdom.[32] Perhaps he even received westernmost Mygdonia from the Persians, who had taken it off the powerful Edonians, to give him control of the northeast coast of the Thermaic Gulf as far as the fertile valley named Anthemus.[33]

As we noted in the previous chapter, according to Herodotus Amyntas apparently offered Anthemus to the former Athenian tyrant Hippias in 510–505.[34] The king may have approached Hippias because the latter sought to re-establish control of Athens, though his move does not mean he was actively seeking an alliance with Hippias, and it is hard to see what gains Macedonia would make.[35] Possibly Amyntas did not possess Anthemus and was advocating a joint campaign to take it.[36] The episode is more likely one in relations between Macedonia and Persia, given that Hippias was pro-Persian, and only a few years later in 490 Darius seems to have tried to return him to power (chapter 4). Thus, Amyntas was using him to ingratiate himself with Darius and win more gains for his kingdom, especially if he had not formally submitted to Persia.[37]

When Amyntas died is unknown. The story of offering Anthemus to Hippias must show he was on the throne around 510, as he was in 499–498 when Bubares left Macedonia, perhaps because the Greek cities in Ionia revolted in that year and his presence was needed there.[38] If we put Amyntas'

Herodotus' account of Amyntas and Alexander: Rosen 1987 and Badian 1994. Skeptical of Alexander's influence on Herodotus is Scaife 1989; cf. Zahrnt 2011.

[32] Hammond and Griffith 1979, pp. 58–59.

[33] Hammond and Griffith 1979, pp. 55–65; see too Xydopoulos 2012b, citing bibliography.

[34] Herodotus 5.94.1, with Rosen 1987, p. 37; Hammond and Griffith 1979, pp. 28–31 and 59; Borza 1990, pp. 117–118; Vasilev 2011a, pp. 101–102.

[35] On Anthemus and Hippias, see especially Xydopoulos 2012b, with pp. 24–31 on territorial gains when Persia acquired the Strymon; cf. Zahrnt, 1984, pp. 332–334, 360, and 365; Tripodi 2007, p. 82; Archibald 2010, p. 332; Müller 2016, pp. 109–110.

[36] Hatzopoulos 1996, vol. 1, p. 174; Xydopoulos 2012b, p. 25.

[37] Hammond and Griffith 1979, p. 59; Zahrnt 1984, pp. 332–334, 360, and 365; Müller 2016, pp. 109–110, but see the remarks of Xydopoulos 2012b, pp. 25–27.

[38] He cannot have overseen Macedonia for a decade after 510 if Amyntas did not submit to Persia: Hammond and Griffith 1979, pp. 59–60; Hammond 1992a, p. 42; see too Borza 1990, p. 10; Vasilev 2015, pp. 124–127.

death at the same time as Bubares left for Asia Minor, then 498–497 would be an accepted window.[39] How Amyntas died is likewise unknown. As we shall see, many of the Argead kings were murdered, but there is nothing to suggest Amyntas suffered this fate. Relations between him and his son and heir Alexander seemed amicable, and even if the reasons for the latter's apparent rebuke of his father at the banquet are true, it was hardly a motive for regicide. Amyntas therefore may be one of the few Argead rulers lucky enough to have died from natural causes.

Amyntas' reign hinged on his dealings with Persia, and we could even call him a pawn in the Great King's expansion. At the same time, he was wily enough to exploit his status with Persia to expand Macedonia's territory, especially after the reduction of Paeonian power, taking care not to act against any Persian interest while advancing his own. Macedonia's growth under Amyntas meant that its involvement in major events in the north Aegean and in Greece was inevitable: thanks to him, the kingdom's rise to influence had begun.

Macedonia under the Argead Kings: The Rise and Fall of an Ancient Superpower. Ian Worthington, Oxford University Press. © Oxford University Press 2026. DOI: 10.1093/9780197668009.003.0004

[39] Justin 7.4.1. See too Hammond and Griffith 1979, pp. 58–59 and 60; Borza 1990, pp. 87–89.

4
Courting the Greeks: Alexander I

Amyntas I was succeeded by his son Alexander, "one of the most prominent and certainly the most intriguing" of the earlier Argead kings (figure 4.1).[1] He was probably born between 530 and 527, based on Herodotus' comment that he was only a youth when he supposedly engineered the deaths of the Persian envoys in Pella in 512, and came to power in probably 498–497.[2] Nothing is known of his birth or upbringing, but since he was later given the epithet "philhellene" or "lover of all things Greek," he had an appreciation of Greek culture and may have had Greek tutors.[3]

Alexander's reign saw truly significant expansion in Macedonia's territory and economy, especially after he took over the silver mines of Mount

Figure 4.1 Alexander I on silver octadrachm
Source: Wikimedia Commons.

[1] Hatzopoulos 2020, p. 125.
[2] Reign: Papastravrou 1936; Cloché 1960, pp. 36–56; Dascalakis 1965, pp. 147–223; Hammond and Griffith 1979, pp. 60–62 and 98–115; Borza 1990, pp. 123–135; Errington 1990, pp. 9–15; Hammond 1992a, pp. 43–47; Sprawski 2010, pp. 138–143; Mari 2011b, pp. 86–88; King 2018, pp. 28–35; Müller 2016, pp. 105–140; see too Karavites 1997; Wirth 1985a.
[3] Dascalakis 1965, pp. 150–151.

Dysorum in the Strymon Valley and began minting his own coinage, and even in the consolidation of the monarch's power at the expense of influential families in various cities as archaeological evidence, discussed further below, suggests. Thucydides even claims that Alexander was the "the first to acquire and make [Macedonia] a kingdom," thus giving him a pivotal role in the creation of the Macedonian state.[4] Alexander also dramatically increased diplomatic and cultural contacts with the Greeks, and many of his successors built on his accomplishments, though it is perhaps going too far to call *him* "the great."[5]

Alexander's early kingship

If Macedonia became a vassal state of Persia under Amyntas, it must have broken free for it to have been subdued when Alexander was king. When though? A plausible time was during the Ionian revolt of 499 to 492, which challenged Persian dominance over the Greeks of Ionia, forcing the Persians to evacuate their European possessions, including Thrace.[6] At the end of the revolt, Darius restored his power in the Hellespont region and returned his attention to Greece, specifically the lands between the Hebrus and the Strymon.

In the spring of 492, Darius sent his nephew and son-in-law Mardonius as general to secure the land and sea route along the north Aegean coast and, according to Herodotus, "subdue as many of the Greek cities as they could...and their land army added the Macedonians to the slaves that they had already, for all the nations nearer to them than Macedonia had been made subject to the Persians before now."[7] Whether Darius' aim was to subjugate all Greece or punish only those who had supported the Ionians, specifically Eretria (on Euboea) and Athens, is uncertain, but most likely it was the latter, given that Mardonius took only a small force with him.[8]

4 Thucydides 2.99.3. Silver mines: Herodotus 5.17.2.

5 Müller 2016, pp. 105–106.

6 Cole 1978, p. 42; Zahrnt 1992, pp. 250–253 (pp. 269–273 on Persian conquests in Thrace); Badian 1994, pp. 116–117; Sprawski 2010, pp. 136–137; Zahrnt 2011, pp. 765–766; Vasilev 2011a, p. 100; Müller 2016, pp. 118–119; King 2018, p. 27; especially Vasilev 2015, pp. 124–126; cf. Moloney 2018, and on events of the revolt, see pp. 127–142; contra Dascalakis 1965, p. 172, that Alexander stayed loyal. The impact of the revolt on Persia's hold in Europe is downplayed by Hammond and Griffith 1979, p. 60; cf. Georges 2000.

7 Herodotus 6.44.1 and see Instinsky 1956 and especially Zahrnt 1992.

8 Zahrnt 1992, pp. 240–244; Vasilev 2011a, p. 100; Vasilev 2015, pp. 142–146, on the reasons for Persian imperialism, citing bibliography (all say focused on Thrace and Macedonia).

Herodotus does not say who was on the Macedonian throne when Mardonius crossed to Greece, but it must have been Alexander I. Hence, we should therefore accept the ninth century AD Byzantine chronicler George Syncellus' claim that Alexander gave "earth and water" to the Persians and in doing so became the Persian king's *hyparchos*, or military commander.[9] In any case, it made sense that early in his reign Alexander would align himself with Persia; hence Bubares' marriage to Gygaea, mentioned in the previous chapter, was perhaps now, in 492.[10] That marriage would strengthen the king's relations with Persia.[11] Perhaps even his ties with Persia allowed Alexander to increase his own power as king at the expense of previously powerful families, a defining moment in the shaping of his *basileia* ("kingship") and that of his successors.[12]

But did Macedonia become a satrapy, since the term *hyparchos* can mean satrap? Herodotus also uses it of governors of areas, and in any case the first documented person to be *hyparchos* was a man named Hecatomnus a century later.[13] This is a long, perhaps suspiciously long, gap from Alexander's time, though he seems to have been included in the Persian Empire's administrative structure.[14] Perhaps, then, Macedonia did not become an actual satrapy but a dependent territory, which may explain why the Greeks did not attack it after the Persian withdrawal in 479 (see below).

Mardonius marched along the coast of Thrace and Macedonia, but his fleet was hit by the region's violent winds off Mount Athos; 300 ships were destroyed, and 20,000 men were lost at sea.[15] To make matters worse, when his army camped in Macedonian territory, it was attacked one night by the

[9] Syncellus p. 469 (Dindorf ed.) = p. 269, 10–11, in the Teubner text of Mosshammer; see too Adler and Tuffin 2002, p. 296. No submission: Errington 1981; Borza 1990, p. 105. Submission: Zahrnt 1992, pp. 245–249; Badian 1994, pp. 109–111; Tripodi 2007, pp. 68–69; Sprawski 2010, p. 137; Zahrnt 2011, pp. 762–763; Vasilev 2015, pp. 110–117; in more detail: Balcer 1988; Xydopoulos 2012b; see too Müller 2016, pp. 121–129, on relations with Persia.

[10] Errington 1981, pp. 139–143; Rosen 1987, pp. 30 and 40 n. 43; Sprawski 2010, p. 137.

[11] Sprawski 2010, pp. 137–138. Xydopoulos 2012b, p. 29, claims that the marriage sealed "Macedon's servitude" to Persia, implying Bubares was in command and that Persia continued to control the shots after Bubares left.

[12] Saripanidi 2019a, pp. 400–404.

[13] Badian 1994, pp. 114–115, on its meaning as satrap.

[14] Hammond and Griffith 1979, pp. 59–60; Pjakowski 1983; Balcer 1988, pp. 1–6; Zahrnt 1992, pp. 247 and 267; Badian 1994, p. 114; see too Tripodi 2007, pp. 68–72 and 72–85; Sprawski 2010, pp. 134–138; Olbrycht 2010, p. 343; Vasilev 2015, p. 116 and especially pp. 155–159; cf. Castritius 1972, pp. 7–9 and 10–11; Heinrichs and Müller 2008, p. 290.

[15] Herodotus 6.44; on the campaign, see Zahrnt 1992, pp. 238–240; Vasilev 2015, pp. 146–159. It may even be now that Mardonius turned Thrace into a satrapy: Castritius 1972, pp. 1–15; Archibald 1998, pp. 87–88.

neighboring Thracian tribe of the Brygi. Mardonius was wounded, and though he managed to overcome his enemy, he was forced to return to Asia.[16]

Two years later, in 490, a Persian navy with Hippias, the former Athenian tyrant, on board crossed the southern Aegean to Euboea, burning Eretria on that island, and then sailed to Marathon in eastern Attica, where it was famously defeated in the battle of Marathon.[17] The Persians attempted to land Hippias but after losing a tooth as he disembarked and taking that as an omen of bad fortune, he quickly jumped back on his ship.[18] That he was backed by Persia may explain Amyntas' diplomatic dealings with him over Anthemus to ingratiate himself with Darius, as we traced in the previous chapter. Any further Persian expeditions were now halted because of Darius' death and eventual succession of his son Xerxes, who made no plans to involve himself in Greece until the late 480s.

The lag time probably allowed Alexander enough independence to conquer territory to his north and the various peoples in it, in the process naming the region "Upper" Macedonia for the first time.[19] Slowly but surely, the Macedonian state was taking shape.

Xerxes' invasion

By 483 Xerxes was intent on crossing the Hellespont to succeed where Darius had failed. Remembering how Mardonius' fleet had been wrecked by storms in 492, the Great King sensibly sent Bubares back to Macedonia in 483 to oversee construction of a canal through the neck of the Athos peninsula, traces of which are visible today.[20] He also sent men ahead of his main army to build a bridge over the Strymon and to arrange supply bases in Thrace and Macedonia. By 480 the canal was completed, and Xerxes crossed the Hellespont on his famous pontoon bridge with a huge land army of perhaps 350,000 troops and fleet of 700–800 ships, marching through Thrace, eastern Chalcidice, and into Pieria.[21] Herodotus comments that the Persian army was so great that it drank the Echedorus (Gallikos)

[16] Herodotus 6.45. On the Brygi: Hammond and Griffith 1979, pp. 60–61 (between Lake Dorian and the Strumitsa valley on the slopes of Mount Orbelus); Vasilev 2015, pp. 101 and 147–152 (in the eastern part of the Chalcidice, perhaps in the vicinity of Lake Bolbe), with additional bibliography.

[17] Herodotus 6.98–114.

[18] Herodotus 6.107.

[19] Hammond and Griffith 1979, p. 64. See too Xydopoulos 2012a, pp. 520–529.

[20] See Isserlin et al. 2008.

[21] Persian Wars: Green 1998; Cawkwell 2005; Will 2010.

River dry—exaggeration surely, but then again, for most of the year nowadays this river is only a trickle of water, so if it were the same in antiquity it may have appeared that Xerxes' men nearly drank it all.[22]

Xerxes camped in Pieria for some days before marching into Thessaly via the Vale of Tempe, a five-mile-long gorge that led directly from the coast to the plain of Thessaly.[23] To stop the Persian advance, a Greek coalition army led by Athens and Sparta took up a position at the Peneus River on the Thessalian-Macedonian border.[24] At this point Alexander I enters the story. He sent envoys to the Greek camp warning that its location was precarious, and Xerxes would easily overcome it.[25] The Athenian Themistocles and the Spartan Euaenetus, the commanders of the Greek force, agreed with his assessment and withdrew to Thermopylae. Herodotus, however, gives the reason for their move as a fear that Xerxes could bypass Tempe and enter Thessaly by other routes, and the Great King may well have subdivided his army to enter Thessaly from different directions.[26]

In the middle of the fourth century Plato's nephew Speusippus, who succeeded his uncle as head of the Academy in Athens, wrote a letter to Philip II praising Alexander I's Argive lineage and crediting him for saving the Greek forces from destruction.[27] Why Alexander warned the Greek army—assuming he did so—is unknown. He may have been acting on Xerxes' orders, given Macedonia's subordinate status, to disperse the Greek force and allow the Persians an uninterrupted march into Thessaly. Another, more plausible, reason was self-serving: the Greek retreat meant that an undefended Thessaly had to move to the Persian side, which thus reduced the chances of fighting close to or even within Macedonia.[28] We should also not reject that Alexander was playing a double game in protecting his realm while endearing himself to the Greeks.[29]

[22] Herodotus 7.127; cf. Justin 2.10.22 (putting the size of Xerxes' army at one million!), with Borza 1990, p. 107.

[23] Xerxes' route in detail: Vasilev 2015, pp. 165–188.

[24] Herodotus 7.173.1–2. On the Greek defense position and role of the Thessalians, see Robertson 1976, pp. 111–116; Vasilev 2015, pp. 188–190.

[25] Herodotus 7.173.3; Speusippus, *Letter to Philip* 3–4.

[26] Zahrnt 1984, pp. 346–357 and 363–364; Sprawski 2010, p. 138; Zahrnt 2011, p. 769. See Borza 1990, p. 108, on the vulnerability of Tempe despite its strong defensive location and Robertson 1976, pp. 117–12, for collusions between Alexander and the Aleuads.

[27] Speusippus, *Letter to Philip* 3, with Natoli 2004, pp. 117–120.

[28] Cf. Wiesehöfer 2017, p. 59.

[29] Dascalakis 1965, pp. 177–179; Errington 1990, p. 11; Borza 1990, p. 108; Hammond 1992a, pp. 44–45; Badian 1994, p. 117; cf. Moloney 2018; contra Karavites 1997, p. 121, and see further Alexander's role at Tempe: Robertson 1976, pp. 119–120; Cole 1978, p. 43; Scaife 1989, p. 131; Vasilev 2015, pp. 189–190.

The Greek army at Thermopylae was eventually outflanked in the famous battle of 480, although the Persian victory was soured by the contemporaneous Athenian naval victory masterminded by Themistocles at Artemisium, and then, a few months later, by the naval triumph at Salamis. Herodotus briefly tells us that during the summer Alexander sent envoys to the cities in Boeotia that had sent troops to Thermopylae as part of an effort to persuade Xerxes they were on Persia's side.[30] Certainly Alexander was firmly pro-Persian at this time, and perhaps in the winter of 480–479 he even minted coins showing himself with a short sword of Persian type, a possible gift from the Great King himself during his stay in Macedonia.[31] We return to Alexander's coinage below.

After the Persian defeat at Salamis, Xerxes fled back to Persia.[32] He left behind his general Mardonius, who kept his men in Thessaly and Macedonia for the winter of 480–479. He was not inactive. During that time, he sent Alexander to Athens to negotiate an alliance between Athens and Persia because of the king's friendship with Themistocles, the architect of the Athenian navy, and especially his privileged status of *proxenos* (friend) and *euergetes* (benefactor) of the city.[33] This status was a major honor conferred on a foreigner for performing a good deed for the people of a city.[34]

The decree bestowing these honors on Alexander has not survived; hence dates and contexts vary from the accession of Xerxes in 486 to after the Persian Wars in the 470s.[35] Of these, the mid-480s was the most opportune time for Alexander and Athens to establish better relations, as Xerxes was busy with various issues, not least a rebellion in Egypt, which was not

[30] Herodotus 8.34, with Dascalakis 1965, pp. 179–183; Karavites 1997, p. 121; Sprawski 2010, p. 139; Vasilev 2015, pp. 198–200. Herodotus' account may have been because the Boeotians were the only Greeks to fight with Persia at Plataea in 479: Herodotus 9.67.1, with Vasilev 2015, p. 200.

[31] Heinrichs and Müller 2008, pp. 285–286 and 291–295; cf. Olbrycht 2010, pp. 344–345; Vasilev 2015, p. 156; but against this argument, see Ferrari 2022 (not a sword but a fold in the garment). On Achaemenid influence on representations of weaponry, see Heinrichs 2017, pp. 84–85.

[32] Herodotus 8.126.1; Justin 2.13.1–3 (Mardonius persuaded him): see Vasilev 2015, pp. 194–197.

[33] Herodotus 8.136, 140–144; Pausanias 7.25.6; cf. Diodorus 11.28.1, but Plutarch, *Aristides* 10.1–2, says nothing of Alexander on this mission, but only that Mardonius sent "letters." See further Dascalakis 1965, pp. 183–192; Cole 1978, pp. 40–43; Borza 1990, pp. 108–109; Karavites 1997, pp. 121–122; Mari 2011b, pp. 86–87; Vasilev 2015, pp. 200–205; Müller 2016, pp. 125–126. On the friendship with Themistocles see Cole 1978, suggesting on pp. 39–40 that they first met at the Olympic Games in which Alexander participated, although this is unlikely as Alexander did not take part till after 480 (see below).

[34] See Wallace 1970; Walbank, M.B. 1978, pp. 2–9.

[35] For example, Wallace 1970, pp. 199–200 and Walbank, M.B. 1978, p. 66 for late 480s; Hammond and Griffith 1979, p. 69 for mid-480s. Badian 1994, pp. 119–123, suggests the titles were bestowed on separate occasions; see too Gerolymatos 1986.

put down till 484.[36] The Athenians probably had a mercenary reason for their benevolence—their need for high-quality Macedonian timber for their fleet.[37] Forests were the backbone of fleets, and not just in antiquity.[38] Themistocles' naval reforms in the 480s led to the creation of a large war fleet whose triremes needed long timbers. Since shipbuilding timber was scarce in southern Greece, the people turned to Macedonia.[39] From there came the firs and pines necessary for planking, masts, and oars, with oak for keels.[40] Since Alexander as monarch owned his kingdom's natural resources, his friendly relations with Persia were not enough for the Athenians to rescind his proxeny status: timber thus trumped treachery.[41] Interestingly, the Persians did not seem to have minded about his relations with the city—or we do not hear of any concern on their part.

In his speech to the Athenians, Alexander warned that it was futile to resist Xerxes and that an alliance with him meant they could still rule according to their own laws and have their sanctuaries restored—an allusion to the Persians' burning of the Acropolis in 480 shortly before Salamis. But a Spartan embassy was also in Athens. Its members argued that Alexander was a tyrant in the service of another tyrant, Xerxes, and warned the Athenians of associating with barbarians. Perhaps more of a reflection of their anti-Persian feelings than being swayed by rhetorical warnings, the Athenians rejected Alexander and told him not to come before them again.[42] These may have been empty words, given their reliance on Macedonian timber, and tacit assurances could have been made, perhaps even as part of a double game Alexander had been playing since the Persian invasion.[43]

[36] Gerolymatos 1986, p. 76. [37] Cole 1978, p. 43.

[38] See Meiggs 1982, pp. 116–153 (his chapter on forests and fleets).

[39] Edson 1970, pp. 25–26; Borza 1990, pp. 108–110; Cole 1978, p. 42; Borza 1987, pp. 33–34 and 41–42; Vasilev 2015, pp. 203–205 (ultimately undecided), though Meiggs 1982, pp. 123–126, argues that timber for Themistocles' fleet came from south Italy.

[40] Borza 1987, p. 36.

[41] Alexander provided timber for the fleet: Hammond and Griffith 1979, p. 69; Borza 1990, pp. 109–110; Müller 2016, pp. 125–127, but see Vasilev 2015, pp. 202–205. Badian 1994, pp. 121–122, cf. pp. 119–126, argues that Alexander may have inherited the proxeny status from his father because of Amyntas' relations with Hippias. This is unlikely, for the Athenians had an aversion to tyranny after the overthrow of the Pisistratids in 510 and so would hardly have granted these favors to Amyntas for favoring of Hippias.

[42] Herodotus 8.140–144; cf. Plutarch, *Aristides* 10.3–6 and Diodorus 11.28.1–3, who say nothing of Alexander speaking. On Alexander feeling "the sting of the Spartan insult and the Athenian rebuke," see Karavites 1997, p. 122. For a discussion of Alexander's speech and adverse response to it, see Scaife 1989, pp. 134–137.

[43] See Dascalakis 1965, pp. 183–192, on Alexander playing a double game.

In 479 the showdown between Mardonius' troops and a Greek army took place at Plataea in Boeotia. After a ten-day standoff in the plain near Plataea because of ill-favored omens, Mardonius decided it was time for action, as his supplies were dwindling; hence he planned a surprise attack on the Greek army at dawn the following day. Herodotus relates that before daybreak on that eleventh day a sole horseman rode from the enemy camp to the Athenian one, with Plutarch adding that he asked to speak to the Athenian general Aristides, whom he knew personally from a visit to Athens.[44] The rider told the Athenian generals he was a Greek and did not want to see Greece enslaved; hence he was risking his life to reveal Mardonius' plan of attack. He also urged the Greeks not to attack first, as the Persians would soon run out of provisions. The rider then identified himself as "Alexander the Macedonian," and as he rode back to his camp, he said he had warned the commanders in order to redeem himself for siding with Persia.

Evidently Alexander's warning and information on the Persian strategy—delivered incidentally only to Aristides, who promptly told the commander-in-chief Pausanias of Sparta because it "was not honorable to conceal the knowledge from Pausanias"—were taken seriously, for at dawn Pausanias switched the Athenian position to the right wing while he and the Spartans stationed themselves on the left.[45] The actual battle took place on the following day. In the fighting Mardonius was killed and the Greeks, principally because of the Spartan troops, overcame the Persians and slaughtered thousands as they tried to escape to their camp. The remnants of the enemy army, about 40,000 men, marched rapidly through Thessaly and Macedonia for Thrace, but as they did so they were attacked and defeated by some Thracians.[46] The fourth-century Athenian orator Demosthenes claimed this defeat was at the hands of Perdiccas II, for which he was rewarded with Athenian citizenship, but Demosthenes is mistaken as Perdiccas' reign came after the Persian retreat.[47]

[44] Herodotus 9.44.1–45.3; Plutarch, *Aristides* 15.2–4.

[45] Quotation: Plutarch, *Aristides* 15.4. New deployment: Herodotus 9.46; Plutarch, *Aristides* 16.1. Warnings taken seriously perhaps because he was their *proxenos*: Gerolymatos 1986, p. 76.

[46] Herodotus 9.89.4, and see Vasilev 2015, pp. 207–211. Aristodemus, *BNJ* 104 F 1.3.1, speaks of Alexander as responsible for the defeat, but he hardly had the manpower.

[47] Demosthenes 23.200; see too Sprawski 2010, p. 140; Mari 2011b, p. 86. Some believe it was Alexander: Dascalakis 1965, pp. 200–201 and 204–205; Edson 1970, p. 26; Vasilev 2015, p. 202. Cole 1977 argues that the error was not the name of the person but the reason for the honor, that Perdiccas was given this status not for anything to do with the Persian retreat but for his actions in the Peloponnesian War (chapter 5), and that Alexander was awarded the less privileged status of *ateleia*: see especially pp. 26–29.

Most scholars dismiss Alexander's apparent secret night visit to the Athenian camp, and with good cause.[48] For one thing, it is odd that the king himself would venture out in darkness with no bodyguards, not to mention how easily he left and returned undetected. Then again, as at Tempe, he may have had a personal interest to play both sides, so perhaps we should not be dismissive of the tale. How and why then did the story originate? Here a case can be made that this story and others involving his Greekness are set against a shift in Macedonia's alignment from Persia to Greece.

The Persian defeat left a power vacuum in the north Aegean and presented Alexander with an opportunity to expand his kingdom. Macedonian troops were included among the contingents supporting the Persian army, which must have stretched his resources, so he was presumably relieved by the Persian defeat.[49] But he was savvy enough to realize that moves in the north beyond anything that Amyntas contemplated would increase his contact with the Greeks. Naturally, they would be suspicious of him and hate him for fighting on the enemy side in the Persian Wars and so block his expansion.

Therefore, in the aftermath of Plataea, we have the context for stories that had a kernel of truth to them but which he embellished to stress his Greekness and pro-hellenism. The first was the fictitious account of the murder of Persian envoys in his father's reign and how he saved Macedonia by marrying off his sister to Bubares, thus transplanting that known marriage from its later date to Amyntas' reign. Likewise, the Greeks' change of positions at Tempe and at Plataea might have been for other reasons but afforded Alexander the kernel of truth to exploit for his story of warning the Greeks there. But stressing his Greekness even more was his controversial participation at the Olympic Games and explanation of his Argive ancestry, which deserves special attention.

Alexander the Olympian

Herodotus tells the story—perhaps originating with Alexander—that the king participated in the sprint race (*stade*) at the Olympic Games at Olympia:[50]

[48] Borza 1982b, pp. 9–10; Scaife 1989, p. 131; Borza 1990, p. 110; Sprawski 2010, p. 139; Zahrnt 2011, p. 773; Vasilev 2015, pp. 205–206. It is believed by Dascalakis 1965, pp. 194–198; Edson 1970, p. 26; Errington 1990, pp. 12–13; Badian 1994, pp. 118–119; Karavites 1997; King 2018, p. 29.

[49] Herodotus 7.185. Alexander supplied cavalry: Rosen 1987, pp. 34–35; King 2018, p. 28; cf. Dascalakis 1965, pp. 193–199.

[50] Herodotus 5.22. On Herodotus' interaction with Alexander and what the king may have told him of this and other events in his reign, see especially Rosen 1987, pp. 25–51; cf. Hammond and

> When Alexander chose to contend and entered the list for that purpose, the Greeks who were to run against him were for barring him from the race, saying that the contest should be for Greeks and not for foreigners [*barbaroi*]; but Alexander proving himself to be an Argive, he was judged to be a Greek; so he contended in the furlong race and ran a dead heat for the first place.

The Olympic Games afforded competitors and visitors, including dignitaries from the Greek states, the chance to mingle with one another against the backdrop of religion and sport. In addition, victors gained widespread fame throughout the Greek world. If Alexander strove to elevate Macedonia's standing in Greece as well as his own Greekness as a "makeover" after Plataea, it made sense for him to be seen at Olympia. But the episode raises all sorts of questions having to do with the outcome of the race, the year he may have participated, Herodotus' veracity, and perhaps most important the ethnicity of the Macedonians, for this is the first time we hear about the Argive origins of the dynasty and thus how Alexander wanted to project his people to all and sundry.[51]

To begin with ethnicity. The other participants in the race—or perhaps even everyone at the games—protested that the king should not compete because he was a "barbarian" and only Greeks could take part in the games. However, Herodotus says that Alexander persuaded the Hellenodicae (Olympic officials) that he was Greek with the story of his descent from the Temenids of Argos in the Peloponnese, and in chapter 1 various reasons were given for the Macedonians being Greek or at least Greek speaking, so the reaction of the critics is surprising.

Perhaps too much has been read into "barbarian" here. Regardless of any messages to the Greeks at Tempe and Plataea, there would have been considerable bias against Alexander, as Medizers (those who had sided with the Persians, or Medes, as the Greeks referred to them, hence "Medize") were treated with contempt by the Greeks and even as criminals in some states.[52] Alexander cannot have been welcomed at Olympia with open arms; hence

Griffith 1979, pp. 98–99; cf. Vasilev 2016. Skeptical of Alexander's influence on Herodotus: Scaife, 1989 (pp. 133–134 on the tale of Olympia); cf. Zahrnt 2011, pp. 761–777.

[51] Dascalakis 1965, pp. 157–167; Hammond and Griffith 1979, p. 60; Errington 1981; Badian 1982a, pp. 34–37; Scaife 1989, pp. 133–134; Borza 1990, pp. 100–113; Hammond 1992a, p. 18; Hatzopoulos 2011b, pp. 56–58; Müller 2016, pp. 120–121; especially Roos 1985; Adams 2003a; Kertész 2005.

[52] Graf 1984.

calling him a barbarian was not necessarily a response to his ethnicity but evidence that he was still seen as a supporter of Persia. To counter this view, Alexander resorted to a robust exposition of his lineage to justify his presence there and ingratiate himself with the Greeks.

Another issue is the race itself. Victors in Olympic events had their names inscribed on Olympic victor lists, including Philip II at the games of 356.[53] Yet Alexander's name is missing from the lists. Why the silence? Two theories have been proposed. First, that in 476 Alexander was honored with a special race in recognition of his warnings to the Greeks in the Persian Wars.[54] Second, Alexander's claim to Argive ancestry was accepted but he was allowed to participate as a "one-off" since only he participated in these games.[55] In both cases, his name would not be on any official records.

The counterarguments are obvious. For one thing, there were other royal competitors in the games, and in 328 we have the first non-royal Macedonian among Olympic victors.[56] But why would a Medized king, who had even fought against Greeks at Plataea, be rewarded with a special race regardless of his warnings? And if the race was an honorary one, why would other competitors have objected to his participation? A clue to solve the dilemma is that the race was a heat in which Alexander finished joint first. Now, if a Greek race finished in a dead heat, it was rerun until there was a single victor; hence Alexander may have tied for first place in a heat and lost out to a faster runner—identity unknown—when it was rerun.[57] Alexander may have conveniently omitted this setback if telling the story to Herodotus, who thus did not mention any loss.

Herodotus does not give a date for these games, and scholarly estimates range from 504 to 476.[58] Of these, the most plausible is 476, the first games after the Persian Wars. It is hard to imagine Alexander competing any earlier, given his siding with the Persians. In addition Herodotus tells us that the Hellenodicae decided that he could compete, but these officials were

[53] Moretti 1957, victories no. 349 (Archelaus, though this was at his own games, as we see in chapter 6) and 434, 439, 445 (Philip), with Roos, 1985, p. 163.

[54] Borza 1990, p. 111.

[55] King 2018, p. 31.

[56] Dascalakis 1965, pp. 161–162; Roos 1985, pp. 163–164, citing cases of other royal competitors. Moretti 1957, no. 463, for the commoner.

[57] See Crowther 2000; cf. Roos 1985, pp. 164–167.

[58] Cole 1978, p. 39 (504 or 500); Dascalakis 1965, pp. 158–159; Edson 1970, p. 37; Hammond and Griffith 1979, pp. 60 and 435; Zahrnt 1992, pp. 253–255 (496); Rosen 1978, p. 7; Badian 1982a, p. 34; Mari 2002, pp. 31–36; Kertész 2005; Müller 2016, p. 121 (476); cf. Errington 1981, p. 143 (after 479); Roos 1985, pp. 167–168 (earlier still); Borza 1990, pp. 111–112 (too difficult to conjecture).

not introduced until after the Persian Wars, perhaps even for the games of 476.[59] Against 476 though is Alexander's age: if he was about 20 when he became king in 498, he would have been in his early forties in 476, which seems old to compete in a foot race. But that is not a compelling argument, for older athletes are known.[60] The same is true in our era: for example, at the 2004 Olympics in Athens, Merlene Ottey (by then representing Slovenia) was 44 years old when she competed in the 100 meters, failing to make the final by a mere 0.03 of a second, and at the 2024 Olympics in Paris, Malindi Elmore of Canada was also 44 years old when she competed in the marathon. Perhaps the other competitors protested Alexander's participation because they were afraid that he would beat them—and indeed, he may have been fit enough to come first equal in a heat, but when it was rerun, he lost to a younger and fitter runner.

To complicate matters Justin speaks of Alexander taking part in "a variety of events," hence not just the sprint.[61] If there was another event, what was it? Possibly it was the pentathlon, as we have some surviving fragments of an ode by Pindar praising Alexander, a "bold-scheming son of Amyntas," for his pentathlon victory.[62] Yet why Herodotus does not say anything about another event is odd, and Pindar's ode may not even refer to the games of 476.[63] But Pindar wrote *something* about Alexander, for in 335 when Alexander the Great razed a rebellious Thebes to the ground, he spared only the temples and one house, which had belonged to Pindar, because he had written a victory ode for his predecessor Alexander I.[64]

We can resolve this inconsistency by considering Alexander I's patronage of another Greek poet, Bacchylides, who wrote an encomium on the king in the context of an imaginary and sumptuous symposium.[65] Possibly his poem evoked the symposium, discussed in chapter 3, honoring the Persian envoys in Amyntas' reign and Alexander's apparent actions at it.[66] If so, then Bacchylides wrote a work drawing on an event that was part of a

[59] Kertész 2005, pp. 188 and 121–122, citing references; cf. Badian 1982a, pp. 34–37.

[60] Moretti 1957, nos. 61, 66, 68, 70, 73, 75 (Hipposthenes of Sparta); nos. 115, 122, 126, 129, 131, 139 (Milo of Croton); nos. 201, 215 (Theagenes of Thasos), cited in Kertész 2005, p. 126 n. 56.

[61] Justin 7.2.14.

[62] Werner 1967, FF 92 and 93, with Hammond and Griffith 1979, pp. 60 and 103; Rosen 1987, pp. 49–50; Kertész 2005, pp. 122–126; Sprawski 2010, p. 142.

[63] Dascalakis 1965, p. 166; Roos 1985, pp. 167–168; Kertész 2005, pp. 122–126.

[64] Arrian 1.9.10; cf. Plutarch, *Alexander* 11.12.

[65] Solinus 9.13, with Fearn 2007b, pp. 37–86.

[66] This point is noted by Pownall 2017, p. 217, though she does not make the connection to Pindar's encomium, as I shall.

series of stories Alexander was circulating to emphasize his pro-hellenism. Likewise, Pindar may have written his Olympic encomium as a literary piece drawing on Alexander's performance at Olympia to praise his patron and emphasize his Greekness.

Scholars have much debated Herodotus' veracity when it comes to Alexander's participation in the games, given the above discrepancies.[67] Indeed, Herodotus played a key role if he visited Macedonia and the king personally told him the stories, knowing they would be retold widely by that historian on his travels.[68] Nevertheless, the issues we have raised do not mean that Alexander did not go to Olympia: the chances are that he did so in 476, as he was eager to distance himself from his Persian alignment by taking part in a panhellenic event that also celebrated victory against Persia.

Further support for this view is Herodotus' tale of Alexander's message before Plataea, in which he said, "I am Alexander, a Greek," not "Alexander the king." We do not have the same appellation in his actions at Tempe or in his embassy to Athens. Perhaps this was because Herodotus had not made up his mind what sort of king he was—a tyrant, a barbarian, or a pro-Hellene.[69] More likely, though, is that he would be proclaiming his Greekness while an ally of an enemy of the Greeks: talking about a Greek ancestry would have been out of place and disbelieved then. Moreover, there was every chance the Persians would defeat the Greeks, and Alexander needed to play both sides.

Alexander's erection of expensive statues, presumably financed by the newly acquired mines at Bisaltia, as we shall shortly discuss, was another way of projecting a Greek image. One was an equestrian statue of himself at Delphi, which has not survived, and he apparently set up a bronze one of Zeus in another panhellenic sanctuary, Olympia.[70] The panhellenic importance of the oracular site of Delphi in the Greek world, like Olympia, was something Alexander carefully calibrated, and he made sure that his statue was next to the victorious bronze serpent memorial set up by the 31 Greek

[67] Dascalakis 1965, pp. 157–167; cf. pp. 110–113; Badian 1982a, pp. 34–37; Borza 1982b, pp. 10–11; Greenwalt 1986, pp. 119–120; Borza 1990, pp. 111–113; cf. Sprawski 2010, p. 142; Scaife 1989, pp. 133–134; Mari 2002, pp. 31–36.

[68] Alexander and Herodotus: Hammond and Griffith 1979, pp. 98–99, though see Scaife 1989; cf. Zahrnt 2011 (both skeptical).

[69] Scaife 1989, pp. 129–137; Borza 1990, p. 112.

[70] Delphi: Herodotus 8.121.2; [Demosthenes] 12.21; Solinus 9.13, with Hammond and Griffith 1979, p. 102; perhaps using ransom money from Persian captives to erect the statue: Errington 1990, p. 12. Equestrian statue: Saatsoglou-Paliadeli 2007, pp. 346–349; Saatsoglou-Paliadeli 2011, pp. 273–274; Paspalas 2011, pp. 181–182 (the statue of gilded bronze). Zeus statue: Hammond and Griffith 1979, p. 103.

states of the Hellenic League for its triumph over the Persians.[71] The clear implication of this act is that he was involving himself in that panhellenic fight for freedom and emphasizing his own brand of Hellenism.[72]

Against this background we can say that Alexander's attendance at Olympia and the projection of his Greekness reflected a reorientation of his kingdom from Persia to Greece, setting that trend for the future. To this we may now turn.

After the Persian Wars

Alexander grasped the opportunity of the Persian withdrawal to expand beyond the Strymon River. His eastern frontier at the time extended into Crestonia (the hilly region between the Axius plain and the Strymon valley) and parts of the Chalcidice, but east of the Strymon lay large timber reserves and silver mines, which Greeks, Thracians, and Persians had coveted for some decades.[73] The reduction in Thracian power was clearly beneficial to him there.

A year or so after the battle of Plataea Alexander made his move. If we accept Thucydides' account of Macedonia's rise, discussed in chapter 2, as chronological, the king's campaign was as follows.[74] He first attacked and expelled Paeonian tribes from the valley of the lower Axius River, and probably at this time their chief citadel, Amydon, was destroyed. Then most likely he drove the Edonians from Mygdonia, east of the Axius between Amphaxatis and the Strymon, before turning west against the Eordoi and expelling them. Next, again likely, he drove the Almopians from north of Edessa. Finally, he conquered the Bisaltae, a Thracian tribe living in the mountainous districts of Crestonia, though whether he expelled them, as he had done other peoples, is not certain.[75] That conquest must have been

[71] Alexander and panhellenic sanctuaries: Mari 2002, pp. 29–46; cf. Müller 2016, pp. 130–133.

[72] Rosen 1978, p. 8; Badian 1982a, pp. 34–37; Sprawski 2010, p. 140; cf. Greenwalt 1986, pp. 119–120; Mari 2002, pp. 37–44; see too Hall 2001. Rosen 1978, p. 8, believes his statue in tandem with his story about his Argive ancestry were enough to persuade the Greeks that the Macedonian kings were indeed of Greek ancestry. Alexander's peddling of Greek patriotism: See too Rosen 1987, pp. 34–35; cf. Castritius 1972, p. 3.

[73] Discussion of their moves in the region and relations with Macedonia lie outside the topic of the chapter; for a survey, see Borza 1990, pp. 116–119. Resources: Borza 1982a.

[74] Thucydides 2.99.4–5, with Edson 1970, pp. 26–29; Hammond and Griffith 1979, pp. 59–64; Zahrnt 1984, pp. 332–334 and 361–363; Rosen 1987, pp. 35–39; Borza 1990, pp. 85–89; Hatzopoulos 1996, vol. 1, pp. 105–119; Vasilev 2015, pp. 205–207; see especially Xydopoulos 2016.

[75] Justin 7.4.1. Edson 1970, p. 28, notes they existed as a distinct people as late as the Roman conquest of Macedonia in 168.

after 460 as the Bisaltae were still minting their own coinage until then.[76] From this last campaign Alexander acquired the mines of Mount Dysorum, which were said to have yielded him one talent a day and became a major income generator for the kingdom—it was these mines that helped him introduce his coinage and finance his two statues.[77]

Alexander's expansion transformed Macedonia in his own time and opened the door to further growth for the kingdom, as archaeology testifies; it is for good reason that Thucydides describes the Macedonian kingdom of his own day as the creation of "Alexander, father of Perdiccas (II), and his ancestors."[78] However, his gains brought him into conflict with Athens. In 478 that city had established a network of allies with itself as the hegemon in an anti-Persian alliance commonly known as the Delian League, given that initially the league treasury was located on the island of Delos.[79] In time, this league grew into a fifth-century empire, and, as we shall see in the following chapter, Athens would eventually go to war with the other military power of Greece, Sparta, which involved Macedonia under Perdiccas II.

Until Alexander's move into the lower Strymon Valley relations between him and Athens had been amicable. That changed in 476 when Cimon, son of the general Miltiades who had masterminded the Athenian victory at Marathon in 490, seized the former Persian supply base Eion, at the mouth of the Strymon.[80] The Athenians went on to expel the last remnants of Persian influence in that area as well as the remaining Thracians, perhaps as far as the future site of Amphipolis three or four miles to its north, and resettled the area.[81] They then spent much of the 470s establishing their hold over the coastline of the Thermaic Gulf while expanding the Delian League.

Cimon's successes made him influential in Athenian public life and caused a corresponding decline in Themistocles' influence as well as an increasing frostiness in relations between Athens and Macedonia.[82] Alexander's actions did not help, for probably in 477, when it was obvious a Persian army was

[76] Xydopoulos 2016, pp. 255–256, suggests 460–450.

[77] Borza 1982a, p. 10 n. 21; cf. Borza 1990, p. 119; Rosen 1987, pp. 45–46. On the identification of Dysorum with Menoikion and Alexander's temporary gain of control of the Pangaeum area, see Picard 2006, though Xydopoulos 2016, p. 264, does not agree with the identification (Flamouri/Vertiskos). See also Kosmidou 2011 for the view that Alexander and the Thracians both made use of the mines.

[78] Thucydides 2.99.3; see too Saripanidi 2019a on the significance of archaeological finds.

[79] On the league see, for example, Meiggs 1972, with pp. 42–49, on its foundation.

[80] Smart 1967 on the capture.

[81] Borza 1990, p. 120.

[82] Cole 1978, pp. 45–46; cf. Edson 1970, pp. 32–33; Borza 1990, p. 120.

not returning to Greece, he took over the Persian enclave at Ennea Hodoi ("Nine Ways"), later Amphipolis, blocking Athenian moves in the region.[83] The Edones, hostile to both Alexander and the Athenians, wrested Nine Ways from him, but by then the damage to the relations between him and Athens had been done.

To make matters worse Alexander offered Themistocles, exiled from Athens in 471, sanctuary at Pydna, which the king had earlier seized to help transport his timber down the Haliacmon, Axius, Strymon, and lesser Loudias Rivers to the coast for export.[84] The two men were likely already friends, but one theory has it that Themistocles was trying to persuade Alexander to support a democratic faction in Argos to counter Athens and Sparta, though this is unlikely.[85] That this was the origin of Alexander's attempt to provide his family with a Greek Argive lineage, as has been suggested, is equally unlikely.[86] Indeed, in about 468 he gave refuge to people from Mycenae after Argos captured and ransacked the city, which would hardly have endeared him to the Argives.[87]

In 465 or 464 the Athenians landed 10,000 colonists at Nine Ways, intent on taking over this swathe of Macedonian territory.[88] They continued their imperialistic ventures in the north Aegean with a force commanded by Conon. In this campaign was the three-year-long siege of Thasos (465–463), ostensibly because the island had rebelled from the Delian League, but the mines on the nearby Thracian mainland were more of a factor—and were also of interest to Alexander. But the Athenians also suffered a reversal when a Thracian force attacked their settlers at Ennea Hodoi.[89] It would not be until 437 that the Athenians captured Ennea Hodoi and refounded it as the colony of Amphipolis. However, Cimon's siege of Thasos was successful; the island surrendered in 463, and the Athenians seized it and the mainland opposite, including the mines.

[83] Hammond and Griffith 1979, p. 102 (Alexander taking Ennea Hodoi between 478 and when Cimon took Eion in 476/5). Cole 1977, p. 31, argues it was not Alexander but Perdiccas who seized Ennea Hodoi, but this is less likely; cf. Borza 1990, p. 121 n. 52.

[84] Thucydides 1.137.1–2. Cole 1978, pp. 45–27, discusses the controversial dates for the exile and argues for the liaison.

[85] Cole 1978, pp. 37–49.

[86] Borza 1990, pp. 121–122. Alexander making up the story of his Argive ancestry: Rosen 1978, pp. 6–11. Sprawski 2021 questions Alexander's responsibility for the story of his Argive heritage and argues it was the product of Greek writers.

[87] Pausanias 7.25.6.

[88] Thucydides 1.100.3; Diodorus 11.70.5, 12.68.2, with Hammond and Griffith 1979, pp. 107–108; Borza 1990, p. 122; Müller 2016, p. 137.

[89] Herodotus 9.75; Thucydides 1.100.3; Diodorus 11.70.5, 12.68.2; Pausanias 1.29.4.

It must have dawned on Alexander by now that the Persian threat to his territory had been replaced by an Athenian one. After all, Cimon's seizure of Eion at the mouth of the Strymon showed that the Athenians were establishing themselves in the north Aegean to secure timber for their fleet, on which their new Delian League was anchored. That may have caused the king to encourage or even be part of a Thracian coalition force against Ennea Hodoi.[90]

However, when Cimon returned home, he was prosecuted for allegedly taking a bribe from Alexander because he had not used the newly acquired territory as a base "to invade Macedonia and reduce a large part of it."[91] Alexander could certainly have bribed him, but the charge was surely political, for Thasos and the mainland opposite were too far east to launch such an invasion—not to mention that the powerful Thracian tribes between there and the kingdom's frontier along the Strymon would not have taken kindly to an Athenian army marching through their territory. Cimon was acquitted but still had to pay an enormous fine of 50 talents.[92] His political enemies were clearly at work against him, but most importantly, for the accusation to have credibility there may have been talk in Athens of invading Macedonia and even of acquiring Crestonia, with its rich silver and timber reserves.[93]

We hear nothing else about Alexander's activities apart from a shadowy campaign against the Eordi, who he expelled—part of a pattern in dealing with conquered peoples—from their area west of Mount Vermion.[94] But to shore up his support in the western mountains, the king may have married, for a later source refers to a certain Derdas who was king of Elimea and a cousin of Alexander I's sons Perdiccas and Philip.[95] Elimea was south of Eordaea and on the route to Thessaly, so a marriage between Alexander (or perhaps his sister) with the royal family of Elimea was a good strategic move.[96]

Thanks to Alexander's harnessing the natural resources of his kingdom, Macedonia became a much stronger state. But the momentum could not be

[90] Cole 1978, pp. 48–49.

[91] Plutarch, *Cimon* 14.2–3, with Hammond and Griffith 1979, pp. 102–103; Errington 1990, p. 14.

[92] Plutarch, *Cimon* 15.1; Plutarch, *Pericles* 10.4–5, with Cole 1978, p. 49 n. 26; Hammond and Griffith 1979, pp. 102–103; Hatzopoulos 2020, p. 34. Mari 2011b, p. 88, notes that "Persian gold" is a topos in the reign of Philip II and appears for the first time here; cf. Hatzopoulos 2020, p. 34.

[93] Borza 1990, p. 123.

[94] Thucydides 2.99.5, with Edson 1970, pp. 27–28.

[95] Scholiast on Thucydides 1.57.3.

[96] Bosworth 1971a, p. 100; Hammond and Griffith 1979, pp. 18–19; Borza 1990, pp. 124–125; Badian 1994, pp. 127–130.

maintained. Numismatic evidence suggests a decline in coinage after about 460, so Alexander may have suffered a reversal later in his reign. Perhaps this was at the hands of Teres, king of the Odrysian Thracians, who had been building up a powerful kingdom east of Macedonia, and his son Sparadocus, who may have eclipsed Alexander's power in the Strymon region after the mid-460s.[97] In addition, at some point Alexander seems to have lost the mines in Bisaltia—how is unknown—since he minted only small coins (tetrobols) for the rest of his reign, as did his successor, Perdiccas II.[98] To Alexander's numismatic reforms we now turn.

The first coinage

The Thracians and the Greek cities of the Chalcidice had been coining for some time, but Alexander's acquisition of the mines at Bisaltia provided him with a major economic boost and allowed him to mint Macedonian coinage for the first time.[99] All these coins were struck at different mints, one of which may have been at Aegae. The date of the first issue is controversial, but it was probably in 479—the timing of the defeat of the Persians, his pro-hellenic moves, and expanding his kingdom is surely not coincidental.[100]

Alexander issued eight- and four-drachma coins (octodrachms and tetradrachms) and four-obol coins (tetrobols) in two different weight standards, which benefited trade, helped pay for his campaigns, and reflected Macedonia's growing position at a geographical and trading crossroads.[101] Hence his coins have been found in hoards in western Asia

[97] Taceva 1992, especially pp. 73–74.

[98] Raymond 1953, pp. 23–24; Price 1974, p. 19; Hammond and Griffith 1979, pp. 119–120; Dahmen 2010, p. 51; Kremydi 2011, p. 163.

[99] Raymond 1953, pp. 43–60; Price 1974, pp. 2–19; Hammond and Griffith 1979, pp. 104–113; cf. pp. 84–86; Borza 1990, pp. 126–130; Hammond 1992a, pp. 41–47; Psoma 1999; Kremydi 2011, pp. 161–163; Müller 2016, pp. 127–128; Heinrichs 2017. See too Taceva 1992; Greenwalt 1994b, pp. 125–131; Prestianni and Tripodi 1996; Caccamo Caltabiano 2007; Heinrichs and Müller 2008; Ferrari 2022; Kosmidou 2011; Kosmidou 2013. On coinage before Alexander in Thrace and Macedonia and its interrelationship in our period, see Raymond 1953, pp. 43–60; Hammond and Griffith 1979, pp. 69–91; Taceva 1992; Lorber 2000; Kosmidou 2011. See also Price 1974, with a succinct discussion on the evidence of coins on pp. 1–24; Dahmen 2010; and Kremydi 2011; cf. Kosmidou 2013, on Macedonian coinage.

[100] Caccamo Caltabiano 2007, p. 763; Heinrichs and Müller 2008, pp. 285–291; Müller 2016, p. 125, though see Taceva 1992, especially pp. 60–61; Lorber 2000, p. 128. Alexander's coinage: Heinrichs 2017.

[101] Hammond and Griffith 1979, pp. 105–106; Kremydi 2011, pp. 162–163; cf. Lorber 2000, pp. 113–133. These are frequently struck from worn and recut dies, indicating their scarce issue was only when need arose: Wartenberg 2002, pp. 85–86. On weight standards in Macedonian coinage, see Raymond 1953, pp. 18–42.

Minor, Jordan, and Egypt.[102] However the light tetrobols were more of a token coinage, as they were used probably for military pay or wages mostly within Macedonia.[103]

The coins were much influenced by Thracian designs and had three major iconographies on their obverse.[104] The first was a rider on a walking horse, in full battle dress, and holding two javelins (Group 1).[105] The second was a rider on foot beside a horse with chlamys (cloak), petasus (hat with broad brim), and two javelins (Group 2).[106] The third was a young rider with petasus, chlamys, two weapons, and a small dog between the horse's hooves (Groups 3–4), which is figure 4.1 in this chapter.[107] On the reverse of the coins was the king's name. The chronology is debated, but the groups are likely not contemporaneous—those of Group 2 (the walking horseman) are like coins of the Bisaltae; hence Alexander may not have adopted that type until after he conquered the region in about 465.[108]

The heroic iconography was followed by Alexander's successors down to Philip II. The rider or hero in Thracian myth was probably both a religious symbol and a portrait of the king as even a superhuman being.[109] The depiction of a hunter in Groups 3–4, accompanied by his hunting dog, perhaps an echo of Homer's Pelasgians or Mycenaean imagery, may also show the ideal model of a king who "shows the same strength (*aretē*) in hunting and warfare," and thus appeals to his subjects in Macedonia, the Greeks, and even elsewhere, given coins circulated widely.[110] The device may even represent Alexander as hunter and protector, especially as he dedicated statues of himself to the gods at Delphi and Olympia.[111] As noted

[102] Kremydi 2011, p. 162, citing evidence.

[103] Dahmen 2010, pp. 50–51; cf. Heinrichs 2017, pp. 90–91. The number of light tetrobols of Perdiccas II found, for example, during the excavations of Olynthus is much smaller than the number of heavier ones: Raymond 1953, pp. 142–143; Psoma 2001, pp. 175–179.

[104] Taceva 1992, especially pp. 64–67; Greenwalt 1997; Greenwalt 1994b, pp. 125–128; cf. Raymond 1953, pp. 43–46; Price 1974, pp. 9–10; Heinrichs and Müller 2008, pp. 295–298.

[105] Raymond 1953, pp. 78–79, nos. 1–7.

[106] Raymond 1953, pp. 100–104, nos. 45–75.

[107] Raymond 1953, p. 126, nos. 109–111 and p. 143, no. 200; Price 1974, pp. 9–10 and 18–19 with plates referenced in these pages; see too Taceva 1992, pp. 64–69; Psoma 1999, especially pp. 274–277; Heinrichs and Müller 2008, pp. 295–298.

[108] Caccamo Caltabiano 2007, pp. 763 and 767–770, citing further bibliography. See too Hammond and Griffith 1979, pp. 102–115; Taceva 1992, pp. 62–63; Greenwalt 1997, pp. 121–133; Lorber 2000, pp. 113–130, with pp. 130–132 on the influence of coinage from Mygdonia and Crestonia.

[109] Hammond and Griffith 1979, p. 110; Greenwalt 1994b, pp. 125–129.

[110] "Ares types": Price 1974, p. 9; hunter: Hammond and Griffith 1979, p. 109; Hammond 1992a, p. 46; and see Taceva 1992, pp. 64–69; cf. King 2018, p. 32. Homeric: Raymond 1953, p. 78, no. 5; Caccamo Caltabiano 2007, pp. 764–765.

[111] Hammond and Griffith 1979, p. 109; protector: Greenwalt 1997, pp. 126–127. The youth has been taken to indicate Alexander's successor—"a young son who is already capable of assuming the

above, the appearance of a short sword on the coins may be Persian influence, even a gift from Xerxes.

A common device on coins was the goat, the mascot of the Macedonians and the dynasty, which associated the king as the founder of Aegae on the site where goats were spotted, and which may even have been part of a trend beginning elsewhere in Thrace and Upper Macedonia.[112] In addition, Alexander issued images of the forepart of a lion, associated with Heracles, an ancestor of the royal house, and a crested helmet, associated with a local Macedonian god (or goddess) of war.[113]

The symbolism of Alexander's coins is obvious: they were testimony to his kingship and the increasing wealth of the kingdom. Thanks to him, successive kings, especially Philip II, made Macedonian coinage the strongest in Europe.

Alexander and the army

We know next to nothing about the Macedonian army before Philip II. Thucydides claims that the cavalry was its only arm and infantry was not needed, which would explain why Alexander sent only cavalry to support the Persians at Plataea.[114] However, it is likely that the force included infantry, probably conscripts, ordinary farmers called up from their fields with little in the way of training and arms; hence they received scant attention in the sources. Mercenaries were used as infantry—Thucydides tells us that Alexander's successor, Perdiccas II, had mostly "barbarians" in his infantry, who were most probably mercenaries.[115] Perhaps those refugees from Mycenae offered a home by Alexander after Argos captured their city were trained in hoplite tactics and added to his army.[116]

Alexander may have introduced military reforms based on a fragment of the fourth-century historian and orator Anaximenes. It speaks of an Alexander who introduced training for the nobility in cavalry warfare and

role of hunter, alongside his father"—and thus the succession of royal power: Caccamo Caltabiano 2007, pp. 764–767 (the quotation on p. 765).

112 Price 1974; Poulios 1993. See too Raymond 1953, pp. 4 and 49–52; Hammond and Griffith 1979, pp. 85–86 and 104–105; but see Lorber 2000, pp. 113–134.

113 Hammond and Griffith 1979, p. 110, where Hammond also discusses other devices with their religious significance.

114 Army under Alexander I: Kalléris 1987 ; Noguera Borel 2007; cf. Sekunda 2010, pp. 446–449; Juhel 2017 ; King 2018, pp. 107–110.

115 Thucydides 4.124.1, 4.125.1.

116 Cole 1978, p. 47; Hammond 1992a, p. 47; Sprawski 2010, p. 142; King 2018, p. 33.

called them Companions (*hetairoi*) and organized the non-nobles into infantry units called Foot Companions (*pezhetairoi*):[117]

> After training the most renowned men to serve as cavalry, he gave them the name of (Companions) *hetairoi*; the majority, that is, the foot, he divided into *lochoi* and *dekades* and other commands and designated them *pezhetairoi* (Foot Companions). He did this in order that each of the two groups, by sharing in the royal Companionship, should be always exceedingly loyal to him.

Anaximenes, frustratingly, does not specify which Alexander he was talking about—I, II, III ("the Great"), or IV. Since the name *pezhetairoi* existed in Philip II's time, when it had come to mean the infantry overall, Philip's son Alexander III and the latter's son Alexander IV must be excluded.[118] Alexander II had a very short and troubled reign of a little over one year (369/8), as we will see in chapter 8, which makes us wonder whether he had the time to introduce military reforms; hence on balance responsibility probably lies with Alexander I.[119] It would make sense for our Alexander to have devoted time to the army given his campaigning, which was on a much grander scale than anything Amyntas had undertaken. Yet he did not leave his son and successor Perdiccas II with a powerful army, as the latter was at times forced to turn to Athens and Sparta for military help. It would not be until Philip II's reign that the infantry and cavalry were regrouped into the formidable army that won victory after victory (see chapter 9).

Alexander the "philhellene"

At some point Alexander I was dubbed "philhellene," or "lover of all things Greek."[120] When and why are unknown. The epithet probably has nothing

[117] Anaximenes, *BNJ* 2 no. 74 F 4, with Williams' commentary (translation: Williams 2006). See too Brunt 1976; Milns 1976; Kalléris 1987; Juhel 2017; cf. Hammond and Griffith 1979, pp. 418–420 and 705–713; Borza 1990, pp. 125–126; Roisman 2010, p. 162; Sekunda 2010, pp. 447–448; Lane Fox 2011b, p. 260; Müller 2016, pp. 223–224. Against Alexander I is Greenwalt 2007, pp. 92–93; cf. Greenwalt 2017. Heinrichs and Müller 2008, pp. 294–295, argue unknowingly that the spear on Alexander's coins was an early sarissa; hence he introduced military reforms.

[118] Arrian 1.28.3 and 7.2.1 implies they had been part of the army for a while, and Demosthenes 2.17 (of 349) refers to them. But Hammond and Griffith 1979, pp. 406 and 705–713, think the fragment refers to Alexander III as does Williams 2006, Anaximenes, *BNJ* 2 no. 74 F 4 commentary.

[119] Noguera Borel 2007 and Greenwalt 2017 argue for Alexander II; contra Kalléris 1987. Summary of scholarship on the attribution: King 2018, p. 126 n. 19 (to which add Greenwalt 2017).

[120] Dio Chrysostom 2.33, with Dascalakis 1965, pp. 201–204; Hammond and Griffith 1979, p. 101; Badian 1982a, pp. 35–36; Borza 1990, p. 113; Sprawski 2010, p. 143; Müller 2016, pp. 134–136.

to do with race or background but arose from his push to enhance the cultural quality of his court, unlike his father, perhaps stemming from his participation in the Olympic Games, statues at Delphi and Olympia, and support of the Greeks at times in the Persian Wars.[121] Alexander also started a trend of favoring Greeks poets and Greek culture at his court. Thus, he invited Hellanicus, Herodotus, Pindar, and Bacchylides of Ceos to Aegae, and all wrote praising him.[122] We commented on Bacchylides' encomium on him above. He also had artists working there, perhaps some who sculpted the remarkable life-size, realistic clay heads found as unique grave offerings in the "Cluster of the Queens" graves close to Rhomaios' tomb at Aegae, and who presumably would have sculpted the equestrian statue of him at Delphi.[123]

The term "philhellene" was first used by Dio Chrysostom in the second century AD; hence, it does not seem to have been bestowed on him contemporaneously.[124] Certainly if it had been granted to Alexander in his lifetime, Herodotus would have mentioned it rather than simply referring to him as, for example, "Alexander the Macedonian" in his anecdote of the king's warning before Plataea.[125] A likely time for the epithet was during the Hellenistic era (323–30), when scholars were writing commentaries on classical authors or adding sobriquets to people with the same names to distinguish them from one another.[126] Since there were four kings in the Argead ruling house with the name Alexander, it may have been in the Hellenistic period that our Alexander was named "philhellene" because of his expansion in relations with the Greeks and growing hellenism of his court, just as Alexander III was perhaps then dubbed "the Great" because of his sensational military campaigns and creation of an empire.

If Alexander were 15 or so when the Persian envoys visited his father in 492 and died in the mid-450s, perhaps 454, he would have been in his late 70s or even 80 at the time of his death. He reigned, therefore, for 44 years. Whether his death was from natural causes or was sudden and violent,

[121] Badian 1982a, pp. 33–34; see too Dascalakis 1965, pp. 209–210; Hammond 1992a, pp. 46–47.

[122] Solinus 9.13, with Dascalakis 1965, pp. 209–210; Hammond and Griffith 1979, p. 103; Hammond 1992a, pp. 46–47; Rosen 1987, pp. 47–50 (after Plataea); cf. Pownall 2017, pp. 215–218. On the Argeads' use of Greek literature, see Pownall 2017.

[123] Hammond and Griffith 1979, pp. 98–104; cf. Saatsoglou-Paliadeli 2011, pp. 273–274.

[124] Errington 1981, p. 139; Errington 1990, p. 13. Evidence: Hammond and Griffith 1979, p. 101 and n. 3; Badian 1982a, p. 46 and n. 19; Sprawski 2013. We should not share the conviction of Dascalakis 1965, p. 201, and see pp. 201–204, that "there is not the slightest doubt that Alexander was called 'philhellene' by the contemporary Greeks."

[125] Herodotus 9.45.3; Plutarch, *Aristides* 15.2.

[126] Badian 1982a, pp. 35–36; Errington 1990, p. 266 n. 14; Sprawski 2010, p. 143; Sprawski 2013.

and hence needed to be avenged, as some sources claim, is unknown.[127] The former is probably closer to the truth. Since many of Alexander's successors were assassinated, our sources, writing centuries later in the Roman imperial period, may have erroneously attributed his death to a "pattern" of political conspiracies. In any case, we cannot expect Herodotus to have said nothing if there had been an actual assassination.

Evaluating Alexander

Alexander was praised by Thucydides as the creator of the greater Macedonian kingdom. Certainly, his union of the major regions of Macedonia, increasing hellenization of his court, introduction of coinage, and even military reforms were no mean feats.[128] The projection of his Greekness was also careful and calculated with an eye on the kingdom's future and his own position. Moreover, archaeological evidence, especially funerary goods, support his changes and contacts with other areas that fashioned developments and even an economic uptick in the period after him. Moreover, if the decrease of wealthy and ostentatious burials in various places in Macedonia, such as Archontiko and Sindos but not the royal capital of Aegae, is anything to go by, it seems Alexander also took measures to reduce the influence of local families there and thus help centralize his own power.[129] In tandem with this aim was arguably his desire to project his Greekness to the Greeks to emphasize that only the king was powerful in his realm.

Yet most scholars see his achievements more modestly, and the later pushbacks of several conquered areas for a return to the status quo undid much of his good work.[130] Likewise, the economic boost he brought from acquiring mines was relatively short-lived once he lost control of Bisaltia and Ennea Hodoi, which led to a reduction in the quality of Macedonia's

[127] Curtius 6.11.26 ("Alexander the ancestor"). Assassinated: Diodorus 15.71.1, 16.2.4; Justin 7.5.4. On his death, see Hammond and Griffith 1979, pp. 103–104; Tripodi 1984; Borza 1990, pp. 133–134; Sprawski 2010, p. 143; Müller 2016, pp. 139–140.

[128] See too the evaluation of him at Dascalakis 1965, pp. 204–208, as the "creator of Macedonian unity."

[129] See, for example, Saripanidi 2017, pp. 117–124 and *passim*; especially Saripanidi 2019a, for example, pp. 402–404 (a narrower elite).

[130] Errington 1981; Badian 1982a, pp. 34–36; Errington 1990, pp. 12–13; Borza 1990, pp. 130–131; Fearn 2007a, cf. Mari 2011b, pp. 85–86; Vasilev 2015, pp. 197–206.

coinage.[131] He was also indebted to Persia, as Justin notes that he "extended his kingdom as much through his own valor as through Persian generosity."[132] Still, when compared to Amyntas and several of his successors, Alexander I was one of the greater kings of Macedonia, and set up the successes of kings like Archelaus and Philip II. He may have modeled his kingship on that of the Persian kings by bringing the power of the king into its own when it came to relationships with nobles and even took advantage of Persian domination to reduce the power of influential families while increasing his own, as the evidence of less extravagant burials before and after his reign, apart from in Aegae, attests.[133] We see his moves to centralize his kingship also in his coinage, which demonstrated his standing in the state, and which succeeding kings followed.[134]

Alexander had several sons, so he may have had more than one wife. Perhaps he was even the first king to practice polygamy, bringing this Persian practice into Macedonian society.[135] Succeeding him was his eldest son, Perdiccas, who took Macedonia far more into the Greek orbit than his father.

Macedonia under the Argead Kings: The Rise and Fall of an Ancient Superpower. Ian Worthington, Oxford University Press. © Oxford University Press 2026. DOI: 10.1093/9780197668009.003.0005

[131] Price 1974, p. 19; Hammond and Griffith 1979, p. 14; Borza 1990, p. 122.
[132] Justin 7.4.2.
[133] Influence of Persia on Macedonia: Olbrycht 2010; Wiesehöfer 2017. His own consolidation of power: Saripanidi 2019a.
[134] Well argued by Heinrichs and Müller 2008.
[135] Carney 2019, p. 10, citing bibliography.

5

Perdiccas II: The Enemy of My Enemy Is My Friend

The period from Alexander I's death to 435 was something of a "dark age" in Macedonian history because of a lack of surviving evidence of events. Alexander had added substantially to his kingdom both territorially and economically and had brought Macedonia into the orbit of Greek affairs thanks to his relations with the Athenians and attendance at Olympia. His successor, Perdiccas, increased his kingdom's contacts with the Greeks, and in expanding and protecting his kingdom he made alliances with powerful cities such as Athens and Sparta as he saw fit. But there were times when Macedonia suffered shortcomings, which may well have strengthened the Greeks' view of it as "a backward entity" and encouraged states like Athens took advantage of it.[1]

The gap years?

Alexander had at least five sons: Perdiccas, Philip, Alcetas, Menelaus, and Amyntas, of whom Perdiccas was the eldest.[2] Exactly when Perdiccas succeeded is controversial.[3] Ancient writers say he reigned anything from 23 to 41 years, and one has him succeeding to the kingship in 461/0.[4] We should expect him to have assumed the throne as soon as his father died, yet his abbreviated name (*PER* initially and then later *PERDIK*) appears on his

[1] Mari 2011b, pp. 88–89 with n. 27 on p. 89.

[2] Herodotus 8.139; Thucydides 2.100.2; contra Justin 7.4.3, who says that Amyntas, son of Menelaus. succeeded him.

[3] See Müller 2016, pp. 144–147, and the commentary of Sprawski and Mojsik 2024 on Nicomedes, *BNJ* 2 no. 772, F 2.

[4] Anaximenes, *BNJ* 72 F 27; Hieronymus, *BNJ* 154 F 1; Marsyas, *BNJ* 135–136 F 15; Nicomedes, *BNJ* 772 F 2; Philochorus, *BNJ* 328 F 126; Theopompus, *BNJ* 115 F 279; cf. *Marmor Parium*, *BNJ* 239 A 58 (41 years). Accession in 461/0: *Marmor Parium*, *BNJ* 239 A 58, with Sickinger's commentary, ad loc.

coinage in about 435, indicating he may have been king in his own right only in that year.[5]

The reason for the lag time from his father's death may be that Thucydides refers to a province "which before had belonged to Philip," presuming a king and at least one governor of an individual area.[6] Accordingly, one theory is that after Alexander died, the Assembly decided that three of his sons, Philip, Alcetas, and Perdiccas, would be kings and gave each of them a realm (*arche*); hence Perdiccas and his brothers ruled jointly.[7] In this hypothesis Philip was the eldest son and received an area probably east of the Axius River including Amphaxitis, which was of great strategic importance.[8] Next in age was Alcetas, whose *arche* is not known, though he had one, as Perdiccas was said to have deprived him of it at an unknown date.[9] Then came Perdiccas. The other two brothers were not considered rulers per se—Menelaus was politically active, acting as Perdiccas' envoy in a treaty between the king and Athens, as we shall see, but does not seem to have had an *arche*. Nor did the fifth brother, Amyntas, who was not involved in public life.[10]

This distribution of power may have taken place since Alexander had expanded Macedonia's territory but then suffered losses later in his reign, not to mention economic reversals, as evidenced in Macedonia's coinage, which was reduced from octodrachms, tetradrachms, and tetrobols to poorer-quality tetrobols without any name inscribed on them until 435.[11] Thus, it may have been thought that one ruler was not enough to maintain and grow the kingdom. But there is no evidence for this arrangement, and we never hear of the Assembly acting in this way other than appointing a regent, which was clearly not the case here, as Perdiccas was not a minor. In any case, three kings jointly ruling what was still not a huge kingdom—or subdividing it into three under each king—does not seem plausible.[12]

Still, after Alexander's I's death there seems to have been a 20-year-long succession struggle involving at least three of his sons, who in the process

[5] Borza 1990, p. 134. Coinage: Raymond 1953, p. 142; Hammond and Griffith 1979, pp. 120–121.

[6] Thucydides 2.100.3; Plato, *Gorgias* 471a–b; cf. Aelian, *Varia Historia* 7.2.41.

[7] Hammond 1992a, p. 71; especially Feil 2023; cf. Goukowsky 1991, pp. 47–60.

[8] Cf. Thucydides 2.100.3, with Goukowsky 1991, pp. 45–47; Müller 2016, p. 145. On Philip's *arche*, see especially Badian 1993, pp. 171–185 and 239–244 (notes).

[9] Cf. Plato, *Gorgias* 471a–b, with Hammond and Griffith 1979, p. 115; Borza 1990, pp. 133–135; Goukowsky 1991, pp. 55–60; Müller 2016, p. 146.

[10] See Goukowsky 1991, pp. 50–55, on Amyntas.

[11] Raymond 1953, pp. 136–138; Hammond and Griffith 1979, pp. 119–121; Psoma 1999, pp. 275–279; Kremydi 2011, p. 163; see Dahmen 2010, p. 51 with n. 41, on the term "tetrobol."

[12] Cf. Cole 1974, pp. 55–57; Errington 1990, p. 15; King 2018, p. 35, arguing that Alexander did try to set up a tripartite division of power for administrative and to foster unity, but it collapsed after his death.

Figure 5.1 Perdiccas II from coin
Source: Wikimedia Commons.

fashioned their own lines of succession until the time of Philip II.[13] If the brothers were at loggerheads with each other—over what is guesswork—then Perdiccas was ruling in his own name by 435, as shown by his name on his coins (figure 5.1). Perhaps he was keen to secure sole rule to ensure that his son Archelaus would succeed him.[14] Further support for 435 comes from Thucydides, who speaks of Athens allying with Sitalces of Thrace against the Macedonian king in 432 and refers to him as someone "who had before been an ally and friend, [and] had now become hostile."[15] This implies Perdiccas was king before that year and had an amicable relationship with the city until 432.[16]

As a result, the years of Perdiccas' reign vary from 23 to 41, based on the assumption that he either succeeded his father immediately or did not rule in his own name until 435 and died in 413.

Perdiccas and Athens

Perdiccas' reign was a tumultuous one, mauled by conflicts with Thrace, Illyria, and Athens.[17] The Athenians especially were proving a threat to

[13] See Goukowsky 1991.
[14] See Feil 2023 on Perdiccas exploiting the foundation myth as given by Herodotus to this end.
[15] Thucydides 1.57.2. [16] Cf. Cole 1974, pp. 55–56.
[17] Reign: Cloché 1960, pp. 57–81; Hammond and Griffith 1979, pp. 115–136; Errington 1990, pp. 15–24; Borza 1990, pp. 134–160; Müller 2016, pp. 141–163; Müller 2017b; King 2018, pp. 34–41; see too Goukowsky 1991, pp. 47–50; Roisman 2010, pp. 146–154; Mari 2011b, pp. 88–91; cf. Cole 1974; Hoffman 1975; Chambers 1986; Chambers 1999.

Macedonia, given their presence along the Thermaic Gulf and in Macedonia and the Chalcidice because of their Delian League.[18] When Macedonia regained possession of the mines of Bisaltia, the safety of the nearby Athenian settlement at Berge (only 25 miles upstream from later Amphipolis) may have caused alarm in both Berge and Athens. After the Athenians won over the small town of Argilus on the Bisaltic coast from Perdiccas to the Delian League, the Athenian leader, Pericles, sent 1,000 cleruchs (settlers) to Berge.[19] The intention must have been to access the area's timber resources and perhaps even to make an alliance with the people of Bisaltia against the neighboring Macedonians and Thracians.

In the 440s, perhaps 446, the Athenians founded what may have been a military colony at Brea (not far from Olynthus), which along with other towns such as Strepsa and Eion paid tribute to the Delian League.[20] Perhaps also in the same year they may have interfered in Macedonian affairs during their siege of the island of Euboea when Pericles allowed anti-Athenian refugees in its town Histiaea to move to Macedonia.[21] Evidently, Pericles clearly thought little of gaining Perdiccas' approval. On the other hand, the resettlement may have been initiated by Perdiccas, as the Athenians were needy of Macedonian timber and could not afford to upset the king.[22]

A clear sign of the Athenians' intentions in the north came in 437 when they took over Ennea Hodoi in Thrace, expelling the Edoni, who had seized it from Alexander I, and refounded it as a fortified colony renamed Amphipolis.[23] As well as being atop trade and communication routes between the coasts of Thrace and Macedonia, Amphipolis gave Athens access to the precious timber of the region, and a garrison was installed in it to ensure control. Perdiccas' reaction is uncertain, but he must have been suspicious,

[18] Hoffman 1975, pp. 364–366; Hammond and Griffith 1979, pp. 115–119; Borza 1990, pp. 135–139; see too Zahrnt 1971, pp. 31–49, on Chalcidian cities being members of the Delian League.

[19] Plutarch, *Pericles* 11.5; see too Meiggs 1972, pp. 538–561 (on p. 550, III no. 50); Borza 1990, pp. 136–137; Roisman 2010, p. 146; Mari 2011b, p. 88; Hatzopoulos 2020, p. 34.

[20] Brea: *IG* i^3 46; Thucydides 4.102.4 ("which they already held"), with Cole 1974, pp. 58–60; Hammond and Griffith 1979, pp. 115–121; Psoma 2009, and Psoma 2011, p. 114 with n. 8, citing further bibliography.

[21] Theopompus, *BNJ* 115 F 387; cf. Thucydides 1.114.3, with Cole 1974, p. 58; Hammond and Griffith 1979, pp. 121–122.

[22] Edson 1970, pp. 25–26; cf. Borza 1987, p. 43; Müller 2016, p. 145. See too Karathanasis 2019.

[23] Thucydides 4.102.2–4; Diodorus 12.32.3, 12.68.1–2, with Meiggs 1972, pp. 83–84; Cole 1974, pp. 58–60 ("a product of calculated diplomacy which exploited the situation to the maximum advantage of Athens"); Hammond and Griffith 1979, pp. 115–121; Meiggs 1982, pp. 121–131 and 356–357; Borza 1990, pp. 137–138; Roisman 2010, p. 146. On Amphipolis throughout antiquity, see Lazaridis 1997; Koukouli-Chrysanthaki 2011.

especially as Amphipolis was not required to pay tribute to the Athenians, a sign of its importance in protecting their interests in the Strymon.[24]

Indeed, Perdiccas may have stopped exporting timber to Athens, despite the impact his move would have had on his finances.[25] His action would explain why in 432 the Athenians allied with his brother Philip and Derdas, king of Elimea (a former ally and even relative by marriage of Alexander I), against the king.[26] Presumably Philip had lost his *arche* by then and sought refuge with Derdas; hence the alliance was plausibly to install Philip on the throne.[27] Since by 432 there was a growing threat of war from Sparta, any successful support of a new king would earn his favor and thus enable access to timber and the rich Strymon basin.[28]

Another worrying factor for the Athenians concerned Potidaea, a colony of Corinth strategically located on the narrow isthmus connecting the peninsula of Pallene, which was receiving support from Perdiccas and Corinth to secede from the Delian League.[29] Some months earlier, in the fall of 433, the Athenians had demanded that Potidaea sever its ties with Corinth and raze its walls, which the Potidaeans had refused to do. Perdiccas' kingdom had been weakened over the past two decades, so he was quick to seize this situation as a means of procuring allies. He sent envoys to Corinth to support the Potidaeans' cause and to Corinth's allies the Spartans, urging them to make war on Athens.[30] His move was meant to counter the hostile Athenian bloc against him, and in doing so he played a role in the outbreak of the Peloponnesian War.

The Athenians responded by sending 30 ships and 1,000 hoplites under the general Archestratus to join their new allies Philip and Derdas in the north.[31] Probably in response to their action rather than before, Perdiccas

[24] Meiggs 1972, pp. 538–561; Errington 1990, p. 17.

[25] Psoma 2001, pp. 105–108; cf. Psoma 1999; contra Roisman 2010, p. 147.

[26] Papastavrou 1957, pp. 257–259; Kagan 1969, pp. 276–278; Meiggs 1972, pp. 196–197; Hammond 1972a, pp. 169–170; Cole 1974, pp. 58–61; Hammond and Griffith 1979, pp. 18, 115, and 122; Badian 1993, p. 173. Hammond and Griffith 1979, p. 122, connect *IG* i^2 53 as a fragment of the alliance with Philip, but against this, see Cole 1974, p. 61; Borza 1990, p. 139 with n. 21. Kagan 1969, p. 277 n. 14, puts the Athens-Derdas alliance as early as 435; contra Cole 1974, pp. 60–61. Elimiote dynasty: Liampi 1998.

[27] Badian 1993, pp. 173–174.

[28] Cole 1974, p. 57. Perhaps even a second Amphipolis might have been founded at the mouth of the Strymon, so Hammond 1992a, p. 82.

[29] Kagan 1969, p. 278.

[30] Thucydides 1.572–5, with Chambers 1986, pp. 140–142; cf. Cole 1974, p. 62; Müller 2016, pp. 149–150. On his need to safeguard Macedonia even if that meant clashing with Athens, see Cole 1974, pp. 57–58; Borza 1990, pp. 140–141.

[31] Thucydides 1.57.6, though Badian 1993, p. 172, suggests the opposition was intended to be more diplomatic and political, not military action; cf. Edson 1970, pp. 33–34.

now sent embassies to the Chalcidians and the Bottiaeans, coaxing them to revolt from Athens and come over to his side.[32] They and the Potidaeans were all located on his borders; hence his new allies would strengthen his position against Derdas and the Athenians. The Chalcidians may have had issues with the Athenians anyway, which Perdiccas was quick to exploit. For one thing, there was Athens' military colony of Brea near Olynthus, which posed a threat to the Chalcidice.[33] For another, the Athenians had treated the mother cities of Chalcis and Eretria harshly in the 440s and the Chalcidians harbored a grudge.[34]

In the meantime, Archestratus led an army from Athens tasked with taking hostages from Potidaea, destroying its walls, and preventing the Chalcidice from revolting. The size of Archestratus' force—30 ships and 1,000 hoplites—was surely too small to fight both Macedonians and rebels simultaneously.[35] He may therefore have expected troops from Philip and Derdas to bolster his numbers. Then again, the Macedonian army was still developing, so he may have believed he had sufficient men to achieve his objectives. Even so, when Archestratus arrived, the Chalcidians were already revolting, and he requested reinforcements from Athens, which sent Callias north with 40 ships and 2,000 hoplites.[36]

The combined army of Archestratus, Philip, and Derdas scored some successes, among other things capturing Therma on the eastern coast of the Thermaic Gulf to cut off Perdiccas from the Chalcidians, whose coastal cities were easy prey for the Athenian fleet.[37] The king, however, persuaded the Chalcidians to abandon their homes and settle together in one inland location at Olynthus. This was to be "a single strong city," so easily defensible, about three miles from the sea, with good fertile land, and he also promised them land in Mygdonia around Lake Bolbe, where they founded Apollonia.[38] The move to Olynthus led to the founding of a federal organization of cities with a powerful army commonly called the Chalcidian League, with Olynthus as capital.[39] If all this really was at the king's instigation to

[32] Thucydides 1.57.5, with Hammond and Griffith 1979, pp. 122–123.

[33] Zahrnt 1971, pp. 215–216; Psoma 2011, p. 114.

[34] Psoma 2011, p. 115.

[35] Cole 1974, p. 62; Roisman 2010, p. 147.

[36] Thucydides 1.61.1.

[37] Thucydides 1.61.2–3.

[38] Thucydides 1.58.2, with Hammond and Griffith 1979, pp. 123 and 192–193; Borza 1990, p. 142. Apollonia: Hatzopoulos 1994c. Note Thucydides' claim that the Olynthians could cultivate Mygdonia "as long as they were at war with the Athenians."

[39] Zahrnt 1971, pp. 49–57; Psoma 2001, pp. 203–221; cf. Papastavrou 1957, pp. 258–260. Not every city in the area was subject to the league: Apollonia's bronze coinage from 400 to 375 shows that it retained its independence: Hammond and Griffith 1979, pp. 192–193.

block Athenian moves in the north, then the formation of this league in 432 was a major coup.[40]

By now, the early summer of 432, Philip, Derdas' brother Pausanias, and the Athenians, with the reinforcements under Callias, were besieging Pydna on the Thermaic Gulf.[41] The aim was to hinder and pressure Perdiccas and his Chalcidian allies as Pydna was only a few hours march from Aegae. But the siege of Pydna dragged on, and when news came that 8,000 troops including 2,000 hoplites under Aristeus of Corinth had arrived to protect Potidaea, the Athenians were forced to come to terms with the king, abandon the siege of Pydna, and rush to Potidaea.[42]

If Perdiccas expected the Athenians to withdraw support from Philip, he would be disappointed. The Athenian army marched around the coast of the Gulf via Beroea and Strepsa (probably Basilika) to Potidaea, bolstered by 600 cavalry from Philip and Pausanias, and laid siege to Strepsa, an ally of Perdiccas.[43] Unsurprisingly, the king immediately ended his short-lived alliance with Athens and marched to defend Potidaea, for some reason appointing the otherwise unknown Iolaus as commander with 200 cavalry, which were stationed not far from Potidaea to attack the Athenian rear.[44] Although Thucydides criticizes Perdiccas for "immediately deserting the Athenians again," Athenian duplicity was to blame for his action.[45] Callias, however, ordered Philip's 600 cavalry to Olynthus to keep Iolaus' cavalry there in check.[46] Then came news that the Athenians had been victorious in battle (though Potidaea did not fall to Athens until winter 430–429), causing Perdiccas and Philip to retreat, so neither cavalry contingent was engaged.[47]

In 431 Perdiccas changed tack and renewed his alliance with the Athenians, not from any feelings of friendship but because of the sudden surge of Thracian power exposing the vulnerability of his borders.[48] In the previous year the Athenians had allied with the powerful Sitalces, who had succeeded Teres as king of the Odrysian tribe in Thrace, to regain influence

[40] Papastavrou 1957, p. 260; cf. Cole 1974, p. 62. [41] Thucydides 1.61.2–3.
[42] Thucydides 1.61.3, with Hammond and Griffith 1979, p. 123.
[43] Thucydides 1.61.4–5, with Hammond and Griffith 1979, p. 123; Borza 1990, p. 143; Badian 1993, pp. 174–179; Roisman 2010, p. 147. Location of Strepsa: Hatzopoulos 1987, especially pp. 22 and 54–60.
[44] Thucydides 1.62.2–3. [45] Thucydides 1.62.1, with Cole 1974, p. 63.
[46] Thucydides 1.62.4. Cole 1974, p. 63 and n. 32, suggests the Athenians exploited two forces of Macedonian cavalry operating on different sides to weaken Macedonia by promoting internal dissension, but this is stretching it. See too Papastavrou 1957, pp. 260–261.
[47] Thucydides 1.62.5–63, with Kagan 1969, pp. 273–285; Meiggs 1972, pp. 309–311.
[48] Thucydides 2.29, with Borza 1990, p. 143; Chambers 1999, p. 217.

in the northern Aegean, and they continued to support Philip's bid for the throne.[49] The Odrysians posed a threat to Perdiccas as they were fierce warriors and their kingdom was wealthy because of a tribute levied on the various cities close to them.[50]

Sitalces' brother-in-law Nymphodorus, a Greek of Abdera, had arranged the alliance between Athens and Sitalces. The Athenians had been suspicious of Nymphodorus but still made him *proxenos* when he got Sitalces to promise to send Thracian troops to help Athens reassert control of the Chalcidice and had granted citizenship to his son.[51] At some point Perdiccas persuaded Nymphodorus and Sitalces to win over the Athenians to him, and for Sitalces to turn his back on Philip. As a result, Philip and his son Amyntas took refuge with Sitalces, who did not seem especially enamored of Philip.

Thucydides adds that Perdiccas made a promise to Sitalces "on condition that he should reconcile him to the Athenians and should not bring back his brother Philip, who was hostile, to make him king; but Perdiccas would not fulfil his promise." Exactly what was this promise is unknown, and various theories have emerged.[52] For example, Thucydides may have made it up to evoke an image in his readers of the king as a liar and unreliable.[53] Perhaps, even, it was to marry one of the king's sisters to the Thracian king, just as in 429 Perdiccas gifted his sister as bride to Sitalces' nephew Seuthes to help persuade Sitalces to end his invasion, though it is odd that Thucydides did not mention something as important as a diplomatic marriage.[54] Other suggestions include Sitalces' obtaining a financial undertaking from Perdiccas or—surely incorrect—Perdiccas promising to return Philip to his *arche*, which by extension would endear him to the Athenians.[55] Most plausible is that the promise was not to undertake any action against Sitalces' new allies the Athenians—thus when Thucydides tells us that Sparta received Macedonian troops for an offensive against Athenian allies in Acarnania

[49] Thucydides 2.95.2–3; Diodorus 12.50.1–4, with Borza 1990; Chambers 1999, pp. 217–218; Psoma 2011, p. 116; Müller 2016, pp. 151–153; especially Mihailov 1977. Sitalces: Archibald 1998, pp. 107–112 and 118–120. Odrysians: Archibald 1998, pp. 93–125, 145–150, and 213–239 (to Alexander the Great); Alexander the Great); Martinez, Mathleux, and Tonkova (eds.) 2015.

[50] Thucydides 2.97.3–4.

[51] Meiggs 1972, p. 216; Kagan 1974, p. 63; Archibald 1998, p. 118.

[52] Thucydides 2.95.1, with Papastavrou 1957, pp. 263–264; Cole 1974, pp. 65–66; Badian 1993, pp. 179–185; Roisman 2010, pp. 149–150; Psoma 2011, p. 116; Vasilev 2011b.

[53] Badian 1993, p. 179, and see pp. 179–185.

[54] Chambers 1999, pp. 218–219.

[55] Chambers 1999, p. 217 (former); Papastavrou 1957, p. 261 (latter); and see Chambers 1999, pp. 219–220, for arguments against.

(in 429), Perdiccas' betrayal triggered Sitalces' invasion.[56] But we should not discount that Thucydides was simply more interested in Sitalces' invasion of Macedonia, to which we turn below, than the promise; hence we shall never know what it was.

After renewing their friendship with Perdiccas in 431, the Athenians gave him back Therma. In return, he seems to have handed over to them the Greek settlement of Methone, close to Pydna.[57] The date is controversial and rests on interpretation of epigraphic evidence dating from 424/3 when the Athenians inscribed in chronological order four decrees to do with Methone, of which only the first two decrees are preserved.[58] The first decree, waiving debts that the Methonians owed Athens, also sets out Athenian relations with Perdiccas over Methone and is generally agreed to have been moved in 430/29, as Methone was then a member of the Delian League.[59] It ordered Perdiccas to allow the Methonians access to the sea and freedom to trade with the interior—presumably when he had controlled Methone he had imposed limits on its trading activities, potentially causing economic strife.[60] In addition, he was forbidden to march an army through the Methonians' lands without their permission, and the Athenians were to settle disputes between the two of them.

Thus, if Perdiccas surrendered Methone to Athens in 431, for the Athenians to impose these terms only a year later must mean that he was interfering in it, and relations were souring between him and Athens. We should not be surprised. Both Methone and Pydna where bases from which an invading army could march into Macedonia, and Methone was the nearest port for the timber reserves of the Olympian-Pierian mountains. Hence, the Athenians' decree was as much for the Methonians' economic well-being and security as for protecting their own interests in the region.[61]

In 431 hostilities began in the Peloponnesian War with a Spartan invasion of Attica. Thucydides tells us that there were three "immediate causes"

[56] Chambers 1999, pp. 220–221, based on Thucydides 2.80.7 and building on Borza 1990, pp. 146–147.

[57] Papastavrou 1957, p. 262; Hammond and Griffith 1979, pp. 124–125; Borza 1990, pp. 148–149; Roisman 2010, p. 148 with n. 11.

[58] *IG* i3 61 = Meiggs-Lewis, no. 65, with Mattingly 1961; Meiggs 1972, pp. 534–537; Cole 1974, p. 66; Hammond and Griffith 1979, pp. 124–128; Errington 1990, p. 20; Hammond 1992a, p. 85; Roisman 2010, pp. 148–149; Ruffing 2017, pp. 128–129.

[59] It could have been 434 because of a reference to the "preceding" festival of Panathenaea, which was held every four years, so either 434 or 430, but the latter is more plausible: Hammond and Griffith 1979, pp. 124–127. The second and perhaps third decrees were moved in 426/5 and the fourth in 424/3.

[60] Suggested by Roisman 2010, p. 149.

[61] Ruffing 2017, p. 128.

of the war, stretching back to 435—the defeat of Corinthian fleets by the Athenians at Corcyra, the Potidaea affair mentioned above, and the Athenian economic sanctions on Megara, which all prompted Corinth to pressure Sparta to declare war. But Thucydides also states that there was only one "truest explanation" for war breaking out, and that was Sparta's fear of the growth of Athenian power.[62] The details of the war, which ended in 404 with the Athenians' defeat and collapse of their Delian League, do not concern us here except when Perdiccas involved himself in them.[63] When he did so, he allied with Athens and Sparta at different times not for any ideological reasons but simply because of a cynical principle: the enemy of my enemy is my friend.

Sitalces' invasion

In the summer of 429, Perdiccas sent 1,000 troops to join the Spartan Cnemus' invasion of pro-Athenian Acarnania, where they were joined by Molossian and Orestian contingents.[64] Presumably Perdiccas defied the Athenians because of how they treated him in their decree over Methone, but he may also have taken advantage of a devastating plague that had swept through Athens the previous year; it killed up to one-quarter of its population, including Pericles, and caused lawlessness and a collapse of societal norms.[65] The Macedonian troops arrived too late to take part in Cnemus' campaign, which in any case was a miserable failure.[66] The Athenian reaction is interesting: they overlooked Perdiccas' support of Sparta as his troops did not actually fight, though it is likely that the Athenians, weakened by the plague, could not engage in any large-scale punitive campaigns.[67]

Then in the winter of 429 Sitalces of Thrace embarked on an invasion of Macedonia, supported by the Athenians, who sent him Hagnon (the founder of Amphipolis) as a military adviser.[68] Sitalces also took with him Amyntas,

[62] Thucydides 1.23.6 (*alēthestatēn prophasin*); cf. 1.144.3 (*anankē polemein*). Events leading to the war: Thucydides 1.57–65. Causes and outbreak: Kagan 1969.

[63] War: Kagan 1969; Kagan 1974; Kagan 1981; Kagan 1987. See in one volume Tritle 2004; Kagan 2005; cf. Meiggs 1972.

[64] Thucydides 2.80.7 ("without the knowledge of the Athenians").

[65] Plague: Thucydides 2.47.3–53, with Kagan 1974, pp. 70–100. Cole 1974, p. 64, connects the plague to Perdiccas' motive in sending troops.

[66] Borza 1990, p. 146.

[67] Roisman 2010, p. 149.

[68] Thucydides 2.95–101; Diodorus 12.50.3–7, with Kagan 1974, pp. 119–121; Müller 2016, pp. 151–153.

the son of Perdiccas' brother Philip—since we never hear of Philip again, he may have been dead by then. That Sitalces intended to depose Perdiccas and install Amyntas on the throne is possible but unlikely—Sitalces never threatened Aegae but operated largely in the Axius Valley, the area that Philip had governed; hence he may have taken Amyntas with him for the psychological effect of showing Perdiccas he could still be threatened by a pretender.[69] After all, if Perdiccas had broken his enigmatic promise to Sitalces of 431, discussed above, then the latter was free to do what he may have promised not to do—back a rival to Perdiccas.[70]

Sitalces had already expanded his kingdom to reach as far north as the Danube and as far east as the Black Sea, so he was clearly ambitious to acquire more lands.[71] If we believe our sources on numbers, he mustered a large army of 150,000 troops, of which roughly one-third were cavalry from his own Odrysians and subject Thracian and Paeonian tribes.[72] He moved down through Doberus in Paeonia into the Axius Valley, devastating the districts of Mygdonia, Crestonia, and Anthemus, sending troops to pin down the Bottiaeans and Chalcidians, and entering Amphaxatis, where he captured several cities and forced the people to flee to strongholds.[73]

Perdiccas would have been in dire straits had an Athenian army joined Sitalces, especially as he had just sent 1,000 troops to Acarnania. But Sitalces received no help from the Athenians. Thucydides claims it was because they thought Sitalces would not come, but they may have been put off by the size of Sitalces' army and misjudged the situation to their later cost.[74] We should also not forget they were still reeling from the plague, for it took them about 15 years to recover and replenish their manpower, to judge by Nicias' remark in the Sicilian debate of 416: "we have but recently recovered from a great plague."[75]

[69] Badian 1993, pp. 179–185; Hammond and Griffith 1979, pp. 127–128; Chambers 1999, pp. 222–224: he may well have been successful in setting up Amyntas in an *arche* since we do not hear of him again.

[70] Hammond 1972a, pp. 153, 169, 200–201; Hammond and Griffith 1979, pp. 128–129; Badian 1993, pp. 180–181 and 184; Chambers 1999, pp. 222–223.

[71] Thucydides 2.96–97, and see Mihailov 1977.

[72] Thucydides 2.98.3; cf. Diodorus 12.50.3, but Mihailov 1977, pp. 244–245, questions the number because of the influence of references to Thrace in drama on Thucydides.

[73] Thucydides 2.100.3–8. Route: Hammond and Griffith 1979, p. 128, with further references; cf. Borza 1990, p. 146 n. 38.

[74] Thucydides 2.101.1, with Badian 1993, pp. 181–185; Chambers 1999, p. 223; cf. Kagan 1974, pp. 120–121.

[75] Thucydides 6.12.1.

Possibly Perdiccas now secured his supply dumps, as Diodorus speaks of him stockpiling grain, and he may even have sent for cavalry reinforcements from his allies in Upper Macedonia.[76] More likely, though, given that even increased numbers would still have been no match for Sitalces' army, Perdiccas cunningly contacted Sitalces' nephew Seuthes and offered him his sister Stratonice in marriage together with a substantial dowry if he could persuade his uncle to withdraw.[77]

The campaign by now had taken up 30 days, including eight in the Chalcidice, where Sitalces had sent perhaps up to his half his men to show his support of Athens. As a result, Sitalces accepted Seuthes' diplomacy, though, according to Thucydides, a shortage of supplies and deteriorating weather as winter approached also motivated him to return home.[78] As agreed, Stratonice married Seuthes, who became Odrysian king in 424 on Sitalces' death.[79] The ties from the political marriage helped to keep Macedonia's eastern border secure for a while, though Sitalces' death marked a substantial decline in Thracian power.

Perdiccas had had a narrow escape, though nothing is known of his activities from now until 424. However, he seems to have taken little heed of the Athenians' terms imposed on him in their first Methone decree, for the second decree issued in summer 426 repeats Methonian grievances against him. Presumably these were about hindering trade and perhaps marching through its territory, yet there is no mention of any Athenian arbitration.

Return to the Peloponnesian War

In 424 Perdiccas, clearly concerned about Athenian inroads into his territory, supported the Spartan general Brasidas' campaign in the north to wrest cities from the Delian League and prevent Athens from obtaining timber around Amphipolis.[80] He even offered to pay half of Brasidas' expenses,

[76] Diodorus 12.50.5 (grain); see Borza 1990, p. 147, for reinforcements.

[77] Thucydides 2.95, 100–101.5. Seuthes was the son of Sitalces' brother Sparadacus: Hammond and Griffith 1979, p. 129.

[78] Thucydides 1.101.5. Cole 1974, p. 65, notes that this campaign, like that of Bubares a century earlier, ended in a wedding—perhaps Herodotus had the wedding of Seuthes in mind when was telling the story of Gygaea and the Persian envoys.

[79] Thucydides 4.101.5. See Borza 1990, p. 148 n. 43; Archibald 1998, pp. 120–125, on Perdiccas' possible involvement in his death.

[80] Thucydides 4.79, with Hammond and Griffith 1979, pp. 129–136; Roisman 2010, pp. 150–151.

perhaps because he did not have enough troops of his own; the Chalcidians, equally wary of Athenian influence in their lands, paid the other half.[81] Perhaps Perdiccas was also quick to throw his weight behind Sparta because he needed a strong ally to campaign against Arrhabaeus, king of Lyncus in Upper Macedonia.[82] The two kings may have been locked in a territorial dispute since Lyncus controlled important inland routes, and bordering Lyncus was Eordaea, which was in Perdiccas' kingdom.

That summer a Spartan army of 1,700 soldiers (1,000 Peloponnesian hoplites and 700 helots, or state-owned serfs) was sent north. One of Perdiccas' friends, Niconidas of Larissa, escorted it through Thessalian territory, ignoring convention, as a Greek state needed permission to march through the territory of another state.[83] Presumably Thessaly, at the time an ally of Athens, would have blocked the Spartans' passage. From there Brasidas moved via Perrhaebia to Dium.[84] The Athenians in response increased garrisons in the Chalcidian towns and unsurprisingly ended their alliance with Perdiccas, declaring him "an enemy and responsible for Brasidas' arrival."[85] Although Perdiccas has been criticized for sacrificing his relations with one major power, Athens, to court another, Sparta, we should not be so quick to judge: if Arrhabaeus was threatening his kingdom, Perdiccas needed to respond any way he could to protect it.[86]

Perdiccas immediately launched his offensive against Arrhabaeus, marching with Brasidas through Eordaea and then over the Kleidi Pass into Lyncus.[87] But when they arrived on the border of Lyncus, contrary to Perdiccas' expectation, Brasidas suggested negotiating with Arrhabaeus rather than attacking him.[88] It seems that Chalcidian envoys had warned Brasidas that Perdiccas was using him; hence Brasidas formed his own plan to win over Arrhabaeus and counter Perdiccas' expansion plans. Arrhabaeus

[81] Thucydides 4.83.5, with Papastavrou 1957, p. 265; Cole 1974, pp. 67–69; Chambers 1986, p. 143; Psoma 2011, p. 116. Perdiccas and Brasidas: Hammond and Griffith 1979, pp. 129–131; Chambers 1986, pp. 143–145; Borza 1990, pp. 150–155. Note Archibald 2010, p. 326, pointing out that Thucydides speaks of the Thraceward region without making clear where Macedonian control ended and "Thrace" began and that the Chalcidice was in "Thrace": Thucydides 4.78.1, 79. 2–3; cf. 5.18.5.

[82] Thucydides 4.83, with Roisman 2010, p. 151; King 2018, p. 38; cf. Papastavrou 1957, pp. 262–263.

[83] Mosley 1973.

[84] Hammond and Griffith 1979, p. 129; Sprawski 1999, pp. 29–31; Graninger 2010, pp. 310–311.

[85] Thucydides 4.82.1.

[86] Critical: Borza 1990, p. 150.

[87] Thucydides 4.83.1–2. See Hammond 1972a, pp. 103–105, for the route; see too Borza 1990, pp. 150–151; Greenwalt 2010, pp. 282–283, on the campaign.

[88] Thucydides 4.83.2–4.

in turn asked for Sparta to arbitrate between him and Perdiccas in their dispute.[89] Perdiccas objected, telling Brasidas he was in the wrong because the king had brought in the Spartans to fight his enemies and was paying half of his expenses.[90]

Perdiccas was in the right, but Brasidas was keen to make his way to the Chalcidice; he went ahead with negotiations and as a result abandoned the campaign. Since Perdiccas could not take on Arrhabaeus by himself, he was forced to do the same, but in justified anger he cut Brasidas' funding from one-half to one-third.[91] Arrhabaeus' position in all this is hard to gauge, but if he were sincere about peace with Perdiccas, he could have turned elsewhere for arbitration.[92]

Brasidas was now free to proceed to the Chalcidice, where he won over Acanthus and Stagira and then advanced on Amphipolis. In a bitter blow for Athens, Amphipolis fell to him in the winter of 423.[93] His attempt to take Eion failed, though, because of the timely arrival of the historian Thucydides as commander of Athenian troops.[94] Thucydides was not able to retake Amphipolis, for which he was exiled and spent the rest of his life roaming Greece and writing his monumental history of the Peloponnesian War (although its account ends at 411).

In the meantime, Perdiccas marched to Amphipolis, presumably to see how he might exploit the situation to his advantage, and, letting some bygones be bygones, helped Brasidas seize Myrcinus, Galepsus, and Oesyme. As Brasidas detached numerous cities from the Delian League over the next months, Perdiccas had good reason to think his future lay with Sparta.[95] But then in the spring of 423 Athens and Sparta agreed to a one-year truce.[96] The latter was no more than a breathing space and was soon broken by Brasidas' actions in accepting the surrender of Scione and Mende in the Chalcidice and reinforcing them with Peloponnesian and Chalcidian troops. In response, the Athenians sent an army to battle him at Mende, but Brasidas decided to renew the earlier campaign with Perdiccas against Arrhabaeus, possibly because the Athenians thought Arrhabaeus could be a

[89] Thucydides 4.83.3. [90] Thucydides 4.83.5.

[91] Thucydides 4.83.6. The break with Brasidas in 423/2: Mattingly 1968, pp. 467–475; Meiggs 1972, pp. 308 and 428–430; Cole 1974, p. 61.

[92] Roisman 2010, p. 151.

[93] Campaign: Thucydides 4.102–108, with Hammond and Griffith 1979, p. 130; Borza 1990, pp. 151–152.

[94] Thucydides 4.106.4.

[95] Cole 1974, pp. 67–78; cf. Müller 2016, pp. 154–155. [96] Thucydides 4.117–119.

valuable counter to Brasidas' and Perdiccas' ambitions.[97] Not to mention Perdiccas showed no qualms in changing sides when it suited him, so Brasidas may also have thought he needed to keep the king and Athens at loggerheads with one another to obstruct Athens' access to timber and indeed the northern Aegean.[98]

Perdiccas and Brasidas marched into Lyncus with an army of 3,000 Greek hoplites, 1,000 Macedonian and Chalcidian cavalry, and contingents of "barbarian" troops, which presumably included some Macedonians.[99] Arrhabaeus' infantry had taken up a position on a hill and his cavalry on a plain beside it, probably just northwest of Monastir near the exit of the Diavat pass.[100] The two sides first sent their cavalry across the plain to fight, followed by the Lyncestian hoplites coming down the hill as backup, but they were routed by Brasidas' army and retreated to higher ground.[101]

Although, Thucydides says, both sides "set up a trophy," Macedonians did not have the custom of setting up victory trophies; hence Brasidas must have been responsible for claiming victory.[102] But then Brasidas and Perdiccas began to bicker with each other as they waited two to three days for Perdiccas' Illyrian allies to join them. The king wanted to attack the Lyncestian villages forthwith, whereas the more cautious Brasidas planned to use the expected reinforcements in the Chalcidice, where an Athenian fleet in the Thermaic Gulf had captured Mende and blockaded Scione. Then came the news that the Illyrians had broken their deal with Perdiccas and joined Arrhabaeus.[103] Their reputation as fierce warriors preceded them, so when they arrived in large numbers Brasidas and Perdiccas retreated.[104]

Unfortunately, communication was not these two leaders' strong suit. They were unable to agree on how to retreat and to where, so both set up their own camps some distance from each other. When darkness fell the already jittery Macedonians panicked and fled for home, with Perdiccas not informing Brasidas of their flight.[105] When dawn broke Brasidas discovered half of the army had deserted him and he was a sitting duck to attacks by

[97] Edson 1970, p. 34. [98] Cole 1974, p. 68; Mari 2011b, p. 90.

[99] Thucydides 4.124.1. Campaign: Thucydides 4.124–129, with Hammond 1972a, pp. 104–108; Hammond and Griffith 1979, pp. 130–131; Borza 1990, pp. 152–153; Psoma 2011, p. 117. Barbarians: Borza 1990, p. 152 with n 53, citing further references.

[100] Hammond 1972a, pp. 104–108, explaining the location here at p. 107; cf. Hammond and Griffith 1979, p. 130.

[101] Thucydides 4.124.2–3. [102] Thucydides 4.124. 4.

[103] Thucydides 4.4.124–125.1 for the disagreements and Illyrian betrayal.

[104] Thucydides 4.125.1. [105] Thucydides 4.125.1–2.

the Illyrians and Arrhabaeus, who had already taken the Kirli Dirven pass, the only exit from the Lyncestian plain. He took the bull by the horns and formed his troops into a defensive square, exhorting them in a rousing speech to fight their way through the pass to the town of Arnisa in Eordaea.[106] Obviously angered at Perdiccas' desertion, he allowed his men to kill any Macedonian cattle they came across and seize as booty anything the retreating Macedonians had left behind.[107]

Thucydides rightly contrasted the panicked retreat of Perdiccas with the disciplined retreat of Brasidas even though faced by superior enemy numbers. But Brasidas should not have plundered Macedonia to the extent that he did, for an enraged Perdiccas turned his back on him and Sparta and began to open negotiations with Athens.[108] Brasidas thus deprived the Spartans of a valuable ally and risked being cut off from Peloponnesian reinforcements reaching him through Thessaly because of Perdiccas' influence there.[109]

A fragmentary inscription, found on the Athenian Acropolis, records a treaty between Athens and Perdiccas, which may date to this time.[110] Among its terms are that both parties have the same friends and enemies, and that Perdiccas export oars only to the Athenians. This exclusivity shows the importance of oars—hundreds of thousands of them were needed for a war fleet.[111] The same stone also records a second decree proclaiming friendship between Athens and Arrhabaeus and asking the Athenians to help reconcile him with Perdiccas. Its remaining lines deal with procedures for implementing the alliance and include a list of signatories of Argeads and others. Many of the names are restored, but the order seems to be Perdiccas; Alcetas, his brother; and Archelaus, his son and successor (from his marriage to a Cleopatra, though we know little about her). The fourth and fifth listed names are missing—perhaps one was Perdiccas' fourth brother, Philip, though he was probably dead by then. The sixth name was the other brother, Menelaus; then came Agerrus, Perdiccas' nephew and Philip's son. These are followed by the names of other men who were not Argeads and who had been hostile to Perdiccas: Arrhabaeus, Derdas (restored), Antiochus of

[106] Thucydides 4.125.2–128.3, with Hammond 1972a, p. 106, on the town; cf. Hammond and Griffith 1979, p. 131; Borza 1990, p. 152.

[107] Thucydides 4.128.4, with Roisman 2010, p. 152.

[108] Thucydides 4.128.5, with Hammond and Griffith 1979, pp. 132–133.

[109] Cole 1974, pp. 68–69; Roisman 2010, p. 152.

[110] *IG* i^3 89 = *SEG* 10, 86.

[111] Timber exclusive to Athens: line 23—Hoffman 1975, p. 361, thinks this clause was the treaty's most important. See Borza 1987, p. 34, for figures; cf. Cole 1977, p. 30; Borza 1990, p. 154.

Orestis, and after them several people who are unknown but were probably barons from Lower Macedonia.[112] Together these names show that Perdiccas had made peace with his brothers and local dynasts and that they supported his rule, which was no small feat.[113]

This important treaty—to judge from the number of signatories—surely "marked a high point in Athenian-Macedonian relations."[114] But because the stone is broken and many of the names are restored, not always with certainty, the date is controversial and ranges from the 430s to 413.[115] Since we know of a break in relations between Perdiccas and the Athenians until the start of the Peloponnesian War in 431, the alliance may be dated to 432 or even 431.[116] Then again, Perdiccas had been an Athenian ally before 432, as we saw above, which could indicate an earlier date.

The common opinion is a date of 423. By then the king had severed relations with Brasidas, who was favoring Arrhabaeus' claims and had a strong army in the north. Hence if the Upper Macedonia cantons banded together with Arrhabaeus or simply declared their independence, Perdiccas would have been in a precarious position. Since the second decree speaks of reconciling Arrhabaeus and Perdiccas, the king may well have been prepared to accept a "non-threatening status quo" to shore up his western frontier.[117] Evidently Athenian diplomacy was successful, since Arrhabaeus was a signatory to the treaty.[118] Moreover, in the following year (422) Cleon was sent by the Athenians as general with an army to regain Amphipolis and requested that Perdiccas bring an army to Eion "in accordance with the terms of alliance" and join him in attacking Brasidas' position there.[119] Perdiccas did not lend Cleon military aid, but he did persuade his friends in

[112] Masson 1998; Hatzopoulos 2000, pp. 112–113. For restorations, see Mattingly 1968, pp. 472–475; Hammond and Griffith 1979, pp. 134–136; cf. Meiggs 1972, pp. 428–430. For a reconsideration of this treaty and especially the names of certain signatories, see now Voller 2025.

[113] Roisman 2010, p. 153. [114] Hoffman 1975, p. 362.

[115] 431: Hoffman 1975, pp. 363–364 Chambers 1986, p. 143. 423/2: Cole 1974, pp. 60–61 and 69; Borza 1990, pp. 153–155 with n. 55 (p. 153) and p. 295; Voller 2025. 422/1: Mattingly 1968, pp. 473–476. 417–413: Lewis in i^3 89. 415: Hammond and Griffith 1979, pp. 134–136. 413: Edson 1970, p. 34; Hammond 1992a, p. 85; cf. Meiggs 1972, pp. 308 and 428–430 (before 433). See too Errington 1990, pp. 15–16; King 2018, p. 50; Roisman 2010, pp. 152–153; Müller 2016, pp. 156–161.

[116] Thucydides 5.6.2 for Perdiccas and Athens becoming closer; see too Hammond and Griffith 1979, pp. 134–135; cf. Borza 1987, p. 44.

[117] Borza 1990, p. 154.

[118] Errington 1990, p. 16, argues that the names show the relative weakness of Perdiccas and the Athenian position of strength in demanding the Macedonian nobility witness the oath. But Roisman 2010, p. 153, is surely right to emphasize that the order of names shows only a growth in influence for Perdiccas, for men like Arrhabaeus and Derdas had been his enemies.

[119] Thucydides 5.6.2.

Thessaly to deny permission for Spartan reinforcements to march through their territory toward Macedonia.[120]

Perdiccas thus gained valuable allies and the Athenians a guaranteed supply of timber. But they may also have detached Bormiscus, Tragilos in Bisaltia, and Heracleum in Pieria, from him, which they added to their league.[121] Heracleum controlled the entry from Thessaly into Macedonia via the Tempe pass and Bormiscus that from the Strymon River into Macedonia via the Rendin pass; hence, given their locations, they were of strategic value to Perdiccas as well. However, he may have had little choice but to agree to these terms.

The treaty imposed an obligation on Perdiccas to support Athenian expeditions, which might indicate that Macedonia joined the Delian League.[122] In support of this interpretation is the fact that he did not coin from about 424 or 423 to 416 or 415, perhaps because hegemonic Athens deprived him of this right. He struck only small tetrobols until 424, more suitable for local commerce than trade, so he had probably lost control of the Bisaltic mines between 452 and 445.[123] But neither of these factors supports his membership in the Athenian league, and in the case of his coinage, other kings also suffered economic reversals. Indeed, there was a devaluation of the coinage toward the end of the century when bronze issues circulated with token values rather than by weight, perhaps due to a shortage of silver, which suggests he had lost control over the Bisaltic silver deposits.[124]

Brasidas managed to make his way to Amphipolis, but in 422 he and Cleon were killed in battle there.[125] An Athenian conservative general named Nicias negotiated a peace in the war, the Peace of Nicias, which was formalized in 421 and was supposed to last for 50 years.[126] Its terms were very general and not every state was happy with it, with the Corinthians accusing the Spartans of betraying their interests and the Chalcidians perhaps even losing their confederacy.[127] In addition, Amphipolis was supposed to be returned to Athens, but its people refused—even by Philip II's time the

[120] Thucydides 4.132.2.

[121] Cole 1974, p. 55 n. 4; Hammond and Griffith 1979, pp. 132–133; Borza 1990, p. 156.

[122] Hammond and Griffith 1979, p. 133.

[123] Hammond and Griffith 1979, p. 120; see especially Psoma 1999.

[124] Price 1974, pp. 16–17 and 20; Psoma 1999, pp. 275–279.

[125] Thucydides 5.7–10; Plutarch, *Nicias* 9.3, with Kagan 1974, pp. 321–330.

[126] Thucydides 5.17–20; Plutarch, *Nicias* 9.3–10.1, with Kagan 1974, pp. 342–345; Hammond and Griffith 1979, pp. 131–132.

[127] Corinthian accusation: Thucydides 5.30.2. Chalcidian cities: Zahrnt 1971, pp. 66–72.

Athenians still wanted it back. It is no surprise that the Peace of Nicias lasted less than two years as the Athenians continued to capture enemy cities.

In 418 the Corinthians joined a new anti-Athenian coalition headed by Sparta and Argos, which appealed to the Chalcidians and Perdiccas to join it—perhaps by exploiting his dynasty's link to Argos.[128] Perdiccas had been firmly on Athens' side for some years, even arranging a treaty between the city and Bottiaean cities south of Lake Bolbe in 422.[129] But now he changed sides again and joined the Argive-Spartan alliance, thus realigning himself to Sparta's cause.[130] He may well have considered Sparta had an advantage over Athens because it was busy reasserting its influence in the north, but interestingly he probably now minted coinage with an Argive Heracles, showing the connection between the royal house, Heracles, and Argos.[131]

Perdiccas' final years

The king kept his dealings with the Spartans and Argives a secret from the Athenians, who had taken steps in spring 417 to counter the Spartan-Argive alliance and were about to send a fleet northward. Perdiccas' joining the coalition deprived them of their main ally in that region, and the fleet never sailed. Unsurprisingly they declared him an enemy and in naval operations in the Thermaic Gulf blockaded Macedonian ports over the winter of 417–416.[132] The blockade was unsuccessful, though, as Macedonia was economically self-sufficient. In the winter of 416–415, the Athenians sent a force of their own cavalry and some Macedonian exiles—perhaps former supporters of Philip and Amyntas—living in Athens to Methone, from where they ravaged Macedonian territory.[133]

Since Perdiccas had abandoned Athens, and Amphipolis remained independent, the Athenians had to find timber elsewhere, so they turned to Italy and Sicily.[134] Their connection with Sicily was soon to turn disastrous. In

[128] Thucydides 5.80.2. Exploiting the link has been disbelieved: Borza 1990, p. 156 n. 61, citing references.

[129] *IG* i³ 76, with Zahrnt 2006a, p. 596. See too Chambers 1993, pp. 325–335.

[130] Cole 1974, pp. 69–70; cf. Kagan 1981, pp. 143–144.

[131] Hammond and Griffith 1979, pp. 120–121 and 132; Roisman 2010, p. 154 with n. 28.

[132] Thucydides 5.83.4. Hammond and Griffith 1979, p. 133, suggest the ports of Heracleum, Methone, and Bormiscus as well as Potidaea.

[133] Thucydides 6.7.3–4; exiles: Cole 1974, p. 70.

[134] Though note the caution of Borza 1990, p. 157 with n. 63.

the winter of 416 there was a public debate in Athens on whether to send assistance to Egesta, then in conflict with its neighbor Selinus, in Sicily.[135] Selinus was an ally of Syracuse, the largest and most powerful city in Sicily, with a formidable navy; hence Athenian support for Egesta had the potential of drawing Syracuse into the conflict when the Athenians could not afford a war on another front. Despite the valid reservations of Nicias, the people in the Assembly were swayed by the charismatic Alcibiades and voted to send a huge armada of 134 triremes, 25,000 hoplites, and 130 supply ships to Sicily.[136] That Athenian force was quickly in trouble thanks to Syracusan attacks, and in 413 it and another fleet and troops sent out later were completely defeated, with the city losing most of its fleet and over 5,000 men.

During this time the Athenians were in desperate need of shipbuilding timber, so they reconciled with Perdiccas. He may have been feeling vulnerable as Spartan influence, and indeed interest, was on the wane in the north, so he made an alliance with Athens.[137] By the summer of 414, we find him serving with the Athenian general Euetion and a Thracian force in an attack on Amphipolis, ultimately to no avail.[138]

That is the last we hear of Perdiccas, for he probably died in 413, perhaps of natural causes as no ancient writer speaks of assassination. The ancient sources give differing lengths for his reign, as noted at the start of this chapter, and the only mention of his death has it in 421–420.[139] This clearly contradicts Thucydides' account of Perdiccas fighting at Amphipolis in the summer of 414.[140] Further, Diodorus says Perdiccas' successor, Archelaus, was already king in the winter of 411 as he was by then besieging Pydna, which is surely correct.[141] Hence the more commonly accepted year of 413 is taken for the king's death.

Evaluating Perdiccas

Of all the Macedonian kings, Perdiccas receives the greatest criticism for his flip-flopping relations with Athens and Sparta, and in the 420s the comic

[135] Thucydides 6.9–25.

[136] Kagan 1981, pp. 157–353, on the Sicilian expedition.

[137] Cole 1974, pp. 70–71; Hammond and Griffith 1979, pp. 133–134; contra Borza 1990, p. 157.

[138] Thucydides 7.9.

[139] *Marmor Parium*, *BNJ* 239 A 61. On his death, see Cole 1974, p. 71 n. 48; Hammond and Griffith 1979, pp. 103–104; cf. Müller 2016, pp. 160–161; King 2018, p. 48 n. 120.

[140] Thucydides 7.9.

[141] Diodorus 13.49.1–2. But Diodorus 14.37.6 says that Archelaus died in 399 after a reign of seven years, thus putting Perdiccas' death in 406, which is too late.

poet Hermippus spoke of the king's ships "loaded with his lies" among goods imported to Athens.[142] Modern scholars largely follow suit when it comes the king's multiple changes of heart and policy.[143] Much of this critical view, however, stems from the bias of Athenocentric sources, for we do not have Macedonian writers who could present a different picture. It is worthwhile wondering whether the bias has anything to do with Perdiccas not engaging with Greek culture as much as Alexander I and Archelaus. Perdiccas was perhaps too busy with internal and external threats to spend undue time on cultural pursuits, though possibly Hippocrates visited the court, and the king patronized the poet Melanippides, who made musical innovations.[144] But both Alexander's and Archelaus' embracing of Greek culture was on a far grander scale than anything Perdiccas did; hence it may have affected Greek authors' views of that king.

Yet the censure of Perdiccas does not reflect the reality of the times. His first concern was the security of his kingdom, something he could not achieve if he stayed only on the side of either Athens or Sparta, as their conflicting interests and fluctuating fortunes in the Peloponnesian War showed. A policy of single alignment was thus impossible; hence he made alliances that best suited himself and his realm—as a pragmatic and sensible king ought to have done. In this respect, he was no different from the Greek states throughout their history who followed a mantra of "The enemy of my enemy is my friend." Perdiccas' changes of alignment are even more understandable as he could not field large numbers of troops; hence he aligned himself with powerful states whose help at the time he needed the most.[145]

Thus, the Athenians' foundation of Amphipolis ended Macedonian attempts to control the territories east of the Strymon, and their founding of Brea was an immediate threat to the kingdom's security. Athens strove to keep Macedonia weak, supporting opponents of the king, just as Perdiccas worked to weaken both Athenian and Spartan influence in the north. No wonder, given his lack of military manpower and the fluidity of his borders, that when he was threatened by Athens, he sought Spartan help, and when

[142] Hermippus, F 63 line 8 in Kassel and Austin 1986, p. 592. For a useful chart of his flip-flops, see Borza 1990, p. 158 (described as "lively diplomatic relations"). Bias of sources: Müller 2016, pp. 141–144.

[143] For example, Cole 1974, pp. 71–72; Borza 1990, pp. 158–160; Roisman 2010, p. 148; Psoma 2011, pp. 118–119.

[144] Pownall 2017, pp. 218–219; Müller 2016, pp. 161–162 (perhaps "cultural policy" is overstatement).

[145] Errington 1990, pp. 18–19; Borza 1990, p. 159.

he thought Sparta was more menacing, he reattached himself to Athens, using the precious timber of Macedonia as an economic weapon. His dealings with both powers thus "make clear his fear for the survival of the Macedonian kingdom should a major southern Greek power establish itself firmly on his frontiers."[146]

Perdiccas does not deserve his bad press. He may not have had the same impact on Macedonia as Alexander I or Philip II, but he was a successful king who strove to protect his kingdom and benefit his people, as to be expected of a king. He showed a clever cunning in his dealings with Greek states that deserves greater praise, and he was able to reconcile his rule with previous opponents, as the list of names in the decree recording an alliance between him and Athens, discussed above, shows. The stability of his monarchy and security of his kingdom were at the top of his list of priorities, and for him the ends justified the means. We should not ask more of a king and leader.

Macedonia under the Argead Kings: The Rise and Fall of an Ancient Superpower. Ian Worthington, Oxford University Press. © Oxford University Press 2026. DOI: 10.1093/9780197668009.003.0006

[146] Errington 1990, p. 18.

6

The Emergence of Regicide: Archelaus

Perdiccas II's successor, Archelaus, took the throne in probably 413 and ruled until 399 (figure 6.1).[1] The former year is not certain, but since he was killed in 399 after ruling, it is said, 14 years, 413 is the most likely accession date.[2] Few details of his reign are known because of the paucity of our sources. He may have modeled himself on his grandfather Alexander I, and his achievements allowed Philip II to build on them and craft a Macedonian Empire.[3] Up until now, kings had succeeded to the throne relatively smoothly and died apparently by natural causes. Archelaus' accession marked a bloody change, for with him regicide became frequent even if a

Figure 6.1 Archelaus from coin
Source: Wikimedia Commons.

[1] Reign: Cloché 1960, pp. 82–103; Hammond and Griffith 1979, pp. 137–141 and 167–168; Errington 1990, pp. 24–28; Borza 1990, pp. 160–177; Müller 2016, pp. 164–193; see too Roisman 2010, pp. 154–158; Mari 2011b, pp. 91–92, and Kanatsoulis 1948; Borza 1993; Greenwalt 2003; Mikrogiannakês 2007; Stewart 2021; Chapinal-Heras 2022.

[2] Diodorus 14.37.5–6; cf. Thucydides 7.9.1; Diodorus 13.49.1–2; cf. Athenaeus 5.217d–e, with Borza 1990, p. 162.

[3] Chapinal-Heras 2022, p. 12; cf. Müller 2016, pp. 164–165, on Alexander I's importance, and for Archelaus' influence on Philip in economic, military, and cultural matters, see Kanatsoulis 1948, pp. 58–112; Mikrogiannakês 2007; Chapinal-Heras 2022.

king had tapped his eldest son as successor.[4] Archelaus' reign therefore was an ominous turning point in the ruthless battle for the throne of multiple heirs from polygamous marriages.

A bloody accession?

In his *Gorgias* Plato gives a damning account of Archelaus' character and how he took the throne. At that point in the work, Socrates and the orator Polus, a former student of Gorgias, are discussing whether Archelaus was happy or wretched, and by extension unjust. Polus calls him "wretched" and "the greatest wrongdoer in Macedonia." He also says that Archelaus had no right to be king as he was an illegitimate son of Perdiccas by a female slave named Simache and murdered all the other claimants, including Alcetas, his uncle, Alcetas' son Alexander, and an unnamed seven-year-old son of Perdiccas and his wife Cleopatra:[5]

> [Archelaus] had no claim to the throne which he now occupies, being the son of a woman who was a slave of Perdiccas' brother Alcetas, and in mere justice he was Alcetas' slave; and if he wished to do what is just, he would be serving Alcetas and would be happy, by your account; but as it is, he has become a prodigy of wretchedness, since he has done the most enormous wrong. First of all he invited this very master and uncle of his to his court, as if he were going to restore to him the kingdom (*arche*) of which Perdiccas had deprived him; and after entertaining him and his son Alexander—his own cousin about the same age as himself—and making them drunk, he packed them into a carriage, drove them away by night, and murdered and made away with them both. And after all these iniquities he failed to observe that he had become a most wretched person, and had no repentance, but a while later he refused to make himself happy by bringing up, as he was justly bound, his brother, the legitimate son of Perdiccas, a boy about seven years old who had a just title to the throne, and restoring the kingdom to him; but he cast him into a well and

[4] See Hatzopoulos 1986; cf. Lane Fox 2011d, pp. 218–219, against which see Greenwalt 1989; Carney 1983, though some analogies need to be viewed with caution.

[5] Plato, *Gorgias* 470d–471c; the quotation is 471a–c. On it see Hammond and Griffith 1979, pp. 135–136; Greenwalt 1989, pp. 23–25; Borza 1990, pp. 161–162; Roisman 2010, p. 154; Müller 2016, pp. 165–169; King 2018, pp. 49–51.

> drowned him, and then told his mother Cleopatra that he had fallen in and lost his life while chasing a goose. So now, you see, as the greatest wrongdoer in Macedonia he is the most wretched of all the Macedonians, not the happiest; and I daresay some Athenians could be found who would join you in preferring to change places with any other Macedonian of them all, rather than with Archelaus!

How accurate are these details? The *Gorgias* was a philosophical work; at this point in it, Archelaus' character is called into question by his supposed heinous acts, but without supporting evidence.[6] Another factor is that the dialogue was written in about 380, by which time Archelaus had been dead for some two decades, yet Polus speaks in the present tense and makes it sound as though the king were still on the throne.[7] Then again, what he has to say about the king would be weakened if his audience knew them to be untrue. There is also the question of legitimacy. Certainly kings had relationships with women not their wives, including slaves, who might well bear them children, but whether a bastard would be an acceptable heir is another matter.[8] In addition, Archelaus is named as a signatory in a treaty between Perdiccas and Athens dated probably to the later 420s, as discussed in the previous chapter—presumably for him to have been included, he must have been thought of as legitimate.[9] Simache, then, might have been a wife of Perdiccas II, possibly from a less elite noble family, in which case Perdiccas is the earliest Argead king we know of who was a polygamist. In turn, non-Macedonian writers, who did not understand polygamy, made her out to be a slave.[10]

If we can query the claim about Archelaus' legitimacy, what about the manner of his accession, as the Platonic extract does not support that he was next in line?[11] Nor does the treaty between Perdiccas and Athens, mentioned above. In the list of signatories of the inscription, Perdiccas is

[6] Cf. Athenaeus 5.217d and 11.506e, who refers to the *Gorgias* and describes Archelaus as of "shameful origin" and a "wretched man."

[7] At Plato, *Gorgias* 470d.

[8] Hammond and Griffith 1979, pp. 154 and 198, would say no, though against this see Greenwalt 1989.

[9] *IG* i[3] 89; cf. Hatzopoulos 1986, pp. 284–285.

[10] Aelian, *Varis Historia* 12.43, with Hammond and Griffith 1979, pp. 154 and 199; Greenwalt 1989, pp. 23–25; Errington 1990, p. 25; Carney 2000, pp. 1 and 17; Müller 2016, p. 167; cf. Chapinal-Heras 2022, pp. 12–13. Note Hatzopoulos 1986, p. 284, who argues that Plato means Alcetas was the rightful heir not of Perdiccas but of Alexander I in the 450s.

[11] Hammond and Griffith 1979, pp. 133–137, questioning it by considering Archelaus' succession.

first, then Alcetas, but Archelaus is third, suggesting that he was somehow subordinate to his uncle. At the time of the treaty Archelaus would have been underage, which means that if his father were to die, a regent or guardian would be required. Perhaps Perdiccas had already arranged for his brother to assume the role of guardian, given he would have been the logical choice, which thus explains Alcetas' position in the list of names—and by extension Archelaus' prompt removal of him.[12] Possibly Archelaus resorted to these murders as he was simply keen to rule in his own right, or he may have wanted to avenge his father's troubles with his brothers—if there was bad blood between them—to stabilize his own kingship.[13]

The Platonic extract is still a valuable insight into an expected father-to-son royal succession now interrupted by a ruler eager for power but not next in line—one of the downsides of polygamy—or even the machinations of influential factions at court jockeying for various claimants to the kingship.[14]

Archelaus as king

In a far cry from Plato's vilification of Archelaus, Thucydides, who may have visited the king's court, spoke favorably though only briefly of him:[15]

> Subsequently Archelaus son of Perdiccas, when he became king, built those [fortresses] that are now in the country, and cut straight roads, and in general organized his country for war by providing cavalry, arms and other equipment beyond anything achieved by all the eight kings who preceded him.

Interestingly, Thucydides says nothing of nonmilitary matters but focuses only on military affairs and preparedness, something he as a general might appreciate.

What did Archelaus do? Building new roads not only helped trade but also allowed soldiers and equipment to move quickly, though "roads" is perhaps

[12] Greenwalt 1989, pp. 19–22 and 34–40; Borza 1990, p. 161; Goukowsky 1991, pp. 43–44; King 2018, p. 50; cf. Hatzopoulos 1986, on regencies.

[13] Errington 1990, p. 25. Note Roisman 2010, p. 154, who states that there is "no decisive argument" for or against the hostile account.

[14] Greenwalt 1989.

[15] Thucydides 2.100.2. Thucydides' visit: Hammond and Griffith 1979, p. 137.

too grand a term for what were probably beaten paths through forests and swamps that bettered the previous tracks used by transhumant herdsmen, especially in Upper Macedonia.[16] Thus, one ran through the Pierian forest from Aegae direct to Pydna, and perhaps there was also one also from Beroea via the Zoödokos Perge into Elimea and from Edessa into Eordaea, as well through the Demir Kapu, which helped keep the Paeonians at bay.[17] The construction of new forts throughout the kingdom also played a role in its defense. At Markova Kula, near Koreshnica, in the Demir Kapu region the remains of a late fifth-century fort have been discovered, which may have been to help protect Pella.[18]

Archelaus' dealings with his army are more shadowy. If Alexander I had introduced reforms to his army, especially the infantry, they were not enough as Perdiccas II had needed to rely on Spartan troops in some of his campaigns, as we saw in the previous chapter. Perhaps drawing on the lessons to be learned from Perdiccas' reign, Archelaus tried to increase his infantry numbers, but his army was still not enough to match the fighting capabilities of the tribes on his borders. Further, in warfare against Arrhabaeus of Lyncestis and Sirras of Illyria, as we shall see, he was forced to seek military support from Derdas of Elimea. It is very unlikely he introduced hoplites into the army, but he may have seen the advantage of Thracian peltasts and perhaps trained his own men in their tactics.[19]

The swift removal of Archelaus' rivals meant that as undisputed king he could turn immediately to the issues that had been plaguing Macedonia. He was perhaps motivated by his firsthand observations of which areas had been weakest under his father's rule.[20] But he was not content merely with border security and Macedonia's relations with its neighbors. He also embarked on a cultural policy far more ambitious than that of Alexander I, making his court a cultural center in the eyes of his own people and, perhaps even more important when it came to the image of Macedonia, the Greeks.

[16] Hatzopoulos 1987, pp. 21–60.

[17] Hammond and Griffith 1979, p. 140; Errington 1990, pp. 25–26. See the discussion of Hatzopoulos 1987—at p. 53 he names Archelaus as builder.

[18] Hammond 1972a, p. 174; Hammond and Griffith 1979, pp. 146–148; cf. Borza 1990, p. 166, though on p. 168 Borza is cautious on the attribution to Archelaus.

[19] Hoplites: Hammond and Griffith 1979, pp. 147–148; contra Roisman 2010, p. 156 and n. 34. But Greenwalt 2007, pp. 87–96, drawing on much of his earlier work, argues uncompellingly that Archelaus introduced army reforms to foster a new hoplite or middle class in Macedonian society that continued to grow over the years to the time of Philip II. He is followed by Chapinal-Heras 2022, pp. 13–14.

[20] King 2018, p. 41.

If Archelaus learned only one lesson from his father's reign, it was the need to get along with that most important of Greek cities, Athens. In 413, the Athenians were still deeply embroiled in the Peloponnesian War against Sparta, and that summer their disastrous two-year-long campaign in Sicily ended with the devastating loss of almost their entire fleet and over 5,000 of their men at Syracuse, forcing them to abandon their expansionist plans in the western Mediterranean.[21] Yet no matter the catastrophe, the Athenians were resilient: they had bounced back from the devastating plague of 429, and now in 413 they resolved to rebuild their fleet. For this, they needed Macedonian timber and pitch, which Archelaus used to his advantage to gain both income and a strong ally against Sparta if the latter resumed its activity in the north.[22]

Two years later, in 411, Athens suffered a short-lived oligarchy, during which time a new fleet, crewed and commanded by exiled democrats and those who could not live in the city under an oligarchy, was based at Samos.[23] In that year Archelaus honored an ancestral tie with the Athenian orator Andocides' family by allowing Andocides to send at his own cost timber for oars and ships to the democratic fleet at Samos, presumably for repairs rather than building actual vessels there.[24] There is no evidence of a treaty; hence Archelaus, who as king owned all of Macedonia's natural resources, made the decision privately.[25]

The Athenians continued to support Archelaus, for in 410 they sent a fleet under Theramenes to support the king's siege of Pydna on the coastline. Alexander I had taken Pydna, among other things because its port was vital to the export of timber and it was a potential base for operations against Macedonia. Its people rebelled against Archelaus—they "would not obey his orders"—so the king besieged it with a large army. When it capitulated, he moved it inland, though some locals remained at the original site, and refounded it as a Macedonian town, now identified with modern Kitros.[26]

The Athenians' did not have a positive view of Archelaus but needed to keep in his good books to ensure timber supplies.[27] That was perhaps why

[21] Thucydides 7.59–71; on the campaign see especially Kagan 1981, pp. 157–353.

[22] Errington 1990, p. 25; cf. Borza 1987, pp. 44–45; Ruffing 2017, pp. 130–131, on prices.

[23] 411 oligarchy: Kagan 1987, pp. 106–273.

[24] Andocides 2.11, with Borza 1987, pp. 44–45; Ruffing 2017, pp. 130–131.

[25] Borza 1987, pp. 44–45.

[26] Diodorus 13.49.1–2, with Hammond 1972a, pp. 128–129; Hammond and Griffith 1979, p. 150. I thank Vivi Saripanidi for the modern location.

[27] Mari 2011b, p. 91, notes the need for the Athenian fleet to help capture Pydna; cf. Hammond and Griffith 1979, p. 137.

in 408 Andocides, who in 411 had suffered exile on the orders of the oligarchs, appealed to return to the city and spoke of his providing timber for the fleet at Samos and of Archelaus' favor in allowing him to do so.[28] Androcides was clever: if the Athenians refused his appeal, Archelaus might view that as a criticism of him. The Athenians also passed a decree in 407/6, of which we have only fragments, congratulating Archelaus (his name is restored) and bestowing on him and his sons the status of *proxenoi* and *euergetai*—"friends and benefactors"—for his good services and benefactions to the city, which of course would be timber, oars, and pitch for shipbuilding.[29]

Also included in these benefactions was the king's allowing Athenian shipwrights to go to Macedonia to build triremes. The location of his dockyards is unknown, but most likely they were in Pieria as that afforded easy access to the sea, although Methone or Pydna and even the new capital, Pella, has been suggested.[30] Building vessels in Archelaus' dockyards made sense as at this juncture of the Peloponnesian War an Athenian army was currently blocked in Mytilene and the Athenians did not have the time to tow the timber to Athens and build there—not to mention the timber fleet would be a sitting duck to enemy vessels.[31]

The construction of vessels in Macedonia may not have occurred just this one time. A group of anchors made of a dark stone found in the Chalcidice and Thessaly suggest Athenian shipwrights were at work in Macedonia and even the Chalcidice on several occasions, with the triremes then sailed or rowed down to Athens with skeleton crews.[32] But at this time, in 406, building vessels where the timber grew was a necessity, and a new fleet of 110 triremes was soon launched, which decisively defeated the Spartan fleet at Arginousae.

Athens' military power came to an end in 405 when an Athenian fleet was wiped out at Aegospotami by a Spartan fleet under Lysander. In 404 the city surrendered to Sparta, and among other things had to dismantle the Delian League. Archelaus now lost Athenian support, but then again,

[28] Andocides 2.11, with Errington 1990, p. 24.

[29] *IG* i[3] 117 = Meiggs-Lewis no. 91, with "Archelaus" and "shipwrights" restored on the fragmentary inscription but universally accepted: Hammond and Griffith 1979, pp. 138–139; Errington 1990, p. 24; Borza 1990, p. 163; Blackman 1990, pp. 47–48, Roisman 2010, p. 155; Müller 2016, pp. 169–171; Ruffing 2017, p. 129; Chapinal-Heras 2022, p. 21. See Meritt 1936 on Archelaus and the Decelean War.

[30] Methone or Pydna: Borza 1990, p. 163 n. 9; Greenwalt 1999, p. 175. Pella: King 2018, p. 42. See too Meiggs 1982, p. 356, on the harbor.

[31] Meiggs 1982, p. 128.

[32] Blackman 1990, p. 48, for references; cf. Borza 1990, p. 164.

the Athenians were no longer a dominant power in the north Aegean and Sparta had no interest in operating there.

Toward the end of Archelaus' reign, perhaps in 400, we hear of his intervention in Thessaly, where the powerful Aleuad family of Larissa sought his help in putting down a democratic movement that had ousted them from power.[33] The source for this political strife is a speech titled *Concerning Administration* (*peri politeias*) addressed to the people of Larissa.[34] The author is unknown: he may have been a contemporary or even the second century AD orator and Sophist Herodes Atticus—though why someone living in Athens centuries later wrote a literary work about fifth-century Thessalian affairs is an argument against a later date.[35] The knowledge of social and economic conditions in Thessaly makes it likely the author was Thessalian and accurate in his details about Larissa at this time.[36] We return to this speech below for its interesting characterization of Archelaus.

The Aleuad appeal to Archelaus was understandable as it was common for states in civil conflicts to seek outside military help or at least arbitration—we saw this when Arrhabaeus of Lyncus invited Brasidas to arbitrate in his dispute with Perdiccas II (chapter 5). The Aleuadae also claimed descent from Heracles, like the Macedonian kings, so Archelaus was quick to respond favorably, which may imply he had bolstered his military to where he felt comfortable intervening in Greece.

The Larissan democrats (of whom the author of the above speech was one, to judge by its content) turned to Lycophron of Pherae and the Spartans for help. This was during the period commonly referred to as the Spartan hegemony of Greece—from the end of the Peloponnesian War in 404 to Sparta's defeat at the battle of Leuctra by Thebes in 371. The Spartans were keen to extend their sphere of influence; hence it is not surprising they agreed to support Pherae. In the end they did not send any help, perhaps because Archelaus died the following year.

Undeterred by the Spartans' offer of support to the Larissan democrats, Archelaus captured Larissa and installed the Aleuad Aristippus as ruler, perhaps even receiving citizenship as a reward.[37] He certainly seems to have enjoyed something akin to a guest friendship with the Aleuadae.[38] But then

[33] Westlake 1993, pp. 51–59; Hammond and Griffith 1979, pp. 140–141; Borza 1990, pp. 164–165; Müller 2016, pp. 184–186; Chapinal-Heras 2022, p. 22. Aleuadae: Sordi 1996, pp. 37–45.

[34] See the exhaustive discussion of Dascalakis 1965, pp. 236–249; cf. Westlake 1993, pp. 52–54; Errington 1990, p. 28 n. 2, Roisman 2010, p. 155 with n. 32; Sprawski 1999, pp. 36–37.

[35] Dascalakis 1965, pp. 239–246, arguing for 404.

[36] Cf. Roisman 2010, p. 155.

[37] Westlake 1993, pp. 56–57; Roisman 2010, p. 155.

[38] Graninger 2010, pp. 309–310.

he set up a Macedonian garrison in Larissa, seized control of the strategically important Perrhaebia, the northernmost Thessalian territory bordering on his kingdom in western Pieria, and took 10 sons of leading men as hostages.

Perrhaebia was strategically important because running through it were the Petra and Volustana passes from Macedonia to the west slopes of Mount Olympus in Thessaly. Acquiring these routes was therefore consistent with Archelaus establishing good defensive positions, although in this case he had done so by exploiting the civil war in Thessaly.[39] Still, he had both shored up his kingdom's southern defenses and interfered in Thessalian affairs, though it is unlikely he ever intended Thessaly to be a province of Macedonia.[40]

On Macedonia's eastern border the independent Thracians were checked by the power of Seuthes. The latter was connected to the Macedonian throne through marriage to Perdiccas II's sister Stratonice, as we saw in the previous chapter, though on his death in about 410 the Odrysian kingdom went into decline until the 360s. But in the west Archelaus inherited Perdiccas' clashes with the Lyncestians under Arrhabaeus and the Illyrian Sirras, who may have been from Lyncestis.[41] In the later years of Archelaus' reign we hear of a war "against Sirras and Arrhabaeus," though the details are unknown.[42] Elimea was also a problem for Archelaus, which he decided to solve diplomatically by marrying his eldest daughter to the Elimean king Derdas.[43] The marriage was a coup as Derdas' namesake father had supported the likely bid of Perdiccas II's brother Philip for the Macedonian throne.[44] However, Archelaus may have had no choice but to resort to diplomacy if he were hard pressed in a war against Sirras and Arrhabaeus, and the marriage may also have played a role in his death as we discuss below.

Coinage

Archelaus was the first king to issue copper coins as well as make some production reforms and introduce a token coinage for everyday life.[45]

[39] Sprawski 1999, p. 36. [40] Westlake 1993, p. 57; contra Borza 1990, p. 165 with n. 14.

[41] Errington 1990, p. 27; Hammond 1966, p. 244; Kapetanopoulos 1994.

[42] Aristotle, *Politics* 5.1311b 12–13.

[43] Aristotle, *Politics* 5.1311b 11–13; date: Hammond and Griffith 1979, p. 139; cf. Borza 1990, p. 164. See too Chapinal-Heras 2022, p. 14; cf. Roisman 2010, pp. 155–156.

[44] Hammond and Griffith 1979, p. 138; Greenwalt 1986, p. 36; Errington 1990, p. 27; Borza 1990, p. 164.

[45] Price 1974, pp. 19–20, with plates referenced in these pages; especially Greenwalt 1994b, pp. 106–119 and 128–129 (on types); see too Kremydi 2011, pp. 163–164.

To judge by the innovations, he most likely regained control of Bisaltia and its silver mines, lost to Perdiccas II between 452 to 445.[46] Among other things, the debased small coinage of Perdiccas became a thing of the past, and a new and more varied series of denominations were introduced, including silver coins such as didrachms, tetrobols, and obols of varying weights.[47] These new coins went beyond stimulating the economy; Archelaus intended them to facilitate trade with Athens, for despite the devastating losses in Sicily the Athenian economy was strong and the city remained the chief trading state in the northern Aegean.[48]

Some of Archelaus' coins bore the same types as his grandfather Alexander I, but a second series with a male head on the obverse and a horse on the reverse may have been a nod to the mythical founder of the kingdom.[49] On the didrachms we have a mounted man with two spears on a cantering horse and a walking, unattended horse, but then a new device is a young male head with short hair in a band and the forepart of a goat with back-turned head (as on the coins of Alexander I). The male head may be a portrait of the king in his youth, and the revival of the goat-head motif was probably due to Archelaus promoting himself as the founder of Aegae—arguably an addition to the foundation myth found in Euripides' *Archelaus*. In addition, he was the first Argead to put on his coins the head of his Temenid ancestor Heracles to emphasize the connection of the royal house with Heracles and Argos.[50]

The income from the sales of timber and pitch to Athens as well as the revenues from the Bisaltic silver mines must have helped Archelaus finance his various initiatives, which included two that would have far-reaching significance for Macedonia: the establishment of a new capital at Pella and cultural activities far beyond anything his predecessors had undertaken.

Pella and Aegae

At some point in Archelaus' reign the capital of Macedonia was relocated from Aegae north to Pella on the central Macedonian plain near the coast of

[46] Hammond and Griffith 1979, p. 138; Hatzopoulos 2020, p. 34.
[47] Kremydi 2011, p. 164. [48] Greenwalt 1994b, pp. 111–116.
[49] Greenwalt 1985a, pp. 45–57; cf. Greenwalt 1997, pp. 128–130; Kremydi 2011, pp. 163–164, citing further bibliography; cf. Borza 1990, p. 173; Dahmen 2010, p. 51.
[50] Kremydi 2011, pp. 163–164.

the Thermaic Gulf. Exactly when is not known, but the consensus is toward the end of his reign, perhaps even 399.[51] It had certainly happened by the 380s if we accept Demosthenes' claim that Philip II's childhood was spent there.[52] Pella's site already had a small settlement on it; hence it was not built from scratch, but Archelaus made it the primary capital as well as the administrative, commercial, military, and even cultural center of the kingdom, and it was probably also home to the royal mint (cf. figures 1a and 1b).[53]

Archelaus had several reasons for where he established Pella, most importantly economic and strategic. In antiquity Pella had a port and lay on the Loudias River, which flowed into the Thermaic Gulf.[54] It was also situated on established communications routes from the Adriatic to Byzantium as well as the northern Aegean and close to a crossing of the Axius River. These factors gave its site the edge over Aegae, given that Macedonia's territory now reached to the Strymon.[55] Archelaus' choice of location thus facilitated trade and commerce.

Another motive was strategic: Pella may have been intended to prevent any threat from Amphaxatis, a base of power from which Philip and Amyntas had likely challenged Perdiccas II for the throne. Hence the new capital was meant to protect Macedonian territory east of the Axius.[56] Its location on the shore of the Thermaic Gulf was also to its advantage as it was less vulnerable to attack, and Archelaus may have built the fortress at Markova Kula, mentioned above, as further protection for the city.

According to Xenophon, Pella was the "largest" of the Macedonian cities.[57] That does not make it a sprawling metropolis. Even in Philip II's era it was quite small compared to a Greek city like Athens despite Philip's expanding it and building a huge palace complex on the middle hill of three hills north of the city. The palace, perhaps built on top of Archelaus' palace (which has yet to be identified), was still within easy reach of the city center

[51] Hammond and Griffith 1979, pp. 139–140; Greenwalt 1999, pp. 166–177, for an earlier date. Hatzopoulos 1987, pp. 41–44, argues that it was Amyntas III who founded the new capital (cf. Psoma 2011, p. 124), but see Hammond and Griffith 1979, pp. 139–140 and 150; Borza 1990, pp. 166–171, 296; Greenwalt 1999; Akamatis 2011; Chapinal-Heras 2022, pp. 19–20. On the name, cf. Kalléris 1988, pp. 245–246.

[52] Demosthenes 18.68.

[53] Greenwalt 1994b, pp. 117–119 citing bibliography, but see Kremydi 2011, pp. 165–167, for multiple mints under Philip II, which may indicate that Archelaus had a similar number. On the site of Pella, see Akamatis 2011, pp. 393–408; Petsas 1978; Lilimbaki and Akamatis 2004.

[54] Strabo 7.20 and 23; cf. Hammond 1972a, p. 148.

[55] Errington 1990, p. 26.

[56] Borza 1990, p. 140; Greenwalt 1999, p. 159.

[57] Xenophon, *Hellenica* 5.2.13. See Hatzopoulos 1987, pp. 42–44, though dating Pella's prominence to Amyntas III.

but distant from the noise and bustle, and in the Hellenistic period following the death of Alexander the Great in 323 the site was even larger.[58] Unfortunately, dating and even identifying buildings are made difficult because the Romans later plundered the city and over the centuries much of its stone was used in nearby villages. But archaeologists have unearthed several superb mosaics from the late Classical and Hellenistic eras and exquisite figurines and jewelry, which testify to the artistic craftmanship and tastes of the Macedonians.

It has been suggested that there were three capitals of Macedonia: Pella, Aegae, and the religious center of Dium in Pieria, the foothills of Olympus. This tripartite division was akin to the Persian Empire, which had several capitals, like Susa, Persepolis, and Babylon.[59] The analogy does not work, not least because the sheer size of the Persian Empire, stretching thousands of miles from Asia Minor to India, made multiple capitals essential. Moreover, a religious center does not make it a capital.

Aegae remained an important secondary royal residence, as archaeology has shown. It had a large, splendid palace, which Archelaus was said to have built and decorated (though little remains) and which Philip II continued.[60] Its existence presumes that the royal family visited and stayed there—as would the courtiers, for at the end of the day power lay with the monarch, wherever he happened to be. Aegae's theater testifies to a buoyant cultural life—it may even have been at Aegae that Euripides' *Archelaus* was performed, which would make sense as Aegae was part of the revised founding myth by Euripides, as discussed in chapter 2. And Aegae was also the site of royal weddings and burials—infamously, its theater was where Philip II was assassinated in 336. In addition, we have dedicatory inscriptions from the sanctuary of the goddess Eucleia ("good fortune") by Eurydice, wife of Amyntas III, and one by Laodice (the name is partially restored), wife of the last Antigonid king, Perseus.[61] Since Eurydice married Amyntas III in the

[58] Hammond and Griffith 1979, p. 197, with references. Palace of Pella: Akamatis 2011, pp. 399–401; Chrysostomou 2018.

[59] Borza 1990, pp. 166–167. On Dium, see Pandermalis 1997.

[60] Archelaus: Aelian, *Varia Historia* 14.17. See Drougou and Saatsoglou-Paliadeli 2004; Drougou 2011; and especially on the palace Kottaridi 2011b; Kottaridi 2020, pp. 140–146; cf. Borza 1990, pp. 254–255; Kottaridi 2002; Lane Fox 2011e, p. 365.

[61] See Oikonomides 1983; Saatsoglou-Paliadeli 2000, especially pp. 392–395, for the dedication by Eurydice, dated between 370 and 340; Kyriakou 2020a; cf. Saatsoglou-Paliadeli 1999, pp. 361–362; Saatsoglou-Paliadeli 2011, pp. 277–278.

late 390s and Perseus was defeated by Rome in 168, we see royal interest at this sanctuary extending well over two centuries.

Philhellenism, or money talks

Archelaus faced fewer security threats than Perdiccas, leaving him free to spend time on cultural pursuits. The measures he took to elevate the cultural acceptance of his court at home and among the Greeks were unprecedented—as was his willingness to spend money to do so.[62] Perhaps he had little choice as the artists he attracted may have rejected less lucrative invitations.

The king hired the famous painter Zeuxis to decorate his new palace at Pella, perhaps with a series of panel paintings as its primary decorations, and in return Zeuxis gifted him a painting of Pan, a deity of particular interest to the Macedonian royal house.[63] Other invited artists probably included the sculptor and architect Callimachus, who is cited in an inscription as producing "temples with fine columns," and is believed to have been the inventor of the Corinthian capital.[64]

Several literati spent time at court, including the tragedians Euripides and Agathon from Athens, the epic poet Choerilus of Samos, and the harp-player Timotheus of Miletus.[65] The king was said not to have reprimanded Euripides for kissing Agathon openly, even though the latter was "already bearded," hence a grown man, which might indicate the king's interest also in Agathon.[66] We should not think anything of this episode, as there seems a tendency to relate "bisexual" incidents to key people, such as the sixth-century Athenian tyrannicides Harmodius and Aristogeiton and even Philip II and Alexander the Great, as part of a "tyrant topos."[67] Archelaus

[62] Cloché 1960, pp. 95–102; Borza 1990, pp. 171–177; Borza 1993; Greenwalt 2003; Müller 2016, pp. 173–175; Hecht 2017; Stewart 2021; Chapinal-Heras 2022, pp. 15–19; see too Saatsoglou-Paliadeli 2007; cf. Pownall 2017, pp 219–221.

[63] Aelian 14.17; Pliny, *Natural History* 35.62, with Hardiman 2010, p. 507, citing further bibliography in n. 7. On patronage, cf. Hardiman 2010, pp. 506–511.

[64] Saatsoglou-Paliadeli 2011, pp. 275–276 with n. 29, though Paspalas 2011, pp. 185–186, is more cautious about Callimachus going north.

[65] Athenaeus 8.345d (Choerilus); [Plutarch], *Moralia* 177b (Timotheus); Aelian, *Varia Historia* 2.21, 13.4; [Plutarch], *Moralia* 177a–b (Agathon); Aelian, *Varia Historia* 13.4; Athenaeus 13.598d–e; [Plutarch], *Moralia* 177a; Aristotle, *Politics* 5.1311b 34–35 (Euripides). For the poets at the Macedonian court, see Dascalakis 1965, pp. 105–110; Harder 1985, pp. 129–137 and 288–290.

[66] [Plutarch], *Moralia* 177a–b.

[67] See Müller 2016, pp. 175–181. "Tyrant topos" (*Tyrannentopos*): Müller 2016, p. 263.

particularly admired Choerilus since he was said to have paid him the large sum of 400 drachmas per day, which the poet frittered away on "delicacies," as he was a "gourmet."[68] The amount perhaps prompted Timotheus' snide comment to Archelaus that he should have been paid more![69]

The most famous artist-in-residence was Euripides, who went to Pella between 410 and 408/7, and remained in Macedonia until he died there, probably in 406.[70] Tradition has it that he was torn to death by dogs—either at Pella by Archelaus' hunting dogs or at Bormiscus or Arethousa by sheepdogs.[71] This story of his demise may not be inaccurate—think of the tragic stories in our times of dogs mauling or killing humans. Euripides wrote several plays at Pella, including his *Bacchae* and now lost *Archelaus*, the latter in perhaps in 408/7.[72] Perhaps even commissioned by the king to celebrate his Greek ancestry, the *Archelaus* adds to the Argead legend, as Euripides changed the mythical founder of the royal house from Perdiccas I to Archelaus.[73]

The choice of poets and artists is interesting, and perhaps Archelaus—and indeed Argead kings in general—wanted only those making innovations in their respective genres, such as Timotheus, who was famous for musical innovations.[74] On the other hand, no patron would spend money on second-rate people but would want only the best in their field. It may be simple coincidence if some happened to be experimenting with new concepts, such as Melanippides in Perdiccas II's time and Timotheus in that of Archelaus. The most important point is that Argead kings were patronizing those who could better their courts and by extension themselves, a push originating with Alexander I.

As well as the financial reward of going to Pella, the court may have afforded intellectuals and artists a haven that Athens, despite it being a cultural

[68] Ister, *BNJ* 334 F 61 (= Athenaeus 8.345d). [69] [Plutarch], *Moralia* 177b.

[70] Stewart 2021; cf. Di Giuseppe 2004. Against Euripides' exile and death in Macedonia or his staying there for more time than necessary to produce his plays, see Scullion 2003.

[71] Athenaeus 13.598d–e, with Hammond and Griffith 1979, pp. 139, 160, and 162; Borza 1990, p. 173 with n. 28.

[72] Harder 1985, pp. 125, 145–147, and 288–290; Stewart 2021, pp. 84–96, on the plays (*Bacchae, Archelaus, Temenus*, and *Temenidae*) and two visits (viewing Archelaus as an "enlightened despot" on p. 81); cf. Borza 1993, pp. 239–240; Müller 2016, pp. 97–100; and see especially Fol 1993; Atkinson 2002; Xanthakis-Karamanos 2012; Allan and Swift 2024.

[73] See Lane Fox 2011d, pp. 209–210, for speculation on how the play was received by the audience.

[74] Argued by Pownall 2017, pp. 225–226, and see *passim* for a survey of the intellectuals with whom they dealt.

powerhouse, could not.[75] Life in the city in the final years of the Peloponnesian War was uncertain and difficult, and after the end of the war the Spartans had installed a brutal oligarchy in the city.[76] The rule of the Thirty, as the oligarchs were known, ended in 403 when democracy was restored, but by then Athens was a very different place—we see this most clearly in the trial and execution of Socrates in 399. Archelaus had also invited Socrates to his court, but the philosopher refused on the grounds he could not return the favor by inviting the king to Athens.[77]

Archelaus also founded a major festival named the Olympia that included dramatic contests in honor of Zeus at Dium.[78] It was said that as a youth the king had won the four-horse chariot races in the games at Delphi and Olympia, though the veracity of our source on this has been doubted.[79] But if Alexander I competed in the Olympic Games, presumably so could Archelaus. Why, then, did he introduce his own festival? It has been suggested it was a "counter-Olympics" to compete with the Greek games and was meant for his own people.[80] This may be true, but what we can say is that a festival to Zeus would have spotlighted again the Greekness of the Macedonians, and Archelaus' Olympics enjoyed a long life of several centuries.[81]

Why did Archelaus pursue these ambitious cultural initiatives? He may of course have simply enjoyed Greek, especially Athenian, culture and wanted more of it at home.[82] But a clue to his thinking lies in the remarkable similarity to the cultural policies of the tyrants of seventh- and sixth-century Greece. Take, for example, Pisistratus of Athens. He seized power in 545 after two failed attempts, died in 528, and was succeeded by two sons until the tyranny was overthrown in 510.[83] Under Pisistratid rule the city

[75] Chapinal-Heras 2022, p. 15 with n. 44. [76] Krentz 1982; Németh 2006.

[77] Aristotle, *Rhetoric* 2.1398a.24; Aelian, *Varia Historia* 14.17; Diogenes Laertius 2.25.

[78] Diodorus 17.16.3; Arrian 1.11.1 (who mistakenly puts the festival at Aegae), and see Hammond and Griffith 1979, pp. 150–151; Hatzopoulos 1982a, pp. 39–41; Badian 1982a, pp. 35–36; Borza 1993, pp. 241–242; Voutiras 2006, pp. 338–339 ; Müller 2016, pp. 181–182; Chapinal-Heras 2022, pp. 17–18.

[79] Solinus 9.16, with Badian 1982a, pp. 35 and 46 n. 16; Fearn 2007a, pp. 116–118; Chapinal-Heras 2022, p. 17 (believed by Hammond and Griffith 1979, p. 150).

[80] Badian 1982a, p. 35; Borza 1993, pp. 237–244. See Greenwalt 2003, pp. 145–148, arguing that the event was for his own subjects as a means of bringing them together, allowing for his own athletes to compete and win renown, and popularizing his rule. Greenwalt 2007 argues the festival was a popular measure to appease a rising hoplite middle class. Alexander and panhellenic sanctuaries: Mari 2002, pp. 51–60, against which, for example, Roisman 2010, p. 156; Chapinal-Heras 2022, p. 17.

[81] Mari 1998.

[82] On Archelaus and Greek culture, see Hammond and Griffith 1979, pp. 149–150; Borza 1990, pp. 171–177; Borza 1993; Greenwalt 2003.

[83] Pisistratids: Andrewes 1956, pp. 100–115; Forrest 1966, pp. 175–190.

prospered economically and socially as well in cultural affairs. Pisistratus was said to have produced the first official text of the Homeric poems, very much a propaganda move given the widespread appeal of Homer, and patronized Thespis, who is credited with inventing the genre of tragedy.[84] It is tempting to connect the way Pisistratus elevated Athens in his recension of Homer, even though that city did not play an important role in the Bronze Age when the Homeric epics were set, to Archelaus having Euripides rewrite the Argead foundation myth to give himself more prominence.

The Greek tyrants' measures were meant to improve the people's lives and garner support for their regimes. The same can be said for Archelaus' "bread and circuses," from stimulating the economy with new coinage and standards to elevating the cultural sway of Macedonia—especially if there was stigma attached to him over the murderous manner by which he became king. It has been thought that his efforts were to turn Macedonia into a Greek state so it could take its place in the Greek world.[85] That is unlikely—after all, he made no attempt to change the customs that the Greeks scorned, such as polygamy.

Likewise, we can reject the theory that he wanted to promote radical political, economic, and social changes to reshape Macedonia and used popular cultural reforms to help offset resistance but was killed before his vision came into being.[86] Presumably, reforms introduced for the betterment of a kingdom and the people's daily lives were not likely to be resisted, and while Archelaus made positive changes for Macedonia they were hardly transformative and not continued by any of his immediate successors. His moves thus stemmed from a desire to emulate not so much Greek cultural life but Athenian and did not carry over into politics—just as the 18th-century Russian nobility's zeal to speak French was not a stepping stone to reforming Russia and making French the official language.[87]

Even so, Archelaus does not seem to have impressed the Greeks.[88] When he intervened in Larissa, the Sophist Thrasymachus of Chalcedon, who lived in Athens, wrote a speech, *On Behalf of the Larissaeans*, in which he said, "Shall we, who are Greeks, be slaves to the barbarian Archelaus?"[89] Admittedly, Thrasymachus was paid to write this oration to galvanize Greek, or at least

[84] Davison 1975. [85] Cf. Borza 1990, p. 171. [86] Greenwalt 2003.

[87] Greenwalt 2003, pp. 150–151, refers to Peter I's Russia and Lous XIV's France; cf. Badian 1982a, p. 39.

[88] Cf. Badian 1982a, p. 35, Borza 1993, pp. 243–244.

[89] Thrasymachus, F 85 B2 in Diels and Kranz 1952; Graninger 2010, p. 311. See the valuable discussion of Dascalakis 1965, pp. 228–236, on Thrasymachus and the setting of the speech.

Spartan, opposition to Macedonia's expansion in Greece.[90] But the division of Greek and barbarian is telling. Likewise, Archelaus is called a "barbarian" in Pseudo-Herodes' speech *Concerning Administration* (*peri politeias*), mentioned above, to contrast him to the "Hellenes" and show him to be unworthy.[91] And in Athens, Aristophanes in the *Frogs* of 405 ridiculed those who had rushed to Macedonia for safety when their city was in the death throes of the Peloponnesian War. Whether this was a criticism of Archelaus or denigration of traitors who fled to a "barbarian" state cannot be determined, but it does show what people thought of Macedonia at the time.[92] "Hellas" and "Macedonia" thus remained two different entities.[93]

Archelaus' death

Archelaus died in 399, probably aged between 45 and 50, and may have been deified.[94] In addition to two daughters, he had at least one grown son, Amyntas, and a toddler son Orestes, who was about three years old when his father died. Orestes' mother was Cleopatra, presumably his father's widow, and it was he who succeeded his father.[95] Why Archelaus preferred his infant son over his older one is unknown. However, his decision shows us that it was king's right to designate his successor regardless of age, in which case the theory that "legitimate" children were only those born *after* the father succeeded to the throne has some merit and would explain Orestes' succession.[96]

Aristotle in the *Politics* gives the fullest account of Archelaus' death in a long passage about the motives of various assassins in killing rulers.[97] He attributes the murder by the king's lover Crataeas because of resentment from homoerotic relationship and perhaps Archelaus' duplicity in retracting

[90] Whether he himself delivered it is unknown—he could not have done so in Athens as he was not a citizen.

[91] At 34–37: see Dascalakis 1965, pp. 246–249.

[92] Aristophanes, *Frogs* 85, but on the passage see Greenwalt 2003, pp. 140–141, that Dionysus' choosing to bring back from the underworld (the plot of the play) not Euripides but Aeschylus shows Aristophanes' contempt for Archelaus. Note also that one tradition has it that Archelaus' dogs were said to have torn Euripides apart, not anonymous dogs: Borza 1990, pp. 175–176.

[93] Cf. Hammond and Griffith 1979, pp. 149–150, and see too the comments of Dascalakis 1965, pp. 41–49, on Hellas and Macedonia.

[94] Hammond 1992a, p. 169 n.2.

[95] Diodorus 14.37.6, with Carney 2000, pp. 21–22, arguing that the two women were one and the same, but Hammond 1979, p. 169 n. 2, thinks it is a coincidence.

[96] Hatzopoulos 1986, p. 283; King 2018, pp. 51–52. On the heirs see Hatzopoulos 1986, pp. 283–286.

[97] Archelaus: *Politics* 5.1311b 9–21, 31–35.

a promise for Crataeas to wed his eldest daughter. Crataeas was obviously noble and important enough to be considered as husband of the princess—the latter was the same one married off to the Elimean king Derdas in return for support against Sirras and Arrhabaeus, as we saw above. At the same time, Aristotle hints at a possible political motive to the assassination by speaking of foreign conspirators who had a grudge against the king:

> Crataeas was always resentful of the association, so that even a smaller excuse became sufficient, or perhaps it was because [Archelaus] did not give him the hand of one of his daughters after agreeing to do so, but gave the elder to the king of Elimea when hard pressed in a war against Sirras and Arrabaeus, and the younger to his son Amyntas, thinking that thus Amyntas would be least likely to quarrel with his son by Cleopatra; but at all events Crataeas' estrangement was primarily caused by resentment because of the love affair. And Hellanocrates of Larisa also joined in the attack for the same reason; for because while enjoying his favors Archelaus would not restore him to his home although he had promised to do so, he thought that the motive of the familiarity that had taken place had been insolence and not passionate desire....Also Decamnichus took a leading part in the attack upon Archelaus, being the first to stir on the attackers; and the cause of his anger was that he had handed him over to Euripides the poet to flog, Euripides being angry because he had made a remark about his breath smelling.

Diodorus gives the alternative version that Archelaus was killed unintentionally during a hunt at the hands of a certain Craterus, "whom he loved."[98] We do not know who Diodorus' source was, perhaps Marsyas, but his version is generally disregarded. To complicate matters further, other ancient writers have the king killed by Craterus also over a souring love affair but then go on to say that Craterus assumed the throne for three or four days before he was killed in a plot.[99] The latter point is surely incorrect and by extension casts doubt on the former. So too do the discrepancies in the killer's name, which is variously given as Crataeas, Craterus, Crateas, or Crateuas, of which the first is usually preferred.[100]

[98] Diodorus 14.37.6.

[99] [Plato], *Alcibiades* 2.141d–e; [Plutarch], *Amatorius* 23; Aelian *Varia Historia* 8.9. On the various theories: Hammond and Griffith 1979, pp. 167–168; Errington 1990, p. 28; Borza 1990, p. 177; Carney 1983, pp. 261–264, Greenwalt 2003, pp. 151–153; Müller 2016, pp. 186–190; cf. Lane Fox 2011d, p. 215.

[100] Craterus in Diodorus 14.37.6; Crateas in [Plutarch], *Moralia* 768f; Crateuas in Aelian, *Varia Historia* 8.9; and Crataeas in Aristotle, *Politics* 5.1311b 9. Hammond and Griffith 1979, p. 167, confidently say, "We may adopt [Crateuas]" without specifying why.

The others connected to the assassin are largely unknown. Hellanocrates of Larissa was perhaps a refugee or a hostage, exiled by the pro-Macedonian faction in Larissa, whom Archelaus received as a hostage a year earlier.[101] Archelaus promised to send him home but kept him at court as a lover, which shows he could control Hellanocrates' movements. Nothing is known of Decamnichus, though a flogging for saying Euripides had bad breath sounds an extreme motive for assassinating a king.[102] It has been suggested these individuals were royal pages, boys aged 14 to 18 who served the king at court, since flogging was one of their punishments. Thus in 330 a page named Hermolaus was publicly flogged and apparently hatched a plot to kill Alexander the Great.[103] But Hermolaus was in the wrong as during a hunt he had speared a boar, robbing Alexander of his regnal right to kill it; hence the king could legitimately punish him. Hermolaus' flogging and that of Decamnichus may only be coincidental, as the latter presumably had not incurred the king's wrath: just because alleged assassination plots have similar traits does not mean they fit the same box or that they had political motives.[104] In any case, the school of royal pages was surely the creation of Philip II, so not existing in Archelaus' time.[105]

It is important to note that Aristotle includes the murder of the king in his account of rulers killed "by insolence" that caused anger on the part of their killers, who acted "for the sake of revenge, not of ambition." Thus, Crataeas was angered to an extent by the breaking of the promise, but his relationship with the king and estrangement "was primarily caused by resentment because of the love affair." Hellanocrates had "the same reason" because the king broke his promise to him, and Decamnichus was angry at being flogged over a personal slight.

Aristotle's account is usually regarded as the most reliable as he may have had a close insight into Macedonian history from his father, a court physician to Amyntas III. But nothing in it suggests a political conspiracy—and if there had been one, what was it about: foreign policy, rival ambitions, or even, as recently argued, aristocratic dissension from infantry reforms that

[101] Hammond and Griffith 1979, p. 168.

[102] Believed by Chapinal-Heras 2022, p. 17.

[103] Arrian 4.10.1–14.4, with Carney 1983, pp. 262–266; cf. Greenwalt 2003, pp. 152–153; Worthington 2014a, pp. 234–235.

[104] Carney 1983, pp. 266–270, makes strained analogies to the murder of the Pisistratid tyrant Hipparchus by the tyrannicides in 514.

[105] Arrian 4.13.1 (Philip's creation); Curtius 8.6.2 (the pages were "customary"), with Carney 2008; Roisman 2010, p. 158; Lane Fox 2011d, p. 215, though Hammond 1992a, pp. 56–57, for example, believes the school was founded by Archelaus.

gave rise to a hoplite or middle class?[106] This last explanation is unconvincing as Archelaus seems to have done nothing to do the army, which remained weak after his death and could not prevent the Spartans' marching through Macedonia (chapter 7). We cannot discount that in the following decades of upheaval after the king's death, which undid almost all his gains, the competing branches of the ruling house and rival factions at court may have brought about his downfall after all.[107] Since a hunt was not just a social activity but brought together king and court in a quasi-political setting, killing a king in that setting may have been a political statement.[108]

On balance, however, the assassination seems to spring from personal reasons as all accounts have the commonality of homoerotic love and hunting, so we should avoid conspiracy theory while acknowledging that there is no compelling explanation for Archelaus' death.[109] Indeed, Archelaus may have been accidentally killed, as hunts were not safe places, and his demise was given a personal or political spin by various writers.

Evaluating Archelaus

Archelaus' ambitions and achievements deserve more than the short summary Thucydides gave them. By the end of the fifth century the king had increased his own status, made his kingdom strong economically, as his new coinage reveals, promoted his court as a cultural center, and contributed to bettering the lives of his subjects. But he had his darker side if we can believe the story of his accession. His assassination, though, made Macedonia vulnerable to a series of succession struggles that undid almost all his gains. Perhaps, then, we should agree with the view that the years after Archelaus show how his achievements were ultimately superficial, and the kingdom was still unable to withstand externally generated crises.[110] If Macedonia had been on the rise under Archelaus, it was about to make a dramatic fall.

Macedonia under the Argead Kings: The Rise and Fall of an Ancient Superpower. Ian Worthington, Oxford University Press. © Oxford University Press 2026. DOI: 10.1093/9780197668009.003.0007

[106] As argued by Greenwalt 2007, pp. 90–91; cf. Greenwalt 2003, pp. 151–153.
[107] Greenwalt 2003, pp. 151–153.
[108] Put forward by Greenwalt 2003, pp. 152–153 and Greenwalt 2019, citing bibliography.
[109] Roisman 2010, pp. 157–158.
[110] Borza 1990, p. 188.

7
The Short Reigns of Five Kings

Thanks to a paucity of sources and chronological issues, the 40 years following Archelaus' death in 399 until the accession of Philip II in 359 are almost completely obscure and present "a historiographical nightmare for the historian of Macedonia."[1] Diodorus, our main source, used the fourth-century universal historian Ephorus, who is generally reliable, while another source, an unnamed chronographer of the Hellenistic era who compiled a list of dates of the kings' reigns, is more suspect because how he worked out these dates is unknown.[2] What we can say is that these four decades were ones of instability, with a rapid turnover of kings, some of whom ruled for only a year or two, punctuated only by the longer reign of Amyntas III (393/2–369/8). In addition, there were threats from the Illyrians and Olynthians in tandem with dynastic struggles between different Argead branches.[3] All of this was a testing time for the economy as well, for some kings never coined, and others issued Archelaus' coin types only rarely and in a debased form.[4]

Four kings over six years

Who succeeded Archelaus is variously given in our sources. In one place Diodorus tells us it was Orestes, who was then murdered by Aeropus, yet elsewhere the same author claims it was Pausanias, who ruled for one year

[1] Borza 1990, p. 180; cf. Lane Fox 2011d, p. 211, "a scholarly minefield," and the exhaustive discussions of March 1995 and Stylianou 1998, pp. 25–132, with Müller 2016, pp. 41–84. On the period, see Cloché 1960, pp. 104–129; Lane Fox 2011d (for 399–369) and Lane Fox 2011b (for the 360s); cf. Lane Fox 2011b, pp. 210–215, specifically on sources. See too Hammond and Griffith 1979, pp. 167–202; Greenwalt 1988; Errington 1990, pp. 27–39; Borza 1990, pp. 177–197; Zahrnt 2006b; Zahrnt 2007; Müller 2016, pp. 194–235; King 2018, pp. 49–69; Hatzopoulos 2020, pp. 35–37.

[2] Chronographers and their use by narrative sources: March 1995, especially Stylianou 1998, pp. 25–132; see his pp. 45–49 on this chronographer's errors.

[3] Goukowsky 1991, pp. 43–60. Two other lines did not survive: those of Philip (wiped out by Perdiccas and Sitalces) and Alcetas (presumably eradicated by Archelaus).

[4] Greenwalt 1994b, pp. 119–120.

before being killed by Amyntas; the last name is echoed in the chronographic source and placed between Aeropus and Pausanias (hence Amyntas II sometimes called "the Little").[5] Inconsistencies between these two ancient writers give us different dates for their reigns, and who was king at any one time has been the subject of much debate and revision.[6] Perhaps even the Macedonians themselves at times were unsure who was king.[7] Lane Fox has recently addressed the controversies in detail, and in my opinion compellingly, and I follow his proposed chronology in this chapter and the following one:[8]

Orestes: 400/399–397/6
Aeropus II: 397/6–394
Amyntas II "the Little": 394/3
Pausanias: 394/3
Amyntas III: 393/2–369/8 (including a two-year challenge from Argaeus)
Alexander II: 369/8
Ptolemy as regent: 368/7–365/4
Perdiccas III: 365/4–360/59

Orestes was a toddler so needed a regent as the age of majority was 18 or even 20.[9] Accordingly Aeropus was selected, possibly by the Assembly.[10] Little is known about him. He may have been a Lyncestian prince or even another son of Perdiccas, though that is less likely as it is based on emending the fragmentary text of the alliance between Athens and Perdiccas, discussed in chapter 5, to read "Areopus son of Perdiccas," and the editor of the inscription shows that the name and patronymic are too long to fit in the space available on the stone.[11] Whatever his lineage, Aeropus was regarded highly as he was chosen to look after Orestes.

[5] Diodorus 14.37.6 (Orestes and Aeropus), 14.84.6, 14.89.2 (Pausanias and Amyntas); see too Hammond and Griffith 1979, pp. 168–172; Hammond 1992a, p. 73; Borza 1990, pp. 178–179; Lane Fox 2011d, pp. 210–213; cf. March 1995; Stylianou 1998, pp. 25–132.

[6] March 1995; Stylianou 1998, pp. 25–132; Zahrnt 2006b; Zahrnt 2007; Lane Fox 2011b; Lane Fox 2011d; Müller 2016, pp. 195–199.

[7] Cf. March 1995, p. 262.

[8] Lane Fox 2011d, pp. 210–213—only slightly different in Hammond and Griffith 1979, p. 168; March 1995 (see his chart on p. 280).

[9] LeBohec 1993a.

[10] Hammond and Griffith 1979, p. 168; Ogden 1999, pp. 8–11, though see Anson 2009, pp. 277–280. Regent: Lane Fox 2011d, pp. 215–216. See too Müller 2016, pp. 195–199, on Orestes and Aeropus.

[11] Prince: Goukowsky 1991, pp. 47–58; Carney 1980a, especially pp. 25–26; Lane Fox 2011d, pp. 217–218. Whether this means the fourth-century Lyncestian brothers had a "model" for the

Orestes ruled from 399 to 397/6 before Aeropus took the throne for himself, presumably by murdering Orestes. If so, he likely had the support of influential barons or companions who wanted a strong king and not an infant.[12] Few details of Aeropus II's reign are known, which may indicate he was not faced with the sort of issues that had plagued his predecessors and that Macedonia was relatively stable under his rule. In 394 he refused the Spartan king Agesilaus' request to permit the latter's army to march through Macedonia, perhaps because Sparta had opposed Macedonia's involvement in Thessaly under Archelaus.[13] However, that summer Agesilaus defied the king and led his army through Macedonia anyway, which showed Aeropus' military strength was no match for a foreign army—and is support for a lack of manpower reforms by Archelaus.[14] When Corinth later revolted from the Spartan hegemony, Aeropus sided with the rebels and prepared to face a Spartan army, but he was outwitted and had to make terms with Sparta.[15]

Nothing else of Aeropus II's reign is known apart from a defeat of the Illyrians, who may have been in search of booty, of uncertain date. He died of sickness in mid-394/3, with Diodorus telling us his son Pausanias succeeded him.[16] But Pausanias may not have ruled solely, because of the presence of a certain Amyntas ("the Little"), who Aristotle tells us was murdered by Derdas and who may have been king at the same time as Amyntas II.[17] Amyntas' father is unknown. Archelaus did marry off his younger daughter to Amyntas—if the latter was his son, presumably the newlyweds were not full brother and sister but were born of two different mothers, since Archelaus was polygamous. If so, this marriage of half-brother to half-sister may have been an attempt to unite the different branch lines.[18]

Pausanias was still in contention for the throne, though, and both he and Amyntas II may have ruled in some type of partnership rather than as

seizure of the Macedonian throne, so Carney, is unknown. Son of Perdiccas based on *IG* i³ 89: Hammond and Griffith 1979, pp. 134–136 and p. 170; see too Hatzopoulos 1986, p. 283; Errington 1990, p. 28; Borza 1990, p. 178; Roisman 2010, p. 158, Lane Fox 2011d, pp. 216–217. Too many letters: Lewis in *IG* i³ 89, p. 105; cf. Lane Fox 2011d, p. 216.

[12] Errington 1990, p. 28. Influence of Companions: Lane Fox 2011d, pp. 218–219.

[13] Borza 1990, p. 178.

[14] Polyaenus 2.1.17, 4.4.3; cf. Plutarch, *Agesilaus* 16.2.

[15] Supposed treaty between Aeropus and Agesilaus: Hamilton, C.D. 1986, p. 240.

[16] Diodorus 14.84.6, with Lane Fox 2011d, p. 215.

[17] Aristotle, *Politics* 5.1311b 3–5, with Hammond and Griffith 1979, pp. 168–169; Hammond 1992a, p. 72 (based on Justin 7.4.3 and Aelian, *Varia Historia* 12.43); Hatzopoulos 1986, p. 282; Borza 1990, p. 178; Roisman 2010, p. 158; Lane Fox 2011d, p. 215; contra Ellis 1971, p. 17; Errington 1990, p. 28.

[18] Ogden 1999, p. 10; cf. Hammond and Griffith 1979, p. 169; Lane Fox 2011d, pp. 216–217. Polygamist: Greenwalt 1989, pp. 22–28; Müller 2016, pp. 62–64.

rivals, as the few coins dating from 394/3 are so similar.[19] This joint rule, to call it that, did not last long. Amyntas II died a violent death within a few months, in 393, assassinated by Derdas of Elimea, leaving Pausanias as king. His days were also numbered, for another Amyntas now came to the fore, a son of Arrhidaeus and grandson of Perdiccas' brother Amyntas, who murdered Pausanias and took the throne as Amyntas III.[20] Given the assassinations of two kings in quick succession, the "new" Amyntas may have been in cahoots with Derdas, as some years later the latter sent Amyntas military support.[21]

Amyntas III's appearance may well explain Amyntas II's nickname of "Little"—Pausanias succeeded his father Aeropus II as king, but Amyntas, son of Menelaus or even Archelaus, also took the throne. They were succeeded by another Amyntas (III). The first Amyntas was nicknamed "Little" perhaps because he was younger or even smaller in size, to distinguish him from Amyntas III.

What caused this spate of regicide? Perhaps it was the "amphimetric" conflict of a polygamous king's children by different mothers, which was endemic in Macedonian royal history.[22] On the other hand, if Aeropus was a Lyncestian prince, perhaps the struggles of the 390s involved members of Archelaus' lowland dynasty (Orestes and Amyntas) against the Lyncestians (Aeropus and Pausanias).[23] What we can say with some certainty is that after half a dozen kings in as many years, the monarchy and the kingdom were in chaos. Perhaps it was now that the Argead foundation legend saw Archelaus replaced by the enigmatic Caranus to bolster the claims of the other family branch under Amyntas III.

Amyntas III: The early years

Amyntas III ruled from 393/2 to 369/8, a longer reign that was certainly needed after the recent upheavals (figure 7.1). However, reconstructing the

[19] Errington 1990, pp. 28–29; Lane Fox 2011d, pp. 212–213. Hammond and Griffith 1979, p. 128, have Amyntas II, Pausanias, and Amyntas III ruling for fragments of the same year, 394/3, whereas Müller 2016, pp. 195–199, spreads their rule between 396/5 and 395/4; cf. March 1995, pp. 259–265.

[20] Diodorus 14.89.2. See Rhodes-Osborne, no. 12, for an inscription naming Amyntas, son of Arrhidaeus, as king of the Macedonians.

[21] Errington 1990, p. 29. [22] Ogden 1999, pp. ix–xx.

[23] Goukowsky 1991, pp. 47–58; cf. Lane Fox 2011d, pp. 217–218.

Figure 7.1 Amyntas III from coin
Source: Wikimedia Commons.

events of his 23 years in power is still problematic.[24] Diodorus, our main source, sums up his reign briefly:[25]

> [Amyntas] was driven from the country when the Illyrians invaded Macedonia. Despairing of his kingdom he presented the Olynthians with a piece of territory bordering their own. At that time, he did indeed lose his kingdom, and may have been driven out to seek refuge with the Aleuadae in Larissa. He was brought back by the Thessalians and ruled in all for 24 years. Some say, however, that after Amyntas had been expelled Argaeus ruled the Macedonians for two years, and only afterward did he recover the kingdom.

Amyntas clearly faced more than his fair share of problems thanks to outside interference in his realm, but it is an understatement to say what we have in the passage is controversial. Amyntas it seems did not rule continuously, for the Illyrians expelled him for some months. He also had to contend with a two-year rule by a certain Argaeus, whose dates range

[24] Following, for example, Lane Fox 2011d, pp. 211–213. But Borza 1990, p. 181, and Müller 2016, pp. 202–204, date the accession to 394/3. Reign: Cloché 1960, pp. 107–121; Hammond and Griffith 1979, pp. 172–180; Borza 1990, pp. 180–189; Roisman 2010, pp. 158–161; Müller 2016, pp. 200–216; see too Greenwalt 1988, pp. 35–44; Zahrnt 2006b; Zahrnt 2007; Lane Fox 2011d, pp. 219–234; cf. Rosenberg 1916; Carney 2019, pp. 17–22.

[25] Diodorus 14.92.3–4 (trans. Errington 1990, pp. 29–30); cf. 15.19.2.

from 387/6 to 385/4 or 385–383, although the former is usually preferred.[26] But was Amyntas exiled once or twice? Who was Argaeus? Did the Illyrians support him against Amyntas? What were the circumstances of Amyntas' alliance with the Olynthians? All these issues are intertwined, and what I give below, again following the chronology of Lane Fox, provides a plausible running order of Amyntas' first years as king.[27] The issues also show that to combat threats to his position and kingdom, he took a leaf from Perdiccas II's diplomatic book by making strategic alliances with whomever when they suited him best.[28]

Not long after he came to the throne Amyntas was expelled to a fort—somewhere, it seems, in Macedonia—after an Illyrian invasion in 393/2, possibly sparked by his coup when he murdered Pausanias. He did not return for some months—three according to Isocrates—thanks to Thessalian help provided by the Aleuadae of Larissa.[29] What this help consisted of is unknown, but perhaps it was diplomatic since the Aleuadae could not, presumably, commit a large force for a pitched battle as they were currently at loggerheads with the Spartans.[30] However, the alliance with the Olynthians, to whom Amyntas gave some of his lands, was not in force at this time but later, as is argued below. Then in 387/6 he was sent packing again by a certain Argaeus and was in exile for two years before recovering the throne in 385/4.

We do not know who Argaeus was. It is an unusual name, and since the first successor of Perdiccas I was also named Argaeus, the Argaeus of Amyntas III's reign may have been an Argead and even another son of Archelaus.[31] His support base is unknown, but it is not likely to have been the Illyrians—the bane of Macedonian kings—as they had less interest in regnal affairs than in plundering the lands.[32] Indeed, Amyntas may have agreed to pay the

[26] Diodorus 14.92.4. Former: March 1995, pp. 261–273 (cf. pp. 280–282 on Argaeus' rule); Lane Fox 2011d, pp. 223–225; Müller 2016, p. 207. Latter: Ellis 1969a, pp. 5–8.

[27] Lane Fox 2011d, pp. 220–225.

[28] Roisman 2010, p. 159.

[29] Isocrates 6.46, with Ellis 1969a; March 1995, p. 274 n. 68; Roisman 2010, p. 159; Lane Fox 2011d, pp. 220–221; cf. Sprawski 1999, p. 45—probably the Aleuadae, or more generally the Larissans, noting that their help shows that the condition of Thessaly at this time "was not too bleak"—and Hammond and Griffith 1979, pp. 172–173. But Heskel 1997a, p. 172, says he was expelled "probably by Macedonian nobles disenchanted with his failure to protect the kingdom from invasion."

[30] See, for example, Westlake 1993, pp. 61–64.

[31] Hammond and Griffith 1979, pp. 175–176, argue that Argaeus was a son of Archelaus, citing in support Theopompus, *BNJ* 115 F 29 about two pretenders to the throne in 359 (Argaeus and Pausanias); cf. Errington 1990, p. 30 n. 15; Goukowsky 1991, pp. 56–57; Heskel 1996, p. 40; Zahrnt 2006b, p. 131; Müller 2016, pp. 207–208, but on the name see the reservations of Lane Fox 2011d, p. 224. Borza 1990, p. 182, merely says that any attempt to identify Argaeus or fix a date for him is impossible.

[32] Hammond and Griffith 1979, p. 172; Greenwalt 1988, pp. 35–37; Errington 1990, p. 30; March 1995, p. 272, for the view, with which I disagree, that the Illyrians backed Argaeus on the

Illyrian chieftain Bardylis a regular tribute to prevent further invasions.[33] Perhaps this arrangement had lapsed, and Philip II promised to reintroduce it to end an Illyrian invasion in 359 (p. 148).

Possibly the Olynthians threw their weight behind Argaeus because they felt aggrieved that Amyntas demanded back the lands he supposedly gave them when he first came power to gain their support against Illyrian threats.[34] But this scenario is unlikely as Amyntas' treaty with them—and the land concessions he made—should be placed later in his reign; hence there was no reason for them to back Argaeus now. Another possibility is the Athenians, who seem to have supported him (if he is the same Argaeus) against Philip II in 359, though why they did so now is hard to fathom. Perhaps even court factions that were hostile to Amyntas supported the pretender, though this is an argument from silence—as with enigmatic factions that may have engineered Archelaus' murder in 399 (chapter 6).

The date and circumstances of Argaeus' seizure of the throne are also controversial because of an apparent doublet in Diodorus, who at one point in his narrative speaks of the Illyrian invasion of 393/2 but later mentions a defeat a decade later at the hands of the Illyrians, followed by Amyntas conceding territory to the Olynthians.[35] The repetition has been taken to mean that the Illyrians invaded twice. But more likely is that Diodorus repeated the same events in abbreviated form because his first mention of them was over 40 chapters earlier in his narrative; hence there was only the one invasion.[36] Diodorus may then have confused and telescoped two different crises: the challenge from Argaeus in the 380s and an Illyrian invasion of Epirus in 385/4 supporting Dionysius of Syracuse's plan to

throne in return for his cooperation with their economic designs, especially if Amyntas were attempting to block them.

33 Diodorus 16.2.2.

34 Ellis 1969a, pp. 5–8; Goukowsky 1991, pp. 56–58; cf. Lane Fox 2011d, p. 223; Psoma 2011, p. 121; Müller 2016, pp. 202–204 (was gifted rather than gave).

35 Diodorus 14.92.3 and 15.19.2–3; he speaks of the archonship of Demostratus, which was 394/3 but also the archonship of Phanostratus, which was 383/2. On the doublet, see Costanzi 1901; Ellis 1969a, pp. 5–7; Hammond and Griffith 1979, p. 174; Borza 1990, pp. 296–297; March 1995, pp. 257–268; Parker 2003, pp. 127–132; Lane Fox 2011d, pp. 224–225, all citing earlier scholarship.

36 Ellis 1969a, pp. 1–3; see too Errington 1990, p. 31 n. 15; Borza 1990, p. 184; March 1995, pp. 269–272; Stylianou 1998, pp. 211–213; Lane Fox 2011d, pp. 224–225; Müller 2016, pp. 202–204; cf. Natoli 2004, pp. 178–180; Greenwalt 2010, pp. 285–286. March redates the Illyrian invasion to 388–387 (p. 272) and argues that it was Argaeus not Amyntas IIII who gave the land grant to the Olynthians (p. 274). Parker 2003, pp. 127–132, and Hammond and Griffith 1979, pp. 174–175, argue, however, against a Diodoran doublet and that both passages refer to different periods, but their views are not held.

install the exiled king Alcetas on the Molossian throne and so establish ports along coastal Epirus.[37]

Also pointing to only the one Illyrian incursion is Amyntas' marriage to Eurydice.[38] She was the daughter of the Sirras who was either Illyrian or Lyncestian and granddaughter of Arrhabaeus of Lyncestis, against whom Perdiccas II and Brasidas had fought.[39] That made her either a Lyncestian or a combination of Lyncestian and Illyrian. Born between 410 and 404, she was the first queen to emerge as a figure in her own right, a "turning point in the role of royal women in Macedonian monarchy."[40]

Eurydice bore Amyntas three sons, Alexander, Perdiccas, and Philip, and one daughter, Eurynoe.[41] Amyntas also had another wife, Gygaea, about whom we know next to nothing, who also bore him three sons: Archelaus, Arrhidaeus, and Menelaus.[42] No ancient source states whether Eurydice was the first or second wife or when he married either—he may even have married both in quick succession early in his reign.[43] Perhaps an argument for Eurydice being the first wife is that Gygaea's sons did not challenge their stepbrothers' succession after Amyntas' death. Later, they may have given Philip II cause for concern after they were offered sanctuary at Olynthus and he demanded their surrender in 349/8.[44] Then again, we cannot discount that Eurydice was Amyntas' second wife and that the king decided her sons should succeed him or even that she was backed by a more powerful faction at court than Gygaea.[45]

[37] Diodorus 15.13, with Greenwalt 2010, p. 285; cf. Hammond and Griffith 1979, p. 173. In the end they were unsuccessful as they were driven out by a Spartan army. Stylianou 1998, p. 193, notes it does not necessarily follow that Alcetas was expelled with them.

[38] Justin 7.4.5.

[39] Epigraphic evidence from Aegae confirms her father was Sirras: Oikonomides 1983. She was probably Lyncestian: Hammond and Griffith 1979, p. 15; Errington 1990, p. 29; Oikonomedes 1982; Greenwalt 1989, pp. 37–44; Greenwalt 2010, pp. 286–287; Lane Fox 2011d, p. 221; Saatsoglou-Paliadeli 2000, p. 392. Illyrian: Papazoglou 1965, p. 150; Badian 1982b, p. 103; Mortensen 1991, pp. 51–55. On her ethnicity, Carney 2000, p. 41 nn. 12–14, concludes she had Illyrian and Lyncestian blood; cf. Carney 2019, pp. 23–24 with n. 46; Müller 2016, p. 213.

[40] Carney 2019, p. 1. On Eurydice, see Badian 1982b; Mortensen 1992; Howe 2018; Carney 2019; cf. Hatzopoulos 1986, p. 281; Carney 2000, pp. 40–48.

[41] Justin 7.4.5. On Eurynoe, see Carney 2000, pp. 39–40, querying the sources on her, and Mortensen 1992, p. 156. On Eurydice and her sons, see Carney 2019, pp. 53–67.

[42] Justin 7.4.5; Carney 2000, p. 47; Mortensen 1992, p. 169; cf. Greenwalt 1988, suggesting she was an Argead, but there is no evidence for this view.

[43] Gygaea first: Ellis 1973, p. 351; Badian 1982b, p. 104; but see Greenwalt 1988, p. 37; Greenwalt 1989, pp. 25–28 and 37–40; Carney 2000, p. 47; Carney 2019, pp. 27–28; cf. Mortensen 1992, pp. 168–169. Müller 2016, p. 213, sits on the fence.

[44] Justin 8.3.10–11, with Ellis 1973; Carney 2019, pp. 22–23.

[45] Promotion: Greenwalt 1989, p. 43, against which see Carney 2019, pp. 29–30, also arguing for factional support. We do not know if there was any resentment on either queen's part, but see Greenwalt 1988, p. 43.

The marriage of Amyntas and Eurydice should be placed soon after his first return from exile, given that it seemed to find favor with the Illyrians, who did not bother him for two decades.[46] This may mean they forced the marriage upon him or that he arranged it to stave off Illyrian threats. The latter is more likely, for their leader Bardylis, a hereditary chieftain of the Dardanians in the area around Kosovo, was in the 390s expanding his state—including taking over the rich silver mines of Damastium. Hence interference in Macedonia was not on his radar.[47] There would also have been too little time for the marriage before Amyntas' expulsion, and presumably the Larissans would not have wanted him living in their city for a long time. Nor can the marriage be later than 390 since their eldest son Alexander (who succeeded his father) was old enough by the mid-370s to sign a treaty with Athens; hence he must have been born by 388 at the latest.[48] Eurydice was also said to have taught herself to read and write when her sons Alexander, Perdiccas, and Philip were adolescents, which likewise suggests an early marriage date.[49]

Amyntas was therefore expelled by Argaeus five years after the start of his reign and was in exile for two. from 387/6 to 385/4.[50] It was probably then and not earlier that he made the alliance with the Olynthians, to which Diodorus refers: its complex and long-term arrangements, discussed below, do not point to a panic measure from a sudden Illyrian invasion at the start of his reign and he would not have needed to make concessions on his return shortly later.[51]

By the 380s Amyntas needed the support of the Chalcidian League, which by then was a powerful entity militarily and economically, as its fine gold and silver coinage shows.[52] To win it over he gave it a border area, which

[46] Isocrates 6.46 (also speaking of one barbarian invasion).

[47] Bardylis was perhaps in his 80s when he was defeated by Philip II in 358 after invading Macedonia in 359, so he may have been active in the 390s: Hammond and Griffith 1979, p. 172; Mortensen 1991, pp. 51–55; Greenwalt 2010, p. 284. Good comments on Bardylis in Howe 2017. Expansion: Hammond and Griffith 1979, pp. 191–192; cf. Wilkes 1995, p. 118.

[48] Carney 2000, p. 41; Mortensen 1992, p. 168; Müller 2016, p. 213 with n. 101.

[49] [Plutarch], *Moralia* 14b–c, with Carney 2019, pp. 28 and 79–81.

[50] Ellis 1969a, p. 7; March 1995, pp. 261–273; Lane Fox 2011d, pp. 221–223.

[51] Diodorus 14.92.3 and 15.19.2, with Lane Fox 2011d, p. 222 (no "Macedonian kingdom in chaos"), but see Zahrnt 2006b, pp. 129–130; cf. Müller 2016, pp. 204–207; Roisman 2010, p. 159; Borza 1990, pp. 182–183; Greenwalt 2010, p. 284, who argues the treaty was to be dated early and that Amyntas was probably hoping to prevent the region's revenues falling to the Illyrians, who were currently minting new silver coins from Damastium and were perhaps trying to build trading links with the Chalcidice via Macedonia.

[52] Hammond and Griffith 1979, p. 193; cf. Parker 2003, p. 132; Zahrnt 2006b, p. 131; Roisman 2010, p. 159; Müller 2016, p. 204.

probably included Anthemus (Galatista).[53] Land grants were not unknown: Perdiccas, we saw, granted land around Lake Bolbe to the Chalcidians, who abandoned their coastal cities and moved to Olynthus. Assuming the chronology is right, Amyntas could not have fled too far away to bring about the alliance, perhaps only to Aegae, given the protection its city walls offered.[54]

The resulting defensive treaty was supposed to last for 50 years.[55] The treaty that exists today is the Chalcidian copy; it is damaged on its front but less so on its back. Each side has a different tone as far as Amyntas' relations with the Chalcidians go: the front shows both parties were equals, but the back appears to give the Chalcidians an advantage.[56] Among other things, it contains various limits on export and import agreements and on alliances, which give us a valuable contemporary glance into aspects of Macedonia's economy.[57] The league was allowed to import pitch and fir, which was the preferred timber as it was lighter and grew in the long lengths needed for warships. Macedonia was allowed to do the same from the Chalcidians—a moot point as the kingdom had its own abundant reserves. Also, both parties were banned from making independent alliances with Amphipolis, Bottiaea, Acanthus, and Mende, showing none of these places was under Amyntas' control at this time.

These provisos led Zahrnt, who personally inspected the inscription, to conclude that the two sides actually represented two separate treaties negotiated at different times and that the back, favoring the Chalcidians, shows their growth in influence during the first 10 years of Amyntas' reign.[58] His arguments have been challenged, and it remains reasonably certain that there was only the one treaty made contemporaneously with Argaeus' coup.[59] Its terms indicate that both sides were not negotiating

[53] Hammond and Griffith 1979, p. 172; Zahrnt 2006b, p. 130; Zahrnt 2007, p. 242; cf. Müller 2016, pp. 204–207.

[54] Saatsoglou- Paliadeli 2011, p. 277, with bibliography in n. 35; cf. Borza 1990, p. 184.

[55] Rhodes-Osborne, no. 12 = Harding, no. 21 (translated as two treaties) = Hatzopoulos 1996, vol. 2, no. 1, pp. 19–20; see too Zahrnt 1971, pp. 81–82 and 122–124; Hammond and Griffith 1979, pp. 172–180; Psoma 2001, pp. 221–225; Zahrnt 2006b, pp. 129–130; see too Millett 2010, pp. 472–475; Lane Fox 2011d, pp. 221–223. Date: Ellis 1969a, p. 3; Lane Fox 2011d, pp. 221–223; King 2018, p. 56, for a date of 393. Hammond and Griffith 1979, p. 173 and Borza 1990, pp. 182–183, favor 391. March 1995, p. 280: somewhere between 393 and 388.

[56] Meiggs 1982, pp. 118–119. But Hammond 1992a, p. 80, believes the phrasing shows this was a pact between equals; cf. Lane Fox 2011d, pp. 223, arguing that it did not give the Olynthians a free hand to do what they wanted.

[57] Millett 2010, pp. 472–474.

[58] Zahrnt 1971, pp. 122–124; cf. Errington 1990, p. 31; Zahrnt 2006b, p. 130 (followed by Harding, no. 21).

[59] Lane Fox 2011d, pp. 222–223.

equally, which would be consistent with Amyntas' need for Olynthian support and the concessions he had to make to gain it.

Amyntas and Sparta

Amyntas evidently had enough troops with him to recover the throne in 385/4.[60] Argaeus' fate is unknown, though he may have fled to Athens, as he was likely the Athenian-backed pretender to the throne when Perdiccas III died in 359.[61] By 383 Amyntas evidently felt safe enough to risk a conflict with the Chalcidians by demanding the return of the land he had earlier ceded to them. Since they were profiting from this area, they refused, and he likely declared war on them, which led to an invasion of his eastern territories and even it seems their capture of Pella. It is ironic that the Chalcidian League had been Macedonia's creation and now it posed a threat to that kingdom.[62]

Amyntas therefore turned to the Spartans for help.[63] Two ancient writers, Xenophon and Diodorus, give us differing details here. Xenophon claims that Amyntas' appeal was supported by envoys from Acanthus and Apollonia, two independent cities in the Chalcidice that were being pressured to join the Chalcidian League.[64] He gives an Acanthian speech to the Spartans that describes Olynthus as a major threat because of its resources, income from harbors, and extension of territory, and that Thebes and Athens, Sparta's rivals in central Greece, could join the Olynthians against Sparta.[65] Diodorus' account is briefer; there is no mention of anyone else but Amyntas influencing the Spartans—he "gathered an army from his own people and forming an alliance with the Spartans persuaded them to send out a general and a strong force against the Olynthians."[66]

These differences have led scholars to question the veracity of Xenophon and to accept Diodorus (via his source Ephorus) that it was Amyntas himself who secured Spartan support.[67] But why did the Spartans agree to

[60] Hammond and Griffith 1979, p. 176. [61] Heskel 1996, especially pp. 39–43.

[62] Psoma 2011, pp. 113–115. See on the following Zahrnt 1971, pp. 81–97; Zahrnt 2007.

[63] Diodorus 15.19.3; cf. Zahrnt 2006b, p. 131.

[64] Xenophon, *Hellenica* 5.2.11–24, with Psoma 2001, pp. 224–225; Zahrnt 2006b, pp. 131–132; Lane Fox 2011d, p. 225.

[65] Xenophon, *Hellenica* 5.2.11–19.

[66] Diodorus 15.19.3; *SEG* 53 (2003), 587, for a possible fragment of the treaty.

[67] Ellis 1969a, pp. 4–5; Zahrnt 2006b, p. 132; Roisman 2010, pp. 159–160; Psoma 2011, pp. 122–123; King 2018, p. 58. See especially the careful discussion of Parker 2003 (excellent speech analysis on pp. 114–126).

help him? Greece at the time was still in the era of the Spartan hegemony (404–371) though Sparta's dominance had taken a tumble until it was restored by the King's Peace of 387, brokered by the Persian king at the cost of Persian interference in Greek politics.[68] The Spartans' relations with Persia made them unpopular, as many Greeks believed they had been betrayed; hence there was the danger that the formidable Chalcidian League, perhaps in tandem with states like Athens, Thebes, and Thessaly, might oppose Sparta. To combat this scenario, the Spartans responded positively to Amyntas' call.

Potential conflict with the Chalcidians supports Amyntas' dealings with Cotys, the ambitious Odrysian king. He aimed to restore a weakened Thrace, which was vulnerable to Olynthian incursion, to its leading position of the fifth century.[69] After Seuthes' death Thrace had been divided between two rival kings, but Cotys reunited it. He may not have been favorably disposed to Amyntas until the latter cannily adopted as his son the Athenian general Iphicrates, who happened to be Cotys' son-in-law, thus exploiting a family connection.[70]

The Spartans sent an army of 3,000 hoplites north in the spring of 382, which took possession of Potidaea, an excellent launching pad for an attack on Olynthus, only eight miles away.[71] The Spartan Eudamidas waited for reinforcements, but as the latter marched north their commander Teuleutias took possession of Thebes and installed a garrison on the Cadmea.[72] Teuleutias then sent orders to Amyntas to hire mercenaries and to "give money to the kings in his neighborhood"—presumably the chiefs of western Macedonia—to gain their alliance.[73] A key ally for Sparta was won over at this time in the shape of Derdas of Elimea and his first-class troops with the argument that the Olynthians could swallow up his kingdom, as they were already doing to Macedonia.[74] Nothing, incidentally, is said of using Amyntas' own troops, which may indicate Teuleutias thought little of them.[75] If so, we again have an argument against Archelaus' increasing infantry

68 Hamilton, C.D. 1986; cf. Borza 1990, pp. 184–185; Lane-Fox 2011d, pp. 225–227.

69 Archibald 1998, pp. 218–222.

70 Nepos, *Iphicrates* 3.2; Athenaeus 4.131a–c (marriage); cf. Aeschines 2.28, with Hammond and Griffith 1979, pp. 176–177 and 195–196. Brother-in-law: Demosthenes 23.129.

71 Hammond and Griffith 1979, pp. 177–178.

72 Diodorus 15.20.1–3, (with Stylianou 1998, pp. 221–224); Plutarch, *Pelopidas* 5–6.1.

73 Xenophon, *Hellenica* 5.2.38.

74 Xenophon, *Hellenica* 5.2.38. Derdas not a subject ally at this time of Amyntas: Hammond and Griffith 1979, pp. 177–178; Errington 1990, p. 34; Zahrnt 2006b, p. 132. Superiority of his troops: Xenophon, *Hellenica* 5.3.1; cf. 5.2.42.

75 Hammond and Griffith 1979, p. 177; Borza 1990, p. 186.

numbers or training his men.[76] Indeed, in the campaigns against Olynthus Amyntas may have had to hire mercenaries if Diodorus' reference to his army "from his own people" was not a full national levy.[77]

The campaigns of 382 and summer 381 against Olynthus were, however, disastrous for Teleutias, whose men fell to Chalcidian cavalry attacks and a barrage of missiles from the defenders of the walls.[78] Sparta was forced to send more troops, this time under one of its kings, Agesipolis, who sensibly coordinated the troops of Amyntas and Derdas as well as the Thessalian cavalry.[79] Agesipolis devastated Olynthians lands and captured Torone before succumbing to a fever, and nothing further is known until Olynthus fell in the fall of 379.[80] The Spartans imposed harsh terms on its people, ordering them to have the same friends and enemies as themselves, be their ally, and give them military assistance; to restore Amyntas' lands (which included Anthemus); and to dissolve the Chalcidian League.[81]

The reduction in Chalcidian power must have been a relief for Amyntas, though the Spartans did little to strengthen his position. Still, the threat from the Chalcidian League was no more, and Amyntas punished Macedonians who had been supportive of Olynthus, including a certain Pausanias—the same man we will meet in 368/7 trying to seize the throne by force.[82] Not everyone was pleased that Sparta had sided with the Macedonian king, but Spartan influence in Greece continued to decline, and the expansionist policies of its king Agesilaus were unpopular.[83] Against this background the power of Athens rose again.

Amyntas, Athens, and Thessaly

In 379 Athenian troops helped the Thebans expel the Spartan garrison from their city.[84] To counter the inevitable Spartan wrath, the Athenians sought

[76] But see Greenwalt 2007—Amyntas III at pp. 91–93.

[77] Diodorus 15.19.3, interpreted as a personal force by Hammond and Griffith 1979, p. 177 n. 3; Hammond 1992a, p. 86; cf. Borza 1990, p. 185 n. 16; Zahrnt 2006b, p. 132.

[78] Xenophon, *Hellenica* 5.2.40–3.3.1–6; Diodorus 15.21. On the chronology of the Olynthian War, see Stylianou 1998, pp. 209–211; cf. Zahrnt 1971, pp. 96–98; Psoma 2001, p. 229.

[79] Xenophon, *Hellenica* 5.3.8–9.

[80] Xenophon, *Hellenica* 5.3.18–19 (Agesipolis); 5.3.26 (fall of Olynthus.

[81] Xenophon, *Hellenica* 5.3.26; Diodorus 15.23.3, with Zahrnt 1971, pp. 91–97; Hammond and Griffith 1979, pp. 173 and 178; Borza 1990, p. 186.

[82] Zahrnt 2006b, pp. 132–134.

[83] See Hamilton, C.D. 1986.

[84] Diodorus 15.25–27, with Stylianou 1998, pp. 230–243.

allies, and in 378/7 formed their Second Athenian League, which grew into a fourth-century empire and boasted the most powerful fleet in the Aegean.[85] Although anti-Spartan and ostensibly intended to protect the freedom of all Greek cities, the league aimed to re-establish Athenian power in the Aegean and recover Amphipolis. For the next several years the Athenians sent several commanders, including Timotheus, to regain Amphipolis, but ultimately to no avail.[86]

Macedonia did not join the Athenians' league.[87] Still, Amyntas read the writing on the wall: since Athens needed Macedonian timber and he, like his predecessors, needed income, he made sure a more than adequate supply was sent to the city between 377 and 373 for its fleet.[88] Thus we have a context for an alliance between Amyntas and Athens of 375 or 373, probably a trade deal for Athens to obtain timber and Amyntas money for military support.[89] The fragmentary inscription that we have of this treaty also features his eldest son, Alexander, as oath taker, whose reign as Alexander II we discuss in the next chapter.[90]

In 371 Sparta and its allies, cooperating with Athens and Persia, invited delegates from the Greek states to meet at Sparta to end their hostilities and renew the King's Peace.[91] Aeschines speaks of Amyntas sending an envoy "whose vote was absolutely under his control" in the proceedings.[92] That Macedonia was present at this Greek congress of states shows Amyntas was taken seriously by the end of the 370s.[93] Macedonia had come a long way from the days of Amyntas I.

Amyntas III apparently voted in favor of a Common Peace, which was what the Great King of Persia had urged, and in which alliance each member state swore an individual oath to the others, among other things to have the same friends and enemies and not to make war on one another.

[85] Diodorus 15.28.2–4, with Stylianou 1998, pp. 249–259. On the confederacy, see Cargill 1981. Its charter: Rhodes-Osborne, no. 22.

[86] Heskel 1997b, pp. 22–52.

[87] Cargill 1981, pp. 85–86.

[88] Athenian reliance in fifth and fourth centuries: Cawkwell 1984; Hamilton, C.D. 1986. On the costs of fleets, see Ruffing 2017, pp. 130–131.

[89] *IG* ii^2 102 = Tod, no. 129 = *SIG*^{3} no. 143 = Harding, no. 43; cf. Xenophon, *Hellenica* 6.1.11, with Cargill 1981, pp. 85–87, on dating (as late as 370–369); cf. Hammond and Griffith 1979, p. 178 (pp. 172–180 in general); Borza 1990, pp. 187; Zahrnt 2006b, p. 136 (noting also that there is no need to connect the alliance to either date but it could be Amyntas reframing his foreign policy in case of renewed Spartan or Athenian aggression on his coastline, though this is doubtful, as Zahrnt admits at pp. 136–138).

[90] Alexander (restored): lines 20–21.

[91] Xenophon, *Hellenica* 6.3; Diodorus 15.38.

[92] Aeschines 2.32.

[93] Zahrnt 2006b, p. 134: "vollwertiges Mitglied der griechischen Staatenwelt" ("a full member of the Greek world").

More surprising, according to the Athenian orator Aeschines, Amyntas "joined the other Greeks in voting to help Athens to recover possession of Amphipolis," despite its proximity to his borders and the threat Athenian possession of it posed to his economic and security interests.[94] Perhaps Amyntas acted to remain close to the Athenians, though his power had not shrunk to where he needed their protection. He did send timber to the house of the Athenian general Timotheus in the Piraeus in about 370, but this was a private agreement rather than a courtship of the city.[95] More likely is that Aeschines was lying to support Athens' claim to Amphipolis in Philip II's time: his speech was delivered in 343 and from 357 to 346 the Athenians had waged war on the king over the city (chapter 9). No other source speaks of Amyntas backing Athens over Amphipolis, and the peace sworn at the congress simply recognized the autonomy of Greek cities.[96]

The demise of Spartan power, the liberation of Thebes, the rise of the Second Athenian League, and Macedonia's alliance with Athens perhaps all influenced Amyntas to turn to protecting his southern border with Thessaly, where internal problems had long been growing. In 404 Pherae, under its tyrant Lycophron, went to war against Larissa, a conflict that was still ongoing in 395 when Larissa received help from a coalition of southern Greeks.[97] In the meantime, Lycophron had been succeeded by Jason, who had expelled the Aleuadae from Thessaly and was intent on establishing the supremacy of Pherae over the entire state.[98]

Despite the Macedonian kings' close ties with the Aleuadae up to now, Amyntas made a treaty with Jason, who was by then *tagos*, a leader of sorts, of all Thessaly.[99] This was probably in 371 after the battle of Leuctra (about 12 kms southwest of Thebes), at which a Theban army of 6,000 troops under the generals Epaminondas and Pelopidas defeated the Spartans,

[94] Aeschines 2.32, with Hammond and Griffith 1979, p. 179; cf. Cargill 1981, pp. 166–167; Hatzopoulos 1985, p. 249; Greenwalt 1988, p. 38; Heskel 1996, p. 39 (pp. 38–52 on the subsequent Athenian effort to regain Amphipolis); Zahrnt 2006b, pp. 133–134; Zahrnt 2007, pp. 242–245; Müller 2016, p. 212.

[95] [Demosthenes] 49.26; see Borza 1987, p. 40; Borza 1990, p. 187.

[96] Xenophon, *Hellenica* 6.3.18–20; cf. Diodorus 15.38.2 (from Ephorus), with Borza 1990, pp. 187–188; Lane Fox 2011d, p. 230. Aeschines accepted by Hammond and Griffith 1979, p. 179; Hammond 1992a, p. 87. See too Jehne 1992.

[97] Sprawski 1999, pp. 24–48.

[98] Jason's life and career: Westlake 1993, pp. 67–125; especially Sprawski 1999.

[99] Diodorus 15.60.2—the only source for this alliance, but Isocrates 5.20 and Arrian 7.9.4 may allude to it: Stylianou 1998, p. 418. After Leuctra: Stylianou 1998, pp. 418–419. See too Westlake 1993, pp. 86–87; Sprawski 1999, pp. 98–99; Zahrnt 2006b, p. 139; Zahrnt 2007, pp. 249–250; cf. Rosenberg 1916, pp. 506–507. On the term *tagos*: Sprawski 1999, pp. 15–17; cf. Robertson 1976, pp. 104–107.

replacing the Spartan hegemony (404–371) with that of the Theban hegemony (371–362).[100] As *tagos* Jason had supreme command of an army of 28,000, which could overcome any neighboring state refusing to pay tribute. It is likely that Jason was an ally of Athens, though he was not content to accept its naval supremacy; hence Amyntas' alliance with Jason meshed with the king's contacts with Athens.[101]

Jason's Thessaly was more powerful than Amyntas' kingdom, and arguably had an edge over Athens since it was not as dependent on imported grain.[102] Amyntas would have recognized Jason's usefulness for his southern border security and even as a possible revenue generator, as Jason was evidently planning a navy, for which he needed Macedonian timber.[103] Possibly Jason agreed to cede northern Perrhaebia to the king in return for timber—and to pry the king away from his Aleuad allies—but the Macedonian-Thessalian alliance ended abruptly in 370 when Jason was assassinated.

Amyntas was also busy elsewhere. A Roman inscription of AD 101, dating from the reign of the emperor Trajan and found in Doliche in northern Perrhaebia, relates to a border dispute between Elimea and Doliche.[104] The final lines refer to a similar arbitration decision between the same two places several centuries earlier by Amyntas. The latter's ruling does not show he had authority over each area, but he was clearly reputable enough to be accepted by both sides, and may even have regained Elimea, though presumably Derdas would have opposed this.[105]

Finally, two later sources refer to an "Amynteion" at Pydna, which indicates that Amyntas received divine honors while alive—if true, he would be the first known Macedonian king to do so.[106] But these two later sources have been queried, and in any case the building in question was only in Pydna, perhaps because of a close relationship between it and the monarchy. Hence divine honors were not bestowed on Amyntas throughout the kingdom.[107]

[100] Leuctra: Xenophon, *Hellenica* 4.4.9–15; Diodorus 15.53–56, with Buckler 1980, pp. 59–66; Stylianou 1998, pp. 386–707. Theban hegemony: Buckler 1980.

[101] Jason as an ally of Athens: Cargill 1981, pp. 83–85.

[102] Sprawski 1999, p. 77; Sprawski 2004.

[103] Xenophon, *Hellenica* 6.1.11.

[104] Wace and Thompson 1910–1911; Rosenberg 1916; Helly 1975; Hammond and Griffith 1979, p. 178; Errington 1990, p. 34; Borza 1990, p. 187; Parker 2003, p. 130; Zahrnt 2006b, pp. 138–139; Lane Fox 2011d, pp. 230–231. For general interpretation, see Lucas 1997, pp. 101–108.

[105] Cf. Rosenberg 1916, pp. 503–507; Zahrnt 2006b, p. 139, on Elimea.

[106] Scholiast on Demosthenes 1.5; Aelius Aristeies, *Oration* 38, 715d Dindorf.

[107] Lane Fox 2011d, pp. 228–229.

Amyntas was said to have died in the same year as Jason of Pherae, which was 370, though 369/8 is more plausible for the king.[108] He was one of the few Argead kings to die of natural causes, as Isocrates claims he "died of old age."[109] This was no mean feat in that day and age, especially as he had faced wars against the Illyrians and Olynthians, expulsion from his kingdom twice, and an assassination attempt that may have involved his wife Eurydice that is better discussed in the following chapter.[110]

Evaluating Amyntas

The argument has been forcefully made that Diodorus unfairly gave Amyntas a bad press and that the spectacular successes of Philip II and Alexander the Great overshadowed his accomplishments, which in turn enabled Philip II to do what he did.[111] We cannot dispute Amyntas' energy, resilience, and courage, against the odds, especially when it came to dealing with powerful neighbors like the Chalcidians and Illyrians. And in economic matters his coinage was an improvement on that of his predecessors.[112] His silver staters showing a mounted hunter clasping a spear atop a rearing horse, and on the reverse a lion continued an iconographic tradition going back to Alexander I depicting the king as hunter and protector.[113] He also stressed Argead legitimacy from Heracles by striking a silver stater with a bearded Heracles wearing a lion skin on the obverse and with a standing horse on the reverse. But as his reign progressed, he had to reduce the weight of his silver coinage, perhaps because he urgently needed revenue to deal with external threats from the Illyrians and the Chalcidian League.

We know next to nothing about Amyntas' measures outside military and economic affairs—he certainly did not have a cultural policy on anything like the scale of Archelaus. He hired Aristotle's father Nicomachus as the

[108] The Parian Marble gives the date of his death in the archonship of Phrasikleides (371/0): *BNJ* 239 A 72; but we should follow Diodorus 15.60.3, who puts it in his account of the year 370/69: March 1995, p. 263. See too Hammond and Griffith 1979, pp. 179 and 249; Stylianou 1998, pp. 32–37.

[109] Isocrates 6.46; echoed in Justin 7.4.8; cf. Diodorus 15.60.3.

[110] His resilience and kingship are seen as miraculous by Hammond and Griffith 1979, p. 180; Borza 1990, p. 188; cf. Zahrnt 2006b, pp. 128–129.

[111] Zahrnt 2006b, especially pp. 127–128 and 140–141; especially Zahrnt 2007; cf. Müller 2016, pp. 200–216, but see the reservations (while acknowledging Amyntas' achievements) of Lane Fox 2011d, pp. 227–234.

[112] Greenwalt 1994b, pp. 120–124; Greenwalt 1988, pp. 39–41; cf. Lane Fox 2011d, p. 228. See too Heinrichs 2012.

[113] Greenwalt 1997, pp. 126–127; see too Greenwalt 1993.

royal doctor at court, just as Amyntas' son Philip II would hire Aristotle to tutor his son and heir, Alexander III (the Great).[114] There is a belief that Amyntas, not Archelaus, made Pella the official royal residence, though there is no hard evidence for this in his time, and both Pella and Aegae were important, relatively large, and prosperous, as archaeological evidence, especially from graves, shows.[115]

Amyntas had a busy reign with its share of successes, but, nevertheless, he protected Macedonia—and his own position—only when he had a strong enough ally like Sparta or Athens supporting him, and his rift with Sparta in the 370s exposed his weakness.[116] His largely defensive strategy left Macedonia vulnerable, especially in its relations with the Greeks, and by the end of his reign he faced problems from marauding Illyrians again. His son and heir, Alexander II, thus did not inherit a stable and secure kingdom.

Macedonia under the Argead Kings: The Rise and Fall of an Ancient Superpower. Ian Worthington, Oxford University Press. © Oxford University Press 2026. DOI: 10.1093/9780197668009.003.0008

[114] Nicomachus: Diogenes Laertius 5.1.

[115] Hatzopoulos 1987, pp. 42–45; cf. Lane Fox 2011d, pp. 229–230. On Aegae, see in particular Kottaridi 2011b; Kottaridi 2020, all citing her extensive work, and on Pella, see Akamatis 2011.

[116] Hamilton, C.D. 1986, pp. 239–245.

8

A Kingdom in Decline: Alexander II to Perdiccas III

Amyntas III fathered at least seven children from two wives: Archelaus, Arrhidaeus, and Menelaus by Gygaea, and Alexander, Perdiccas, Philip, and Eurynoe (his only daughter, it seems), by Eurydice.[1] Of these, it was the three sons by Eurydice who succeeded their father, first Alexander II, then Perdiccas III, and finally, by force of circumstance, Philip II. From Amyntas III's death to Philip II's accession in 359, Macedonia experienced a series of upheavals and varying fortunes thanks to the Illyrians, Thracians, Chalcidians, Spartans, and Athenians.[2] In addition, the end of the Spartan hegemony in 371 and era of the Theban hegemony (371–362) brought about changes in relations between Macedonia and Thebes, as we shall see.[3]

In this chapter I continue following the chronology of Lane Fox for the three kings prior to Philip II:[4]

Alexander II: 369/8
Ptolemy as regent: 368/7–365/4
Perdiccas III: 365/4–360/59

Alexander II

As the eldest son of Amyntas, Alexander II came to the throne in probably 369 and ruled until 368 (figure 8.1).[5] He was in his early twenties if he was born after his father became king in 393 and of age to have been co-oath taker in Macedonia's alliance with Athens in the middle to later 370s, as

[1] Justin 7.4.5. [2] Cf. Consolo Langher 2007 (mostly Philip II).
[3] Hatzopoulos 1985.
[4] Lane Fox 2011d, pp. 210–213—only slightly different in Hammond and Griffith 1979, p. 168; March 1995 (see his chart on p. 280).
[5] Diodorus 15.60.3; cf. Justin 7.4.8, with Stylianou 1998, pp. 35–36; Lane Fox 2011d, p. 211.

Figure 8.1 Alexander II from bronze coin
Source: Wikimedia Commons.

noted in the previous chapter.[6] Alexander became king uncontested, a fairly rare occurrence in more recent Argead history, perhaps because Amyntas had given him prominent roles to help stave off opposition from his many sons.[7]

Alexander faced several threats during his short reign, not to mention economic woes, as shown by his minting of only bronze coins and no silver ones.[8] On coming to power he stopped an Illyrian invasion, perhaps brewing since the end of his father's time, by resorting to bribery.[9] He was said to have handed over his younger brother Philip to the Illyrians, perhaps on this occasion, and presumably as a hostage.[10] We should be skeptical of this account, as Philip was surrendered to the Thebans less than a year later, as we see below, leaving little time for him to return from Illyria and be sent off again—or for the Illyrians to hand him over to Thebes for that matter—and

[6] *IG* ii^2 102 = Harding, no. 43, with Cargill 1981, pp. 85–87, on dating (as late as 370–369).

[7] Hammond and Griffith 1979, p. 181, for the view that he was elected by the Assembly; contra Borza 1990, p. 189.

[8] Reign: Cloché 1960, pp. 121–125; Hammond and Griffith 1979, pp. 172–184; Wirth 1985a; Roisman 2010, pp. 161–162; Lane Fox 2011b, 257–260; cf. pp. 210–213; Müller 2016, pp. 216–229; Greenwalt 2017; Carney 2019, pp. 33–37. Economy: Hammond and Griffith 1979, p. 192; Greenwalt 1994b, pp. 124–125.

[9] Justin 7.5.1. Müller 2016, p. 217, suggests the payment was to deter an invasion rather than to buy off one that was happening.

[10] Diodorus 16.2.2; Justin 7.5.1, accepted by Hammond and Griffith 1979, p. 181; March 1995, p. 270; Lane Fox 2011b, p. 257, Müller 2016, p. 218; Greenwalt 2017, p. 88; contra the skepticism of Borza 1990, p. 189 n. 28; cf. Müller 2016, pp. 217–218.

when speaking of Philip's time in Thebes, no ancient writer mentions anything about a previous hostage period.

Alexander had scarcely dealt with the Illyrians when a pretender named Pausanias challenged him. The chronology of events is controversial, and Pausanias' attempt to seize the throne may even have occurred in the reign of the next ruler, Ptolemy, which we discuss below.[11] But it makes more sense to place Pausanias' attempt within the context of a new king settling onto the throne and the chaos of an Illyrian incursion. Apparently backed by a Greek force, Pausanias took control of territory southeast of Anthemus, Therma (close to Thessaloniki), and Strepsa, all near the eastern Thermaic Gulf, as well as "certain other places when the Macedonians were not united but most of them favored Pausanias."[12] These were probably the same places the Olynthians had taken 15 years earlier.

We do not know who Pausanias was. He may have been another son of Archelaus or the son of the Pausanias who was king in 394–393 before his murder at the hands of Amyntas III, as we saw in the previous chapter.[13] More likely he was Archelaus' grandson, who had been living in exile in the Chalcidice after Amyntas III expelled him from Macedonia.[14] By now the Olynthians were starting to recover from their earlier defeat at the hands of the Spartans, and after the latter's loss of hegemony in 371, they had rebuilt the Chalcidian League. Hence, they may have offered Pausanias refuge, thinking that he would be a useful ally against Athenian expansion in the north, which was increasing by the end of Amyntas' reign.[15]

Pausanias was a serious contender for the throne, even minting his own coinage and connecting himself to the dynasty with the device of the walking horse used by Archelaus and his descendants.[16] Fortunately for Alexander, the Athenians had recently sent the general Iphicrates north in an attempt to recover Amphipolis.[17] Amyntas' widow Eurydice, who seems

[11] I follow the chronology of Lane Fox 2011b, pp. 257–258, with his emendation of the Aeschines passage. Hammond and Griffith 1979, p. 184, for Pausanias' attempt during the regency of Ptolemy over the young Perdiccas III.

[12] Aeschines 2.27.

[13] Hammond and Griffth 1979, p. 184, suppose him to be a son of Archelaus, against which see Goukowsky 1991, pp. 59–60; Müller 2010 (a companion), p. 167; Lane Fox 2011b, p. 258.

[14] *Suda*, s.v. "Karanos"; cf. Aeschines 2.27, who merely says he was an exile at the time, with Hammond and Griffith 1979, pp. 176 and 184; Hatzopoulos 1985, pp. 248 and 250–251; Borza 1990, p. 193 (putting Pausanias in the reign of Ptolemy).

[15] Zahrnt 1971, pp, 97–104 and 124–127; see too Hatzopoulos 1985, p. 251 with n. 44; Psoma 2011, p. 125.

[16] Miller, M.C.J. 1968, pp. 23–25; doubted by Borza 1990, p. 194 n. 44.

[17] Aeschines 2.28, with Heskel 1997b, pp. 42–43.

to have gained influence at court after her husband's death, summoned Iphicrates to meet her, presumably at Pella, and by reminding him that Amyntas had adopted him as his son secured his help.[18] Iphicrates expelled Pausanias and his men from the kingdom to Kalindoia (Kalamoton).[19] It thus appears Eurydice was responsible for saving the throne. Perhaps Alexander was still in the west and preoccupied with the Illyrians, leaving his eastern flank vulnerable, which by extension helps place Pausanias' attempt early in his reign.[20]

At any rate, with threats to his kingship now over, Alexander turned to affairs further afield. In the late summer of 369, following on from his father's attempt to shore up his southern border, he involved himself in Thessalian affairs.[21] There the Aleuadae of Larissa sought his help to win control of the Thessalian League.[22] The king was agreeable, although his army was perhaps not up to a prolonged campaign, especially as Pherae was now controlled by Jason's successor, Alexander (not to be confused with the Macedonian king), who prepared to invade Macedonia. King Alexander, however, moved too quickly for him. He seized Larissa and Crannon, with supporters of the Aleuadae in both cities welcoming him as a liberator, but instead of handing over the cities to the Thessalians, as he had earlier promised, he installed garrisons in them.[23]

The Aleuadae had no desire to see the tyranny of Alexander of Pherae replaced by that of Alexander II, so they appealed to the Thebans for help.[24] The latter—still hegemons of Greece—were opposed to Athenian expansion in the north and welcomed the opportunity to intervene in Macedonian affairs.[25] Their general Pelopidas was sent north in the spring of 368, where he and his army easily took Larissa from Macedonia's control, though no alliance was made with Alexander of Pherae.[26] Then Pelopidas' attention

[18] Aeschines 2.28, with Greenwalt 1988, pp. 41–43. The actual location of Eurydice at the time is unknown: Carney 2019, p. 66.

[19] Aeschines 2.27–29; Nepos, *Iphicrates* 3.2; cf. Hatzopoulos 1985, pp. 249–251; Greenwalt 1988, p. 42; Mortensen 1992, pp. 157–159; Heskel 1997b, pp. 22–28 and 41–43; King 2018, p. 62; Müller 2016, pp. 210–211; Carney 2019, pp. 64–67.

[20] Cf. Lane Fox 2011b, p. 258. In the west: Greenwalt 2017, p. 88.

[21] Buckler 1980, pp. 112–113; Hatzopoulos 1985, pp. 251–253; Stylianou 1998, pp. 449–450; Lane Fox 2011b, pp. 258–259; Müller 2016, pp. 219–221; Greenwalt 2017.

[22] Diodorus 15.61.3–5; cf. 15.67.3, with Westlake 1993, pp. 129–131; Graninger 2010, p. 312. League: Sordi 1958; Westlake 1993.

[23] Diodorus 15.61.5; cf. 15.67.3, with Müller 2016, p. 220.

[24] Plutarch, *Pelopidas* 26.1.

[25] Buckler 1980, p. 114.

[26] Diodorus 15.67.4; Plutarch, *Pelopidas* 26.2, with Westlake 1993, pp. 131–134; cf. Hatzopoulos 1985, p. 252; Müller 2016, pp. 221–222.

was diverted to Macedonia, where the king was suddenly faced by a new challenger to the throne, Ptolemy; in response, Alexander II asked Pelopidas to arbitrate between them.[27]

Who was this Ptolemy? Presumably this was Ptolemy of Alorus, who was probably one of Amyntas III's three ambassadors to the Athenians named in the treaty struck with Athens in the middle to later 370s.[28] If so, he would have held a trusted place at court. But Diodorus calls him "son of Amyntas," which is highly doubtful as he is not named along with the six sons of Amyntas.[29] Indeed, Diodorus indicates that Amyntas III had only three sons (Alexander, Perdiccas, and Philip), and Justin does not name him either.[30] The addition "of Alorus" surely refers to that town, now Kypseli-Neochori, about 20 miles northeast of Aegae; hence he came from there.[31] If so, he was not an Argead but a trusted nobleman, who may have been the husband of Amyntas' daughter Eurynoe and so brother-in-law to Alexander by a marriage arranged by Eurydice.[32] Since we do not hear of any challenges by the sons of Gygaea, Ptolemy may have thrown his weight behind Alexander II in a fashion similar to Philip's II's generals supporting Alexander III when Philip was murdered in 336.[33]

Alexander and Ptolemy were clearly disputing the throne, but when Pelopidas decided in favor of Alexander, Ptolemy left the kingdom.[34] Why he left so meekly is unknown; it may be that Pelopidas threatened to do

[27] Plutarch, *Pelopidas* 26.3, with Buckler 1980, pp. 115–116; Lane Fox 2011b, p. 259.

[28] *IG* ii^2 102 = Tod, no. 129 = *SIG*^{3} no. 143 = Harding, no. 43, and see previous chapter.

[29] Diodorus 15.71.1. Hammond and Griffith 1979, p. 182, make him a son of Amyntas the Little, hence Amyntas II, and Ogden 1999, p. 14, a son of Amyntas III, but there are no grounds for either: Borza 1990, p. 190; Lane Fox 2011d, pp. 231–233; see further Anson 2009, pp. 282–283; Müller 2016, pp. 224–229. Goukwsky 1991, pp. 44–45, makes him an otherwise unknown brother of Gygaea, but there is no evidence for that either. Stylianou 1998, pp. 465–466, suggests that he could have been a younger brother of Amyntas and uncle of the three princes. Site of Alorus: Hatzopoulos 1987, pp. 36–39.

[30] Diodorus 15.60.3; Justin 7.4.5 (the six sons named above from two wives).

[31] Diodorus 16.2.4. But Stephanus of Byzantium, s.v. *Aloros*, claims that citizens of the city of Azorus were also called "of Alorus." Azorus was in Pelagonia (cf. Strabo 7.7.9); hence Diodorus could be mistaken in his attribution of Alorus, and Amyntas therefore married his daughter to a Pelagonian nobleman, perhaps as part of a strategic alliance.

[32] Greenwalt 2010, pp. 286–287; King 2018, p. 61. Eurynoe: Carney 2000, p. 40; cf. Carney 2019, p. 70 with n. 53. Ptolemy of Alorus is nowhere named as the husband of Eurynoe. But Diodorus 15.71.1, 77.5 identifies him as a brother of Alexander II (hence, also of Perdiccas III and Philip II), which most scholars take to mean "brother-in-law" (since he is not listed among the children of Amyntas). Hence, the assumption that this Ptolemy was married to Eurynoe: Carney 2000, pp. 39–40; Carney 2019, pp. 58–64

[33] Greenwalt 2010, p. 287.

[34] Plutarch, *Pelopidas* 26.4; cf. Diodorus 15.67.4, with Buckler 1980, pp. 113–114 and 117–119; Müller 2016, pp. 221–222; King 2018, p. 61; contra Hatzopoulos 1985, pp. 252–254; Stylianou 1998, p. 423.

away with him. On the other hand, he may have had a tacit agreement with Pelopidas to support his claim again or even to be made guardian of the underage Perdiccas (Amyntas' second son), who was next in line to the throne. Pelopidas now made a treaty with Alexander II, thus furthering Theban ambitions in Macedonia and weakening the king somewhat by forcing him to follow a pro-Theban foreign policy.[35] Among other things the Theban general demanded that he restore some exiles and surrender 30 noble sons, who included his younger brother Philip (the future Philip II) and who were all sent to Thebes as hostages.[36] The known departure of Philip for Thebes at this time precludes his being sent to the Illyrians in 369 during Alexander's first year of rule.

Alexander II did not last much longer. He was assassinated the following year (or possibly spring of 367), apparently at the instigation of the returned Ptolemy of Alorus and even with the connivance of Eurydice, while watching a war dance at a festival.[37] The martial setting of the dance provided a first-class opportunity for an assassin to get close enough to kill a king.[38] Demosthenes names a certain Apollophanes of Pydna as involved in the assassination.[39] Who this man was and whether Pydna, which was currently not part of Macedonia, was taking any lead in removing the king are unknown, and Demosthenes may well be mistaken or guilty of falsehood. A more important question is whether Ptolemy had a role in the assassination. He does not seem intent on becoming king, as he did not mint his own coins.[40] Nor does he seem concerned that Alexander's approach to the Illyrians differed from that of Amyntas III, as has been suggested, and so decided it was in the kingdom's better interests to remove Alexander.[41] After all, he did not embark on a radically new policy, and he surely would not have been appointed guardian of the young Perdiccas, as we discuss below, if he were suspected of murdering his predecessor.

[35] Cf. Müller 2016, pp. 221–222.

[36] Diodorus 15.67.4; Plutarch, *Pelopidas* 26.4; Justin 6.9.7, 7.5.2–3, with Lane Fox 2011b, p. 259. Philip was a hostage in Thebes between 369 and 367: Aymard 1954, especially pp. 23–26.

[37] Marsyas, *BNJ* 135–136 F 11 (= Athenaeus 14.629d); Diodorus 15.71.1; Plutarch, *Pelopidas* 27.2; Justin 7.5.4–5 (but at 7.4.8 Justin says Amyntas died of old age). Hammond and Griffith 1979, p. 181 with n. 2, believe the festival was the Xanthica held in the spring, hence accept a date of spring 367 for the assassination.

[38] Carney 2019, p. 35 with n. 13.

[39] Demosthenes 19.194–195.

[40] Hammond and Griffith 1979, p. 183; Anson 2009, p. 282; Lane Fox 2011b, p. 260; cf. Greenwalt 2017, p. 89

[41] Greenwalt 2010, pp. 287–288, on the Illyrian factor.

More likely is that Ptolemy was falsely implicated in assassination rumors by his association with Eurydice, who is much maligned in the sources.[42] Justin, for example, tells us that she and Ptolemy had a pact to kill Amyntas, marry each other, and make Ptolemy king, but Eurynoe foiled their plan.[43] Nonetheless, Eurydice was said to have married Ptolemy, who was still married to Eurynoe, unless she had died by then.[44] The images of Ptolemy as a scheming manipulator who married Eurydice in hopes of gaining the throne, given her influence at court, or of Eurydice as a ruthless adulteress and murderer are highly suspect—as has been adroitly put, the sources are "poppycock."[45] After all, Audata, one of Philip II's early wives, adopted the name "Eurydice" and would surely not have done so if it called to mind a namesake traitor.[46]

The marriage of Eurydice and Ptolemy is also suspect: did it, for example, take place after Amyntas III's death or Alexander's murder?[47] Ptolemy left the kingdom after the arbitration of Pelopidas, but he may have been among the exiles whose return Pelopidas ordered.[48] If so, a marriage may have taken place then. Yet why would Eurydice marry her husband's alleged assassin—unless to ensure the safety of her remaining sons, whose welfare was of concern to her and whose claim to the throne she championed over their stepbrothers?[49] Moreover, Justin claims that she also killed Perdiccas, whereas we know he died in battle against invading Illyrians (see the section on Perdiccas below).[50] Perhaps the origins of these stories lie in a smear campaign by Gygaea's sons, who may have had their eyes on the throne once Amyntas died, and who seem to have given Philip II cause for con-

[42] Carney 2019, pp. 54–58 and 68–70; cf. Roisman 2010, p. 163; Lane Fox 2011b, pp. 231 and 261–262. See also on the biased sources: Badian 1982b; Mortensen 1992, pp. 156–163; Howe 2018; Carney 2019, pp. 67–75; cf. Saatsoglou-Paliadeli 2000.

[43] Justin 7.4.7. On the episode, see Hammond and Griffith 1979, pp. 181–182; Badian 1982b, pp. 99–100; Borza 1990, pp. 192–193; Mortensen 1992; Carney 2019, pp. 54–55; cf. Lane Fox 2011b, pp. 261–262; Howe 2018, pp. 16–18.

[44] Carney 2019, pp. 60–64, on the marriage, arguing that it was a possibility; cf. Lane Fox 2011b, pp. 261–262.

[45] Hammond and Griffith 1979, pp. 182–183 (quotation on p. 183); Mortensen 1992, pp. 156–164; Carney 2000, pp. 42–44; Roisman 2010, p. 161; cf. Lane Fox 2011d, p. 231 (hostile sources having origins in the "scandalous" Theopompus). Ogden 1999, p. xix, argues marrying widowed queens was designed to establish a claim to the throne.

[46] Badian 1982b, pp. 104–105.

[47] Mortensen 1992, pp. 165–166; Stylianou 1998, pp. 456–457; Greenwalt 2010, p. 287.

[48] King 2018, p. 62.

[49] Mortensen 1992, especially pp. 165–167, on marrying Ptolemy and promoting her family; see too Hatzopoulos 1986, pp. 281–282; Roisman 2010, p. 162; Müller 2016, pp. 225–226; Greenwalt 2017, p. 88; Carney 2018, pp. 29–31; Carney 2019, p. 63.

[50] Justin 7.5.6–8.

cern. If they were slandering Eurydice at this time, it is tempting to connect her dedication to the goddess Eucleia ("fair repute") at Aegae to combat them.[51]

Alexander II's brief and turbulent reign was marred by several factors, not least his error in not executing his rivals. In addition, his involvement in Thessaly, though for the right reasons of border protection, backfired on him spectacularly, and his military could not cope with his involvement on several fronts.[52] In light of this, it is unlikely that he made improvements to his infantry. If so, then the Alexander who introduced the foot companions (*pezhetairoi*) was Alexander I (chapter 4).[53]

Ptolemy

There is nothing to suggest that Ptolemy himself wanted to rule. Indeed, the coins over the next three years bear Perdiccas' name, so Ptolemy can only have been regent to the young Perdiccas, as our sources state.[54] Still, he faced his fair share of troubles.[55] At some point friends of the deceased Alexander II appealed to Pelopidas for help against Ptolemy. Pelopidas was in Thessaly at the time, but he marched with a force of mercenaries to Macedonia, perhaps taking advantage of the uncertainty in the kingdom.[56] Ptolemy quickly bought off the mercenaries but was "afraid of the name and reputation of Pelopidas" and agreed to be regent for Perdiccas and made an alliance with Thebes.[57] He handed over 50 hostages including his own son Philoxenus (by

[51] [Plutarch], *Moralia* 14b–c, and see Greenwalt 1988, p. 42; Saatsoglou-Paliadeli 2000, p. 395. See too on the dedication: Mortensen 1992, pp. 163–165; Carney 2019, pp. 82–92; Lane Fox 2011b, p. 262. This context fits better than 368 to celebrate the safeguarding of the throne after the expulsion of Pausanias. Saatsoglou-Paliadeli 2011, p. 277, suggests the thank-offering was for her overcoming her illiteracy.

[52] Heskel 1997a, p. 175.

[53] Greenwalt 2017 argues that Alexander's measures transformed the Macedonian state but were overshadowed by the more transformative ones of Philip II, an extension of Greenwalt 2007 (pp. 92–93 on Alexander II). But he packs too much into Alexander's short reign, nor can Alexander's foreign policy be used to explain that he changed the status of these troops, certainly an *argumentum e silentio*.

[54] Aeschines 2.29; Diodorus 15.71.1, 15.77.5; Plutarch, *Pelopidas* 27.3; cf. *Marm. Par.*, *BNJ* 239 A74; see Hammond and Griffith 1979, pp. 183–184; Lane Fox 2011b, p. 260. Coinage: Hammond and Griffith 1979, p. 183; Anson 2009, p. 282; Lane Fox 2011b, p. 260; cf. Greenwalt 2017, p. 89. We can hardly agree with Borza 1990, p. 193, that the next three years belonged to the reign of Ptolemy *and* Eurydice.

[55] Ptolemy: Hammond and Griffith 1979, pp. 184–185; Hatzopoulos 1985, pp. 253–254; Roisman 2010, pp. 162–163; Lane Fox 2011b, pp. 260–262; cf. pp. 210–213.

[56] Plutarch, *Pelopidas* 27.3; see Borza 1990, p. 194; Lane Fox 2011b, pp. 260–261.

[57] Plutarch, *Pelopidas* 27.3.

Eurynoe?), who joined the earlier ones in Thebes.[58] That alliance presumably explains Ptolemy's snub of Athens by allying with Amphipolis in 366/5 and taking hostages from there, perhaps even in a bid to seize Amphipolis for himself, as they would give him leverage.[59] But shortly after his envoy Harpalus took charge of the hostages, Iphicrates caught up with him and seized them; they were eventually sold back to the Amphipolitans.[60]

Pelopidas' insistence on the surrender of Ptolemy's son might have been to prevent Ptolemy putting Perdiccas to death and then defying Theban interests in the north. But Ptolemy stayed loyal to the Thebans, supplying them with timber, as their general Epaminondas planned a fleet to challenge Athenian naval superiority.[61] Ptolemy's action may have led to the release of Philip from Thebes since hostages were no longer necessary to ensure good behavior.[62] However, we do not hear of any others being released, so Philip more plausibly returned home when Perdiccas III came to the throne in 365.

In the summer of 365 Ptolemy was assassinated either by Perdiccas himself, according to Diodorus, or as part of a plot orchestrated by Perdiccas.[63] Nothing is said of any involvement of Eurydice. Perhaps Perdiccas wanted to avenge his brother Alexander or had been simply biding his time till he came of age, for if he were born by 383, he would have been 18 in 365.[64]

Perdiccas III

Perdiccas III ruled for six years, from 365/4 to 359 (figure 8.2).[65] Like many of his predecessors he was an intellectual, who had ties with philosophers

[58] Plutarch, *Pelopidas* 27.3–4, with Hammond and Griffith 1979, p. 185; Errington 1990, p. 36; Graninger 2010, pp. 312–313. Lane Fox 2011d, pp. 232–233, says that if born to Eurynoe, Philoxenus would be very young (between two and eight years), so perhaps he was a son by a previous marriage.

[59] Hostages: Demosthenes 23.149; cf. Liddel, D64, pp. 277–280. See further Heskel 1997b, pp. 44–45; contra Buckler 1980, pp. 122–123, who suggests that it was loyalty to Thebes; cf. Hatzopoulos 1985, p. 254; King 2018, p. 63.

[60] Heskel 1997b, pp. 45–46.

[61] Hatzopoulos 1985, pp. 254–256; Lane Fox 2011b, pp. 262–263. This agreement is dated to the start of Perdiccas' reign by Hammond and Griffith 1979, pp. 185–188.

[62] Lane Fox 2011b, p. 263.

[63] Diodorus 15.77.5 under 365/4 Diodorus 16.2.4 under 360/59; cf. Scholiast to Aeschines 2.29 for a plot.

[64] Hammond and Griffith 1979, p. 185; cf. Borza 1990, pp. 194–195.

[65] Reign: Cloché 1960, pp. 125–129; Hammond and Griffith 1979, pp. 185–188 and 207–208; Borza 1990, pp. 195–197; Roisman 2010, pp. 163–164; Lane Fox 2011b, pp. 262–269; Müller 2016, pp. 229–235.

Figure 8.2 Perdiccas III from coin
Source: Wikimedia Commons.

in Athens including Plato, and he offered residency at Pella to Plato's student Euphraeus of Oreus (on Euboea).[66] The story goes that a haughty Euphraeus told Perdiccas' companions they could not dine with the king if they did not know geometry and philosophy—if true, Alexander I's work to hellenize his court had long come to fruition.[67]

Macedonia was still economically hard pressed, as shown by the poor state of its coinage.[68] Perdiccas did strike coins of good quality, but he could not do so on any great scale.[69] A turning point for the economy was the arrival of the Athenian Callistratus of Aphidna, the architect of the peace between Athens and Sparta of 371. Callistratus had been exiled in 361/0; he went to Pella and helped the king double the kingdom's revenue from its harbor dues to 40 talents annually.[70] Some of this was surely used to combat another Macedonian weakness, its army, for by the end of Perdiccas' reign he may have had as many as 10,000 troops, a substantial increase from the days of Amyntas III.[71]

[66] Hatzopoulos 1996, vol. 1, p. 178; Natoli 2004, pp. 23–32; Lane Fox 2011b, pp. 263–264; Müller 2016, pp. 230–232. Euphraeus may even have been sent to further Athenian interests at the Macedonian court: Dusanic 1980.

[67] Cf. Speusippus, *To Philip* 12; Plato, *Letter* 5, with Natoli 2004, pp. 31–35, believing the story. Importance of Greek education: Roisman 2010, p. 163.

[68] Hammond and Griffith 1979, p. 192; Greenwalt 1994b, p. 125; Heinrichs 2012.

[69] For one of his tetradrachms with a beardless Heracles, see Price 1974, plate X.52.

[70] [Aristotle], *Oeconomicus* 2.1350a 16–23, with Hammond and Griffith 1979, p. 187; Borza 1987, p. 41; Lane Fox 2011b, p. 266; Müller 2016, p. 232.

[71] Numbers: Hammond 1992a, p. 78; cf. Borza 1990, p. 196. Greenwalt 2007 argues they stem from policies of previous kings to boost hoplite numbers and spawn a new middle class.

Perdiccas' reign was too short to help Macedonia recover from the setbacks of the previous two rulers in foreign policy. He was a supporter of Thebes and probably supplied timber for Epaminondas' planned fleet, given that an inscription of the Boeotian League honors Athenaeus, son of Demonicus of Macedonia, for "services rendered"—presumably the transport of Macedonian timber.[72] In return the Thebans probably now released his brother Philip, aged 16 or 17, as a sign of good faith. When Philip returned home Perdiccas gave him "some territory," perhaps the strategically important region of Amphaxatis, where Philip was said to have kept a force of men that enabled him to take the throne when Perdiccas was killed in 359.[73]

Perdiccas' relationship with the Athenians was uneasy mostly because of his association with Thebes, though they may have thought he, like Ptolemy, had designs on Amphipolis. In 364 Iphicrates' replacement, Timotheus, son of Conon, commanded a fleet in the Thermaic Gulf to increase Athenian presence in the north. He seized various coastal town such as Pydna and Methone, which thus created a launching point for an offensive on Aegae.[74] In addition, the Athenians gained influence in parts of Upper Macedonia. A decree of 365/4, for example, records a king of the Pelagonians as a proxenus and benefactor of Athens, and another decree of 362 honors Menelaus the Pelagonian (probably a mercenary leader) for his services on Athens' side in warfare against the Chalcidian League and Amphipolis.[75]

In late 364 or early 363 the Athenians were able to impose terms on Perdiccas.[76] Among other things, he was required to help Timotheus against Olynthus and elsewhere in the north and supply the Athenian army with Macedonian cavalry—nothing is said of Macedonian infantry, which was still subpar compared to the cavalry. Timotheus' plan was to capture Olynthus first to block its Chalcidian support, which was also advantageous to Perdiccas as the Chalcidian League posed a threat to Macedonia.[77] In

[72] *SEG* 34 (1984), 355; Roesch 1984; cf. Lane-Fox 2011b, pp. 262–263 (but dating this to spring 365, when Ptolemy was still alive, to show Perdiccas' leaning to Thebes); Müller 2016, p. 232.

[73] Athenaeus 11.506e from Carystius.

[74] Demosthenes 2.14, 23.149–51; Dinarchus 1.14, 3.17 (Methone and Pydna); Diodorus 15.81.6; Isocrates 15.108, 113; Rhodes-Osborne, no. 38. See with Hatzopoulos 1985, p. 253 n. 66 and pp. 254–255; Errington 1990, p. 37; Müller 2016, p. 232. The chronology of Timotheus' Chalcidian campaigns is uncertain: See Heskel 1997b, pp. 31–35 and 49–50 (363–362); cf. Stylianou 1998, pp. 503–505 (chronographic notes).

[75] Hammond and Griffith 1979, p. 186, with references.

[76] Hatzopoulos 1985, pp. 254–256 Psoma 2001, pp. 235–236; Psoma 2011, p. 126. Heskel 1997b, p. 31, argues, however, for the second half of 365.

[77] Heskel 1997b, p. 47.

364/3 Timotheus seized Potidaea and Torone to cut Olynthus' communications lines with the Gulf of Torone and peninsula of Pallene, but, ultimately, he failed to take Amphipolis.[78]

Perhaps pressure from Thebes compelled Perdiccas to sever contacts with Athens in 363.[79] But Epaminondas' death at the battle of Mantinea in 362 brought with it the downfall of the Theban hegemony; the following year an Athenian army marched against Perdiccas to seek revenge. Its general Callisthenes arranged an armistice, but shortly after, he was executed in Athens; Perdiccas, without missing a beat, switched allegiance to the Chalcidian League.[80] He sent troops to help Amphipolis against Athens and installed a garrison there as protection.[81] Athenian influence in the region thus suffered a decline, and Amphipolis was still garrisoned when Philip II assumed the throne in 359.

The reality of the times and Perdiccas' policy toward the Athenians is shown by a newly discovered inscription in the city of Dikaia (Nea Kallikrateia), north of Potidaea and west of Olynthus, which refers to Perdiccas as "ruler" of nearby territory and arbitrator after civil strife.[82] The strife is unknown, but presumably it happened in the war between Athens and Olynthus in the second half of the 360s, and Dikaia may have divided into pro-Athenian and pro-Chalcidian factions. The inscription tells us Perdiccas had the right to execute anyone "rejecting oaths and pledges." Presumably the latter were supporters of Timotheus, so we can see why the king would accept the arbitration, given his relations with Athens.[83]

In the summer of 362/1 Potidaea requested more settlers from Athens, perhaps as security against Chalcidian attacks or even to block Perdiccas from wresting control of it from Athens.[84] The townspeople of Pydna and Methone, given their strategic locations, may also have been uneasy about Perdiccas making a move on them, and to highlight their friendship to Athens they issued coins with an owl on the reverse, calling to mind the famous Owls of Athens.[85] The fear was well placed, for in 362 Perdiccas began to reassert control of his coastline, and by the fall of 362 he had recovered Methone, though he failed at Pydna.[86]

[78] Isocrates 15.113; Diodorus 15.81.6.
[79] Hatzopoulos 1985, pp. 255–256.
[80] Cf. Aeschines 2.30, with Heskel 1997b, pp. 32–36.
[81] Diodorus 16.3.3, with Heskel 1997b, pp. 50–51; Lane Fox 2011b, p. 265.
[82] Voutiras and Sismanides 2007; cf. Lane Fox 2011b, pp. 265–266; Psoma 2011, p. 130.
[83] Lane Fox 2011b, p. 266.
[84] Tod 2, no. 146; *IG* ii/iii^2 114; cf. Psoma 2011, p. 130.
[85] Hammond and Griffith 1979, pp. 192 and 193 n. 1.
[86] Heskel 1997b, p. 52.

One aspect of Perdiccas' reign we can address here is a possible alliance with the Molossian king of Epirus, then facing threats from the Illyrians, which may have included Perdiccas' brother Philip's marriage to the young Epirote princess Olympias.[87] She and Philip were on the island of Samothrace for a religious ceremony in about 360, and it has been argued that the contract was arranged in secret in case of Illyrian reprisals against Macedonia.[88] The betrothal at this time, let alone the secrecy, seems far-fetched. Such a politically charged arrangement could surely not have been kept secret, and Philip married Olympias only in 357, so why was there this long wait? It is better to accept the common opinion that Philip met the young princess on Samothrace by chance and that in 357 he made an alliance with the king of Epirus that included marrying Olympias.

By 360 Perdiccas was faced with threats from the Illyrians under Bardylis.[89] The situation echoed the 390s, when Amyntas bought off a similar threat by paying them a tribute—perhaps that had become an ongoing payment that Perdiccas or even Alexander II had ended; hence Bardylis now wanted its return and booty. In addition, Macedonia's western flank was still unsecured, and its westerly neighbors the Molossians of Epirus had their hands full protecting their lands against the Illyrians.[90] In the east the Chalcidian League remained a constant concern for Macedonia, as was Thrace. The following year everything came to a head when, to protect his borders, Perdiccas decided to engage the menacing Illyrians first.

In spring 359, he marched out against Bardylis and his men, but in what must have been a major battle he and 4,000 troops were killed.[91] His untimely end plunged Macedonia into chaos, with Diodorus exaggeratedly claiming that it was now "a slave to the Illyrians."[92] To make matters worse, the Paeonians massed to invade from the north, and a hostile Athens supported a pretender to the throne, Argaeus, probably the same man who had ruled for two years in Amyntas III's reign (chapter 7).[93] Finally, another pretender presented himself, Pausanias, likely the same man who had

[87] At the time she may have been named Polyxena and changed her name to Olympias when they later married: Heckel 1981a.

[88] Greenwalt 2008, especially pp. 85 and 91–97; Carney 2000, p. 63.

[89] Hammond and Griffith 1979, p. 188.

[90] Hammond 1967, pp. 528–529; Hammond and Griffith 1979, p. 185.

[91] Diodorus 16.2.4–5; Polyaenus 4.10.1. Justin 7.5.6–8 wrongly says he was murdered by Eurydice. See Hatzopoulos 1982a for the death in 360.

[92] Diodorus 16.1.3.

[93] Diodorus 16.2.5–6. Argaeus: Heskel 1996.

challenged Ptolemy of Alorus.[94] Pausanias was supported by Berisades, the king of western Thrace, for when Thrace's king, Cotys, had been assassinated in 360, the Athenians weakened that kingdom by encouraging his three sons to rule different parts of it.[95]

Perdiccas' short reign had seen conflict with both Athens and Thebes and a failure to protect the kingdom from the interference of both those powers. In addition, the Illyrians had returned to the sorts of plundering raids that had characterized their dealings with previous kings, but this time killing the monarch in battle. To make matters worse, Perdiccas' son, Amyntas, was not old enough to succeed in his own right.[96] Macedonia's fall at the end of Archelaus' reign seemed inconsequential to the security crisis it now faced. Against this ominous background Philip II assumed the throne and turned Macedonia into a superpower in the Greek world. In the process, as Diodorus rightly claims, he "made himself the greatest of the kings in Europe in his time."[97]

Macedonia under the Argead Kings: The Rise and Fall of an Ancient Superpower. Ian Worthington, Oxford University Press. © Oxford University Press 2026. DOI: 10.1093/9780197668009.003.0009

[94] Theopompus, *BNJ* 115 F 29 with the commentary of Morison 2008 ad loc.; Diodorus 16.2.6, and see too Borza 1990, pp. 178–179.

[95] Lane Fox 2011e, pp. 336–337, accepts Cotys was still alive and was the backer.

[96] Justin 7.5.8 (an infant—*parvulus*).

[97] Diodorus 16.95.1–2.

9

Philip II and the Remaking of Macedonia

The heyday of Macedonia, as we saw in the first chapter, came with Philip II, whose reign was the most transformative for his kingdom until Alexander the Great established a Macedonian Empire. We have more ancient evidence for Philip's life and reign than his predecessors, but, frustratingly, it too has its limitations.[1] Aside from a limited number of inscriptions and numismatic evidence, our main literary sources, Diodorus and Justin, wrote centuries after the events in question—Diodorus in the first century BC and Justin anywhere from the second to fourth centuries AD. Justin's work was not original, as it was an epitome of a lost first century BC work by Gnaeus Pompeius Trogus. To these we can add other writers, such as the biographer Plutarch of the first to second century AD, whose life of Alexander contains some information on Philip. These accounts are also tainted as they drew on much earlier works, especially the fourth-century Theopompus of Chios, who wrote a *Philippica* (*History of Philip*) in 58 books in which he was highly critical of the king.[2] We also have important contemporary speeches by several Athenian orators, principally Demosthenes and Aeschines, though their veracity is also called into question as they present a slanted view of the king and his aims.[3]

Philip has been the subject of several books; this chapter and the following one can treat only the more important aspects of his reign to show his innovations, his debt to previous kings like Alexander I and Archelaus, his impact on Macedonia, and the legacy he left to his son Alexander.[4]

[1] For a discussion of the ancient sources, including epigraphic and numismatic, see Worthington 2014a, pp. 311–319; Müller 2016, pp. 74–84; especially Baynham 2003 and Zambrini 2007, all citing further bibliography, to which add Worthington 2022b.

[2] See, for example, Shrimpton 1977; Flower 1994; cf. Müller 2016, pp. 50–52. On later traditions hostile to Philip, see too Asirvatham 2008; Asirvatham 2010b. Theopompus was criticized even in antiquity: see Speusippus, *Letter to Philip* 12, with Natoli 2004, ad loc.

[3] Buckler 2000.

[4] Philip's reign: Momigliano 1934; Wüst 1938; Cloché 1955; Cloché 1960, pp. 132–246; Ellis 1976; Cawkwell 1978a; Hammond, and Griffith 1979, pp. 203–698; Tsimboukides 1985; Wirth 1985b; Hammond 1992a, pp. 100–119 and 137–187; Hammond 1994; Worthington 2008a; Squillace 2009; Gabriel 2010; Müller 2010; Worthington 2014a (comparing and contrasting him to Alexander); Müller 2016, pp. 236–276; King 2018, pp. 70–106; Anson 2020; see too Cook 2005; Anson 2008b; Lane Fox 2011e; Lane Fox 2011f.

Philip's accession

Philip was born in either 383 or 382 and was the youngest of the three sons of Amyntas III and Eurydice (figure 9.1).[5] His two brothers, Alexander II (369–368) and Perdiccas III (368–359), were both kings who met with untimely ends, as we saw in previous chapters. Between 369 and 367 Philip had been a hostage in Thebes as part of an arrangement between Alexander II and the Theban general Pelopidas to stave off challenges from Ptolemy.[6] While there, he stayed in the house of either the general Epaminondas or the politician Pammenes, and among other things had watched the daily training of the crack infantry corps known as the Sacred Band. He was also said to have learned from Epaminondas about shock tactics and how to combine infantry and cavalry.[7] Equally important, his time in Thebes showed him that even a small state could dominate Greek affairs if it had a powerful enough military and proper leadership—and from 371 to 362 Greece had been under the Theban hegemony.

When he returned home in Perdiccas III's reign, Philip was supposedly given territory—perhaps strategic Amphaxitis—and troops, perhaps because

Figure 9.1 Silver tetradrachm of Philip II
Source: Wikimedia Commons.

[5] Birth and youth: Worthington 2008a, pp. 14–17.

[6] Diodorus 16.2.2 and Justin 7.5.3; Plutarch, *Pelopidas* 26.5; Aymard 1954, pp. 15–36; Hatzopoulos 1996, vol. 1, p. 178; Worthington 2008a, pp. 17–19.

[7] Diodorus 15.67; Justin 6.9.7, 7.5.2; cf. Plutarch, *Pelopidas* 26.5. Hammond 1997b; cf. Hammond and Griffith 1979, p. 425.

of what he had learned about military matters in Thebes.[8] Probably during that governorship Perdiccas arranged for Philip to marry Phila, daughter of Derdas II of Elimea.[9]

Since Perdiccas III's son Amyntas was not old enough to succeed in his own right when his father was killed, it fell to the Assembly to appoint a regent. Justin claims that Amyntas' uncle Philip "was guardian for the minor rather than king himself" for some time, and the third-century biographer Satyrus says that Philip reigned for 22 years.[10] Since Philip died in 336, some scholars argue that he was regent for two years and king from 357.[11] But Diodorus states that he was made king on Perdiccas' death, which we should accept.[12] Among other things, the dire situation facing the kingdom then was unprecedented, and our trust in Justin's accuracy is affected by claiming that Perdiccas was assassinated and that Philip was challenged by his three stepbrothers (the sons of Gygaea).[13] More importantly, we have no coins with Amyntas' name on them but only that of Philip.[14]

A date of middle to late 360 is possible for Philip's accession based on an inscription from the village of Oleveni (three miles south of Monastir).[15] Also, Diodorus has Philip reigning for 24 years, and Justin for 25 years.[16] However, the figure in Justin is normally read as an ordinal; hence Philip's reign ended in its 25th year and the Oleveni inscription might not refer to Philip II but Philip V (221–179). The common opinion is that Philip became king in 359. The heir Amyntas, incidentally, remained at court and never seems to have challenged his uncle.

Philip's first year

In comparison with its Balkan neighbors, Macedonia was weak in the 360s, and in 359 it was in crisis.[17] It was disunited; there was no centralization

[8] Athenaeus 11.506e, and see Worthington 2008a, pp. 19–20. Lane Fox 2011e, p. 336, suggests Amphipolis as a possibility.

[9] Athenaeus 13.557c (from Satyrus). Phila: Carney 2000, pp. 59–60.

[10] Justin 7.5.9–10; Satyrus in Athenaeus 13.557b, with Tronson 1984, pp. 120–121.

[11] Hatzopoulos 1982a, p. 42; Pafford 2011; Hatzopoulos 2020, pp. 135–137.

[12] Diodorus 16.1.3. [13] Justin 7.4.5, 8.3.10.

[14] Hammond and Griffith 1979, pp. 208–210; Worthington 2008a, pp. 20–22.

[15] Lines 11–16: See Hatzopoulos 1982a; Hatzopoulos 1995; cf. Lane Fox 2011e, pp. 335–336.

[16] Diodorus 16.1.3, 2.1, 95.1, 17.1.1; Justin 9.8.1.

[17] See Hammond in Hammond and Griffith 1979, pp. 189–200; cf. Lane Fox 2011e, pp. 335–339.

of the capital at Pella; its economy had suffered recently; it was prone to incursions by various tribes on its borders as well as interference in its domestic politics by cities such as Athens and Thebes; its king and 4,000 troops had just been killed in battle against plundering Illyrians led by Bardylis—the same one who had been plaguing Macedonia since the days of Amyntas III; the Paeonians were massing to invade; and two separate pretenders, one backed by Athens and the other by Berisades of Thrace, were vying for the throne.

Philip, however, "was not panic-stricken by the magnitude of the expected perils, but, bringing together the Macedonians in a series of assemblies and exhorting them with eloquent speeches to be men, he built up their morale."[18] Speed and decisiveness were of the essence to combat the multiple threats.[19] He first made an alliance with Bardylis, which may have included paying them a tribute and marrying his granddaughter Audata (from his second marriage), and then bribed the Paeonians and Berisades to abandon their plans.[20]

The Athenians were more of a problem as they had already landed Argaeus the pretender—perhaps the same man who had taken the throne during Amytas III's reign—with 3,000 troops at Methone to march on Aegae.[21] Bribery would not work with them, but there was one thing they had been craving for decades: Amphipolis. Philip cunningly removed the Macedonian garrison there to make it seem that the Athenians were finally going to get the city back.[22] As he anticipated, the Athenians withdrew support for Argaeus, who still set off for Aegae with some followers but was ambushed by the king and no doubt put to death.[23] To maintain good relations with the Athenians, Philip now concluded a peace with them.[24]

Philip saved Macedonia in a few weeks, but his actions were meant simply to buy him time. He had no intention of honoring any of the deals he

[18] Diodorus 16.3.1.

[19] Worthington 2008a, pp. 23–25; Lane Fox 2011e, pp. 337–345; Worthington 2014a, pp. 29–30; Müller 2016, pp. 237–239; cf. Ellis 1970.

[20] Illyrians: Justin 9.8.1; Athenaeus 13.557c; see further Carney 2000, pp. 57–58. Bribery: Diodorus 16.3.4–5; Justin 7.6.1–4.

[21] On Argaeus, see Heskel 1996; Lane Fox 2011e, pp. 337–338.

[22] Diodorus 16.3.3–4. He may also have done so because he needed troops to use against Argaeus: Lane Fox 2011e, p. 338.

[23] Diodorus 16.3.5.

[24] Cf. Heskel 1996, pp. 50–51. Philip was supposed to have promised Amphipolis to Athens in return for Pydna as part of a "secret agreement," so Demosthenes 2.6–7, but this is surely a falsehood to make the king duplicitous: de Ste. Croix 1963; cf. Worthington 2008a, p. 41.

made but to protect his borders as never before. For that he needed a better army, and he now turned to military matters.

Philip's military reforms

The Macedonian army was not strong and had suffered a devastating blow at Bardylis' hands. Regardless of whether Alexander I and Archelaus had introduced some military reforms, Philip went much further, perhaps influenced by his time in Thebes.[25] Indeed, his military reforms continued throughout his reign, creating a formidable army that also became the backbone of the state.[26]

Most revolutionary was the change from the Greek hoplite style of fighting, where the infantry of both sides fought each other in close combat while the cavalry bore down on the enemy flanks.[27] Instead, Philip trained his cavalry to attack first, arranging them in squadrons (*ilai*) of about 200 men, followed by the infantry, a shock-and-awe tactic that demoralized and trapped an enemy between two offensive lines.

Although Philip made some reforms to his cavalry, perhaps creating the fast, mounted scouts (*prodromoi*) that Alexander relied on so heavily in Asia, he was mostly concerned with his infantry. Until now the bulk of infantrymen appear to have been poorly trained farmers drafted into service as needed. Philip abolished this form of conscription so that farmers were able to remain working their lands and hence benefit themselves and the economy. In their place he recruited full-time soldiers, who underwent arduous training.[28] For example, they went on forced marches of 300 stades (roughly 30 miles) from plains to high mountain passes, carrying all their

[25] Aymard 1954; Hammond 1997b; cf. Hatzopoulos 1996, vol. 1, p. 178; Worthington 2014a, pp. 27–29. Howe 2017 argues that Philip was also influenced by Illyrian military practices stemming from his time as a hostage of the Illyrians, but it is unlikely he spent time in Illyria, as discussed in chapter 8.

[26] Philip's military reforms: Hammond and Griffith 1979, pp. 405–449; Hammond 1992a, pp. 100–106; Lloyd 1996; Lonsdale 2007, pp. 37–42; Worthington 2008a, pp. 26–32; Gabriel 2010, pp. 62–92; Sekunda 2010, pp. 449–452; Worthington 2014a, pp. 30–38; King 2018, pp. 107–114; Ferguson and Worthington 2024, pp. 57–71; cf. Lane Fox 2011f, pp. 374–377. Army and state: Errington 1990, pp. 229–249; Hatzopoulos 1996, vol. 1, pp. 443–460; cf. Errington 1978.

[27] On Greek warfare, see, for example: Hanson 1989; Van Wees 2000; Van Wees 2004; Rawlings 2007; cf. Lonsdale 2007, pp. 22–44.

[28] Karunanithy 2013, pp. 19–39 and 174–175 (marching with weapons); cf. Hatzopoulos 1996, vol. 1, pp. 451–452. Demosthenes 18.157 says Philip ordered his troops to carry 40 days' worth of food, so these training exercises may have lasted that long.

equipment and rations and learning to forage, so were self-sufficient.[29] The infantrymen, or phalangites, were organized into a phalanx line of varying depths from eight to 32 men composed of different units, often with specific functions.[30] They were supported by lighter-armed troops or peltasts, who were to stop enemy cavalry and infantry attacking the phalanx's flanks or rear.

Philip had noted that the regular Greek hoplite was encumbered by a panoply of a bronze cuirass, greaves, a bronze helmet with narrow visor (allowing only limited vision), and a round, heavy shield (*hoplon*). He therefore gave his heavy infantry lighter armor of a cuirass, greaves, a small shield carried over one shoulder, a short sword, and a lightweight, iron, open-faced helmet.[31] Likewise he introduced new arms and armor for the heavy cavalrymen of a metal helmet, cuirass, greaves, a round shield, spear, and sword, while the light cavalrymen had lighter armor as they usually threw javelins or fired arrows before fighting at closer quarters.[32]

The most fearsome new infantry weapon was the sarissa. This was a pike some 18 feet long and weighing probably 14 pounds, which at one end had a razor-sharp blade and at the other a sharpened spike.[33] Its length and weight meant that both hands were required to wield it; hence the shield was carried on the shoulder. As the phalangites approached an enemy line, the first three ranks lowered their weapons to charge, while those in the fourth and fifth lines started to lower their sarissas, and the remaining men kept theirs upright until needed and as protection against missiles (figure 9.2).[34] Because the sarissa projected well in front of each soldier, enemy troops could not reach the Macedonians before they were impaled on the blade.

There was, however, a major weakness to the phalanx: it needed space and level ground to operate effectively, and Greece was not known for large flat battlefields free of ditches, ravines, depressions, ridges, and riverbeds.

[29] Polyaenus 4.2.10. That self-sufficiency extended to logistical and supply personnel, including surveyors, road builders, doctors, siege craft builders, and repairers of arms and armor: Karunanithy 2013, pp. 164–170 and 209–223. See further, Taylor 2020; cf. Anson 1985b.

[30] Organization: English 2009a, pp. 10–16 and 110–120; Sekunda 2010, pp. 456–458; cf. Bosworth 1988, pp. 266–271.

[31] On infantry equipment, see English 2009a, pp. 16–25; cf. Hatzopoulos 2001, pp. 61–66 and 80–84; Karunanithy 2013, pp. 100–115; Sekunda 2013, pp. 78–87.

[32] Hammond and Walbank 1988, p. 541 with n. 1, citing references for the functions of the light cavalry; see further Hatzopoulos 2001, pp. 32–54; Sekunda 2013, pp. 67–77.

[33] Polybius 18.29.1–5. On the sarissa, see Sekunda 2001, and especially Noguera Borel 1999; Anson 2010; cf. Hammond 1980b.

[34] Cf. Polybius 18.29.2–30.4.

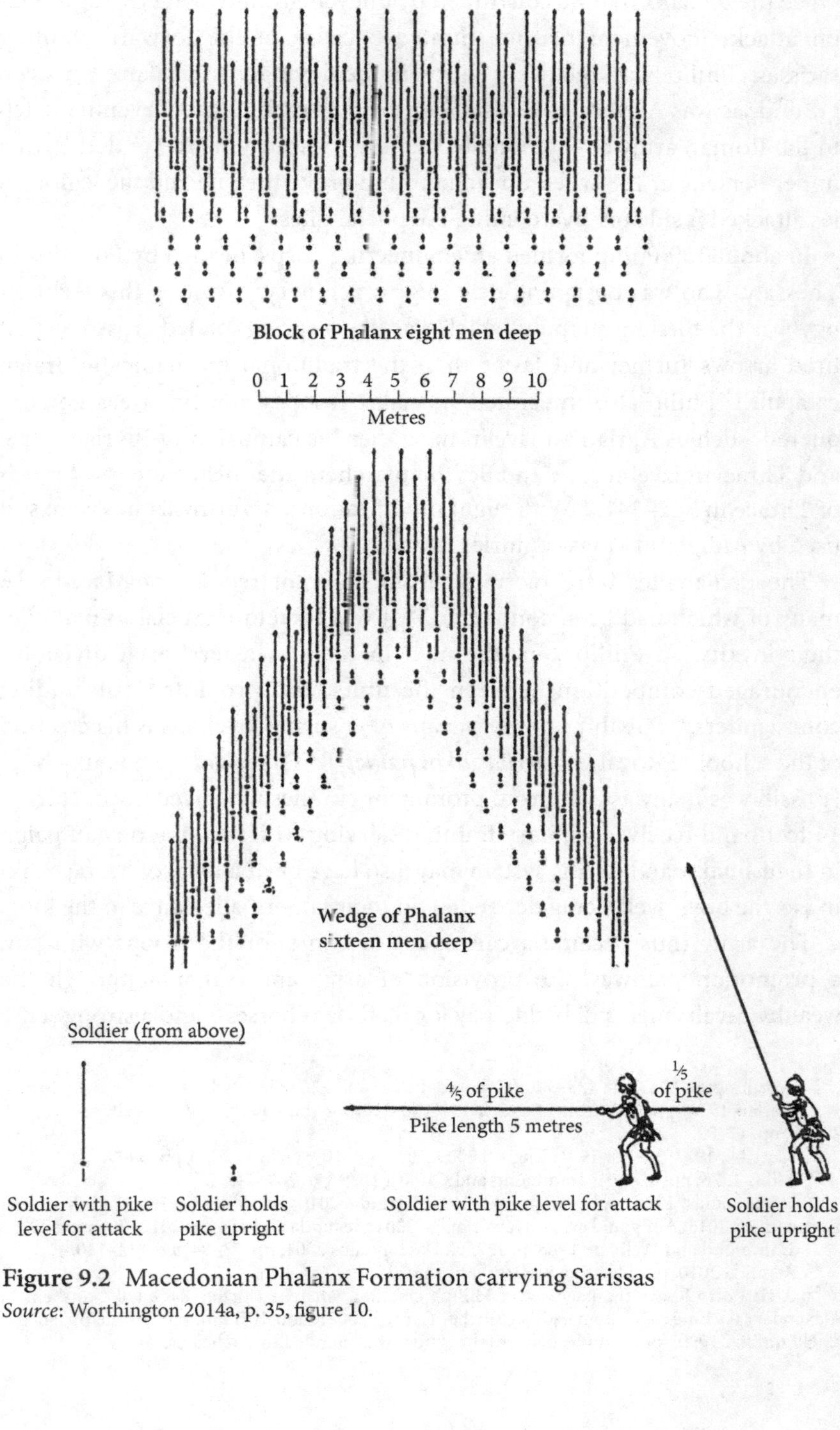

Figure 9.2 Macedonian Phalanx Formation carrying Sarissas
Source: Worthington 2014a, p. 35, figure 10.

Once the phalanx line was disrupted by uneven ground or there was a side-on attack, movement became limited because of the forward-pointing sarissas. Philip was relatively lucky in deploying his phalanx on even ground, as was Alexander in Asia, but the fearsome phalanx eventually fell to the Roman army at Cynoscephalae under Philip V in 179 and at Pydna under Perseus in 168 when uneven ground broke the line and the legionaries attacked it side on, overcoming the phalangites.[35]

In about 350 Philip formed an engineering corps, headed by Polyidus of Thessaly, who was designing new siege machinery.[36] Among this technology was the torsion catapult, which was like a spring-loaded crossbow that fired arrows further and faster than the traditional mechanically drawn catapult.[37] Philip also integrated specialist troops from the areas he conquered, such as Agrianian javelin men after his campaign in Illyria in 358, and Thracian javelin men and Scythian archers after his conquest of much of Thrace in 342–341.[38] With slight modifications, his army tactics were still used by Antigonid kings centuries later.[39]

The phalangites were recruited from different regions of Macedonia, many of which had been conquered.[40] It was therefore crucial to maintain their loyalty, so Philip kept the men in their own territorial divisions, encouraged competition between the units, and promoted outstanding commanders.[41] Possibly another means of ensuring loyalty was his creation of the school of Royal Pages (*basilikoi paides*).[42] The pages were young boys (possibly as many as 200) from prominent families who lived at court from 14 to 18 and received military training, serving with the king on campaign in their final year. But this system may also have been a form of hostage taking as the boys' well-being depended on their fathers' allegiance to the king.

The army thus became a career and a home for the troops with pay, a promotion pathway, the provision of arms and armor—although the wealthy cavalrymen still had to pay for their own horses—and a strong sense

[35] Worthington 2023, pp. 133–140 (Cynoscephalae) and 226–231 (Pydna).

[36] Garlan 1974, pp. 202–244; Marsden 1977, p. 212, for the date. On siege craft, see English 2009b, pp. 17–32.

[37] Marsden 1977; Keyser 1994; English 2009a, pp. 100–109; Gabriel 2010, pp. 88–92.

[38] Milns 1976, pp. 97–101; Hammond and Griffith 1979, pp. 709–713.

[39] Hatzopoulos 1996, vol. 1, pp. 443–460; Sekunda 2010; cf. Milns 1976; English 2009a; Karunanithy 2013. Antigonid army: Hatzopoulos 2001; Sekunda and Dennis 2012; Sekunda 2013.

[40] Hammond and Walbank 1988, p. 477; cf. Hatzopoulos 2001, pp. 73–84 and 133–140.

[41] Sekunda 2010, p. 454, citing bibliography in n. 28.

[42] Arrian 4.13.1 says the pages were Philip's creation, whereas Curtius 8.6.2 talks of them in Alexander III's time as "customary." See further Carney 2008; though Hammond 1992a, pp. 56–57; cf. Hammond 1990, for example, believes the school was founded by Archelaus.

of esprit de corps.[43] In return, Philip expected obedience and loyalty: soldiers who lacked discipline or were derelict in their duty were flogged or even executed.[44] The end result was an army that was without equal in the ancient world until the Roman era, while Philip proved to be a superb general and leader.[45] Not that Philip resorted to fighting at all costs, for he always placed more stock in his diplomatic skills.[46]

Expansion in Greece

In the following year, 358, Philip ended the threats from the Paeonians and Illyrians.[47] He led 10,000 infantry and 500 cavalry—presumably this early on in his reign he had hired some mercenaries to boost his numbers—against the Paeonians and defeated them. Possibly he reduced Paeonia to some type of vassal, giving him a buffer zone between Macedonia and the farther tribes of the Danube, and used Paeonian troops in his army.[48]

He then turned to the Illyrians, defeating them in a hard-fought battle at Lake Lychnitis (Ochrid), in which 7,000 were killed before Bardylis surrendered.[49] Among the terms Philip imposed on him were that the Illyrians had to leave various Upper Macedonian cities so that the native peoples as far north as Lake Lychnitis, including those of Orestis, were subject to the king.[50] Philip's victory also secured his northwest border, and for the first time in its history united Upper and Lower Macedonia, centralizing Pella as capital.[51] Although Upper Macedonia gave him trouble throughout his reign, for the present his northern and northwestern frontiers were secure.[52]

[43] On promotion, see Karunanithy 2013, pp. 154–157. A hypaspist, or "shield bearer," perhaps introduced toward the end of Philip's reign and akin to special forces, was paid one drachma a day, which was more than a Greek hoplite soldier, who was paid five obols daily (a drachma was six obols) and a cavalryman three drachmas. Pay rates are better documented under Alexander: Sekunda 2010, pp. 465–466.

[44] Aelian, *Varia Historia* 14.48.

[45] For Philip as general and his military accomplishments: Ashley 1998, pp. 111–162; Griffith 1980; and especially Gabriel 2010.

[46] On which, see Ryder 1994.

[47] Diodorus 16.4.2–7, 8.1, with Worthington 2008a, pp. 33–35; Worthington 2014a, pp. 38–39; Müller 2016, pp. 241–242.

[48] Merker 1965, pp. 43–44.

[49] Worthington 2008a, pp. 33–35; Worthington 2014a, pp. 38–39. Battle against Bardylis: Hammond 1989a; Gabriel 2010, pp. 105–109.

[50] Diodorus 16.8.1. [51] See Ellis 1980.

[52] Bosworth 1971a but see now Heckel 2017 (drawing implications mostly from Alexander's reign). Frontier: Dell 1970; Hammond 1981.

This was the start of an expansion of the kingdom and stimulation of its economy that built on what Alexander I, Archelaus, and even Amyntas III had done, though Philip's policies were far more ambitious and wide-sweeping.[53]

In the same year the king made an alliance with the Aleuadae of Larissa, who, in echoes of their relations with previous kings, had appealed to him for help against Pherae. Thessaly of course was a vital buffer state between Macedonia and Greece, and Philip attached special importance to it throughout his reign.[54] The Larissans had earlier blocked Jason of Pherae's attempts to overcome them, but Jason's sons had taken over from their father. Although Amyntas III had made an alliance with Jason, Philip responded favorably to the Aleuadae, seeing the means to shore up his southern border and obtain Thessaly's horses for his cavalry.[55]

Part of the alliance was his marriage to a Larissan lady named Philinna (his third wife), who bore him a son, Arrhidaeus, the following year.[56] Philip may even have been made a citizen of Larissa after the marriage so that their children would be legal citizens of Larissa.[57] In all, Philip married seven times without ever divorcing a wife, taking polygamy to a new level. The only source naming all seven wives is a fragment of Satyrus, which is quoted in an even later writer Athenaeus of the second century AD.[58] There is some confusion on the order of his first three wives, but it is generally accepted that Phila, Audata, and Philinna were in that order.

Then in 357 came an alliance with Epirus on his southwest border that included his most famous marriage, to Olympias, niece of the Molossian king Arybbas, so his fourth wife.[59] But 357 was the year that Athens declared war on him over Amphipolis. Athens' hegemony over its naval league gave it the strongest fleet in the Aegean and substantial military manpower, so

[53] Succinct summary by Lane Fox 2011f, pp. 367–385; cf. Ruffing 2017, pp. 132–133.

[54] Westlake 1993, pp. 160–216; Sprawski 2005; Sprawski 2003, pp. 61–64; Badian 1999, pp. 109–122; cf. Graninger 2010.

[55] Griffith 1970, pp. 67–80; Ehrhardt 1967.

[56] Athenaeus 13.557c, though Justin 9.8.2, 13.2.11 calls her a whore; cf. Plutarch, *Alexander* 77.1, but see Hammond and Griffith 1979, p. 225; Carney 2000, pp. 61–62.

[57] Badian 1999, p. 115.

[58] Athenaeus 13.557b–e; cf. 13.560c. See in detail on Satyrus' list, Tronson 1984; cf. Hammond and Griffith 1979, pp. 214–215 and 220–230; Carney 2000, pp. 51–81; Hatzopoulos 2020, pp. 138–142. The fragment is quoted in full and its context discussed at Worthington 2008a, pp. 172–174.

[59] Athenaeus 13.557c; Justin 7.6.10–12; cf. Diodorus 19.51.1, with Carney 2000, pp. 62–67 and 79–81 (Olympias in Philip's reign), and especially Carney 2006; Müller 2016, pp. 243–244; cf. see Carney 2003b. Carney (correctly) disputes that Philip changed her name to mask her Epirote status, against Heckel 1981a.

those factors, in tandem with the strategic location of Amphipolis, meant that Philip could never allow its return to the city. In addition, he had designs on the rich mines at Crenides, founded by the Thasians on the urging of the same Callistratus of Aphidna who had helped Perdiccas III in 361, and only 40 miles to Amphipolis' east. A delegation from Amphipolis appealed to Athens for help, but Philip neatly thwarted any relief force by sending a letter to the Athenians saying that he would give them the city once he took it.[60] They believed him, only to discover they had been duped when it fell to him in summer 357 and he held onto it; that left them no choice but to go to war.[61]

The Chalcidian League, with its army of 10,000 infantry and 1,000 cavalry, did not trouble Philip, enabling him to spend the next years ridding the coastline of Greek influence. The league was perhaps ambivalent because it was not on friendly terms with Athens after the latter founded a settlement at Potidaea, a little over a mile from Olynthus, in 361 and captured Torone on the tip of the middle prong of the peninsula. Philip first moved against Athens' ally Pydna, which soon fell to him.[62] The Athenians then sought an alliance with Olynthus and opened negotiations with Grabus of Illyria.[63] But Philip thwarted this threat by offering to take Potidaea from Athenian control and give it and Anthemus to the Olynthians. In response, they made a treaty with him in the winter of 357–356 and ended any contact with Athens.[64]

To neutralize any other threat from the Athenians, the king may have been behind a revolt of several of their allies known as the Social War, which ended in a rebel victory the following year.[65] In the meantime, Philip took Potidaea, giving it to Olynthus, and then seized Crenides and the mines there.[66] Renamed Philippi, it became a significant revenue source for him.[67] In the same year his chariot won victory at the Olympic Games, for

[60] [Demosthenes] 7.27; Demosthenes 23.116. On Amphipolis and Philip, see also Hammond and Griffith 1979, pp. 351–356.

[61] Aeschines 2.70, 3.54; Isocrates 5.2; Diodorus 16.8.2–3, with Worthington 2008a, pp. 40–42; Müller 2016, pp. 245–247; cf. Lane Fox 2011e, p. 346.

[62] Theopompus, *BNJ* 115 F 30a–b; Diodorus 16.8.3.

[63] See Rhodes-Osborne, no. 53; cf. Liddel, D83, pp. 330–332.

[64] Rhodes-Osborne, no. 50; cf. Diodorus 16.8.5, with Worthington 2008a, pp. 42–43.

[65] Cawkwell 1962a; Cargill 1981, pp. 178–185; Worthington 2008a, pp. 43–45; Worthington 2013, pp. 65–67; cf. Harding, no. 72; Liddel, D90, pp. 356–358.

[66] [Demosthenes] 50.46; Isocrates 8.24; cf. Diodorus 16.8.6–7, with Hammond and Griffith 1979, pp. 187–188.

[67] Hammond and Griffith 1979, pp. 70–72; cf. pp. 358–361; Worthington 2008a, pp. 45–46; Müller 2016, p. 249.

which he struck a series of tetradrachms showing the head of Zeus on the obverse and the Macedonian rider carrying the victory sign of a branch on the reverse. And to cap off an eventful year came the news that Olympias had given birth to a boy, Alexander.

As Philip was systematically taking control of his entire coastline, he suffered a personal setback at the siege of Methone—the last enclave of Greek influence—during the winter of 355–354 when he was shot in the eye by an arrow.[68] His doctor saved his life, but the king was blinded in that eye. Still, Philip maintained the siege, and Methone fell in the summer of 354.

By then clashes between Larissa and Pherae diverted his attention to his southern border. As he marched into Thessaly to assist Larissa, Lycophron of Pherae appealed for help to a new ally, the state of Phocis. Since 355, the latter had been at war with the Amphictyonic League, an ancient body of about two dozen states that administered and protected the oracle of Apollo at Delphi. The prelude to the war occurred a year earlier in 356, when the Phocians protested a fine, though tensions were also at play between league members Thebes and Sparta. When a Phocian army seized Delphi, the league declared a sacred war (the third such one) to liberate the oracle and punish the Phocians, and hostilities broke out in 355.[69]

In 353, Phocis agreed to help Pherae against Philip and dispatched an army, which he easily overcame. That prompted the Phocian general Onomarchus to march to Thessaly with 20,000 infantry and 500 cavalry. He lulled Philip into a crescent-shaped valley, where he had hidden infantry and stone-throwing catapults on the surrounding hillsides, and in a fierce attack routed the Macedonian army.[70] Surprisingly, Philip's men did not regroup but fled back to Macedonia, leaving the king no choice but to follow, though he vowed to return.[71]

Philip's defeat encouraged the Illyrians, Paeonians, and Arybbas of Epirus to reassert their independence, while Cersebleptes, king of eastern Thrace, and the Olynthians, despite their recent diplomatic ties to Macedonia, entered negotiations with the Athenians. Philp did not take his

[68] Demosthenes 18.67; Theopompus, *BNJ* 115 F 52; Diodorus 16.31.4, 35.5–6; Duris, *BNJ* 76 F 36 (javelin); Justin 7.6.13–1. Siege: Worthington 2008a, pp. 47–49; cf. Müller 2016, p. 250.

[69] Third Sacred War: Buckler 1989; cf. Worthington 2008a, pp. 53–57, 85–88, and 99–103; Worthington 2013, pp. 93–97 and 153–155. Previous sacred wars (in 595–586 and in the mid-fifth century): Parke and Boardman 1957; Davies 1994.

[70] Diodorus 16.35.2; Polyaenus 2.38.2, with Worthington 2008a, pp. 57–59; especially Gabriel 2010, pp. 127–132.

[71] Diodorus 16.35.2, and see Worthington 2014a, pp. 44–45.

surprise defeat lying down. The following year, 352, he marched an army of 20,000 infantry and 3,000 cavalry into Thessaly and got his revenge: in battle at the Crocus Field, near the coast of Magnesia, he defeated a Phocian army under Onomarchus, killing 6,000 of their number, including the general, and executing 3,000.[72]

Pherae now surrendered to Philip. The king allowed the tyrant rulers Lycophron and his brother Peitholaus, together with 2,000 mercenaries, to depart unharmed and married Nicesipolis of Pherae (his fifth marriage), later naming their daughter Thessalonice ("Thessalian Victory").[73] But Lycophron and Peitholaus joined the Phocian side, and the Pheraeans continued to resent him. Crucially for the king, though, was that Larissa, on behalf of the Thessalian League, elected him archon of Thessaly, which gave him access to Thessalian troops, income from the state's harbor and market taxes, and the means to be part of Thessaly's official deputation on the Amphicytonic Council.[74] The "barbarian" king now held a Greek office.

A new Greek initiative

Philip's predecessors had had dealings with various Greek states but remained largely out of Greece itself. Philip changed that. The reaction to his defeat in 353 may have brought a surprising realization that his power was still precarious. The sacred war endangered Thessalian stability, and hence his southern border, and afforded those states fighting against Phocis the possibility of rallying under Athens against him. He therefore resolved to steer Macedonia from its role in northern Greek matters into one in central and southern Greece.[75] And in doing so he needed to keep the army on campaign and winning to avoid any repeats of 353.[76]

After the battle of the Crocus Field Philip had executed 3,000 captives by drowning them and crucifying the corpse of Onomarchus, both

[72] Diodorus 16.35.3–6, with Worthington 2008a, pp. 62–64.

[73] Tyrants' flight: Diodorus 16.37.3, 39.4 (the Athenians offered them citizenship: Liddel, D110, pp. 417–419). Marriage: Athenaeus 13.557c; [Plutarch], *Moralia* 141b–c, with Carney 2000, pp. 60–61.

[74] Hammond and Griffith 1979, pp. 220–221; Worthington 2008a, pp. 64–66; Müller 2016, p. 254; see too Westlake 1993, pp. 196–216.

[75] Worthington 2008a, pp. 61–62; Worthington 2014a, pp. 49–50. See too Buckler 1996; cf. Lane Fox 2011e, pp. 350–357.

[76] See Worthington 2003a, pp. 94–96.

punishments meted out for temple robbery. Macedonia was not a member of the Amphictyonic League and had played no part in the Third Sacred War, but Philip's actions showed he was setting himself up as a defender of Apollo on behalf of all Greeks. That was why on his return to Thessaly in 352 his troops wore crowns of laurel—"as though the god were going before."[77] There are interesting affinities here with Alexander I, who had offered help, albeit nonmilitary, to the Greeks in the Persian Wars—except Philip's military might made his intention transparent. For the next several years the Third Sacred War largely centered on skirmishes between Phocian and Boeotian troops, but Philip's assistance was still welcomed.

The king followed his victory at Crocus Field by marching to Thermopylae, the strategic pass that allowed direct access from northern to central Greece. His arrival was too close for comfort for the Athenians, for he could march through Thermopylae and thence into Attica. Therefore, despite the city's financial strife, the statesman Eubulus sent 5,000 men and 400 cavalry to block the king at the pass.[78] Philip had the choice of forcing his way through or circumnavigating the pass, both of which would take time and leave him vulnerable to attack. In the end, he decided to reassert his influence over those who had shown their disloyalty the previous year, so he returned to Pella.

A blitzkrieg followed. First Philip dealt with Cersebleptes of Thrace, who was intriguing with the Athenians.[79] The latter always had to rely on imported grain to meet their needs, given that Attica could not produce enough to feed the population. Most of the grain came from the Black Sea region (now Ukraine and Crimea), so of paramount importance was the protection of the Chersonese, a vital area on the grain route, which influenced Athenian foreign policy.[80] Since the Chersonese was part of Cersebleptes' realm, the Athenians were careful to maintain a good relationship with him.

In tandem with Byzantium and Perinthus in Cersebleptes' kingdom, and Amadocus the king of central Thrace, Philip besieged Cersebleptes at Heraion Teichos ("Hera's Wall") on the coast of the Sea of Marmara during the winter of 352. Cersebleptes surrendered in 351, after which Philip

[77] Diodorus 16.35.5; cf. Justin 8.2.3–4.

[78] Diodorus 16.73.3, 38.1; Demosthenes 19.84, 319, with Worthington 2008a, pp. 66–68; Worthington 2013, pp. 108–109

[79] Worthington 2008a, pp. 68–69.

[80] See Harding 1995; Badian 1995.

visited the Olynthians to re-establish relations.[81] The Chalcidian League, however, did not remain loyal for long, hardly a surprise given its history with Macedonia.[82]

Fast campaigns against the Paeonians, Illyrians, and Arybbas of Epirus followed, though few details are known.[83] Philip did not expel Arybbas but took his 12-year-old nephew and heir to the throne Alexander (Olympias' younger brother, so Philip's brother-in-law) to Pella.[84] There is a story that Philip had a sexual affair with the boy. This is dubious and seems to be part of the hostile tradition of the "tyrant topos."[85]

By 351 Philip had restored control over all who had defied him in 353, not to mention securing all his borders and extending his influence in Thrace and central Greece.[86] In the same year the Athenian orator Demosthenes, Philip's most vocal opponent and Greece's foremost orator, delivered his *First Philippic* in the Assembly, the first of several speeches denouncing the king. He urged the Athenians to fight him before it was too late and muster a standing army in the city ready to deploy when necessary and send a strike force to operate in the north, neither of which the Athenian could afford, so his speech failed.[87] He also compared the king's breakneck speed in taking places and making policy with the slowness of the Assembly, an omen of things to come.[88]

From the fall of Olynthus to peace with Athens

The Olynthians' profession of friendship to Philip in 351 was hollow, as at some point they gave asylum to his two stepbrothers, Menelaus and Arrhidaeus, from their father's marriage to Gygaea—the third, Archelaus, was supposedly killed by Philip when he took the throne.[89] Archelaus must have been perceived as a threat; presumably so were the other two, especially if they had Olynthian support; hence Philip demanded their

[81] Cf. Demosthenes 1.12–13; Theopompus, *BNJ* 115 F 127, with Worthington 2008a, p. 69.
[82] Chalcidian League in time of Philip: Zahrnt 1971, pp. 104–111; Psoma 2011, pp. 132–134.
[83] Cf. Demosthenes 1.13; Isocrates 5.21, with Worthington 2008a, pp. 69–70.
[84] Errington 1975, pp. 41–50; Badian 1999, p. 116.
[85] Justin 8.6.4–7, with Müller 2016, p. 263, and see pp. 72–73; cf. Worthington 2008a, p. 70.
[86] Hammond 1992a, p. 198.
[87] Cf. Liddel, D108, pp. 409–413, and in detail Worthington 2008a, pp. 70–73; Worthington 2013, pp. 116–122. On Demosthenes, see Worthington 2013; cf. Worthington 2000.
[88] Demosthenes 1.12–13.
[89] Justin 7.6.3; cf. 8.3.10.

surrender.[90] The Olynthians refused, so he invaded the Chalcidice in the fall of 349, taking several towns and causing the people to turn to Athens for help.[91]

In response, Demosthenes delivered two speeches (called *Olynthiacs*) in support of the Olynthians, though he exaggerated the danger from Philip by claiming that if he were not stopped in the north he would march on Athens.[92] The first *Olynthiac* failed, but the second persuaded the Athenians to send Chares and 2,000 Thracian mercenaries to Olynthus. However, Philip was no longer there. He had marched to Thessaly after hearing the news that Pherae had welcomed back Peitholaus and was poised to revolt.[93] He overcame Pherae, spent the winter in Pella, and returned to the Chalcidice in March of 348 to besiege Olynthus.

Since Chares had returned home once he discovered Philip was on longer in the Chalcidice, the Athenians sent Charidemus (then based in the Chersonese) with 4,000 mercenary soldiers and 150 cavalry to Olynthus' aid.[94] But then Philip captured Olynthus' port of Mecyberna, only five miles from the city, and issued an ultimatum to the Olynthians: "either they should stop living in Olynthus or he should stop living in Macedonia."[95] This dangerous escalation led Demosthenes to deliver his third *Olynthiac*, successfully persuading the Athenians to dispatch Chares with 2,000 citizen infantry and 300 cavalry to Olynthus.[96] This force was delayed for some 40 days because of the northerly Etesian winds (the Meltemi), and when it arrived Olynthus had already fallen.[97]

It must have been a tough siege to judge by the sling bullets and bolt-heads with Philip's name (*Philippou*) on them that have been discovered.[98] Many of Olynthus' inhabitants were killed in the fighting along with Philip's stepbrothers, while some captives, including Athenian troops, were sent to Macedonia to work as slaves in the mines and fields.[99] Olynthus itself

[90] Ellis 1973; cf. Hammond and Griffith 1979, pp. 699–701.

[91] Campaign: Worthington 2008a, pp. 74–82; Gabriel 2010, pp. 150–157; Müller 2016, pp. 255–257, with Cawkwell 1962; Carter 1971; Zahrnt 1971, pp. 115–119.

[92] Ryder 2000, pp. 49–50, 54–57; Worthington 2013, pp. 132–141.

[93] Demosthenes 1.22, 2.11; cf. Diodorus 16.52.9. See too Badian 1999, pp. 117–120.

[94] Philochorus, *BNJ* 328 F 50; Diodorus 16.52.9.

[95] Demosthenes 9.11.

[96] Worthington 2013, pp. 139–141.

[97] The Athenians have been condemned for not doing more to help Olynthus and stop Philip, but that is unfair: Cawkwell 1962, pp. 130–140; Worthington 2008a, pp. 80–82.

[98] Marsden 1977, pp. 213–215. Demosthenes, unsurprisingly, claims that the city fell by treachery: Demosthenes 8.40, 19.265, 342, 18.48; cf. Diodorus 16.53.2, but see Ryder 1994, pp. 231–232.

[99] Philochorus, *BNJ* 328 FF 50–51 and 156; Diodorus 16.53.2–3, 55.1; Justin 8.3.11; cf. Demosthenes 9.26.

was razed to the ground and the Chalcidian League was dismantled once and for all, while Philip absorbed the Chalcidice into his rapidly growing kingdom.[100]

The Athenians braced for Philip's wrath, but to their surprise he sent them a letter of friendship claiming, remarkably, that he wanted to end the war over Amphipolis. Why he sought peace at this time is not known.[101] Possibly he had concerns about Athens and Thebes uniting against him, but more likely is that he did not want Thebes to regain its power in central Greece once the Third Sacred War came to an end.[102] In Athens Philocrates of Hagnus proposed that the people should hear his terms, but he was unsuccessful because of a sudden turn in the events of the sacred war. The final years of that war and the negotiations leading to peace between Athens and Philip in 346 are intertwined, as we shall now see.[103]

The sacred war, as mentioned above, had involved mainly Phocian and Theban clashes following Onomarchus' death at Crocus Field in 352 as the Athenians and the Spartans, who had their own problems, mostly remained aloof.[104] In the summer of 347 the Phocian army invaded Boeotia, forcing the struggling Thebans to appeal for help to Philip. He was apparently pleased they were in dire straits, thus supporting the view that he favored Athens above them.[105] But he did not want to make his attitude known; hence he sent only a token force under his general Parmenion; the annoyed Thebans turned to the Athenians and Spartans, offering them key towns around Thermopylae to block Philip from central Greece.

Philip maintained his diplomatic overtures to Athens, and in 346 on the motion of the same Philocrates the Athenians sent an embassy of 10 men

[100] In a speech delivered in 341, Demosthenes maintained that Philip destroyed all the cities of the Chalcidian League—"I don't say anything about Olynthus and Methone and Apollonia and 32 cities on the coast of Thrace [the Chalcidice], all of which he destroyed with such cruelty that a visitor would be hard pressed to say whether they had ever been lived in" (9.26). This is unlikely, as the region was of benefit to the Macedonian economy.

[101] Ellis 1976, pp. 101–103; Hammond and Griffith 1979, pp. 329–347; Ellis 1982a; Worthington 2008a, pp. 82–85.

[102] Cawkwell 1980; Ryder 1994, pp. 251–257; see too Worthington 2008a, pp. 84–85, 86, 88, 90, 95, 98–99, 100–101, 142.

[103] The principal contemporary sources for the peace negotiations and the end of the war are the two speeches *On the False Embassy*, which Demosthenes and Aeschines gave at Aeschines' trial in 343, and their speeches in the "Crown" trial of Demosthenes in 330. The information in them is often distorted because of their personal enmity and different attitudes to the peace: Buckler 2000, pp. 121–132 and 148–154; Worthington 2008a, pp. 89–90; cf. Müller 2016, pp. 257–262.

[104] Hamilton, C.D. 1982.

[105] Diodorus 16.58.3.

including Demosthenes to Pella to discuss peace with him.[106] After discussions on which states would be allies of the two parties, including Phocis, Amphipolis, and Thrace, it returned to Athens to report.[107] Shortly thereafter an embassy from Macedonia arrived in Athens to reconfirm the king's terms and receive the Athenians' oaths to the peace. Despite opposition during a debate in the Assembly, the Athenians swore their oaths to the Macedonian envoys and sent a second embassy of the same 10 men to Pella to receive the king's oath.[108]

Major delays now occurred as Philip had recently marched into Thrace against Cersebleptes, defeating him, and turning him into his vassal.[109] He did not return to Pella for two months, where the embassies from Sparta, Thebes, Thessaly, and—significantly—Phocis were patiently waiting for him. They wanted to find out what his plans were for the war and for Greece, especially the Peloponnese, where an ambitious Sparta was out to reduce Theban influence there.[110] Philip kept his cards close to his chest, but he underestimated Demosthenes, who backed him into a corner by arguing that the Athenian prisoners from Olynthus should be returned immediately to show the king's good intentions toward the city.[111] Philip needed to keep them as bargaining chips, so he could only promise to return them within a couple of months. Then he swore his oath, and the bilateral Peace of Philocrates ended the war between the two states—with the Athenians still unsuccessful in their attempt to reclaim Amphipolis.[112]

Philip next moved south, ostensibly to deal with the Phocians. Back in Athens the ambassadors on the second embassy reported to the Assembly, which decided to send a third embassy to Philip, extending the peace to his descendants. But at Chalcis on Euboea the embassy turned back to Athens at the shock news that the Phocians had turned their backs on Athens and

[106] Demosthenes 19.12–13; Aeschines 2.18; cf. Liddel, D 125, pp. 461–463, with Hammond and Griffith 1979, pp. 336–340; Harris 1995, pp. 55–62; Worthington 2008a, pp. 90–92; Worthington 2013, pp. 164–168; Müller 2016, pp. 257–259.

[107] Worthington 2008a, pp. 91–92, on the allies.

[108] Liddel, D130, pp. 477–487, with references; cf. Liddel, D133, pp. 492–496; see in detail Cawkwell 1960; Hammond and Griffith 1979, pp. 328–347; Harris 1995, pp. 63–77; Efstathiou 2004; Worthington 2008a, pp. 93–95; Worthington, 2013, pp. 168–170.

[109] Worthington 2008a, p. 92.

[110] Worthington 2008a, pp. 95–97; Worthington 2013, pp. 171–175.

[111] Worthington 2008a, pp. 88–89 and 97–98.

[112] Worthington 2008a, pp. 98–100; Worthington 2013, pp. 175–176. Peace: Cawkwell 1978b; Ellis 1982a; Sawada 1993.

Sparta and handed over Thermopylae to Philip, formally surrendering to him and not to the Amphictyonic Council.[113]

The Athenians sent a fourth and final embassy to Philip, which attended an Amphictyonic Council meeting to debate the Phocian punishment.[114] Some members wanted to throw the Phocian men from the top of the Phaedriades cliffs above Delphi for their sacrilegious seizure of the oracular site and temple robbery. Philip, however, insisted on moderation—which presumably explains why the Phocians surrendered, as they were "victims of necessity, [so] struck a bargain for their lives and capitulated."[115]

As thanks, Philip received the two Phocian votes on the Amphictyonic Council and was elected president of the Pythian Games at Delphi, which had not been held in the dozen years that the Phocians had occupied Delphi.[116] The king was now a force with which to be reckoned in central Greek affairs.[117] But the Peace of Philocrates was soon in trouble, thanks to Demosthenes, whose jingoistic rhetoric painted the king as a threat not only to Athens but also the whole of Greece.

The uneasy peace

Philip's peace settlement was supported by many smaller Greek cities, but Athens and Thebes were dissatisfied with it, with the Athenians even vowing not to send an official delegation to the Pythian Games.[118] Philip did not take this rebuff lying down. He sent them an embassy that included some Amphictyonic Council members, so they appeared to be snubbing the council. Demosthenes, reading the writing on the wall, delivered his *On the Peace*, arguing that attendance at the games was necessary to avoid a possible sacred war against the city, but alluding to warfare against Philip at some future point.[119] He now began to work toward an alliance with Thebes, showing once more that the staple of Greek interstate relations was the

[113] Demosthenes 19.61; Aeschines 2.130; Justin 8.6.1, with Worthington 2013, pp. 177–179.

[114] Aeschines 2.139, with Worthington 2008a, pp. 101–103.

[115] Justin 8.5.3. Among other things, Phocis lost its membership of the council; the Phocian state had to repay the money stolen from the treasuries and could not own horses and arms again until it had done so; and all towns in Phocis except Abae (which had condemned the seizure of Delphi) were razed and their populations relocated to new villages: Worthington 2008a, p. 102.

[116] Diodorus 16.59.4–60; Justin 8.5.4–6; cf. Speusippus, *Letter to Philip* 8, with Natoli 2004, pp. 139–140.

[117] Cf. Buckler 1996.

[118] Worthington 2008a, pp. 103–104.

[119] Demosthenes 5.13–14. Background and speech: Worthington 2013, pp. 183–186.

enemy of my enemy is my friend.[120] After the games Philip returned to Pella but stationed a garrison in Nicaea, to the east of Thermopylae, to control the pass. His move suggests an intention to return to Greece; hence the Peace of Philocrates was not an exit policy, as has been argued, but more of a lull until the king regrouped.[121]

In 345 Philip campaigned against Pleuratus of Illyria, during which he broke his right collarbone.[122] Undaunted, he founded a series of defensive military outposts along his northwest border with Illyria, at places such as Astraea, Dobera, Kellion, and Melitousa.[123] He settled people from different parts of his kingdom in these new towns, but if we believe Justin, they were clearly loathe to go, as they "looked wistfully now at the tombs of their forefathers, now at their ancient family deities, now at the houses in which they had been born and had themselves produced children, sorrowing at one moment for their own fate for having lived to see that day, and at the next for that of their children, for not having been born after it."[124] All this suffering may have been embellished, however, to portray the king in a bad light, as we find a similar description a century later when Philip V transplanted some of his subjects to the borders of Paeonia.[125]

Then in 344 Philip decided it was time to deal with Thessaly once and for all after a member of the Aleuadae named Simus struck his own coinage at Larissa. Simus' action was akin to declaring himself king, something Philip could not allow, especially as he was *tagos* of Thessaly. In a radical change of attitude, he expelled the Aleuadae and took over Thessaly. He set up garrisons in various cities and reintroduced the original four tetrarchies, or districts (Thessaliotis, Pelasgiotis, Hestiaiotis, and Phthiotis), appointing a governor over each one who answered only to Philip.[126] Unsurprisingly, Demosthenes accused Philip of enslaving the Thessalians, yet Isocrates said that he treated them fairly.[127] Since no one likes to be conquered and Isocrates was friendly with the king, even writing to him after the Peace of Philocrates urging him to unite the Greeks and invade Persia, we should favor Demosthenes' view.[128]

[120] Cawkwell 1963; Trevett 1999. [121] Ellis 1977; cf. Borza 1990, pp. 228–230.
[122] Worthington 2008a, pp. 108–109.
[123] Papazoglou 1988; Siganidou 1993. Border: Dell 1970; Bosworth 1971a.
[124] Justin 8.5.7–6.2; cf. Demosthenes 19.89, with Ellis 1969b; Worthington 2008a, pp. 109–110.
[125] Polybius 23.10.1–16; Livy 40.3.3–4. Rhetorical exaggeration: Hammond 1992a, p. 360.
[126] Worthington 2008a, pp. 110–111.
[127] Demosthenes 18.295; cf. 19.260, 6.22, 9.26; Isocrates, *Letter* 2.20.
[128] Isocrates' *To Philip* (5).

In the same year Philip sent an embassy to Athens headed by his friend Python of Byzantium requesting changes to the Peace of Philocrates. He stressed his friendship to the people but wanted to turn the bilateral peace into a Common Peace, which he had been against in 346.[129] His motive is unknown.[130] Perhaps it was because the Athenians had recently sent an embassy of support to the Peloponnese, where Philip was intent on expansion.[131] Possibly he was alarmed because of a Persian embassy in Athens soliciting help to recover a rebellious Egypt. There was always the danger that the Athenians could ally with the powerful Persians against Macedonia, and although the Persian request was denied, the Athenians emphasized their friendship to Persia.[132]

But Philip's plan to change the peace backfired when Demosthenes addressed the Assembly with his *Second Philippic*. In full fearmongering mode, Demosthenes warned the people that a change to the peace meant that their allies could make their own pacts with Philip and affect the hegemony of their league.[133] Demosthenes was supported by the equally hawkish Hegesippus, and accordingly the Athenians proposed that they and Philip would control their own possessions and any state excluded from the peace in 346 was to be independent but receive military support if ever attacked. Philip was never going to agree: the first stipulation allowed Athens to reassert its claim to Amphipolis, Pydna, Potidaea, and Methone, and the second prevented Philip expanding into the key areas of Thrace and the Chersonese, which had not been party to the peace.

Unsurprisingly, when Hegesippus took these amendments to Pella, Philip threw him out of his palace. Still, the Athenians were right to be suspicious of Philip: he had made the first move to change the peace and in a manner that would weaken them, and he had duped them before. It was a different Philip now from the one who had turned back from Thermopylae in 352; he had had a major policy shift toward the Greeks, as we discussed above, and seemed set on expanding his influence beyond anything his predecessors had envisaged.[134]

129 [Demosthenes] 7.21. Müller 2016, p. 262, places Python's embassy in the fall of 343.

130 Worthington 2008a, pp. 112–114; Lane Fox 2011e, pp. 355–356; Worthington 2013, pp. 191–194.

131 Demosthenes 18.295; cf. 19.260, 6.22, 9.26.

132 Cf. Buckler 1994.

133 Demosthenes 6.2.17–19, with Worthington 2008a, pp. 113–114. Speech: Worthington 2013, pp. 195–198.

134 Ellis 1976, pp. 86–87; Hammond and Griffith 1979, p. 280; Ryder 1994, p. 243; contra Buckler 1996, p. 83 and *passim*; cf. Buckler 1994.

A further break in relations between Macedonia and Athens came in 343 when the architect of the peace, Philocrates, was indicted for not acting in the city's best interests—in other words, for proposing peace in the first place.[135] He fled into exile and was condemned to death in absentia. Then in the fall of 343 Demosthenes impeached his political archrival Aeschines, a former actor and now an influential statesman, who had served on the first two embassies to Philip in 346 and had counseled moderation in relations with the king.[136] Demosthenes accused him of misconduct on the second embassy and for misleading the Athenians about the peace, alleging that Aeschines had been bribed by the king to mask the latter's true intentions.[137] The allegation had some credence as sources claim that Philip spent huge sums on bribes during his reign and that his successes were due to bribery.[138]

The charge was of course personal, designed to remove Aeschines from public life. Demosthenes' prosecution speech and that of Aeschines in his defense from the resulting "false embassy" trial have survived but are riddled with distorted facts and slanderous information.[139] With only circumstantial evidence and mostly mudslinging, it is not surprising that Demosthenes lost the case—although only by a narrow margin of 30 votes out of 1,501 jurors.[140]

The condemnation of Philocrates and trial of Aeschines, which were yardsticks of the Athenian attitude to Macedonia, perhaps prompted Philip to make a sudden and disastrous move. He tasked a former Athenian citizen named Antiphon to set fire to the dockyards at the Piraeus, home to the Athenian navy.[141] Antiphon was caught, tried, and executed. Demosthenes is the source of the account, so if he is credible, Philip may have tried to neutralize the navy before embarking on an invasion of Thrace, which he knew would concern the Athenians because of its proximity to the grain route. But before that campaign, and still in 343, problematic relations with

[135] Demosthenes 19.116–119; Aeschines 2.6, 3.79; Hyperides 4.29–30, with Worthington 2008a, pp. 114–115.

[136] Harris 1995; Lane Fox 1994. On the rivalry with Demosthenes: Buckler 2000.

[137] See further on the background and charges: Ellis 1976, pp. 151–153; Harris 1995, pp. 115–120; Ryder 2000, pp. 58–72; Worthington 2008a, pp. 115–116; Worthington 2013, pp. 201–209, and in detail Buckler 2000, pp. 121–132 and 134–140.

[138] Demosthenes 18.295–296; Theopompus, *BNJ* 115 F 237; Diodorus 16.53.2.

[139] The name comes from the titles of their speeches: see Buckler 2000, pp. 148–154; Worthington 2013, pp. 202–209; Müller 2016, pp. 259–262; cf. pp. 50–56, on sources.

[140] Plutarch, *Demosthenes* 15.5; [Plutarch], *Moralia* 840c.

[141] Demosthenes 18.132–133; cf. Dinarchus 1.63; Plutarch, *Demosthenes* 14.5, with Worthington 2008a, p. 119.

Epirus forced him to intervene decisively in its affairs.[142] In 350 he had taken the young Alexander of Epirus to Pella, as we mentioned above. In 343 he came of age, and it was probably now that Philip expelled Arybbas and made Alexander king.[143]

In mid-342 Philip departed for Thrace, leaving behind his 14-year-old son Alexander under the tutelage of Aristotle. His official reason for going there was to support several cities on the Hellespont that Cersebleptes had recently attacked, but few would think he was not out for conquest. The Thracian campaign was a model of swiftness and efficiency: within 11 months he had defeated Cersebleptes and taken over much of Thrace, doubling his kingdom's size. The details of the campaign are given only briefly by Diodorus, who tells us that Philip overcame the Thracians in several battles, imposed a tithe tax on them, installed garrisons in a number of key towns, and created the position of general (*strategos*) to administer Thrace.[144] Here Philip was following a precedent he set in Thessaly when he had appointed governors over its four districts. He then made an alliance with the seminomadic Getae people, who lived between Thrace and the Danube basin, marrying their king Cothelas' daughter Meda.[145] This was his sixth marriage—despite the gap of ten years since his last marriage it was still in keeping with his policy of political marriages.

Macedonian influence now extended as far north as the Istrus (Danube) River. Where would he turn to next? That question was likely in the residents' minds of the last remaining independent Greek cities to his east, Perinthus (Marmaraereglisi), Selymbria (Silivri), and Byzantium (Istanbul). But it was the deteriorating relations with Athens that set the background to his next actions. When Athenian settlers in the Chersonese suffered a territorial dispute with their neighbors in Cardia (one of his allies in the Peace of Philocrates), the Athenians sent Diopeithes with a contingent of troops as protection. That caused Philip to dispatch troops to the strategically important island of Euboea off the coast of eastern Attica, to assist towns eager to rebel against Athens and so divert the city's attention from the north.

[142] Worthington 2008a, pp. 116–117.
[143] [Demosthenes] 7.32; Theopompus, *BNJ* 115 F 206–207; Diodorus 16.72.1; Justin 8.6.4–7.
[144] Diodorus 16.71.1–2, with Worthington 2008a, pp. 122–125; Gabriel 2010, pp. 182–185. On Philip and Thrace, see Badian 1983.
[145] Athenaeus 13.557d; on Meda, see Carney 2000, pp. 67–68.

Diopeithes raided Cardian territory and even robbed merchant ships bound for Macedonia, causing the king to send protest letters to Athens and demand his recall.[146] At an Assembly Aeschines advised recalling him, but Demosthenes delivered a fiery speech, *On the Chersonese*, claiming that Philip was an enemy of democracy and if the Athenians did not act immediately against him he would conquer Greece and destroy Athens.[147] His scare tactics worked, and Diopeithes remained in place. When Philip a little later sent soldiers to assist Cardia, another Assembly was held at which Demosthenes delivered his *Third Philippic*, in much the same vein as *On the Chersonese*.[148] He successfully persuaded the Athenians to send embassies to the Greek states and even Persia calling for war against Philip, and a fourth (and final) *Philippic*, probably delivered after these embassies returned, called on the Athenians to maintain their resolve of resisting the king.[149]

Philip in the meantime suffered a reversal of fortune in Euboea, where Athenian troops expelled pro-Macedonian rulers in several cities and Callias, the former ruler of Chalcis, returned and founded a Euboean League. It did not ally to Athens, but nevertheless Attic security was no longer compromised.[150] But Philip's activities in Thrace and the Chersonese and the Athenians' actions against him put both powers on a collision course that ended with war once more between them.

Macedonia under the Argead Kings: The Rise and Fall of an Ancient Superpower. Ian Worthington,
Oxford University Press. © Oxford University Press 2026. DOI: 10.1093/9780197668009.003.0010

[146] Demosthenes 9.17–18, 20–21, 30–31, 71–72, 18.136; [Demosthenes] 12.3–4.
[147] Worthington 2008a, pp. 126–127. Speech: Worthington 2013, pp. 216–220.
[148] *Third Philippic*: Worthington 2013, pp. 221–224.
[149] Worthington 2013, pp. 224–228 (also arguing it was a genuine speech of Demosthenes). See too Harding 1995; Badian 1995.
[150] Worthington 2008a, p. 128.

10

Macedonian Hegemony and Asian Horizons

Philip decided the time had come to invest the last three Greek cities in his lands. With 30,000 infantry he marched to the Hellespont to besiege Perinthus, leaving behind his 16-year-old son Alexander as regent of his kingdom.[1] The siege proved impossible because the city was built in terraces running up a steep hillside; every time Philip's siege engines breached the walls of one terrace the defenders simply retreated up to the next one, piling rubble behind them to block the attackers.[2] The Perinthians also received supplies and military assistance from Byzantium and Persia, with Persian troops even raiding Thrace, while the strength of the nearby Athenian fleet at Elaious blocked the king from deploying his small navy.

In August or early September Philip left half of his force at Perinthus and led the rest against Selymbria and Byzantium.[3] What happened at Selymbria is unknown, but he failed to take Byzantium thanks to its thick walls, which defied even his new torsion catapults. Philip's attack on Byzantium threatened the grain route through the Hellespont, though, prompting Chares, who had succeeded Diopeithes on the latter's recent death, to sail to Byzantium, where more ships and Athenian troops joined him.

Philip then sent another (and final) letter to Athens, criticizing the people for their hostile actions in the Chersonese and lending military support to Byzantium.[4] He held fast at Byzantium while the Athenian grain fleet of 230 vessels with its precious cargo was assembling close to the mouth of the Propontis (Sea of Marmara), after which Chares would escort it to Athens. While the ships were being loaded, the king struck: his admiral seized the grain ships while he captured their crews. He released 50 ships that

[1] Alexander's regency: Worthington 2008a, pp. 130–131.

[2] Diodorus 16.74.2–76.4; Justin 9.1.1–7; cf. Plutarch, *Alexander* 70.5, with Worthington 2008a, pp. 131–132; Gabriel 2010, pp. 190–194.

[3] Worthington 2008a, pp. 132–133; Gabriel 2010, pp. 194–198.

[4] Liddel, D158, pp. 571–574, with references.

belonged to Byzantium, Rhodes, Chios, and Cos but destroyed the remaining 180, which were Athenian, using their timber for his siege engines, and sold their grain for 700 talents—a substantial gain for his coffers.

When news of the grain fleet's fate reached Athens, Demosthenes persuaded the Athenians to smash the *stele* (stone) recording the terms of the Peace of Philocrates, a symbolic action to show the end of an alliance and the start of warfare.[5] It is possible, however, that Philip had already gone to war against them in 341 without their realizing it: in a speech attributed to Demosthenes, Philip was said to have scolded the Athenians, saying, "By the gods as my witnesses, I will deal with you about these matters," which may show his declaration of war.[6] In support of this interpretation is his referring to the captured ships as "prizes of war" before that news reached Athens.[7]

Final days of Greek freedom

When Chares blockaded the Macedonian fleet in the Propontis, Philip had to make a difficult decision. He did not want to return home and leave his ships behind, nor did he want to risk a battle with so few men. Therefore, he abandoned the siege of Byzantium and cunningly arranged for a letter ostensibly to his general Antipater to fall into Chares' hands with the news that he was sailing to Thrace because of a sudden revolt there.[8] Chares fell for the hoax and left at once for Thrace, only to discover he had been tricked when the Macedonian fleet sailed out of the Propontis and returned with Philip to Pella.

En route, Philip mounted a swift offensive on the Scythians south of the Danube (Rumanian Dobruja), killing many of their men, including their king Abreas and capturing 20,000 horses and the same number of children and women.[9] As he traveled through Thrace the independent Triballi

[5] Bolmarcich 2007; see too Liddel, D159, pp. 574–577.

[6] [Demosthenes] 12.23; translation Buckler 1996, p. 88; cf. Philochorus, *BNJ* 328 F 162, and see Buckler 1996, pp. 87–89, on this being the declaration.

[7] Philochorus, *BNJ* 328 F 162, with Worthington 2008a, pp. 133–134.

[8] Theopompus, *BNJ* 115 F 217; Frontinus 1.4.13; Justin 9.2.1, with Worthington 2008a, p. 134.

[9] Justin 9.2.1; cf. Diodorus 16.1.5, with Worthington 2008a, pp. 138–140. See in depth Bloedow 2002 (skeptical), against which see now Bichler 2017.

people of the Danube area refused to let him pass without paying a toll.[10] In a bitter battle he suffered a serious wound when, apparently, the sarissa of one of his men accidentally speared his horse and kept going into one of the king's legs. Losing much blood, he was carried from the battlefield while the Triballi made off with all the booty from his Scythian campaign. He spent the winter of 340–339 recovering but limped for the rest of his life.[11]

Philip now faced a problem in his war against Athens because if he marched into Greece with an army, the Greeks might unite against him. The problem solved itself when the Amphictyonic Council, after some diplomatic wrangling, declared a sacred war (the fourth) against the west Locrian city of Amphissa and appointed Philip as commander of its army.[12] Now with a legitimate reason for marching into Greece, Philip intended to end his war with the Athenians and deal with the Thebans, who had recently seized the fortress of Nicaea that controlled Thermopylae, expelling its Macedonian garrison and installing their own.[13] He therefore decided it was time to bring Greece under Macedonian control once and for all.[14]

In the spring of 338, Philip moved into Greece and established a camp at Cytinium, six miles north of the Gravia Pass en route to Amphissa. Instead of attacking that city in the sacred war, however, he surprised everyone by turning southeast down the Cephissus Valley, through Phocis, to the Boeotian border, where he seized Elatea. He was now only two to three days' march from Athens. From there he sent an embassy to the Thebans with various terms: the Thebans were to maintain their friendship with him, join him in attacking Athens or at least allow his army passage through Boeotia to the Attic border, and surrender Nicaea to the Locrians since Nicaea lay in their state.[15]

The Athenians feared the worst. An emergency Assembly was called at which Demosthenes advised the people, among other things, to put aside their long-standing enmity with Thebes and send him there to broker an alliance against Philip. In a dramatic passage of a defense speech that he

[10] Philochorus, *BNJ* 328 F 54; Marsyas, *BNJ* 135–136 F 17; Justin 9.3.1–3; cf. Demosthenes 18.67; Diodorus 16.1.5, with Worthington 2008a, p. 140.

[11] [Plutarch], *Moralia* 331b, with Riginos 1994, pp. 116–118. For an alternative description of the wound, see Gabriel 2010, pp. 13–14.

[12] Background: Aeschines 3.115–121; Demosthenes 18.140–155; cf. Liddel, D161, pp. 581–585, and in detail Londey 1990; cf. Harris 1995, pp. 126–130; Worthington 2008a, pp. 136–137 and 140–141; Worthington 2013, pp. 237–241.

[13] Philochorus, *BNJ* 328 F 56.

[14] Buckler 1996.

[15] Demosthenes 18.152–158, 168, 174–175, 178, 211–215; Theopompus, *BNJ* 115 F 328; Diodorus 16.84.3–85.1; Justin 9.3.6, with Worthington 2008a, pp. 141–142.

gave in 330, titled *On the Crown*, he described the shocked reaction in the city when the news broke that Philip had seized Elatea, claiming that no one was able to speak and that he was the only person who advised the people in "the very midst of the horrors."[16]

If Demosthenes had planned a union with Thebes since 346, that planning paid off now.[17] He appeared before the Theban Assembly, where despite ominous warnings from Macedonian envoys and the frightening presence of Philip's army on their doorstep, he persuaded the Thebans to ally with Athens against Macedonia.[18] But the alliance was costly: among other things, the Athenians had to agree to the Thebans having sole command of the army and sharing command of the combined fleet as well as pay for one-third of the costs of land operations and for all naval engagements.

A force of Theban infantry and 10,000 Athenian-hired mercenaries commanded by Chares and the Theban Proxenus was deployed to the Gravia Pass, while another joint force was posted 20 miles away at Parapotamii on the Boeotian border.[19] Only some Peloponnesian states had thrown their weight behind Athens and Thebes, so it was really those two cities that carried the fight to Philip. The king sent his own embassies to the other Greeks, but if he expected them to scurry to his side, he was disappointed, as only a few responded positively. After some minor skirmishes in and around the Cephissus Valley Philip arranged for a letter claiming he was leaving for Thrace to fall into the hands of Chares and Proxenus.[20] They never seemed to suspect his duplicity, despite his earlier hoax at the Propontis, so perhaps the sources have confused the earlier incident with this one or vice versa and given us the two. Either way the Greeks relaxed their guard, enabling Philip's general Parmenion to attack Chares and seize the Gravia Pass. Parmenion then moved to Amphissa, which surrendered to him, thereby ending the Fourth Sacred War.

[16] Demosthenes 18.169–173; Diodorus 16.84.2–5; Plutarch, *Demosthenes* 18.1, with Liddel, D163, pp. 589–593; cf. Worthington 2008a, pp. 142–144; Worthington 2013, pp. 242–243—the passage is quoted on pp. 242–243.

[17] Trevett 1999; Worthington 2008a, p. 138; contra Cawkwell 1963; Cawkwell 1969; cf. Guth 2014.

[18] Aeschines 3.137–151; Demosthenes 18.168–188, 211–217; cf. Dinarchus 1.12; Diodorus 16.85.1–4; Plutarch, *Demosthenes* 18.1–2; Plutarch, *Phocion* 16.3; Justin 9.3.4–6, and see Worthington 2008a, pp. 144–146; Worthington 2013, pp. 244–245, though note Guth 2014 and especially Brun 2022, pp. 312–319, on Demosthenes creating "fake news" over his role in the alliance.

[19] Worthington 2008a, p. 145.

[20] Polyaenus 4.2.8. Professor Carol King points out to me that falling for the same trick could be evidence of a doublet.

In the meantime, Philip had overcome the Greek force at Parapotamii, which fled to the plain of Chaeronea, close to Thebes. The Thebans had deliberately chosen this plain as a fallback position because of its topography. At only two miles wide, with hills on its northern and southern sides and several rivers dissecting it, Philip would face difficulties deploying his cavalry and even his phalanx line effectively. There the Greeks prepared to fight for the freedom of Greece.

The battle of Chaeronea

Philip fielded an army of 30,000 infantry (including 24,000 Macedonians) and 2,000 cavalry, while the Greeks roughly equaled him at 30,000 infantry and 3,800 cavalry, including the elite 300-strong Theban Sacred Band.[21] Philip and the hypaspists were on his right flank with the elite Companion Cavalry commanded by his 18-year-old son Alexander on his left flank. The Macedonian phalanx battalions formed the center. The Greek right flank was stationed by the Cephissus River on the plain's eastern border with the Boeotians and the Sacred Band on its far right. The Athenian force of 6,000 troops (including Demosthenes, whose shield bore the phrase "Good luck") were positioned on the left flank by the Haemon (Lykuressi) stream. The other Greek allies made up the center.

Philip's cavalry was indeed hindered because of the narrowness of the plain and its marshy areas. In addition, he had to decrease the depth of his phalanx, thus reducing its mass and force of its charge, because the Greek line stretched almost the plain's width. The Greeks' strategy was a frontal charge with their right flank, which would then pivot to push the Macedonian left onto the boggy ground and even into the Cephissus. To prevent this, Philip came up with a three-phase strategy to open gaps in the enemy line through which his men could charge and encircle the Greeks.

The actual fighting took place in early August.[22] Philip's first phase began with his men marching toward their enemy at an acute angle, with the right flank closer to the Greeks than the left. When the Macedonian right met the Athenians on the Greek left, Philip brought the second phase of his strategy

[21] Diodorus 16.85.2, 85.5, 86.1; Plutarch, *Demosthenes* 17.3; Plutarch, *Alexander* 12.5; Justin 9.3.9.

[22] Diodorus 16.85–87; Plutarch, *Alexander* 9.2–3; Justin 9.3.8–11; Polyaenus 4.2.2, 7, with Hammond and Griffith 1979, pp. 596–603; Worthington 2008a, pp. 147–151; Gabriel 2010, pp. 214–216. See also Hammond 1973. Date: Plutarch, *Camillus* 19.5, 8.

into play by suddenly moving sideways to the right with the rest of his line following suit. The Athenians thought he was retreating and moved to stay with him. In doing so they opened a gap toward the Greek center, which the other allied troops scrambled to plug, but the Sacred Band followed orders and stood fast on the far right.

Alexander on the left flank now swung into action. Diodorus states that he was next to Philip's "most seasoned generals," probably Parmenion and Antipater.[23] Leading the cavalry, they galloped through the gap between the Sacred Band and the rest of the Greek line, wheeling around to encircle the band and cutting it down to the last man before attacking the other Boeotian troops.[24] Philip's feigned retreat had by now reached the Haemon, where he initiated his third phase. He suddenly turned back, and his superior troops plowed into the startled Athenians and allied center before they had the chance to regroup. The Greeks suffered dreadful casualties—the Athenians alone had 1,000 killed and 2,000 taken prisoner, while the survivors, including Demosthenes, managed to struggle over the Kerata Pass to Lebadea (Levadia) in Boeotia, and thence to their homes.

Philip's actions after the battle are controversial. One ancient writer speaks of him bursting into tears as he walked the battlefield and came upon the corpses of the entire Sacred Band, then ordering a statue of a lion to be set up on that spot to memorialize their bravery (figure 10.1).[25]

However, another account claims Philip got so drunk the night of his victory that he mocked the prisoners. He sobered up when an Athenian captive, the orator Demades, asked him, "O King, when Fortune has cast you in the role of Agamemnon, are you not ashamed to act the part of Thersites?"[26] Agamemnon was leader of the Greeks in the Trojan War, and Thersites was publicly slapped down for not knowing his place. Whether either story is true is not known, but the first has more credibility as there was a lion monument set up at Chaeronea, which was broken in the Greek War of Independence and restored to what we see today. The critical Theopompus may have been responsible for the second anecdote to tarnish the king.[27]

[23] Diodorus 16.86.1. On Antipater, see Baynham 1994b. On Parmenion, see Bearzot 1987.

[24] Diodorus 16.85.5–87; Plutarch, *Alexander* 9.2, with Rahe 1981; Sears and Willekes 2016.

[25] Plutarch, *Pelopidas* 18.5. Monument: Pausanias 9.40.10. But on the monument, see Ma 2008.

[26] Theopompus, *BNJ* 115 F 236 (= Athenaeus 435b-c); Diodorus 16.87.1–2; Plutarch, *Demosthenes* 20.3; cf. [Plutarch], *Moralia* 715c; contra Justin 9.4.1–3. See further, Worthington 2008a, pp. 152–153.

[27] Worthington 2008a, pp. 153–154.

Figure 10.1 Lion of Chaeronea
Source: Wikimedia Commons.

Philip's victory at Chaeronea was a watershed in Greek history. To the Athenian orator Lycurgus, the freedom of the Greeks also died in the battle, and Justin remarked that "for the whole of Greece [Chaeronea] marked the end of its glorious supremacy and of its ancient independence."[28] Demosthenes, his anti-Macedonian policy ruined, now kept a lower profile in Athenian public life, but eight years later, in 330, the battle was reshaped significantly. In that year, Aeschines indicted Demosthenes' crony Ctesiphon for proposing that the orator be awarded a gold crown among other things "because he consistently spoke and acted in the best interests of the people."[29] The case came to court, with Demosthenes delivering the major defense speech *On the Crown*.[30] Aeschines focused on Demosthenes' anti-Macedonian stance throughout his career and the flawed alliance with Thebes in 339 that led to Chaeronea.[31] Demosthenes rebutted Aeschines' assertions by crafting a "rhetoric of defeat" that the Greeks had done the right thing in fighting Philip for the cause of freedom, matching the patriotic standard of their ancestors in the Persian Wars; hence even though they lost the battle they could add another glorious episode to their history.[32] His rhetoric worked: the jurors overwhelmingly acquitted him.

Philip now faced two challenges. One was reconciling the Greeks to Macedonian rule. The second was how to react to the worrying prophecy he had received before the battle:[33]

> From the battle on Thermodon [Chaeronea] may I be far removed,
> To behold it like an eagle in clouds and upper air.
> Tears are for the conquered there, and for the conqueror, death.

It was a prophecy that came true two years later.

[28] Lycurgus 1.50; Justin 9.3.11. End of Greek freedom: Cawkwell 1996.

[29] Aeschines 3.49. Other charges: Aeschines 3.11, 32–48. Background: Sawada 1996; Buckler 2000; Worthington 2013, pp. 294–306.

[30] We have Aeschines' prosecution speech *Against Ctesiphon* (3) and Demosthenes' defense speech *On the Crown* (18), although surely revised after oral delivery given their length: On both, see Worthington 2013, pp. 296–305; cf. Buckler 2000, pp. 148–154.

[31] For example, Aeschines 3.49–167.

[32] Demosthenes 18.63, 66–68, 192–195, 199, 206, 245–246, 208, 270–275. On the rhetorical manipulations and audience memory of the period, see Worthington 2022a; cf. Crick 2022.

[33] Plutarch, *Demosthenes* 19.1.

Hegemon of Greece

Philip followed his victory at Chaeronea by a flurry of diplomatic activity. He began by imposing terms on the states that had earlier defied him and ending his second war with Athens.[34] He dealt with the Thebans first, among other things abolishing their hegemony of the Boeotian League; installing an oligarchy of 300 men supported by a garrison in the city; demanding a ransom for the soldiers killed at Chaeronea apart from the Sacred Band; selling the survivors as slaves; and returning to Athenian control the town of Oropus on the Boeotian-Attic border, long a bone of contention between Athens and Thebes.[35] With the Peloponnesian states, Philip installed oligarchies and garrisons in Corinth, Chalcis, Ambracia, and probably Megara, which also isolated the Spartans, who had been causing instability in the Peloponnese for some time.[36]

The Athenians naturally feared the worst. Demosthenes and Hyperides introduced various emergency measures such as evacuating the countryside; calling up all men to age 60 into the army; sending the women, children, and sacred objects to the Piraeus; and granting citizenship to metics (resident aliens) and freedom to slaves to help defend the city.[37] There was no need. Philip sent Demades to Athens to assure the people of his goodwill, followed by Alexander no less with the ashes of the Athenian dead from Chaeronea and the 2,000 captives—unransomed.[38] The Athenians sent an embassy to Philip to hear his terms, which included giving up their league and influence in the Chersonese; perhaps at this time they granted him citizenship and a statue.[39] Whether these honors had any influence on Philip is unknown, but the resulting treaty was one of friendship and alliance, and he took no measures against their democracy or anti-Macedonian politicians and allowed them to keep their navy.[40]

[34] Roebuck 1948; Worthington 2008a, pp. 154–163.

[35] Diodorus 16.87.3; Pausanias 4.27.9–10, 9.1.8, 6.5, 37.8; Justin 9.4.6–10, 11.3.8; see too Roebuck 1948, pp. 77–80; cf. Hammond and Griffith 1979, pp. 610–612; Ryder 1994, pp. 244–247; Worthington 2008a, p. 154.

[36] Diodorus 16.89.3 wrongly dates this to 337/6. On the Peloponnesian settlement, see Roebuck 1948, pp. 83–89; Ryder 1994, pp. 241–242; Worthington 2008a, pp. 157–158; cf. Hamilton, C.D. 1982, pp. 81–83.

[37] Lycurgus 1.16, 36–37, 41; Demosthenes 18.248; [Demosthenes] 26.11; [Plutarch], *Moralia* 848f–849; Liddel, D167a–c, pp. 603–611; see too Hammond and Griffith 1979, pp. 596–603.

[38] Diodorus 16.56.6–7, 87–88.2; Pausanias 7.10.5; Justin 9.4.4–5.

[39] Liddel, D180, pp. 654–659, though it is unlikely these honors were in the following year or even 336; a post-Chaeronea relief is more plausible.

[40] Liddel, D171, pp. 620–624. Possible fragment of this treaty: Worthington 2008b.

Philip's dealing with Thebes and with Athens could not have been more markedly different. Yet he had been at war with Athens twice in his reign, and there were times when that city and Demosthenes' rhetoric had thwarted his plans.[41] Perhaps he favored the Athenians over the Thebans because he needed their navy for an invasion of Asia he was now planning, or he simply wanted to curtail Theban power in central Greece. Curiously, despite his philhellenism and contacts with Athenian intellectuals, he never visited Athens, and it had been Alexander, not the king, who led a deputation to the city.

Philip made Corinth his base while settling affairs in the Peloponnese and then summoned representatives there from all Greek states to announce a Common Peace.[42] This was an agreement whereby each Greek city swore a separate oath of allegiance to the other cities and to Macedonia, promising to have the same friends and enemies, not to conclude an alliance with a potential enemy, and not to engage in subversive activities. If it did so, then the other states could launch attacks on it—a deterrent that would keep them in check—as Philip intended in his call for such a peace.[43]

Philip also created a council (*synedrion*) of the Greek states, excluding Macedonia, under a hegemon, which was to discuss military, domestic, and foreign issues relating to Greece, with decisions binding on all members. Philip knew his Greek history: previous common peaces had been short-lived because of the distrust that the poleis had of each other. His peace, however, was revolutionary because it exploited the rivalries of the Greeks for each other, because it was backed by his military force, and because the council gave the Greeks some semblance of autonomy.

The following spring of 337, the league met in Corinth, where the states swore their oaths to each other, to Philip, and significantly to his descendants—and elected him hegemon of the council even though Macedonia was not a member.[44] The Greeks called Philip's arrangement the Community of the Greeks (*to koinon ton Hellenon*), but it is given the

[41] Worthington 2008a, pp. 155–157; cf. Cawkwell 1980, pp. 100–110; Ryder 1994 (Philip and Athens on pp. 251–257).

[42] Diodorus 16.89.1–2; Justin 9.5.1; cf. [Demosthenes] 17.1. The Spartans refused him on the grounds that "what was imposed by a conqueror was not peace but servitude": Justin 9.5.3.

[43] Ryder 1965, pp. 102–106; Perlman 1985; Perlman 1986; Worthington 2008a, pp. 158–171; Worthington 2014a, pp. 99–101; Dmitriev 2011, pp. 67–90; Müller 2016, pp. 267–268. Common Peace: Ryder 1965; Jehne 1994.

[44] Rhodes-Osborne, no. 76, with commentary (pp. 376–379); Harding 1985, no. 99, pp. 123–125; Liddel, D172, pp. 624–628.

modern name of the League of Corinth.[45] It became a blueprint for similar leagues by some Antigonid kings long after him, and thus it can be said that it forever altered the face of Greek politics.

Asian horizons

At this same spring meeting of the league, Philip announced his intention to invade Persia. His reasons were to liberate the Greek cities of Asia Minor from the Persian rule imposed on them in 386 by the King's Peace and to punish the Persians for their invasion of Greece in the early fifth century—especially for their looting of Athens and burning of the Acropolis.[46] That Philip made Athens front and center in this panhellenic campaign helps to explain why he did not punish the city as he had Thebes after Chaeronea and then only months later seek revenge on its behalf.

Possibly Philip had been thinking about invading Asia since the Peace of Philocrates in 346, when Isocrates wrote to him to unite Athens, Thebes, Sparta, and Argos against Persia.[47] Presumably Isocrates would not have voiced this plan if Philip had not already had Persia in his sights.[48] Diodorus in the context of 346 claims that Philip "was ambitious to be designated general of Hellas in supreme command and as such to prosecute the war against the Persians."[49] But in 346 Philip was savvy enough to know an invasion was impractical; Greece was not likely to remain passive during his absence and, more importantly, he did not control Thrace, which was strategically necessary to protect his rear.

Why Persia? Perhaps Philip sought revenge for the Persians' assistance to Perinthus and Byzantium in 340 and even retaliation for their overlordship of Macedonia back in the days of Amyntas I and Alexander I.[50] Perhaps he intended to topple the Persian Empire and establish an absolute monarchy

[45] *P. Oxy.* 12 (*BNJ* 255), 5, with Hammond 1991. See too Diodorus 16.89.1–3; Justin 9.5.1–7. See too the works cited in the preceding note.

[46] Diodorus 16.89; Justin 9.5.4–7, and see Worthington 2008a, pp. 160 and 166–169; Worthington 2014a, pp. 103–105; Müller 2016, p. 268. Polybius 3.6.12–13 states that Philip used the excuse of panhellenism to hide his intent. Panhellenic propaganda: Faraguna 2003, pp. 107–115. See too Bloedow 2003—a war of revenge and conquest.

[47] Isocrates had been advocating an invasion since 380 in his *Panegyricus*: 4.16–17, 99, 173. Cawkwell 1978a, p. 111, also suggests that in 346 Philip wanted an alliance as well as peace with Athens as he had decided by then to invade Persia.

[48] Lane Fox 2011e, p. 354.

[49] Diodorus 16.60.4–5.

[50] Arrian 2.14.5. Revenge: Squillace 2010, pp. 76–80.

in a new empire, though this is doubtful.[51] We should also not discount the need to keep the army on campaign and even a thirst for personal glory. But more plausible is that by 337 he was facing a shortage of liquid capital, given that the Macedonians practiced a rolling economy. Despite the income from taxes Philip imposed on various areas he conquered, as we have noted, the loss of his Scythian booty to the Triballi in 339 must have been a major blow as he had no chance to recoup it before his campaign in Greece the following year that led to Chaeronea and now the establishment of the League of Corinth.[52] Indeed, when Alexander became king in 336, he was said to have found a mere 70 talents in the treasury and supplies for only 30 days, and had to borrow 800 talents.[53] The resources of the Persian Empire were enormous, though Philip may have intended to campaign only in Asia Minor, where winning over the Greek cities there would still bring him an influx of new wealth.[54]

Since Philip knew the Greeks would be unconcerned about his financial circumstances, he proposed the campaign as a panhellenic one of liberation and revenge. The Greek representatives in Corinth had no choice but to vote for his plan and elect him commander-in-chief. Accordingly, he sent an advance force of 10,000 Macedonian and mercenary soldiers to Asia Minor in 336 to prepare the way for the main army he would personally lead that summer.[55] He never did: before its departure he was assassinated.

Philip's last marriage and death

Philip married for a seventh and final time in the summer of 337. His bride was a young Macedonian noblewoman, Cleopatra, the ward of the powerful baron Attalus.[56] Apparently he married her out of love, in contrast to his previous marriages, but then again, since his wives were getting older he may have wanted more heirs, especially as he was about to leave for Asia.[57]

[51] Fredricksmeyer 1982; cf. Brunt 1965.

[52] Taxes: Lane Fox 2011f, pp. 377–379.

[53] Onesicritus, *BNJ* 134 F 2 (= Plutarch, *Alexander* 15.2); [Plutarch], *Moralia* 327d–e. He compared his wealth in a speech of 324 with what it was in 336: Arrian 7.9.6; Curtius 10.2.24.

[54] Worthington 2008a, pp. 167–170.

[55] Diodorus 16.91.2, 17.2.4; Justin 9.5.8.

[56] Athenaeus 13.557d; Diodorus 16.93.9; Justin 9.5.8–9, with Carney 2000, pp. 70–75; Worthington 2008a, pp. 172–174. Arrian 3.6.5 says that he renamed her Eurydice after the marriage; cf. Heckel 1978. However, the renaming is most likely Arrian's error: Badian 1982b.

[57] Athenaeus 13.557b–e; cf. 13.560c, quoting Satyrus' biography. Other reasons for marrying now: Worthington 2008a, pp. 172–174; cf. Carney 2000, pp. 73–74.

The marriage was said to have upset Olympias, who disliked Philip anyway and was forever nagging her son about him.[58]

We do not know much about relations between Philip's wives. They all seemed to have been treated as equals, though possibly Olympias had special standing as the mother of the heir apparent. Plutarch speaks of "quarrels which took place in the women's apartments" of the palace because of Philip's marriages and love affairs.[59] We have no idea if these quarrels were regular, and the first six wives may have bonded because they were all foreign and so homesick or lonely.[60]

At the wedding banquet of Philip and Cleopatra, Attalus drunkenly prayed that the newlyweds might produce a legitimate heir, a slur aimed at Olympias, who came from Epirus, and Alexander.[61] After a furious exchange between Alexander and Attalus, a drunken Philip ordered his son to apologize and, when he refused, drew a sword on Alexander and seemed ready to use it on him. But then he fell over a table, to which his son supposedly said: "Here is the man who was making ready to cross from Europe to Asia, and who cannot even cross from one table to another without losing his balance."[62] Attalus' comment may have been nothing more than a taunt, but it was enough for Alexander and Olympias to storm off to her brother, Alexander of Epirus.[63] She was said to have urged him to make war on Philip, but he remained loyal to the king, for which Philip rewarded him with the hand of his daughter Cleopatra (by Olympias, hence Alexander of Epirus' niece) with the wedding set for the following summer.[64]

At some point Alexander left Epirus to go to the Illyrians. Perhaps worried that he was trying to gain their support, given their history with Macedonia, Philip recalled him, though there is no mention of wanting to bring back Olympias to Pella.[65] Relations between father and son never

[58] Cf. Plutarch, *Alexander* 9.5–6.

[59] Plutarch, *Alexander* 9.5–6. See Athenaeus 13.557d and 560c for the view that this marriage caused a rift in Philip's household, with Heckel 1981b; Worthington 2008a, pp. 175–176.

[60] Mortensen 1999, though there is nothing to support her view that "a generally harmonious picture interspersed with occasional rows seems far more likely than the conditions of endless upheaval painted by Plutarch" (p. 805). On Philip's wives, see Carney 2000, pp. 51–81, which Mortensen follows.

[61] Plutarch, *Alexander* 9.5–6, with Worthington 2008a, pp. 176–178.

[62] Plutarch, *Alexander* 9.10; Justin 9.7.4; contra Athenaeus 13.557e, who omits the incident with Philip.

[63] Plutarch, *Alexander* 9.4–5; Athenaeus 13.557d; Justin 9.7.5. Attalus' taunt: Worthington 2008a, pp. 277–278.

[64] Diodorus 16.91.4; Justin 9.7.7, 9.6.1, 13.6.4. On this Cleopatra, see Carney 2000, pp. 75–76.

[65] [Plutarch], *Moralia* 179c; see further Plutarch, *Alexander* 9.6–14; Justin 9.7.6.

recovered, though—not that they had ever been particularly close, given Philip's years of campaigning away from home. Alexander even called his physical fitness tutor Leonidas his foster father.[66]

Late in 337 Philip arranged the marriage of his eldest son Arrhidaeus to a daughter of Pixodarus, the ruler of Caria in Asia Minor, who wanted to rebel against Persian control and sought an alliance with Philip.[67] For some reason Alexander was affronted and sent word to Pixodarus that he wished to marry his daughter.[68] Alexander was in the wrong as only kings arranged marriages of family members, and a furious Philip had no wish for his heir to "marry the daughter of a mere Carian, who was no more than a slave of a barbarian king."[69] He exiled several of Alexander's close friends as punishment and abandoned the alliance with Pixodarus.[70]

In 336 Philip sent the vanguard force to Asia Minor to win over the Asiatic Greeks, and several cities and islands revolted from Persia.[71] That summer the wedding of the princess Cleopatra and Alexander of Epirus was held at Aegae, and the day after was given over to celebratory athletic games. Given that dignitaries from the Greek states were present at both events, Philip presumably intended the games as a "media event" showcasing Macedonia's position in the Greek world, the League of Corinth, and the forthcoming Asian expedition.[72]

Also telling of Macedonia's power was the likely completion by now of the Philippeion ("Philip's building") at Olympia (figure 10.2). Pausanias tell us that the king commissioned this monument after the battle of Chaeronea, planning it to be finished by the 111th Olympic Games in Olympia in 336—the same year as the events at Aegae.[73] The circular Philippeion had an external row of 18 columns and an internal one of nine, and housed statues of Philip, his mother and father Eurydice and Amyntas III, Alexander, and Olympias.[74]

[66] Plutarch, *Alexander* 5.7.
[67] Plutarch, *Alexander* 10, with Worthington 2008a, pp. 178–180.
[68] Plutarch, *Alexander* 10.1–5. [69] Plutarch, *Demosthenes* 10.3.
[70] Arrian 3.6.5; Plutarch, *Alexander* 10.1–4. The whole affair is doubted by Hatzopoulos 1982b, against which see French and Dixon 1986; Ruzicka 2010; and now Kuzmin 2024.
[71] Worthington 2008a, pp. 180–181. [72] Cf. Diodorus 16.91.5–6.
[73] Pausanias 5.17.4, 5.20.9–10. On the building, see Miller, S.G. 1973; Townsend 2003; especially Schultz 2007; cf. Worthington 2008a, pp. 164–166; Hardiman 2010, pp. 508–509; Saatsoglou-Paliadeli 2011, pp. 279–280.
[74] Despite the strained relations between Olympias and Philip she was always going to be part of the family group as all five statues were planned at the same time: Schultz 2007, pp. 208–209 and 213–216.

Figure 10.2 The Philippeion
Source: Wikimedia Commons.

The Philippeion's eye-catching shape was like no other monument at Olympia; hence visitors from all over the Greek world would see it and understand its message, just as the Greeks understood the message of his return to Thessaly in 352 when his men wore laurel crowns in the Third Sacred War.[75] Indeed, in choosing Olympia Philip gave a nod to Alexander I and even Archelaus: if the former had initially been rebuffed when trying to compete in the Olympic Games and the latter had been prevented from taking part in them and so founded a "counter Olympics," then Philip made Macedonia's presence there undeniable. We return to this building below as it has implications for the theory that Philip saw himself as divine.

The games at Aegae following the wedding of Alexander of Epirus to Cleopatra were held in the theater (figure 10.3). They were preceded by a procession featuring statues of the 12 Olympian gods, one of Philip, and finally Philip in person flanked by his son Alexander and Alexander of Epirus.[76] They stood in the performance area (orchestra), acknowledging

[75] Lane Fox 2011e, p. 366.

[76] Diodorus 16.92.5, 95.1; Justin 9.6.1. Philip's statue has wrongly been taken to indicate that he believed himself divine: Worthington 2008a, pp. 228–233.

Figure 10.3 Aegae theater
Source: Sean Burke/Alamy Stock Photo.

the excited crowd before the two Alexanders stepped aside and Philip ordered his bodyguard to do the same so he could "show publicly that he was protected by the goodwill of the Greeks, and had no need of a guard of spearmen. Such was the pinnacle of success that he had attained."[77] It was his last order. Out of the blue one of his bodyguards, Pausanias of Orestis, leaped forward and stabbed him to death.[78]

Pausanias fled but fell over a vine and three of the guards speared him to death. In the meantime there was chaos in the theater and even a fear that Alexander could also be murdered because "all of Macedonia was ablaze with discontent and was looking to Amyntas and the sons of Aeropus."[79] But Antipater managed to calm the horrified spectators by swiftly proclaiming

[77] Diodorus 16.93.1–2.

[78] Aristotle, *Politics* 5.1311b 1–3; Diodorus 16.93–94, 17.2.3–6; Plutarch, *Alexander* 10.4–7; Justin 9.6.4–7.14; cf. Arrian, *BNJ* 156 FF 9 and 22.

[79] Arrian 1.25.1–2; Curtius 6.9.17, 10.24; [Plutarch], *Moralia* 327c; cf. Justin 12.6.14, with Worthington 2008a, pp. 187–188. See now Hatzopoulos 2021.

Alexander king.[80] Shortly afterward, the new king convened an Assembly, where he swore the customary oath that he would rule according to the laws; in return the people—including the army in Asia—swore their oath of allegiance to him.[81]

Why did Pausanias kill Philip? Our ancient accounts differ widely, as do modern scholars.[82] Aristotle, relying on Alexander himself, claimed that Pausanias acted out of jealous rage because Philip had ended a homoerotic relationship with him some time previously and taken up with another man. In other words, Pausanias' motive was personal, and he acted alone, perhaps even on the spur of the moment. Yet why would he wait for as long and take his revenge in so public an arena? Moreover, his acting alone or on a whim conflicts with Plutarch's claim that "it was Olympias who was chiefly blamed for the assassination, because she was believed to have encouraged [Pausanias] and incited him to take his revenge, but a certain amount of accusation was also attached to Alexander."[83] Likewise Justin, who states that "it was also believed that Pausanias had been suborned by Olympias, mother of Alexander, and that Alexander was not unaware of the plot to murder his father."[84] Plutarch and Justin thus give us a conspiracy that involved Olympias and perhaps even Alexander.

Regicide had a long history among the Argeads, as we have seen. Although conspiracy theory is always dubious, there are grounds for arguing a plot here. To begin with, Justin's account goes on to say that Olympias and Alexander feared that if Philip and Cleopatra had a son, he would threaten Alexander's succession. These fears may go back to Attalus' taunt about a legitimate heir at the wedding banquet of 337, assuming it has not been blown out of proportion—in fact a few days before the wedding of Cleopatra to Alexander of Epirus, Philip's new wife had borne him a daughter, so a son might well have soon followed.[85] Rather like Eurydice, Amyntas

[80] Justin 11.1.7–10. [81] Diodorus 17.2.1–2.

[82] Badian 1963; Fears 1975; Hammond and Griffith 1979, pp. 684–691; Hammond 1980c; Develin 1981; Carney 1992 (cf. Carney 1983, pp. 263–264); Hammond 1994, pp. 170–176; Badian 2007; Worthington 2008a, pp. 181–186 (cf. Worthington 2013, pp. 267–271; Worthington 2014a, pp. 112–115); Antela-Bernárdez 2012; Lindholmer 2016; Müller 2016, pp. 271–276; Heckel et al. 2017; Hatzopoulos 2020, pp. 142–147; Hatzopoulos 2021. Still the best and most thorough study is Ellis 1981, who leans toward a personal motive on Pausanias' part but concludes that all explanations are only theories.

[83] Plutarch, *Alexander* 10.6. [84] Justin 9.7.1; see also 9.7.1–11.

[85] Athenaeus 13.557e (see note 62). Pausanias 8.7.7 and Justin 11.2.3 (cf. 9.7.3) have it that Cleopatra gave birth to a son, Caranus, and Justin 12.6.14 claims that the daughter was killed; Diodorus 17.2.3 merely says Cleopatra bore a child (he uses the neuter noun *paidion*). Since we know that Cleopatra did give birth to a daughter and that Olympias killed both mother and

III's wife, supporting her sons at court and keeping their path to the throne unblocked, Olympias was always doing the same for Alexander: if we believe Plutarch, she poisoned Arrhidaeus, who was the eldest son of Philip and so the expected successor.[86] If she meant to kill him she was unsuccessful, but perhaps the poison led to his apparent mental incapacity that forced Philip to set him aside and make Alexander the heir apparent. Arrhidaeus would eventually become king on Alexander's death in 323 (chapter 12).

Yet why would Alexander worry about Philip and Cleopatra having a son? Alexander was clearly next in line, for he had been regent in 340 when Philip went to Thrace and had led an army against the Maedians of the upper Strymon Valley to put down their revolt.[87] In 338 he had been given an important military command at Chaeronea, and shortly after the battle led a guard of honor to Athens. Moreover, in 336 he was 20 years old—even if Cleopatra had a son, he would not come of age for at least 18 years. But there was the possibility of Alexander's succession being challenged by a group of disenchanted barons, who may even have been behind Philip's assassination to maintain their influence.[88] Attalus was obviously one. He clearly did not support Alexander given his hope for an heir of Macedonian blood; hence Alexander might well have to fight for his throne.

In addition, Alexander may have further resented his father when he was told that he would remain in Macedonia as regent and deputy hegemon of the League of Corinth while Philip marched with the army to Asia. While Alexander was growing up, he likely admired his father and strove to emulate him, but in later years, despite his father's trust in him as heir, that feeling changed to resentment.[89] He also felt marginalized as the king kept something of an inner circle with Parmenion, Antipater, and Attalus, but excluded his heir from it. He had twice tasted battle by now, in 340 against the Maedians and in 338 at Chaeronea, distinguishing himself on both occasions, and he apparently told his friends that the more Philip conquered, the less there would be left for him to do.[90] And in 330 Alexander visited the oracle of Zeus Ammon at Siwah in Egypt and asked the priest

daughter upon Philip's death, there is not enough time for her to have been pregnant twice. On Europa, see Carney 2000, pp. 77–78.

86 Plutarch, *Alexander* 77.8, and see Carney 2018, pp. 31–33, on Olympias as "succession advocate."

87 Plutarch, *Alexander* 9.1, with Hammond and Griffith 1979, pp. 557–559; Worthington 2008a, pp. 230–231.

88 Bosworth 1971a.

89 Fredricksmeyer 1990.

90 Plutarch, *Alexander* 5.4.

whether all the murderers of his father had been punished.[91] This episode is a full six years after Philip's assassination, suggesting that there was still a lingering suspicion he had some role in it, and that only a god's word would exculpate him. The motive for Philip's assassination will likely never be known, but we should not outrightly reject the notion of a conspiracy.

Philip's tomb and divinity?

Alexander arranged Philip's burial at Aegae, site of royal burials—in haste as the new king had to attend to an immediate revolt of the Greeks from the League of Corinth and a purge of opponents.[92] Philip's body along with his arms and armor were burned on a pyre, after which the bones were taken down, washed in wine, wrapped in a purple robe, and placed in a gold larnax, or box. The larnax was put inside a stone sarcophagus and then interred in a tomb. During raids by the Galatians in the 270s the tomb was protected by a covering of earth to form a tumulus, 13 meters (43 feet) high and 100 meters (328 feet) in diameter (figure 10.4).[93]

The tomb's location was forgotten over the centuries. Aegae itself was for some time thought to be Edessa, until it was positively identified as the modern hamlet of Vergina, whose largest tumulus was thought to be man-made and covering a tomb.[94] The tumulus was excavated from 1977 to 1978 by Manolis Andronikos, who in one of the most important archaeological finds of the twentieth century discovered in it four tombs. One of them—Tomb II—had a main chamber and a smaller antechamber, neither of which had been plundered. In Tomb II's main chamber was a stone sarcophagus containing a larnax with skeletal remains on which traces of cloth were visible. Forensic tests confirmed wine on the bones, consistent with how they were washed and wrapped in purple after the corpse was burned on the pyre.

There were also exceptional grave goods, including a magnificent gold wreath of oak leaves and flowers, silver drinking vessels and containers,

[91] Plutarch, *Alexander* 27.8–10; cf. Diodorus 17.51.2–3; Curtius 4.7.27; Justin 11.11.2–12.

[92] Worthington 2008a, pp. 187–189; Worthington 2014a, pp. 112–115. In Athens, Demosthenes proposed honors for Pausanias the assassin: Liddel, D182, pp. 662–664.

[93] Galatian invasions: Hammond and Walbank 1988, pp. 251–258; Hammond 1992a, pp. 298–302.

[94] Hammond 1972a, pp. 53–67; cf. Zahrnt 1984, pp. 355–357; Hatzopoulos 2020, pp. 8–11 and 14, with further references.

Figure 10.4 Vergina tumulus
Source: Creative Commons License; flickr, Patrick Janicek.

arms and armor, and five small carved ivory heads thought to be Philip, Alexander, Amyntas III, Eurydice, and Olympias—the same royal family as in the Philippeion. The ivory head believed to be that of Philip is of a bearded adult male and has marks around the right eye that might have been deliberately fashioned to show trauma consistent with the wound received in the siege of Methone in the winter of 355-354 (chapter 9). In the antechamber was another sarcophagus with a larnax containing female skeletal remains as well as a Scythian *gorytos* (quiver), which still had the remains of 74 arrows in it.[95]

Many scholars accept that Tomb II is the resting place of Philip II and one of his wives, though probably just as many favor the occupants to be Philip III and his wife Eurydice and for Philip II to have been buried in Tomb I. Time and space preclude detailed discussion here, but a recent detailed examination of the grave goods in tandem with forensic

[95] Andronikos 1979; Andronikos 1980; Andronikos 1987; Andronikos 2004. See too Borza 1990, pp. 256–266; Drougou and Saatsoglou-Paliadeli 2004; Saatsoglou-Paliadeli 2011, pp. 282–286; Hatzopoulos 2020, pp. 147–161; cf. Kottaridi 2020, all citing bibliography.

Figure 10.5 Facial reconstruction of Philip II
Source: Worthington 2014a, p. xv, figure 1.

examinations of the bones argues overwhelmingly in support of Philip II.[96] Among other things, the skull was reassembled, and the face reconstructed by a British forensic team (figure 10.5).[97] The result shows a male with a damaged right eye in keeping with the eye wound Philip suffered at Methone. The face of Philip II, if this is it, is indeed that of a warrior king.[98]

The identity of the female occupant of the antechamber is not known, but her bones had also been wrapped in a gold and purple cloth, and the weaponry suggests it was Philip's sixth wife Meda since Macedonian women did not fight and had no armor in their graves, whereas Scythian women were warriors.[99]

[96] Lane Fox 2011c; cf. Hammond 1978; Hammond 1992a, pp. 26–31; Worthington 2008a, pp. 233–240; Hatzopoulos 2020, pp. 147–161, all citing further bibliography. For the skeptical view, see, for example, Borza 1990, pp. 260–266; Borza and Palagia 2007; Gill 2008 (inscriptions on silver plate from the tomb were introduced by Alexander III and not used by Philip II); cf. Palagia 2017, pp. 157–160.

[97] Musgrave et al. 1984; Prag 1990a; Prag 1990b.

[98] Note Kottaridi 2020, pp. 145–155.

[99] See Saripanidi 2020 for the lack of arms in female Macedonian burials.

Philip's tomb has provoked another controversy, however, for in front of it was found the foundation of a *heroon*, a small shrine set up to worship the deceased. Macedonian kings received all sorts of honors of a religious nature and were likely semidivine while alive, but several sources apparently claim that Philip had pretensions to personal divinity while living.[100] Diodorus, for example, tells us, as mentioned above, that Philip's statue in the procession at Aegae followed those of the 12 gods, which were "adorned with a dazzling show of wealth to strike awe in the beholder," and that the king's statue was "suitable for a god...so that the king exhibited himself enthroned among the twelve gods."[101] In addition, the Athenians apparently worshiped Philip in the sanctuary of Heracles by the Acropolis; Amphipolis and Philippi were said to have cults to him; there was a statue of him in the Temple of Artemis at Ephesus; and there were altars to Zeus Philippios at Eresus on the island of Lesbos.[102]

Added to these examples is the Philippeion at Olympia. It was built in the sacred *temenos* alongside monuments honoring gods and heroes, including the famous statue of Zeus (one of the wonders of the ancient world), and was thought to have been a temple because the statues were made of chryselephantine (gold and ivory), materials used for cult statues. If so, it appears that Philip was establishing his own cult and may have seen himself as divine.

All these examples can be questioned. Diodorus does not refer to Philip's statue as an *agalma* (the Greek word for a cult statue) but an *eikon*, which was simply a secular statue of a person. The focus of Diodorus' passage is on the lavishness of the statues, with that of Philip expensively adorned to make it no different from those of the gods. Indeed, if the treasury was in the red by now, as mentioned above, the lavishness displayed was a clever move on Philip's part to project his apparent wealth and mask the motive behind the panhellenic invasion of Asia to an audience from all over Greece.

Likewise, Philip's statue at Ephesus was merely honorary, not religious, and the king's name linked to that of Zeus at Eresus indicates a worship of Zeus as Philip's protector. The evidence for the Athenians is very late, and it is perhaps confused with a proposal in 323 by the Athenian orator Demades

[100] See Fredricksmeyer 1979; Baynham 1994a; cf. Worthington 2008a, pp. 227–232; Lane Fox 2011e, pp. 361–363.

[101] Diodorus 16.92.5.

[102] Athenians: Clement, *Protrepticus* 4.54.5. Amphipolis: Habicht 1970, pp. 11–17; Fredricksmeyer 1979, pp. 50–51. Philippi: *SEG* 38.658. Ephesus: cf. Arrian 1.17.11.

to recognize Alexander the Great as a 13th god.[103] Finally, the Philippeion was a secular, not religious, building, for recent analysis of the statues' mountings shows they were not chryselephantine but made of stone, probably marble, that was gilded.[104] In addition, the building was a *tholos*, or round one, a shape that was generally not religious in function, nor did it have an altar (*bomos*) or hearth (*eschara*) to worship any individual. Even more important is that Eurydice and Olympias, whose statues stood next to that of Philip, were never divine, so why would only Philip's statue have anything to do with a personal cult?

There are therefore no compelling grounds for Philip's divinity, and any such megalomania on his part goes against the pragmatism that underscored his entire reign.[105] Possibly our later sources were unduly influenced by the Hellenistic and Roman practice of carrying statues of rulers into a theater as part of a ruler-cult and hence saw Philip's statue and thus the king as proof of his own godhead.[106]

Economy and coinage

Philip's military successes, including the unification of Macedonia, rippled into far wider-ranging economic reforms than any of his predecessors.[107] After the defeat of the Paeonians in 358, for example, he was able to gain access to the trade route along the Axius Valley to Dardania in the north. The defeat of the Illyrians in the same year enabled him to take over the rich gold and silver mines at Damastium, which also enabled him to fulfill that all-important duty of paying the army.[108] Mines became one of the economic mainstays of his kingdom, which is why after taking Potidaea in 356 he seized Crenides in the Mount Pangaeum region of western Thrace. He

[103] See Liddel, D197, pp. 706–710, citing references.

[104] Schultz 2007, pp. 220–221. Other examples of gilded statues included Praxiteles' portrait of Phryne (Pausanias 10.15.1), and that of Alexander I at Delphi.

[105] Lane Fox 2011e, p. 364, is rightly cautious about the literary sources but does say that the Philippeion and the palace of Aegae can point to something superhuman on Philip's part; cf. Mirón Pérez 2000, p. 51, stating that the building housed a dynastic cult.

[106] Chaniotis 2003. See too Mari 2008 on ruler cult.

[107] Ellis 1977; Ellis 1980. Philip's economic reforms: Hammond and Griffith 1979, pp. 657–671; Montgomery 1985; Hammond 1995b; Worthington 2008a, pp. 7–8, 30, 33–34, 40, 45–48, 50, 78–79, 110, 117, 124, 135, 168–169, and 196–197; cf. Millett 2010; Ruffing 2017.

[108] Cf. Lane Fox 2011f, pp. 367–368.

renamed it Philippi after himself and received from its mine the enormous annual revenue of 1,000 talents.[109]

Macedonia's abundant timber reserves had long been coveted by Greek states. Philip followed in the footsteps of his predecessors by always ensuring a market for his timber. In addition, he drained swampy ground and cultivated the marshy plain of Crenides.[110] This was part of a land reclamation policy to produce more landholdings and income for farmers and by extension his kingdom's economy. Archelaus built roads, but Philip undertook a more ambitious program of road construction.[111] These new roads and even towns that were built, not least along his northwest border with Illyria, were for security and economic reasons: they promoted urbanization, with smaller towns becoming larger urban centers with their own administrative and social structures.[112] And he spent time enlarging Pella, especially its market area, to make it the economic center of his kingdom.[113]

Philip could also draw on fresh revenues from the areas he conquered. In particular, the office of archon of Thessaly, which he received in 352, gave him income from that state's harbor and market taxes, and he also received tribute payments from the people of Pherae that they had formerly paid to their tyrants. The conquest of the Chalcidice in 348 earned him money from its timber and mineral resources, especially the gold and silver mines at Stratonici, and probably when he established Alexander on the throne of Epirus in 343, he received some income from its pastureland and timber. Another significant source of revenue would have been the tithe tax he imposed on Thrace after his conquest in 342.

But there was a downside. Macedonia had a rolling economy, whereby the proceeds from one campaign helped to pay for the next one. When Philip was campaigning successfully and winning booty, the coffers were full—and the army was paid. But it was a different story when they were empty. The loss of his booty from the Scythian expedition of 340, outlined above, would have been a substantial blow, and he may even have lost the 700 talents he made from the captured Athenian grain fleet.[114] Hence his need for liquid capital may explain his focus on Asia for booty and the

[109] Diodorus 16.8.6. [110] Theophrastus, *Nature of Plants* 5.14.5–6.

[111] See Hatzopoulos 1987—at p. 53 he names Archelaus as builder.

[112] Papazoglou 1988; cf. Siganidou 1993.

[113] Kottaridi 2011b, pp. 328–332, argues he did so also to make the city something of an "ideal state" based on Greek models.

[114] Theopompus, *BNJ* 115 F 292.

reason why Alexander was said to have found a depleted treasury when he became king in 336.

Much of the gold and silver was used for coinage. Rather than just having one mint, Philip decided to use several throughout his kingdom. The main mint was probably at Pella, but he also struck coins in Amphipolis and Philippi (formerly Crenides).[115] Philip's stimulation of coinage, thanks to his acquisition of various mines, was a tremendous boost for his kingdom's economic standing. Whereas kings had been coining since the days of Alexander I with some interruptions, it was Philip who introduced gold coins and restored silver coins after Alexander II had coined only in bronze, and likewise Perdiccas III after an initial run of silver didrachms.[116]

Philip's coinage was influenced by his predecessors, especially Archelaus, but on a greater scale.[117] He issued a new large bronze coin of a smaller denomination than his silver ones as well as commemorative coinage. Thus, when his horse won a race in the Olympic Games of 356, he minted at Pella a silver tetradrachm coin. On its obverse was the head of Zeus and on the reverse a victorious jockey and horse, with the king's name *Philippou.* In 348 he celebrated the fall of Olynthus at the festival honoring Zeus at Dium and fashioned another silver tetradrachm, this time with his portrait on it and an upraised hand, perhaps as if addressing a crowd in victory.[118] And probably in 345 he proclaimed his success in liberating Delphi from Phocian control and his presidency of the Pythian Games with a new gold stater. This had the head of Apollo with a laurel wreath on the obverse and a two-horse chariot with a charioteer, under which is the inscription *Philippou* (of Philip), on the reverse.[119] Called the "Philip," it replaced the Persian daric that had been the main gold coin in circulation.

Philip was innovative when it came to using iconography to support his kingship. He was the first king to put the head of Zeus on the obverse of his tetradrachms to show the chief god in the Macedonian pantheon underpinning his kingship, something that continued with Alexander the Great. And

[115] Cf. Le Rider 1980; cf. Kraay 1976, pp. 138–147; Kremydi 2011, p. 166. There seems to have been no mint at Aegae, even though it was a royal center, and Philip was said to have added to the palace there: Kottaridi 2011b; cf. Lane Fox 2011e, p. 365.

[116] On Philip's coinage in general, see Le Rider 1977; Poulios 1993.

[117] Hammond and Griffith 1979, pp. 662–666; Greenwalt 1994b, pp. 105–119; especially Le Rider 1977; Price 1979; Touratsoglou 2003; cf. Montgomery 1985, especially pp. 44–45. For the coins, see Price 1974, pp. 20–24, with plates referenced in these pages.

[118] Le Rider 1977, p. 506; Poulios 1993, p. 88; Lane Fox 2011e, p. 361.

[119] Kremydi 2011, p. 166 with n. 31, on dating.

in retaining the horseman introduced by Alexander I, Philip's horseman does not have two lances but the raised right hand, which may be a greeting or a gesture of benevolence.[120]

Philip's coins are important evidence not only for the strong state of the kingdom's economy but also for its expansion, as they were meant to compete with and eventually replace the coinages of regions he conquered, such as the Chalcidice, Thessaly, and even Epirus.[121] Although Philip did not appear to have left the treasury in good shape, his economic initiatives made the kingdom more prosperous than before.

Evaluating Philip

Philip was about 46 years old when he was assassinated.[122] Even a cursory comparison of Macedonia in 359 and in 336 brings him solidly out of the shadow of his more famous son. By 336 Macedonia was on the road to empire as Philip had more than doubled its size to as far east as the Hellespont, including all Greece; correspondingly increased its population; united Upper and Lower Macedonia and centralized the monarchy at Pella; carried out longer-ranging and more permanent economic reforms; and devised plans for the invasion of the Persian Empire.

Worthy of special attention is Philip's military reforms that resulted in a formidable army and dramatically increased manpower reserves. In 359 he had about 10,000 infantry and 600 cavalry, but in 336 that number had risen to 24,000 infantry and 3,000 cavalry.[123] The ineffectual conscript force was a thing of the past; now there was a professional, well-trained and well-equipped defensive and offensive force that was also an integral part of the state, militarily and economically.[124] Its success dovetailed with the need to keep it on campaign, hence more imperialistic ventures.[125] And its fearsome reputation had a long life: after the battle of Pydna in 168, the victorious Roman general Lucius Aemilius Paullus remarked he had never been as afraid as when he saw the Macedonian phalanx bearing down on him.[126]

[120] Caccamo Caltabiano 1999, p. 199 ("a charismatic gesture of the king's benevolence").
[121] Cf. Hammond and Griffith 1979, pp. 662–666.
[122] Justin 9.8.1 says he was 47, but he means in his 47th year; hence Philip was 46.
[123] Diodorus 16.4.3, 17.7.5.
[124] Errington 1990, pp. 229–249; Hatzopoulos 1996, vol. 1, pp. 443–460; cf. Errington 1978.
[125] Worthington 2003a. [126] Plutarch, *Paullus* 19.2.

Philip also maintained the tradition of a cultured court, and the arts also played into the manner of his kingship.[127] He famously hired Aristotle to tutor Alexander from 342 to 340, and Aristotle may even have remained in Philip's employment since he did not open his own school in Athens until 335. Philip also patronized the historians Callisthenes of Olynthus, Anaximenes of Lampsacus, and Theopompus of Chios, who wrote about Macedonia, perhaps echoing Archelaus' patronage of Euripides and refashioning the origins of the Argead line.[128] Philip and Theopompus presumably had some disagreement, and Theopompus clearly did not believe in not biting the hand that feeds you, for the tome that he produced was an attack on Philip and his morals.[129]

Philip enjoyed personal contacts with leading Athenian orators and philosophers.[130] Plato had a special relationship with Macedonian kings: Perdiccas III patronized his Academy, and our Philip was said to have "honored" the philosopher when he died in 347, whatever that meant.[131] The king was also attracted to rhetoric, of which the most famous teacher was the Athenian Isocrates. The two of them corresponded, and Isocrates saw Philip as someone who could end disunity in Greece and in his *Panegyricus* of 380 and again in his *To Philip* of 346 he advocated a panhellenic invasion of Persia under Philip, though Philip was not swayed.

Dramatic performances of Greek classics continued, but Philip made a subtle change by having them performed at royal weddings, after military victories, and at symposia, rather than only in a theater.[132] Presumably for reasons of time, an entire play was not performed in a non-theatrical setting; hence the actor Neoptolemus performed only part of a tragedy at a lengthy symposium the night before Philip's murder, and Alexander the Great recited only some lines of Euripides' *Andromeda* at a symposium the night before his death.[133] Evidently, Greek tragedy was deadly at times.

[127] Saatsoglou-Paliadeli 2007; see too Markle 1976. Convenient summary of Philip and Greek culture: Pownall 2017, pp. 222–223.

[128] Their works exist only as fragments today. Callisthenes: *BNJ* 124; Anaximenes: *BNJ* 72; Theoompus: *BNJ* 115. I find it hard to agree with Pownall 2017, pp. 225–226, that the Argead kings were deliberately selective in wanting to invite only those who were "innovative in their respective genres." In Philip's case, he may have simply wanted a prose history of his kingdom written by respected figures.

[129] See further on Theopompus, Shrimpton 1977; Flower 1994. On later hostile traditions to Philip, see Asirvatham 2008; Asirvatham 2010b.

[130] Markle 1976; cf. Worthington 2008a, pp. 121–122.

[131] Theopompus, *BNJ* 115 F 294.

[132] Csapo 2010, pp. 172–178.

[133] Neoptolemus: Diodorus 16.92.3 (who speaks of "well received pieces" pertinent to the Persian campaign). Alexander: Nicobule, *BNJ* 127 F 2.

Philip certainly had his personal faults, but his achievements and generalship outweighed them, and he was always the traditional warrior king, in the process losing an eye, shattering a collarbone, and suffering a major wound that made him limp for the rest of his life. He was a great ruler, as were some of his predecessors such as Alexander I, who expanded the kingdom east and west, Archelaus, who among other things won back lost areas, expanded into Thessaly, and inaugurated a sweeping cultural policy, and even Perdiccas III, who dealt well with Athens and Chalcidians. Their achievements in part enabled Philip to do what he did.[134]

But Philip's legacy transcends his predecessors, as he left Alexander a kingdom boasting a formidable army, economic strength, secure borders, enormous expansion of territory, hegemony of Greece, dynastic stability, and readiness to invade Asia.[135] Alexander's reign would have been quite different without his father's successes:[136] Thanks to Philip, Macedonia became a superpower in the Greek world and the Macedonians recognized their new status, a far cry from mere decades earlier when they were prey to foreign invasions and looked down upon by Greeks south of Mount Olympus.[137]

Macedonia under the Argead Kings: The Rise and Fall of an Ancient Superpower. Ian Worthington, Oxford University Press. © Oxford University Press 2026. DOI: 10.1093/9780197668009.003.0011

[134] Cf. Zahrnt 2006b, pp. 127–128; Consolo Langher 2007; Anson 2008b.

[135] Comments on Philip's legacy: Worthington 2008a, pp. 194–208; Worthington 2010a; Gabriel 2010, pp. 243–251; Worthington 2014a, pp. 115–119; see too Zahrnt 2009.

[136] See Diodorus 16.95, on Philip's achievements, clearly echoing Theopompus, *BNJ* 115 F 27, asserting that Europe had never produced a man like Philip. Justin 9.8 was even more laudatory in a long necrology comparing Philip and Alexander: See Worthington 2010a. Alexander praises Philip's accomplishments in a speech supposedly given before his troops at Opis in 324: Arrian 7.9.2–5; Curtius 10.2.23–4.3.

[137] See Worthington 2014a, pp. 105–109 and 300–302.

11

Alexander the Great: King of Macedonia and Ruler of Asia

Building on his father's accomplishments, Alexander III made Macedonia a truly intentional power by forging an empire from Greece to India and showing great leadership skills and strategic genius in someone so young. His empire was arguably without parallel in antiquity because, although the Roman Empire was more extensive, it took centuries to reach its height and was the product of many generals and emperors, whereas Alexander was one man and took 10 years to create the empire. Moreover, his campaign, one of the most celebrated of antiquity, also has lessons for today's military operations by demonstrating how a foreign army can survive in distant, hostile, and unknown lands as well as the value of personal leadership.[1]

Ancient evidence for Alexander is more plentiful than for Philip II, but it is controversial. None of the roughly 40 contemporary accounts of his reign and persona are extant—what we have from them are some 400 quotations and paraphrases in the major narrative sources who wrote hundreds of years after his era.[2] These were Diodorus Siculus (first century BC); Quintus Curtius Rufus (middle to later first century AD); Arrian (second century AD); and Justin (sometime in the second to fourth centuries AD), who wrote an epitome of a lost first century BC work by Gnaeus Pompeius Trogus. To these we can add other writers, such as the biographer Plutarch (first to second century AD), who included a life of Alexander in his series of prominent Greeks and Romans.[3] The veracity of sources is a major issue in Alexander studies, for we do not know how carefully later writers used earlier sources, especially as the latter often disagreed on Alexander's life and reign; hence getting to the real or historical king is fraught with difficulty.

[1] Ferguson and Worthington 2024.

[2] *BNJ* nos. 117–153, all translated in Robinson 1953, with roughly one-quarter translated in Worthington 2011. The latter also contains a selection of modern scholars' works on various aspects of Alexander's reign, as does Griffith 1966.

[3] For a discussion of the ancient sources, including epigraphic and numismatic, see Worthington 2014a, pp. 311–319; Müller 2016, pp. 74–84; especially Baynham 2003; Zambrini 2007, all citing further bibliography, to which add Worthington 2022b.

Many books have been written on Alexander; hence no single chapter can do him justice.[4] Because of his importance as an Argead king and how he altered the Macedonian monarchy, he must be included in any history of that dynasty. However, since almost all his reign took place in Asia, so outside Macedonia, the subject of this book, this chapter gives only a broad description of his campaign; its primary focus is to assess him as an Argead king and what he did for Macedonia, as well as mentioning Macedonia and Greece during his time in Asia.

Birth and youth

Alexander was born in 356, the son of Philip II and Olympias (figure 11.1). He had a brother who was one year older, Arrhidaeus, the son of Philip and Philinna of Larissa, but for some reason Alexander was the preferred heir. He was always destined for superhuman status if we believe the stories about his divine conception, such as Olympias' dream that during a storm a thunderbolt from Zeus fell into her womb and impregnated her or how Philip caught her having sex with a huge snake—Zeus in disguise—and not long after she became pregnant with Alexander.[5] Likewise, the day he was born the temple of Artemis at Ephesus burned down because, it was said, the goddess was helping to birth him at Pella. The Magi at Ephesus believed the temple's destruction was symbolic and "ran around slapping their faces and lamenting aloud that on this day had been born only sorrow and great calamity for Asia."[6]

Another story tells of the taming of Alexander's horse Bucephalas ("Ox-head"). A Thessalian horse trader had brought horses to Pella including a black stallion, which reared up violently whenever anyone tried to ride

[4] Biographies: Seibert 1972; Lane Fox 1973; Green 1974; Bosworth 1988; Hammond 1989b; Hammond 1997c; Cartledge 2003; Nawotka 2010; Briant 2010; Worthington 2014a. Other studies: Fuller 1960; Engels, D. 1978; Goukowsky 1978; Sekunda and McBride 1984; Holt 1989; Bosworth 1996a; Fraser 1996; Sekunda and Warry 1998; Holt 1989; Holt 2003; Holt 2005; Chugg 2006; Heckel 2006; Thomas 2006; Lonsdale 2007; Heckel 2008; Ogden 2011; Anson 2013; Holt 2016; Ferguson and Worthington 2024. Succinct treatments: Jähne 1978; Keegan 1987, pp. 74–87; Devine 1989a; Strauss 2003; Gilley and Worthington 2010; Müller 2016, pp. 282–306; Worthington 2017; King 2018, pp. 151–177. See also the essays in edited books such as Griffith 1966; Bosworth and Baynham 2000; Roisman 2003a; Heckel and Tritle 2009; Carney and Ogden 2010; Worthington 2011; Baynham and Wheatley 2014; Ogden 2024.

[5] Plutarch, *Alexander* 2–3, for the various stories, with Worthington 2014a, pp. 90–97; Müller 2016, pp. 278–282, on Alexander's youth.

[6] Hegesias, *BNJ* 142 F 3 (= Plutarch, *Alexander* 3.5–9).

Figure 11.1 Bust of Alexander the Great (Pella)
Source: Creative Commons License.

him. Alexander, although only a boy, noticed that the horse was spooked when his shadow fell in front of him. He persuaded his father to let him ride the animal and turned the horse to face the sun so that his shadow fell behind him; now calm, Bucephalas allowed Alexander to ride him, while a tearful Philip predicted that Macedonia would never be big enough for his son.[7]

Much in these stories is fanciful. Alexander's mother was Olympias; he did bring Achaemenid rule in Persia to an end, and he did have a horse named Bucephalas, which died of wounds suffered in India in 326. But can we really believe that Olympias was impregnated by a snake or a thunderbolt or that a seasoned horse trader along with Philip and various cavalrymen could not see that Bucephalas was startled by his own shadow? The stories were arguably put out by Alexander as his Asian campaign progressed to claim he was always destined for greatness.

[7] Plutarch, *Alexander* 3.

In 342 Philip hired Aristotle to tutor the 14-year-old Alexander.[8] Perhaps because of Olympias' influence over her son, Philip sent Aristotle and Alexander to live in the Precinct of the Nymphs at Mieza in the Gardens of Midas. Alexander was already a precocious boy, and for three years Aristotle taught him biology, ethics, literature, mathematics, medicine, philosophy, politics, rhetoric, and zoology. When Alexander left for Asia he took with him a retinue of philosophers, civilian naturalists, and *bematistai* (surveyors), who provided him with intellectual stimulation and recorded all manner of information about the areas through which they marched.[9] He also took with him Aristotle's edition of Homer's *Iliad*, which he was said to have kept under his pillow along with a dagger.[10] This is surely false as the work would comprise two dozen or more papyrus rolls, a lot to slip under a pillow! That story, like the ones of Alexander's conception and birth, belongs to the realm of legend.

As we saw in the previous chapter, in 340 as regent of Macedonia, Alexander defeated the Maedians, and in 338 had an important cavalry command at the battle of Chaeronea and diplomatic role to Athens afterward. Yet Philip seems not to have included Alexander in the invasion of Asia. Given the young heir was making a name for himself on the battlefield, we must assume he felt slighted and may even have conspired against his father. But Philip's assassination in 336 and Antipater's speedy acclamation of Alexander as king maintained dynastic stability and gave the 20-year-old the throne.

The first campaigns

The new king was immediately faced with a revolt of the Greeks from the League of Corinth. After burying his father at Aegae, he went to Greece, winning over "some cities by diplomacy, others by striking fear into them, and others by the actual use of force."[11] At Corinth he re-established the league along with the plan to invade Persia. He also conducted a series of purges that lasted into the following year of possible opponents including Attalus,

[8] Plutarch, *Alexander* 7.2–5; cf. 8.1–2.

[9] Badian 1991; see too Tritle 2009.

[10] Plutarch, *Alexander* 8.2.

[11] Diodorus 17.3.6–4.9 (quotation); Arrian 1.1.2–3, with Fuller 1960, pp. 81–83; Bosworth 1988, pp. 188–192; Ashley 1998, pp. 165–167; Worthington 2014a, pp. 126–127.

who at the time was a commander of the advance force in Asia Minor.[12] In the meantime, Olympias likely killed Philip's seventh wife Cleopatra and their baby daughter, though Alexander spared his half-brother Arrhidaeus perhaps because of a closer familial bond. Within a year of becoming king, and with speed reminiscent of his father, Alexander had thus reasserted Macedonian hegemony of Greece.

Rather than leave for Asia, in 335 Alexander campaigned in Thrace and Illyria, probably to accustom his men to their new commander and king. With 15,000 infantry and 5,000 cavalry he left for Thrace in the spring of 335.[13] He defeated several Thracian tribes, including the Triballi, thus revenging Philip's defeat at their hands in 339, apparently killing 3,000 of them but losing only 11 of his own cavalry and 41 infantry.[14] These numbers are questionable, as is the case in all his battles, as our ancient writers routinely increase enemy numbers and casualty rates while decreasing those of the king's army to make his victories all the more impressive.[15]

In Illyria Alexander faced tougher foes, including Cleitus, king of the Dardanians and probably the son of Bardylis. In tandem with the Taulantii (around Tirana) and the Autariatae (in modern Bosnia) peoples, Cleitus threatened the vital northwest frontier with Macedonia.[16] Alexander's campaign against him turned out to be a major one, and at one point he was surrounded by the enemy and extricated himself with difficulty. He was gaining the upper hand when news reached him that the Thebans had again revolted—the first was a year earlier as part of the Greek insurrection against Macedonian rule. Now they were calling on the Greeks to join forces against the "tyrant" of Greece and even supporting Amyntas, next in line to the throne in 359, who was perhaps planning a coup.[17]

Alexander was forced to abandon his Illyrian campaign and let Cleitus escape, who fortunately did not bother him again. The king marched on Thebes with 30,000 infantry and 300 cavalry, covering 250 miles of rugged terrain including the Pindus range in only 13 days. They were already in

[12] Diodorus 17.2.4–6, 5.1–2; Curtius 7.1.3; Justin 11.5.1. Purges: Ellis 1982b, pp. 69–73; Worthington 2014a, pp. 121–123.

[13] Campaign: Diodorus 17.8.1–2; Arrian 1.1.6–13; Plutarch, *Alexander* 11.5; Justin 11.2.8, with Fuller 1960, pp. 219–226; Bosworth 1988, pp. 28–32; Hammond and Walbank 1988, pp. 32–55; Ashley 1998, pp. 167–175; Worthington 2014a, pp. 128–130; English 2011, pp. 19–32.

[14] Arrian 1.2.7.

[15] Hammond 1989c; cf. Hammond 1992a, pp. 129–136.

[16] Arrian 1.5–6, with Hammond 1974; Hammond 1977; Bosworth 1982; Hammond and Walbank 1988, pp. 39–48; English 2009b, pp. 25–34; King 2018, pp. 138–141.

[17] Diodorus 17.9.5; cf. Arrian 1.7.1–2; Justin 11.2. Amyntas: Worthington 2003b.

Boeotia when the Thebans learned of their approach and thought at first it was Antipater from Macedonia. They refused to surrender, so Alexander besieged the city. After some costly setbacks thanks to the spirit of the defenders he and his men fought their way into the city, slaughtering 6,000 Thebans and taking 30,000 prisoners, before razing the city to the ground.[18]

Interestingly, Alexander left standing only the temples as well as the house of the poet Pindar because of his encomium to Alexander I, which we discussed in chapter 4. Despite his treatment of the enemy, his admiration of courage and sense of honor showed itself during the taking of Thebes.[19] One of his men had raped a noblewoman, Timocleia. She lured him down a well by telling him she had thrown all her treasure down it, and after he climbed down, she pelted him with stones and killed him. Brought before Alexander, she defiantly told him that she would rather die than suffer the same thing again. Impressed by her courage, he spared her life.[20]

Alexander had thus proved himself as a general and king, displaying the leadership skills and bold, quick thinking that became his legendary trademarks. His merciless punishment of the Thebans showed the Greeks what would happen to anyone defying Macedonian rule and set a pattern for the rest of his reign: if anyone crossed him, redemption was out of the question.

Now it was time to put Philip's grand plan into action. Alexander returned to Pella for the remainder of 335, and in the spring of 334, aged only 22, he led an army of as many as 40,000 infantry and 5,000 cavalry across the Hellespont to Asia.[21] He left behind Antipater as regent (*epitropos*) of Greece and deputy hegemon of the League of Corinth along with a force of 12,000 infantry and 1,500 cavalry.[22] Philip may have envisaged a campaign only in Asia Minor, but Alexander showed his intention was different: before he landed in Asia he threw a spear, so the story goes, into foreign soil to show he intended to take Persia "by the spear."[23] His action would fundamentally change the nature of the monarchy, as we discuss in chapter 11.

[18] Diodorus 17.8.2–14; Arrian 1.7–9; Plutarch, *Alexander* 11.7–13; Plutarch, *Demosthenes* 23. 1–3; Justin 11.3.6–4.8, with Fuller 1960, pp. 85–88; Bosworth 1988, pp. 32–33 and 194–196; Hammond and Walbank 1988, pp. 56–66; Ashley 1998, pp. 175–181; Worthington 2003b; English 2009b, pp. 34–40; Worthington 2014a, pp. 131–135; King 2018, pp. 142–146.

[19] Honor: see Roisman 2003b.

[20] Aristobulus, *BNJ* 139 F 2b (= [Plutarch], *Moralia* 259d–260d); Plutarch, *Alexander* 11.12.

[21] Numbers: Fuller 1960, p. 88; Green 1974, pp. 156–158; Hammond 1989b, pp. 67–68. Fuller 1960, Appendix 2 (pp. 153–157), lists Alexander's officers and their commands. On his army, see Sekunda and McBride 1984; Sekunda and Warry 1998; English 2009a.

[22] Diodorus 17.17.4–5. Antipater: see Baynham 1994b; cf. Gilley and Worthington 2010.

[23] Diodorus 17.17.2. Brunt 1965 argues that Alexander's invasion was merely his inheritance from Philip, but see Fredricksmeyer 1982; Fredricksmeyer 2000; Heckel 2003b, and especially Degen 2019; cf. Austin 1993; Zahrnt 1996.

Ruler of Asia

The Persian Empire was divided into 20 satrapies or regions, established by Darius I, and stretched from Turkey to present-day Pakistan (what the Greeks called "India"), including Egypt and Syria.[24] From its most westerly palace center, Sardis (Sart in Turkey), to its most easterly, Persepolis (northeast of Shiraz in Iran), was roughly 2,000 miles; hence Alexander's communication and supply lines, not to mention his manpower and leadership skills, would be tested. But by 330, just four years later, he had conquered all and was calling himself Ruler of Asia, and in 325 he sailed down the Indus into the Southern Ocean believing that India was his.

Within weeks of landing, Alexander had "liberated" the Greek cities of Asia Minor from Persian rule, though they now had to pay tribute to him and were perhaps forced to join the League of Corinth, and defeated the Persians in the battle of Granicus (Biga) River.[25] Successful sieges of Miletus and Halicarnassus followed as he marched south.[26] Then in the summer of 333 he "undid" the fabled Gordian Knot at Gordium to fulfill the legend that whoever did so would rule Asia—a deliberate psychological tactic to alarm the Persians.[27] That same year he faced the Great King himself, Darius III, a leader of some renown, at Issus.[28] Darius had a huge army of 100,000 to 150,000, but in battle there Alexander's strategy was to capture or kill Darius, thus disheartening his troops and overcoming them.[29] The Great King fled the battlefield, leaving Alexander as victor.

[24] On Persia see, for example, Briant 2002; Waters 2014; Brosius 2020; cf. Strauss 2003, pp. 147–149.

[25] Diodorus 17.19–21; Arrian 1.12.8–16; Plutarch, *Alexander* 16; Justin 11.6.8–13; Polybius 12.19.1, with Fuller 1960, pp. 147–154; Bosworth 1988, pp. 39–44; Ashley 1998, pp. 187–202; Lonsdale 2007, pp. 97–104; Heckel 2008, pp. 46–51; Worthington 2014a, pp. 144–149; in depth: Badian 1977; Devine 1986a; Devine 1988; Hammond 1980d; Matthews 2008; English 2011, pp. 33–60; Ferguson and Worthington 2024, pp. 116–120. Alxander and the Asiatic Greeks: Badian 1966; Hammond and Walbank 1988, pp. 72–76; Bosworth 1988, pp. 250–258; Faraguna 2003, pp. 109–115; Nawotka 2003; Kholod 2010; Kholod 2013.

[26] Miletus: Diodorus 17.22; Arrian 1.18.4, 1.19.1–8; Plutarch, *Alexander* 17.2, with Bosworth 1988, pp. 46–47; Ashley 1998, pp. 204–206; English 2009b, pp. 41–46; Worthington 2014a, pp. 152–153; Ferguson and Worthington 2024, pp. 121–123. Halicarnassus: Diodorus 17.23.4–27; Arrian 1.20.2–23.8; Curtius 5.2.5, 8.1.36; Plutarch, *Alexander* 17.2; with Fuller 1960, pp. 200–206; Bosworth 1988, pp. 47–49; Ashley 1998, pp. 206–210; English 2009b, pp. 47–55; Worthington 2014a, pp. 154–156; Ferguson and Worthington 2024, pp. 123–124.

[27] Aristobulus, *BNJ* 139 FF 7 and 7b (= Plutarch, *Alexander* 18.2–4); Arrian 2.3.7; Justin 11.7.16, with Worthington 2014a, p. 159, and see Fredricksmeyer 1961; Frei 1972; Roller 1984.

[28] Nylander 1993; Badian 2000; Briant 2010, pp. 42–44 and 48–52; especially Briant 2015.

[29] Diodorus 17.31–6; Arrian 2.6–11; Curtius 3.3–4, 7–11; Plutarch, *Alexander* 20; Justin 11.9; cf. Polybius 12.18.2, with Fuller 1960, pp. 154–162; Bosworth 1988, pp. 60–62; Ashley 1998, pp. 222–235; Lonsdale 2007, pp. 80–86; Heckel 2008, pp. 57–65; Worthington 2014a, pp. 165–171; Ferguson and Worthington 2024, pp. 127–131; in depth: Murison 1972; Devine 1985a; Devine 1985b; Hammond 1992b; English 2011, pp. 71–109. Size: English 2011, pp. 75–77 and 83–84.

Figure 11.2 The Alexander Mosaic
Source: Creative Commons License; flickr, Steven Zucker, smarthistory cofounder.

A postscript to the battle may be mentioned. Although Alexander and Darius never fought each other, a contemporary painting perhaps by Philoxenus of Eretria showed Alexander on Bucephalas charging at Darius, their eyes fastened on each other, as Macedonian soldiers wielding sarissas surround the Great King's chariot. This painting—surely for propaganda purposes—became a model for the famous "Alexander mosaic," which was found in the House of the Faun at Pompeii in 1831 (figure 11.2).[30]

To win control of the entire eastern Mediterranean seaboard Alexander marched into Phoenicia (Lebanon), where several cities, such as Byblos and Sidon, surrendered to him, but he faced fearsome resistance at Tyre, and only conquered the city six costly months later.[31] As he continued south, Gaza also resisted him, but this time the siege was shorter though equally brutal.[32] In November Alexander swept into Egypt, where its satrap Mazaces surrendered to him.[33] He was never crowned pharaoh but took on

[30] See in detail Cohen 1997; see too Paliadeli 2019, connecting its composition to the frieze of Tomb II at Vergina.

[31] Diodorus 17.40.2–46.6; Arrian 2.18.3–24.6; Curtius 4.2.8–4.18; Plutarch, *Alexander* 24.4–25.3; Justin 11.10.10–14, with Fuller 1960, pp. 206–216; Romane 1987; Bosworth 1988, pp. 65–67; Bloedow 1990; Ashley 1998, pp. 237–249; English 2009b, pp. 56–84; Worthington 2014a, pp. 173–178; Ferguson and Worthington 2024, pp. 136–140.

[32] Diodorus 17.48.7; Arrian 2.25.4–27.7; Curtius 4.6.7–31; Plutarch, *Alexander* 25.4, with Fuller 1960, pp. 216–218; Bosworth 1988, pp. 67–68; Romane 1988; Ashley 1998, pp. 249–251; English 2009b, pp. 85–101; Worthington 2014a, pp. 178–179, Ferguson and Worthington 2024, pp. 140–141.

[33] Alexander in Egypt: Bosworth 1988, pp. 68–74; Worthington 2014a, pp. 179–184. See too Burstein 1994; Bloedow 2004; cf. Bowden 2014.

all the attributes of that position, including divine status. He then visited the Oracle of Zeus Ammon in the Oasis of Siwah (Libyan Desert), where the priest allegedly told him he was a son of Zeus; this was a turning point in his pretensions to personal divinity, and from then on he viewed Philip as merely his mortal father.[34] Another feature of his time in Egypt was the founding of what became the premier city of the Hellenistic period, which he named after himself: Alexandria.[35]

In the spring of 331, Alexander left Egypt, appointing a man named Cleomenes as overseer, who quickly became powerful and unpopular.[36] The king returned to Tyre, where he supposedly received a letter from Darius offering various terms, including that Alexander marry his daughter Stateira, recognize the Great King as his friend and ally, and receive all lands west of the Euphrates.[37] Alexander refused: he wanted total conquest. The two kings faced each other in battle again on either the last day of September or the first day of October 331 at Gaugamela (Tell Gomel, 70 miles northwest of Irbil, the capital of Iraqi Kurdistan).[38] Both commanded large armies: Darius' of 100,000–150,000 and Alexander's of perhaps 40,000 infantry and 7,000 cavalry, which was outflanked by Darius' line.[39] Again outnumbered and facing war elephants for the first time as well as a unit of 200 scythed chariots, Alexander used the same strategy as at Issus against Darius. The latter again fled as Alexander bore down on him, followed by his men. This victory gave Alexander Persia, and he now began to call himself Ruler of Asia.[40]

Three months later Alexander had seized the Persian capital of Babylon along with its enormous treasury of 40,000 talents of gold and silver bullion.[41] From there he marched to another Persia capital, Susa, and another great treasury. Throughout his campaign the amount of money and treasure

[34] Burstein 1991 on not being crowned pharaoh. Siwah and divinity: Bosworth 1988, pp. 278–290; Worthington 2014a, pp. 265–269; cf. Hamilton, J.R. 1953; Goukowsky 1978, vol. 2; Badian 1981; Fredricksmeyer 1981; Fredricksmeyer 2003; Bosworth 1996c; Müller 2016, pp. 287–289. See also Anson 2003; Collins 2014. Cf. Mari 2008; Dreyer 2009.

[35] Worthington 2016, pp. 135–146; see too Howe 2014. Alexandria: Fraser 1972; Grimm 1998, for example.

[36] Cleomenes: Vogt 1971; Burstein 2008; Baynham 2015.

[37] Diodorus 17.39.1–2; Arrian 2.14; Curtius 4.1.7–14; cf. Diodorus 17.54.1–5; Curtius 4.5.1–8; Justin 11.12; Plutarch, *Alexander* 29.7–8.

[38] Diodorus 17.56–61; Arrian 3.8–15; Curtius 4.9–10.12, 4.12–16.33; Plutarch, *Alexander* 31–33; Justin 11.13–14.7, with Fuller 1960, pp. 163–180; Bosworth 1988, pp. 76–85; Ashley 1998, pp. 257–269; Lonsdale 2007, pp. 127–134; Heckel 2008, pp. 75–80; Worthington 2014a, pp. 188–193; Ferguson and Worthington 2024, pp. 142–147; in depth: Griffith 1947; Marsden 1964; Devine 1975; Devine 1986b; Devine 1989b; English 2011, pp. 110–137. Routes of Alexander and Darius: Bosworth 1988, pp. 79–80, citing bibliography.

[39] Differing numbers: Arrian 3.8.6; Diodorus 17.53.3; Curtius 4.12.13; Plutarch, *Alexander* 31.1; cf. English 2011, pp. 110–115. Order of lines: English 2011, pp. 121–129.

[40] Lonsdale 2007, p. 156. See too Wirth 1971.

[41] Arrian 3.16.3–5; Curtius 5.1.17–45.

Alexander seized from the Persian capitals was practically unimaginable. Some he sent back to Greece, but he kept huge sums for himself, and spent a fortune on religious events, founding cities, and gifts to friends and his men.[42] At Susa he discovered treasures seized by the Persians when they sacked Athens in 480 and returned them in keeping with Philip's original reason for the invasion.[43]

Alexander was now anxious to take control of Persepolis, the symbolic heart of the Persian Empire where at its palace the Great King's subjects would bring him tribute and pledges of loyalty.[44] He was blocked en route at the Persian (Susian) Gates by Ariobarzanes, satrap of Persis.[45] He was pinned down for one month before learning of a path that led behind Ariobarzanes' camp, enabling him to take some men to its far end and attack Ariobarzanes from the front, back, and even the sides where he had stationed troops. It was a brilliant victory, a testament to Alexander's skill, patience, and boldness.

Alexander finally reached Persepolis at the end of January 330. As revenge for what the Greeks had suffered during the Persian Wars, he allowed his men to run riot, killing and raping military and civilian people and looting indiscriminately.[46] As the men prepared to leave in May of 330 to hunt down Darius, the palace burned to the ground, arguably a symbolic act on Alexander's part to show the Achaemenid Empire was no more and that his panhellenic mission was accomplished.[47]

Alexander never took the Great King alive. After some close encounters, he found Darius at Hecatompylus (Qumis), the capital of Parthia, treacherously murdered.[48] But then Bessus, satrap of Bactria, who had fought with Darius at Gaugamela and may even have condoned the act of regicide,

[42] See Holt 2016, estimating between 180,000 and 200,000 talents in money, let alone precious artworks, gold plate, jewelry, etc.

[43] See Finn 2014.

[44] See Cahill 1985.

[45] Diodorus 17.68.2–7; Arrian 3.18.1–9; Curtius 5.3.17–4.34, with Fuller 1960, pp. 228–234; Heckel 1980a; Bosworth 1988, pp. 90–92; Ashley 1998, pp. 274–277; Speck 2002; Worthington 2014a, pp. 202–204; Ferguson and Worthington 2024, pp. 148–151; see too Howe 2015a.

[46] Diodorus 17.70.1–6; Curtius 5.6.1–8 (Alexander ordered his men not to violate the women); Plutarch, *Alexander* 37.3–5, with Worthington 2014a, pp. 204–206, and especially Seibert 2004–2005.

[47] Other explanations include accidentally burning it to the ground or even because of some form of PTSD on Alexander's part (Morrison 2001): Arrian 6.30.1; Curtius 5.8.11; Plutarch, *Alexander* 38.8, with Borza 1972; Hammond 1992c; Sancisi-Weerdenburg 1993; Briant 2010, pp. 107–111; Wirth 1993; Bloedow and Loube 1997 (limitations of archaeological evidence); Morrison 2001; San José Campos 2021; cf. Seibert 2004–2005.

[48] Diodorus 17.73.3; Arrian 3.21.10; Curtius 8.16–17; Justin 11.15.5, with Worthington 2014a, pp. 209–211. On Darius' death, see Antela-Bernárdez 2023.

declared himself Great King, taking the name Artaxerxes (V).[49] For the security of his Macedonian Empire, Alexander had to take down Bessus, which meant marching into Bactria and hence a new war and a new strategy.

Bactria consisted of what today is Afghanistan, Tajikistan, and Uzbekistan, north of the Hindu Kush (what the Greeks called the Caucasus) and south of the Oxus or Amu Darya River. Sogdiana (sometimes Sogdia) comprised Uzbekistan, Tajikistan, Kazakhstan, and Kyrgyzstan. Their mountainous topography as well as deserts and plains pushed Alexander and his men to their utmost—more than in Persia—as the natives anchored their resistance in guerrilla warfare and could easily disappear across the steppes. Yet Alexander's generalship and strategic skills were as much in evidence in Central Asia as they had been in Persia, though they are countered by disturbing changes in his personality and increasing brutality.[50]

In late winter 329 Alexander's army crossed the 11,000-foot high Khawak Pass over the Hindu Kush, suffering badly from frostbite, snow-blindness, and even eating their pack animals raw when supplies ran out.[51] They arrived about 80 miles from Bessus' position, who fled north across the Oxus River into Sogdiana. His flight allowed the king to take over Drapsaca (Kunduz in northeastern Afghanistan) and with it almost all Bactria. Shortly after Alexander crossed the Oxus, Bessus was betrayed and handed over to Alexander: he was whipped and sent to Bactra (Balkh), the capital of Bactria, where his nose and ears were sliced off, and thence to Ecbatana for impalement.[52]

That success did not end Alexander's troubles, for there now erupted a large-scale revolt of Bactria and Sogdiana led by two Sogdian chieftains, Spitamenes and Dataphernes. This included the massacre of Macedonians Alexander had stationed at Samarkand in southeastern Uzbekistan, capital of Sogdiana.[53] For the next three years Spitamenes' guerrilla raids cost the

[49] Arrian 3.21.1, 4; Curtius 5.9.2–8. A fragmentary Aramaic inscription calls him "Artaxerxes the king": See Briant 2010, pp. 178–179. Related to Darius: Arrian 3.21.5.

[50] Alexander in Bactria and Sogdiana: Fuller 1960, pp. 234–245; Bosworth, 1988, pp. 97–119; Ashley 1998, pp. 282–305; Sidky 2000, pp. 37–86; English 2011, pp. 158–174; Worthington 2014a, pp. 211–235; Müller 2016, pp. 296–300; Ferguson and Worthington 2024, pp. 181–196; especially Holt 1989; Holt 2005; see too Bloedow 1991; Holt 1986; Rtvladze 2007; Vacante 2012; Iliakis 2013; and the essays in Antonetti and Biagi 2017; cf. Howe 2015b.

[51] Arrian 3.28.4–291; cf. Curtius 7.3.21 (a fortnight to cross).

[52] Arrian 3.30.4–5; Curtius 7.5.38–39.

[53] On terms like "revolt" or "rebellion" wrongly applied to Alexander's campaign in Bactria and Sogdiana, see Howe 2015b. But this is a matter of semantics: See Ferguson and Worthington 2024, pp. 186–187; cf. Lonsdale 2007, pp. 95–97.

invaders dearly.[54] The end of the revolt came when Spitamenes was betrayed by his allies the Massagetae, who sent his head to Alexander.[55] The latter then combined both areas into one satrapy simply called Bactria.

During all this time, disturbing aspects of Alexander's character appeared. Thus, in the winter of 330–329 at Phrada (Farah) the capital of Drangiana (southwestern Afghanistan), a conspiracy was apparently hatched against the king that was said to have involved Philotas, the commander of the Companion Cavalry. He was executed, but so too was Philotas' father, the general Parmenion, even though he was in Ecbatana 800 miles away.[56] (We return to this episode below in the section "Evaluating Alexander.") Another disturbing aspect to Alexander's character can be seen at Maracanda in the summer of 328.[57] There the king and Cleitus, another general, got into a drunken argument, with Alexander killing Cleitus in cold blood.[58] This unheroic act, given that Cleitus was unarmed, was a stark contrast to the value Alexander attached to honor in his life.[59]

In the spring of 327 the king married the young Bactrian noblewoman Roxane at Maracanda, whom he had met a short time earlier.[60] He did so probably for a pragmatic reason, as he was now set on invading India and wanted her father, the powerful baron Oxyartes, to keep the new satrapy passive.[61] But the marriage did not sit well with his men because of her Bactrian lineage, for in marrying her Alexander would change the bloodline of the Argeads once he had a son.

From Maracanda Alexander returned to the capital, Bactra, where his credibility as king and general was further tested. First, he attempted to enforce *proskynesis* (genuflection), an Asian custom whereby the Great King's

[54] Bosworth 1988, pp. 110–117; Ashley 1998, pp. 292–294 and 297–300; Vacante 2012.

[55] Arrian 4.17.4–7; Curtius 8.3.1–6.

[56] Diodorus 17.79–80; Arrian 3.26–27; Curtius 6.7.1–7.2.38; Plutarch, *Alexander* 48–49; Justin 12.5.1–8, with Bosworth 1988, pp. 101–104; Worthington 2014a, pp. 216–220; deeper analysis: Badian 1960; Heckel 1977; Rubinsohn 1977; Adams 2003b. On conspiracies, see Badian 1964; Badian 1996; cf. Heckel 2003a; Heckel 2009.

[57] The chronology of the next several months is controversial, as our sources have little happening in 328 compared to 327 and possibly some of the events of the latter year took place in 328: see Bosworth 1981.

[58] Arrian 4.8.1–9; Curtus 8.1.19–51; cf. Justin 12.6.1–12; Plutarch, *Alexander* 50–52.7; on the episode: Bosworth 1996a, pp. 100–108; Heckel 2008, pp. 100–104; Worthington 2014a, pp. 225–228; in depth: Carney 1981; Bosworth 1996b; Tritle 2003.

[59] Roisman 2003b—on the Cleitus incident, see pp. 288 and 319–320.

[60] Arrian 4.19.5–20; Curtius 8.4.21–30; Plutarch, *Alexander* 47.7–8, with Renard and Servais 1955 on the Macedonian ritual followed in the marriage. On Roxane, see Carney 2000, pp. 106–107 and 146–148; Chugg 2006, pp. 164–184; Ogden 2011, pp. 124–133.

[61] Holt 1989, p. 66.

subjects prostrated themselves before him and he in return blew them a kiss.[62] To Greeks the act was blasphemous as they did not worship living beings. Then one night at a symposium the court historian and tutor of the royal pages, Callisthenes, refused to prostrate himself; Alexander admonished him, but Callisthenes retorted that he was leaving "the poorer for a kiss."[63] His defiance had a ripple effect among the men forcing, Alexander to abandon his attempt.[64]

Bactra was also the scene of another conspiracy involving some of the royal pages, who plotted to kill the king while he slept.[65] Alexander foiled the attempt by staying up all night drinking.[66] When he found out about it, he had all the pages tortured, urging them to implicate Callisthenes, who had defied him in his the *proskynesis* attempt: none did.[67] Still, Alexander had Callisthenes executed.[68] As noted above, once Alexander was crossed, redemption was impossible.

Believing that Bactria was now his, Alexander embarked on his next campaign in the spring of 327: the conquest of India.[69] Here the invasion was characterized by extreme brutality, including the slaughter of all who resisted him. Alexander fought only one battle in India, against the raj Porus, at the Hydaspes (Jhelum) River in 326.[70] It was another brilliant victory for Alexander, which the king celebrated by founding two new cities: Nicaea ("Victory City," perhaps Jalalpur) on the battle site, and Bucephala (Jhelum), honoring Bucephalas, which had died from battle wounds.[71] He

[62] Herodotus 1.134 says they prostrated themselves; the Persepolis Treasury reliefs illustrate bowing and blowing a kiss; see Briant 2010, p. 123.

[63] Chares, *BNJ* 125 F 14a (= Plutarch, *Alexander* 54.5–6); Chares, *BNJ* 125 F 14b (= Arrian 4.12.3–5).

[64] Arrian 4.10.5–12.5; Curtius 8.5.9–12; Plutarch, *Alexander* 54.3–6; Justin 12.7.1–3, with Bosworth 1988, pp. 284–287; Bosworth 1996a, pp. 109–112; Matarese 2013; Worthington 2014a, pp. 233–234; but see now Bowden 2013, for a skeptical approach to the whole incident including Callisthenes' involvement.

[65] Arrian 4.14; Curtius 8.6–8; Plutarch, *Alexander* 59, with Bosworth 1996a, pp. 112–114; Worthington 2014a, pp. 234–235; in depth: Carney 1980b; Borza 1981; Golan 1988.

[66] Aristobulus, *BNJ* 139 F 30 (= Arrian 4.13.5).

[67] Arrian 4.14.1; Curtius 8.6.24.

[68] On Alexander's relations with Callisthenes: Brown 1949.

[69] Alexander in India: Narain 1965; Bosworth 1983; Dobbins 1984; Bosworth 1988, pp. 119–139; Bosworth 1996a; Ashley 1998, pp. 306–341; Bosworth 2003; Heckel 2008, pp. 112–131; English 2011, pp. 175–215; Worthington 2014a, pp. 235–261; Müller 2016, pp. 300–303; Ferguson and Worthington 2024, pp. 197–209; and the essays in Antonetti and Biagi 2017 and in Ducoeur and Muckensturm-Poulle 2023. See too Howe 2008 on sources.

[70] Lead-up and battle: Diodorus 17.87–89.3; Arrian 5.8.4–19; Curtius 8.13–14; Plutarch, *Alexander* 60; Justin 12.8.1–7, with Fuller 1960, pp. 180–199; Devine 1987; Bosworth 1996a, pp. 9–20; Ashley 1998, pp. 318–329; Heckel 2008, pp. 115–120; English 2011, pp. 192–215; Worthington 2014a, pp. 243–250; Ferguson and Worthington 2024, pp. 199–204. Location: Arrian 5.11.1.

[71] Chares, *BNJ* 125 F 18; Onesicrius, *BNJ* 134 F 20; Arrian 5.19.4; Curtius 9.1.6; Plutarch, *Alexander* 61.1; Justin 12.8.8; on the founding of Bucephala, see Miller 1994.

also had struck two commemorative coins (the "Porus medallions"), depicting scenes from the battle.[72]

But the battle marked the zenith of the Macedonian invasion of Asia. After 70 days marching through drenching monsoon rains, suffering terribly from disease, snakebites, and weariness, the men had had enough. At the Hyphasis River, the second to last one of the Punjab, the respected battalion commander Coenus pleaded with Alexander to stop.[73] For three days the troops held out, until Alexander ended the mutiny by proclaiming the daily auspices were unfavorable for continuing eastward.

A brutal campaign against Malli (Malavas) people in the lower Punjab region followed.[74] When the Mallians made a final stand in the city of Malli (perhaps Multan), Alexander besieged it, and to encourage his men he climbed a scaling ladder to the battlements. But as the men followed him, their weight broke the ladder and the king with perhaps three others were marooned atop the wall.[75] He jumped down into the enemy's midst, preferring a heroic death than being picked off and was badly wounded when an arrow penetrated his armor.[76] His frenzied troops smashed their way into the town and massacred all the defenders, but it took several weeks for him to recover.

In July 325 Alexander realized his dream of sailing down the Indus into the Southern Ocean, where he built altars on a small island to Ocean and Earth to mark the southern boundary of his empire.[77] But by now the Indians had had enough of the invaders and a major revolt of India broke out, encouraged by Brahman ascetics whom Alexander's men had grossly mistreated.[78] Alexander and his men were forced to leave; as they did so, Bactria also revolted, thus undoing the king's gains in Central Asia—and there would be a further revolt after his death, when many of his settlers,

[72] See in detail Holt 2003; cf. Miller 1994.

[73] Diodorus 17.94.5; Arrian 5.25–27; Curtius 9.2.11–3; Justin 12.8.10–16, with Bosworth 1988, pp. 132–134 (downplaying the episode); Worthington 2014a, pp. 251–253; see too Holt 1982; Carney 1996. Howe and Müller 2012 argue that Alexander manipulated the mutiny so he could retreat, which seems unlikely as he was surely wanting to reach the Ganges.

[74] Diodorus 17.98–9; Arrian 6.6–11; Curtius 9.4.26–5.21; Plutarch, *Alexander* 63.2–14; Justin 12.9.1–4, with Fuller 1960, pp. 259–263; Bosworth 1996a, pp. 133–145; Ashley 1998, pp. 333–338; English 2009b, pp. 135–140; Worthington 2014a, pp. 253–256.

[75] Arrian 6.9.2–3; Curtius 9.4.30; Justin 12.9.5–13. Alexander climbing up himself: Arrian 6.7.5.

[76] Aristobulus, *BNJ* 139 F 46 (= Plutarch, *Moralia* 341c); Ptolemy, *BNJ* 138 F 25 (= Arrian 6.10.1); cf. Diodorus 17.99.3; Curtius 9.5.9–10; Plutarch, *Alexander* 63.6.

[77] Diodorus 17.104.1; Arrian 6.18.5–6.19.5; Curtius 9.9.1–27; Plutarch, *Alexander* 66.1–2.

[78] Bosworth 1998.

unhappy with the harsh conditions, returned home.[79] He began the long march westward but chose to take about 30,000 of his men and their Asian wives through the notorious Gedrosian Desert (Makran in Baluchistan). In terrible conditions—searing heat by day and freezing cold by night—as many as one-third of his men perished, and one night a flash flood swept away their wives and baggage train.[80]

Eventually, Alexander emerged from the desert and continued his march to Susa and Opis, where in the midsummer of 324 he faced another army mutiny.[81] Among other things, the men were critical of his pretensions to personal divinity, mockingly telling him that if he wanted to go to Arabia, he could go with his father Zeus.[82] Once again, he regained the men's confidence and proceeded to Ecbatana, where his boyhood friend, closest confidant, and likely lover Hephaestion fell ill and died.[83] Alexander was grief stricken and increasingly isolated: the loneliness of power.[84]

Finally, in early 323, Alexander reached Babylon, from where he planned to launch an invasion of Arabia. But after a drinking party one night he toasted "the health of everyone at the dinner, as many as twenty altogether, and he received the same number of toasts from everyone," then collapsed.[85] He died less than two weeks later, on June 11, a few weeks shy of his 33rd birthday.[86] There was a suspicion that he was poisoned, based on anecdotes such as the Athenian orator Hyperides proposing honors for a certain Iolaos for poisoning the king, or Olympias later desecrating the grave of Iolaos in

[79] See Iliakis 2013, especially pp. 137–190 (first revolt) and pp. 190–193 (second revolt); see too Goukowsky 1981 on the first revolt; cf. Sidky 2000, pp. 90–92.

[80] Bosworth 1988, pp. 142–146; Ashley 1998, pp. 342–343 and 345–348; Worthington 2014a, pp. 261–263. March and presentation in the sources: Bosworth 1996a, pp. 169–183. On Alexander's personal reason for the march to try to outdo Cyrus the Great and Semiramis, the queen of Assyria, see Brosius 2003.

[81] Diodorus 17.109.2–3; Arrian 7.8.1; Curtius 10.2.13–3; Plutarch, *Alexander* 71.2–9; Justin 12.11–12.10, with Bosworth 1988, pp. 159–162; Worthington 2014a, pp. 277–281; especially Olbrycht 2008; cf. Carney 1996.

[82] Diodorus 17.109.2; Arrian 7.8.3; Justin 12.11.6. Changing composition of the army: Bosworth 1980, pp. 13–20.

[83] Diodorus 17.110.7–8; Arrian 7.14.1; Plutarch, *Alexander* 72.2; Justin 12.12.11–12 with Worthington 2014a, pp. 282–283. Hephaestion: see Chugg 2006, pp. 64–130; Ogden 2011, pp. 155–167; Müller 2015; Müller 2018; cf. Reames-Zimmerman 1999.

[84] Badian 1964.

[85] Nicoboule, *BNJ* 127 F 1 (= Athenaeus 10.434c); cf. Ephippus, *BNJ* 126 F 3 (= Athenaeus 10.434a–b).

[86] *Ephemerides*, *BNJ* 117 F 3b (= Plutarch, *Alexander* 76–77.1); cf. Diodorus 17.117.1–3; Arrian 7.25–26.3; Justin 12.13.7–16.1, with Bosworth 1988, pp. 171–173; Worthington 2014a, pp. 293–297. Time: Depuydt 1997. See too Bosworth 1971b on Alexander's death.

revenge for his killing her son.[87] But there is often a coupling of the sudden death of prominent historical figures with conspiracy theories, and even our ancient writers do not accept that Alexander was poisoned.[88] More likely his excessive drinking, punishing lifestyle, and numerous wounds combined to bring about his end from acute alcoholic pancreatitis. Roxane was still pregnant when he died: with no clear heir, the battle for control of his empire began, as we discuss in the next chapter.

Alexander's conquests were on an unparalleled scale in less than a decade, and at such a young age he far exceeded any Macedonian king before or after him. In addition to establishing a vast empire from Greece to India, he helped to spread Greek culture throughout the Middle East and Asia, the eastern half of that empire.

Macedonia during Alexander's absence

Alexander had made Antipater his deputy in Macedonia and Greece—a logical choice given he was in his sixties and had much military and diplomatic experience. Exactly what his status was cannot be determined, as our sources are contradictory: he was a governor or a general, in command of Macedonia, or simply entrusted to manage Macedonia and Greece.[89] He was not an actual regent, but he did manage the kingdom, and as deputy hegemon of the League of Corinth he could oversee affairs in Greece and levy troops when necessary. He also had 12,000 infantry and 1,500 cavalry under his command.[90] That he did not need to raise an army until 331 shows that Alexander's scare tactic in the razing of Thebes had cowed the Greeks, which was just as well as the king's frequent demands for reinforcements from Antipater may have strained the latter's manpower and even his ability to hold Greece in check.[91]

[87] Plutarch, *Moralia* 849f and Justin 12.4.1–9 for the former and Diodorus 19.11.8 for the latter; cf. Oikonomides 1987. The so-called "Last Days and Testament" of Alexander that survives in the *Metz Epitome* and some *Alexander Romances* speaks of his being poisoned, but that is unlikely: see Heckel 1988.

[88] Diodorus 17.118.1; Curtius 10.10.14.19.

[89] Governor: Curtius 4.11. General: Diodorus 17.118.1. In command of the kingdom: Justin 11.7.1. Entrusted with affairs: Arrian 1.11.3.

[90] Diodorus 17.17.3, 5; see Baynham 1994b, pp. 337–338; cf. Hammond 1992a, pp. 171–172.

[91] Bosworth 1986, especially pp. 7–8; contra Billows 1995, pp. 183–212.

That hold faltered in 331 when Antipater was forced to deal with a revolt in Thrace orchestrated by its governor, Memnon, and a war in Greece when Agis III of Sparta declared against Macedonia and called on the other Greeks for support. Antipater settled the first issue diplomatically.[92] But he led an army of 40,000 into Greece and defeated Agis (who had received next to no aid from the other Greeks) in battle at Megalopolis in 330.[93] Probably Sparta now became a member of the League of Corinth. From then until 324 the Greeks remained passive, though Antipater was careful to maintain garrisons and support tyrannies in Peloponnesian cities and expel any opponents to ensure Macedonian hegemony.[94] Indeed, Macedonian rule enabled the Greeks to enjoy a period of peace after decades of unrest, given the bellicose behavior of the Greek cities toward one another, and economic upset.[95] That subservience to Macedonia was shown in 324, when Alexander's treasurer Harpalus, who had been accused of corruption, fled to Athens to raise a Greek revolt against the king.[96] But Antipater's hardline policy toward the Greeks was such that Harpalus was imprisoned on the orator Demosthenes' urging and subsequently fled, his mission a failure.

Antipater had an amicable relationship with Alexander, at least by letter, even deferring to the king about the punishment of the Spartans in 330, although Alexander apparently scorned Antipater's success against Agis and called it "a battle with mice."[97] But Antipater was mistrusted and denigrated by Olympias, though why we do not know for sure, who wrote letters of complaint about him to her son in Asia—and in return he maligned her.[98] After the defeat of Agis III she returned to Epirus, perhaps because its king Alexander, the husband of her daughter Cleopatra, had died, and both women formed a faction against Antipater in 325.[99] Still, he maintained his loyalty to Alexander and Macedonia remained on an even keel under him. However, in 323 Alexander summoned Antipater to Babylon, perhaps intending to replace him with the general Craterus, but Antipater sent his son Cassander instead. The latter arrived shortly before Alexander died, but

[92] Aeschines 3.165; Diodorus 17.63.1; cf. Baynham 1994b, pp. 339–340.

[93] Megalopolis: Diodorus 17.63.4; Curtius 6.1.1–15; Justin 12.1.6–11; Plutarch, *Agis* 3.

[94] Diodorus 18.56.1–4, 56.7, 70–71; [Demosthenes] 17.4, 7, 10, 16.

[95] See Worthington 1994; cf. Cawkwell 1996.

[96] Harpalus affair: Worthington 2013, pp. 310–324; see too Blackwell 1998; cf. Worthington 1994.

[97] Plutarch, *Agesilaus* 15.2.

[98] Diodorus 18.49.4; Arrian 7.12.6–7; Plutarch, *Alexander* 68; see Baynham 1994b, pp. 343–346.

[99] Plutarch, *Alexander* 68.3.

no moves were made against Antipater.[100] Our story of Macedonia after Alexander's death will continue in the following chapter, in which Antipater and Craterus will play no small role.

Alexander's impact on the Macedonian monarchy was profound. To be fair, he was having to chart his own course in trying to rule a large, multicultural subject population. But his lordship of Asia was based not on legitimacy, like the Achaemenid kings with their connection with Ahura Mazda, the Zoroastrian god of light, but on force. When the king first crossed the Hellespont he threw a spear into the foreign soil, claiming all Asia as his "spear-won territory."[101] He intended therefore to topple the Achaemenid dynasty and rule by right of conquest.[102] The Successors who carved up Alexander's empire following his death and established the great dynasties of the Hellenistic period, which we deal with in chapter 12, likewise ruled their lands—including Macedonia—"by the spear."[103] This right to rule by force, a product of Alexander's campaigns, became the norm and fundamentally changed the Argead monarchy and the whole kingdom.

Evaluating Alexander

Almost all of Alexander's reign was spent in Asia, so his activities there cannot really be separated from what he did for his kingdom in any evaluation of him. He was a great general, strategist, and, despite two mutinies, leader of men, showing these attributes in his early campaigns of 335 to help protect his kingdom.[104] And despite always being outnumbered—at Issus in 333, for example, Darius' army numbered probably 100,000 to 150,000 and Alexander's 40,000—he always won, helped immeasurably by his army's training and trust in him.[105] The strategic principles he followed are lessons that can be applied throughout the ages as they lie at the heart of warfare: using all force at the decisive place and time; launching the maximum force in battle at the points that would bring victory even if it brought disadvantage

[100] Plutarch, *Alexander* 74.2. [101] Diodorus 17.17.2.
[102] See, for example, Schmitthenner 1968. [103] Cf. Diodorus 19.105.3–4.
[104] Generalship: See Ferguson and Worthington 2024, pp. 263–307 (with reference to leadership and strategy today), with Fuller 1960, pp. 281–305; Burn 1965; Keegan 1987, pp. 13–91; Cartledge 2003, pp. 157–188; Strauss 2003; Lonsdale 2007, pp. 45–158.
[105] On his army, see Sekunda and McBride 1984; Sekunda and Warry 1998; English 2009a. Casualty figures in his battles: Hammond 1989c, pp. 57–62.

elsewhere; moving rapidly and not wasting time; using the element of surprise; and ensuring an enemy is pursued or captured.[106]

Alexander was constantly faced by major challenges, such as his continually expanding frontiers and the fact that there had never been a king of Macedonia who was also ruler of Asia. Still, he introduced measures to administer his sprawling empire and to benefit trade, communications, and security, all of which led to revenue flowing into Macedonian state coffers.[107] Less successful were his attempts to bind the people together under his rule. His decision, for example, to use local nobility as satraps disgruntled his men, and his predilection for all things Greek offended locals, who saw their own customs and even culture disregarded.[108] Even his attempt to dress in a hybrid form of dress that included Macedonian and Persian clothing backfired on him, with his men seeing him as less of a true Macedonian warrior king. Then again, we wonder whether Alexander could ever have ruled such a culturally dissimilar empire and exercised "command *and* control."[109]

When it came to his own kingdom Alexander is found wanting. The Macedonians had known him as king for only two years before he embarked for Asia, and he showed no intention of returning home—he was poised to invade Arabia on the eve of his death and may even have been considering a campaign in the western Mediterranean, perhaps against Carthage. In addition, while in Asia he had asked Antipater for reinforcements several times, which may have stretched the latter's manpower resources. Antipater had managed to send him troops, but if Agis III had united the Greeks in 331, Antipater would have faced no small challenge. Although the army was a different beast by the end of Alexander's reign thanks to the inclusion of thousands of subject peoples in it, there was no guarantee that had the king lived and embarked on other campaigns he would not have needed more troops from Antipater.

True, Alexander was in close contact with Antipater about affairs in Macedonia and Greece. But while Antipater was an excellent regent, he was not the king, and letters as opposed to personal presence were surely not enough. In addition, the people back home would have heard the worrying stories of their king's growing orientalism, including the marriage to Roxane

[106] On Alexander's methods and today's practices, including what can be learned from him, see Ferguson and Worthington 2024.

[107] Badian 1965; Higgins 1980; Bosworth 1988, pp. 229–250; Hammond 1992a, pp. 205–236; Briant 2010, pp. 67–138; Worthington 2010b.

[108] Worthington 2014a, pp. 185–187.

[109] See Ferguson and Worthington 2024, pp. 218–230.

that changed the Argead bloodline.[110] They would have heard stories of his pretensions to personal divinity and his emotional behavior, including his murder of Cleitus and putting Callisthenes to death. Then there were Alexander's relations with his senior staff, especially Parmenion, which grew strained over time. Indeed, wary of one general becoming too popular with his troops, Alexander may have begun to promote divisiveness among his senior staff to ensure they did not try to overthrow him and have separated individual leaders from units of troops.[111]

True, Alexander sent home huge sums of money seized from the great palace treasuries at Babylon, Susa, Ecbatana, and Persepolis, all of which benefited Macedonia's economy. Nor did he neglect to erect monuments back in his kingdom—for example, the bronze monument of the fallen cavalrymen at the battle at Granicus River carved by Lysippus at Dium.[112] In addition, the returning veteran soldiers came with their own wealth thanks to their pay and generous bonuses from the king, which may even have elevated them into a higher social class and contributed to local communities. But Alexander kept a lot of the money and treasure he seized for his personal fortune and spent enormous sums on gifts to friends and his army and building projects, almost always in Asia. Perhaps a sign of the Macedonians' dissatisfaction is that the mints at Pella, Amphipolis, and Philippi produced no coins of Alexander after Issus.[113] What coins were minted were on Alexander's orders; almost all coins with his head on them are posthumous, minted by his successors during the wars that broke out on his death, as we mention in the next chapter.[114]

There seems little doubt that Alexander took greater care over the eastern half of his empire than the western—perhaps this was proof of his faith in Antipater to keep the peace. But in 325 on his return from India Alexander plunged the whole empire into some chaos by issuing his so-called "Dissolution Decree," which ordered all satraps and governors to disband their mercenary armies.[115] That led to thousands of ex-mercenaries wandering the eastern half of the empire pillaging and looting to survive, as well as several thousand returning to Greece and collecting together at Taenarum in the

[110] Hammond 1992a, pp. 226–231; cf. Wiesehöfer 2017, pp. 60–61, on his orientalism.
[111] Heckel 2009; cf. Heckel 2000.
[112] Aristobulus, *BNJ* 139 F 5 (= Plutarch, *Alexander* 16.15).
[113] Bosworth 1988, pp. 244–245.
[114] Coins: Dahmen 2007; Meeus, 2009; especially Stewart 1993.
[115] Diodorus 17.106.3, 17.111.1, with Worthington 2014a, pp. 263–264.

Peloponnese, thus providing a ready supply of men should any ambitious satrap or governor decide to challenge the king.

To combat this threat and the social upheaval, in 324 at Susa Alexander proclaimed his "Exiles Decree," ordering all Greek exiles excluding murderers, anti-democrats, and the Thebans (probably because of their defiance in 335), to return to their homes, and authorizing Antipater to use force against any city refusing to comply.[116] This unilateral decision ignored the provisions of the League of Corinth allowing the cities autonomy in their domestic affairs, so it is not a surprise that the cities, worried about the social and economic chaos generated by tens of thousands of returning exiles, especially as Greece was still recovering from a famine, sent embassies of protest to Alexander at Babylon in 323. He denied all their requests, a clear sign of his disinterest in the west. The Greeks, however, took advantage of his death shortly afterward to ignore his decree, and only Tegea in Arcadia allowed its exiles to return.[117]

Alexander's campaigns also changed relations between monarch and the Greeks of Asia Minor. Previous Argead kings had had dealings with them, with Pixodarus even trying to arrange a martial pact with Philip II, but for the most part the Asiatic Greeks were left to their own devices and lived under Persian rule until Alexander. Not that they gained autonomy. It is likely that he made them members of the League of Corinth and they paid a tribute to him, thus becoming his subjects and a source of income at least until his death.

Was the undisputed military greatness and leadership prowess of Alexander enough for him to be called *great*? Of course, there were four kings named Alexander, and just as Alexander I was dubbed the "philhellene," perhaps to distinguish him from the others, so Alexander III may have been nicknamed "great" to set him apart from his namesakes because of his conquests. But the word "great" makes someone sound better than others, as has been the case with Alexander. However, when we factor in the other aspects of kingship—diplomacy, administration, attention to kingdom and dynasty, as well as the human element—a different image of the king emerges.

As a man there was a growing paranoia and loss of reason as the campaign progressed further east, as we see in the Philotas affair, murder of

[116] Diodorus 18.8.4, with Bosworth 1988, pp. 220–228 and 223–224; Zahrnt 2003; Dmitriev 2004; Worthington 2014b.

[117] Rhodes-Osborne, no. 101, with Worthington 1993.

Cleitus, and likely reaction to Callisthenes' defiance over the *proskynesis* attempt.[118] And surely the greatest failing of his personality was his pretension to personal divinity, especially after the visit to the Oracle of Zeus Ammon in the Oasis of Siwah. But the most signal failing of Alexander as king was not producing an heir—or rather, leaving Roxane still pregnant when he died.[119] Antipater and Parmenion had advised him to marry even before he left for Asia—good advice, which an Argead king ought to have followed for the well-being of his kingdom, given that dynasty's history.[120] Then again, who would have made a good match at that time is unknown.[121] But Alexander knew the history of his predecessors, so he was aware of the chaos caused by multiple heirs, or even worse, when there was no clear heir.

That was why after a spectacular rise to imperial power Macedonia slumped dramatically on Alexander's death, losing its empire, and surely supporting the view that Philip II was a better king for his kingdom than his more famous son.[122]

Macedonia under the Argead Kings: The Rise and Fall of an Ancient Superpower. Ian Worthington, Oxford University Press. © Oxford University Press 2026. DOI: 10.1093/9780197668009.003.0012

[118] Possibly also the sudden death of Coenus who had voiced opposition to Alexander at the Hyphasis River should also be considered as a retributions: Arrian 6.2.1; Curtius 9.3.20, with Worthington 1999. In disagreement: Holt 2000.

[119] Cf. Baynham 1997; Bosworth 2002, p. 30.

[120] Diodorus 17.16.1–3.

[121] Baynham 1997.

[122] Worthington 2008a, pp. 204–208; Worthington 2014a, pp. 115–119 and 302–309. See too Squillace 2015. Perhaps the most extreme view of the king is seen in the title of Grainger 2007: *Alexander the Great Failure*.

12
The End of the Argeads—and the Antigonids

Alexander's death in Babylon in 323 led to the collapse of the Macedonian Empire. Forty years of bloody warfare waged by his former senior staff in pursuit of their own slices of that empire now followed. Still, thanks to Alexander, the east was opened up as never before as far as trade, communications, social and cultural exchange, and travel were concerned, and a byproduct of his campaigns was the spread of Greek civilization in Asia.[1] His death brought in a new age, the Hellenistic, in which Greek language and culture spread far and wide and the Greeks of the Mediterranean learned to become part of a much bigger world.[2] The period was also one of great cultural activity, with the epicenter for literary and scientific studies and advances no longer Athens but the Museum and Library at Alexandria, closely followed by Antioch and Pergamum.[3] Macedonia did not have the same sway compared to kingdoms such as the Ptolemaic in Egypt and Seleucid in Syria; its hold over Greece was no more, and there was a return to many of the dynastic and internal issues that existed before the days of Philip II.

Alexander's corpse

When Alexander died, the story goes that his senior staff crowded around his deathbed at Babylon and asked to whom he was leaving his empire, receiving the reply, "To the best man."[4] This puzzling response—if it is

[1] Cf. [Plutarch], *Moralia* 328c–329d.

[2] On the Hellenistic era, see as starting points Tarn and Griffith 1952; Green 1990; Braund 2003; Bosworth 2007; Adams, W.L. 2007; Adams, W.L. 2010; and the essays in Erskine 2003 and Bugh 2007.

[3] On which, see, for example, Fraser 1972; Erskine 1995; Grimm 1998; MacLeod 2000.

[4] Ptolemy, *BNJ* 138 F 30 (= Arrian 7.26.3); see too Diodorus 18.1.4; Justin 12.15–8 ("the most deserving"). On the last words, see Antela-Bernárdez 2011.

historical—hardly settled the issue, as everyone thought he was the best. At the same time, a non-Argead was not a likely successor, and thus a pregnant Roxane's son—if she bore a son—should not become king. Indeed, if she were to bear a daughter, there was still Alexander's older half-brother Arrhidaeus (the son of Philip and Philinna of Thessaly), although he suffered from some incapacity that had made Philip set him aside as heir.[5]

Alexander had given his signet ring (the seal of authority) to Perdiccas, his second-in-command, to ensure the smooth running of the imperial administration when he fell ill.[6] Because of that, Perdiccas called a meeting of the senior staff to decide what to do at this time of crisis facing the monarchy.[7] Our sources give us an often confused and contradictory account of the decisions made by these men at Babylon, but the generals decided to divide the empire among themselves.[8] Arrhidaeus was in Babylon, but Perdiccas, who wanted to be made regent of Roxane's unborn son—everyone seems to have expected the child to be male—had not invited him to the meeting.

Perdiccas' ambition was almost realized, until the troops outside the palace burst inside it and demanded that Arrhidaeus to be proclaimed king as Philip III.[9] In the meantime Nearchus, Alexander's admiral, suggested Heracles, Alexander's illegitimate son from his relationship with Barsine, who was only a young boy at that time.[10] But because Heracles was a bastard, he was not considered as ruler in place of a legitimate Argead, and clearly the men regarded Arrhidaeus as a true Argead who deserved their loyalty, unlike Heracles or Roxane's child. The impasse was then heightened by Ptolemy, who spoke against Arrhidaeus and, if we can believe Curtius, Heracles and Roxane's baby, because her Bactrian birth would make Alexander's heir only half-Macedonian.[11] Instead he proposed the generals

[5] Diodorus 18.2.2; Plutarch, *Alexander* 77.5, with Worthington 2008a, p. 175.

[6] For example, Curtius 10.5.4; Justin 12.15.12; Nepos, *Eumenes* 2.1. On Perdiccas and his ambition, see further Badian 1967; Rathmann 2005.

[7] Cf. Bosworth 2002, pp. 29–34.

[8] Arrian, *BNJ* 156 F1, 1–8; Diodorus 18.3.2–5; Curtius 10.6–10.8 (the most details on events at Babylon); Justin 13.2.1–4.25; on the source problems, especially relating to chronology, see Bosworth 2002, pp. 29–44; Roisman 2012b, pp. 61–71.

[9] Curtius 10.7.1–2; Justin 13.2.8; cf. Arrian, *BNJ* 156 F 1, 1: "Arrhidaeus was proclaimed king, and his name was changed to Philip."

[10] Curtius 10.6.10–12. Justin 13.2.6–8 has Meleager putting Heracles and Arrhidaeus forward, but Justin has probably confused Meleager with Nearchus. On Barsine, see Carney 2000, pp. 100 and 104; Chugg 2006, pp. 131–143; Ogden 2011, pp. 139–142. On Heracles, see too Tarn 1921; Brunt 1975. Heracles was either 17 (Diodorus 20.20.1) or 15 (Justin 15.2.3) in 310.

[11] Curtius 10.6.12–15; Justin 13.2.11–12; cf. Pausanias 1.6.2.

form an advisory body to administer the empire, with all of them on an equal footing.[12]

But then the rank and file grew violent, threatening their leaders and causing chaos that lasted almost a week as infantry and cavalry units supported one former commander over another. Finally, a compromise was reached to reconcile the men. Philip III would be sole king until Roxane gave birth; if it was to a boy he would rule jointly with Philip, and Perdiccas and a battalion commander named Meleager would be guardians of the two monarchs.[13]

With peace among the ranks restored, Perdiccas wasted no time in putting Meleager to death and calling another meeting of the senior personnel at which a division of the empire was thrashed out with himself as sole guardian of the king.[14] Interestingly, Philip, though adult and married, "seems to have been treated as a permanent minor."[15] Other men who also gained included Ptolemy, who took over Egypt and adjoining portions of Arabia, and Libya (putting Cleomenes to death shortly after he arrived in the country); Antigonus Monophthalmus ("the one-eyed"), who was reconfirmed as satrap of Greater Phrygia, Lycia, and Pamphylia; Lysimachus, who received Thrace; and Antipater, who shared Greece and Macedonia with another general, Craterus. When Roxane gave birth to a son a few months later, the dual monarchy came into being of Philip III (Arrhidaeus) and Alexander IV.[16] As a further sign of their kingship, both kings received a royal bodyguard, normally composed of seven-handpicked men; four were assigned to Philip III and three to Alexander IV.[17] The senior staff who now controlled the divided old empire are commonly called the Successors, but they were really satraps until the deaths of the two kings.[18]

The Athenians seized upon Alexander's death to unite many Greek cities under them in a revolt from the Macedonian hegemony in what is

[12] Curtius 10.6.15; Justin 13.2.11–12. [13] Roisman 2012b, pp. 71–81.

[14] Arrian, *BNJ* 156 F 1, 5–8; Dexippus, *BNJ* 100 F 8; Diodorus 18.3.1–4; Curtius 10.10.1–4; Justin 13.4.5, 9–25, with Anson 2014, p. 22. On the settlement, see in detail Errington 1970; Billows 1990, pp. 52–58; Bosworth 1993; Bosworth 2002, pp. 29–63; Meeus 2008; Waterfield 2011, pp. 19–29; Anson, 2014, pp. 14–28; Worthington 2016, pp. 71–83.

[15] Carney 2000, p. 134.

[16] At that time, she was either five months pregnant (Curtius 10.6.9) or eight (Justin 13.2.5); cf. Errington 1970, p. 58, for her giving birth in September.

[17] See Burstein 1977; Heckel 1980b.

[18] Alexander had an illegitimate son named Heracles by Barsine—born the same year he married Roxane (327)—but because of his status Heracles was never taken seriously; see further Brunt 1975.

commonly called the Lamian War.[19] Antipater countered by leading an army into Greece, but he was defeated at Thermopylae by a Greek army commanded by the Athenian general Leosthenes and blockaded in the Thessalian town of Lamia for the winter of 323–322. It seemed the Greeks were gaining the upper hand, but then Leosthenes was killed in fighting, Antipater was rescued and made his way safely back to Macedonia, and Craterus with the 10,000 veterans that Alexander had discharged at Opis landed in Greece. With these reinforcements, Antipater marched into Greece in 322, and that August he defeated the Greeks in battle at Crannon in Thessaly.[20]

With Macedonian rule over Greece restored, Antipater installed garrisons in key towns and punished the Athenians as ringleaders, setting up a garrison in the Piraeus and restricting their democracy by imposing a wealth requirement for citizenship that saw thousands of citizens disfranchised and even forced to move elsewhere.[21] He also demanded the surrender of anti-Macedonian politicians—Demosthenes fled the city, but he was hunted down on the island of Calauria (Poros) and to prevent capture committed suicide.[22]

The Successors' ambitions for greater slices of territory, not to mention distrust of each other, soon led to the disregard of Perdiccas and four decades of warfare, with minor interruptions from equally ephemeral settlements, as the Hellenistic kingdoms of Macedonia, Egypt, and Syria took shape.[23] The settlement at Babylon in 323 lasted no more than two years because of warfare over Alexander's body, which had been embalmed and lay in state at Babylon while an elaborate funeral hearse was built to transport it for burial at Aegae—the tradition that Alexander wanted to be buried in Siwah is doubtful.[24] Two years later the hearse was built and the funeral cortège set off, but at Damascus Ptolemy stole his corpse in the

[19] Lamian War: Diodorus 18.9–13, 15–18.6; Arrian, *BNJ* 156 F 1, 9; see too Liddel, D199, pp. 714–718, with Lehmann 1988; Schmitt 1992; cf. Hammond and Walbank 1988, pp. 107–117; Anson 2014, pp. 33–41; Worthington 2021, pp. 24–26. Nomenclature: Ashton, 1984.

[20] Diodorus 18.17.1–8.

[21] Worthington 2021, pp. 27–28.

[22] Plutarch, *Demosthenes* 29.4, with Worthington 2013, pp. 335–337.

[23] Seibert 1983; Hammond and Walbank 1988, pp. 117–244; Sidky 2000, pp. 101–128; Bosworth 2002; Braund 2003; Adams, W.L. 2007; Bosworth 2007; Bennett and Roberts 2008–2009; Adams, W.L. 2010; Waterfield 2011; Anson 2014; Roisman 2012b; King 2018, pp. 205–234; cf. Stewart 1993, and the essays in Hauben and Meeus 2014. On their distrust of each other and the influence Alexander played in it, see Heckel 2000.

[24] Diodorus 18.3.5, 28.3; Curtius 10.5.4; Justin 12.15.7, 13.4.6, with Badian 1967, pp. 185–189; Erskine 2002, p. 171; Meeus 2008, pp. 66–68; Worthington 2016, p. 78. Accepted by Bosworth 2002, p. 219.

summer or early fall of 321.[25] Perdiccas invaded Egypt in the name of the kings to retrieve Alexander's body, though this was an excuse for him to take over Egypt. His campaign was a disaster, and he was killed by some of his own men, after which Ptolemy made his peace with the two kings.[26] He then buried Alexander's corpse first in Memphis and then some years later in Alexandria when he made that city his capital.[27]

In the early fall of 320 the Successors, apart from Ptolemy, met at Triparadeisus in upper Syria and worked out a new settlement.[28] This time Antipater, now in his eighties, attended, but Eurydice, Philip III's wife, caused trouble when she was passed over as guardian of the two kings and sought out the support of the army.[29] At no point was Roxane consulted despite being the late king's widow and mother of potentially the next king. Antipater was able to restore order, primarily by promising the men pay that had been neglected. Antipater was named guardian (*epimeletes*) of Macedonia and Greece and of the two kings, while the others were reconfirmed in their lands or had more added to them, especially Antigonus Monophthalmus, who was satrap of Phrygia and general of Asia. The settlement made Antipater the most powerful man in the west, and Antigonus in the east.

Antipater then returned to Macedonia with Philip III, Alexander IV, and Roxane. But Philip and Alexander were never taken seriously as kings. Nor indeed was Roxane a factor, presumably because of her Bactrian ancestry—in stark contrast to the influence that Amyntas III's wife Eurydice and Olympias exerted.[30]

Final fall: The end of the Argead dynasty

When Antipater died in 319, his son Cassander expected to assume his father's position, but Antipater before his death had tapped a former

[25] Diodorus 18.28.2–3; Arrian, *BNJ* 156 F 9, 25; Pausanias 1.6.3, with Worthington 2016, pp. 94–95.

[26] Diodorus 18.28.2–3, with Erskine 2002, pp. 163–167; Worthington 2016, pp. 129–131.

[27] Worthington 2016, pp. 129–139.

[28] Diodorus 18.39; Arrian, *BNJ* 156 F 9, 34–38; Polyaenus 4.6.4, with Waterfield 2011, pp. 66–68. Discussion: Errington 1970; Billows 1990, pp. 64–71; Roisman 2012b, pp. 136–144; Landucci Gattinoni 2014.

[29] Diodorus 18.39.1–4; Arrian, *BNJ* 156 F 9, 31–33, with Errington 1970, p. 67. See further Roisman 2012b, pp. 136–142 and 157–158.

[30] Cf. Carney 2000, pp. 146–148; see too Mirón Pérez 2000.

infantry commander named Polyperchon, then in his sixties, to succeed him, with Cassander as his second-in-command.[31] An incensed Cassander, however, plotted with Ptolemy, Antigonus Monophthalmus, and Lysimachus to usurp him, but other commitments on their part forced Cassander to turn to Eumenes, the satrap of Cappadocia.[32] In retaliation Polyperchon invited Olympias, who had moved to Epirus after Alexander the Great's death, to return to the court and become guardian of her grandson until he came of age.[33] She was hostile to the family of Antipater, of course, and eventually, in 317, she led troops against Philip III, who with Eurydice had marched out to do battle—unusually for a woman at this time, she had been trained to fight.[34] Their army, however, mutinied, allowing Olympias to return to Pella in triumph: she promptly had Philip III stabbed to death while Eurydice committed suicide by hanging herself.[35]

These actions and Olympias' subsequent killing of Cassander's brother Nicanor and 100 Macedonian nobles she personally hated did not sit well with Cassander. In fear of her life, Olympias fled to Pydna, taking with her Alexander IV, Roxane, and various supporters. Cassander besieged Pydna, and when it fell, he executed Olympias and ordered her corpse to be unburied, which also stigmatized her family.[36] Alexander IV, now only seven or perhaps eight years old, was thus sole king. Cassander assumed guardianship of him, but then he married Thessalonice, a half-sister of Alexander the Great (the daughter of Philip II and his fifth wife, Nicesipolis of Pherae), to bind himself closer to the Argead dynasty. He then imprisoned Alexander and his mother at Amphipolis.[37] Now married to an Argead, Cassander also arranged the burial of Philip III and Eurydice at Aegae, presumably on behalf of the young Alexander IV.[38] It was now, incidentally, that Cassander refounded Thebes, destroyed by Alexander III in 335, and built a new city at the head of the Thermaic Gulf, which he named after his wife – Thessalonica, the modern Thessaloniki.[39]

[31] Diodorus 18.48.4–5.

[32] Diodorus 18.49.3, 18.54.3, 18.57.2; cf. Nepos, *Eumenes* 6.1.

[33] Diodorus 18.57.2; cf. 18.49.4, with Carney 2006, pp. 68–72. Perhaps around this time Polyperchon, as a propaganda move against Cassander and his allies, manufactured the alleged will of Alexander that among other things called for Roxane's son to be king: See Heckel 1988.

[34] Athenaeus 13.560f; cf. Carney 2006, p. 74 with nn. 50–51.

[35] Diodorus 19.11.2–7.

[36] Diodorus 19.51; Justin 14.6.6–12; Pausanias 9.7.2 (stoning); cf. 1.11.4. Unburied: Diodorus 17.118.2; Justin 14.6.6–12, with Carney 2006, pp. 85–87.

[37] Diodorus 19.52.4; Justin 14.6.13.

[38] Diodorus 19.52.5; on the burial cf. Kottaridi 2020, pp. 13–21.

[39] Thebes: Diodorus 19.53.2, 54.1; Pausanias 9.7.1. Thessalonica: Diodorus 19.52.2.

Cassander's rule was not a disaster for Macedonia, and he was influenced by Philip II and Alexander III.[40] He had to fend off challenges from Polyperchon, who refused to take his usurpation lightly, but his greatest foe was Antigonus Monophthalmus, who also had his eye on the Macedonian throne. From 315 to 311 a coalition of Cassander, Ptolemy, and Lysimachus waged war on Antigonus.[41] At the battle of Gaza in 311 Ptolemy decisively defeated Antigonus' son Demetrius, and a new settlement of the Successors was arranged that was supposed to stay in force until the then 13-year-old Alexander IV came of age.[42]

But a single Argead king ruling all territories and served by satraps was no longer tenable, even though Alexander was seen as a king by having a royal bodyguard.[43] In Egypt there is mention of him as Alexander IV on an inscription, and a colossal statue of a boy pharaoh from Karnak is believed to be Alexander IV.[44] Nevertheless, in the spring of 310 Cassander conveniently forgot Olympias' act of regicide five years earlier and had Alexander and Roxane poisoned by their jailer, with the other Successors breathing a sigh of relief.[45] The boy king was probably buried in Tomb III at Aegae, next to his grandfather Philip II, as among other things the cremated bones of a young boy around 13 were found in a silver hydria crowned with a gold oak wreath, but Roxane's burial spot is unknown.[46]

The discovery in the 1960s of the enormous Kasta burial mound near Amphipolis—the largest tumulus yet found in Greece—sparked speculation that it was the burial place of Roxane as it dates from the final quarter of the fourth century.[47] But the Amphipolis tomb, as it is often called, has three chambers, and in the third or burial one skeletal remains of five people of various ages, including a baby were found, so it is hard to connect Roxane to this tomb. Other suggestions have been Hephaestion or even Olympias, although either is unlikely.[48] The sheer size of the burial mound, which is surrounded by a wall 158 meters (518 feet) in diameter and three meters (10 feet), high shows that the occupants were wealthy, important,

[40] Cf. Landucci Gattinoni 2010.

[41] The Third War of the Successors: Diodorus 19.57.2–62, with Hammond and Walbank 1988, pp. 150–162; Anson 2014, pp. 129–149.

[42] Diodorus 19.105.1.

[43] Burstein 1977; Chugg 2006, p. 179; Heckel 1980b.

[44] Discussion at Chugg 2006, pp. 180–182.

[45] Diodorus 19.105.2; see too Justin 15.2.5; Pausanias 9.7.2, with Hammond and Walbank 1988, pp. 164–167; cf. Müller 2016, p. 309. Diodorus 19.105.3–4 for the relief of the others.

[46] Alexander IV: See, for example, Borza 1990, pp. 257–258; Chugg 2006, pp. 182–183; Ogden 2011, p. 127.

[47] See in detail Chugg 2021.

[48] See Chugg 2021 arguing for Olympias.

and surely of the nobility, though not necessarily royalty. It would be nice to say this is Roxane's final resting place, but current evidence makes this only a speculation.

What we can say with certainty is that with Alexander IV's murder in 310 the Argead dynasty, established by Perdiccas I in the mid-seventh century, came to an end. In 306 the remaining Successors finally called themselves kings, and as we shall see a new dynasty came to rule Macedonia, the Antigonid.[49]

However, three other men with Argead blood in their veins deserve mention. The first is Heracles, whom Nearchus had supported at the Babylon meeting, as we saw above. In his struggles against Cassander, Polyperchon had exploited Heracles' Argead heritage and even brought him to Greece. But when in 309 Cassander and Polyperchon came to terms and the latter was given land in Macedonia and made governor of the Peloponnese, he ordered Heracles and Barsine to be strangled to death.[50] He may have been buried in the sanctuary of Eucleia at Aegae.[51] The other two half-Argeads are Cassander's sons from his marriage to Thessalonice, Antipater I and Alexander V, who ruled briefly during the following Antigonid dynasty, and who are discussed in the next section.

Conclusion: Continuum in Macedonian history

In the introduction I said that the rises and falls of the following dynasty, the Antigonid, in the Hellenistic era play a role in combating the view that the Argead period between Alexander I and Philip II was one of decline. If we drew a "graph" of the Argeads and the Antigonids, it would show a remarkable similarity in rises, falls, rises again, and then collapse—in 323 after Alexander's death and in 168 with its conquest by Rome. Yet when we bring out the Argeads from the shadow of their interactions with other powers, we can appreciate their actions and policies for their kingdom. Likewise, when we do the same with the Antigonids from the shadow of

[49] Hammond and Walbank 1988, pp. 164–167; Carney 2021.

[50] Diodorus 20.28.1–2; Justin 15.2.3 (before killing Alexander IV and Roxane); Pausanias 9.7.2 (poisoned). On the killing of Alexander and Heracles, see Hammond and Walbank 1988, pp. 165–168.

[51] See Kyriakou 2020b.

Roman imperialism, we see kings who also did well for their kingdom and enhanced it, as the following brief survey demonstrates.[52]

The Antigonid dynasty traced its origins back to Antigonus I Monophthalmus, who before his death in 301 had vied for the Macedonian throne along with his son Demetrius I Poliorcetes ("the besieger").[53] But there was always turmoil in Macedonia, which never exerted the same influence and soon lost its hegemony over Greece after Alexander the Great's death in 323. Cassander managed to bring some stability to the monarchy but after he died of tuberculosis in 297 the kingdom was hurt by three unremarkable kings in as many years. The first was Cassander's son Philip IV, who succumbed to tuberculosis four months later, at which time Cassander's and Thessalonice's young sons Antipater I and Alexander V—the half-Argeads—took the throne, with their mother as regent.[54] In 295 Antipater I murdered her and overthrew his brother so he could rule in his own name. He did not survive much longer, as Alexander V sought help from Demetrius Poliorcetes and Pyrrhus of Epirus, and the following year Pyrrhus expelled Antipater and made Alexander V sole king.

But Demetrius also had his eyes on the throne. In that same year, 294, he lulled Alexander into a trap, killed him, and thus took the throne as Demetrius I.[55] Antipater I then fled Macedonia to the court of his father-in-law, Lysimachus of Thrace, but received no support there. In the meantime, in 288 Lysimachus and Pyrrhus invaded Macedonia, expelled Demetrius, and divided up the kingdom between them, with Lysimachus putting Antipater I to death. There were now no other contenders for the throne from the Argead line.

For the next several years Macedonia was in the hands of Lysimachus of Thrace, Pyrrhus of Epirus, and after them Ptolemy Ceraunus (the eldest son of Ptolemy I of Egypt), but fortunately in 277 Demetrius I's son Antigonus II Gonatas took the throne after some struggles. His long reign until 239 brought a rise in Macedonia's economy, military, and border security against the Illyrians, as well as a careful domestic and foreign policy,

[52] See further Worthington 2016, pp. 108–112, 116–120, 125–128, 170–173, 176–178, 181–183; Worthington 2023, pp. 34–39.

[53] Antigonus I: Billows 1990; Champion 2014.

[54] Plutarch, *Demetrius* 36.1, with Hammond and Walbank 1988, p. 210 n. 3.

[55] Demetrius I Poliorcetes: Hammond and Walbank 1988, pp. 219–229; Waterfield 2011, pp. 186–190 and 193–196; Wheatley and Dunn 2020; Worthington 2021, pp. 94–100.

which included growing influence in Greece, and dynastic stability.[56] Macedonia's fortunes were on the rise again, but Gonatas' son and successor, Demetrius II, brought them sharply down. King for only a decade (239–229), he was at war with a group of central Greek states known as the Aetolian League for most of his reign and died in a Dardanian invasion.[57] His son Philip was too young to succeed him, and with the hostile Aetolian League compromising Macedonia's southern border, the situation was not greatly different from what the kingdom had faced in 359 before Philip II became king.

The young heir was acclaimed king as Philip V, but Antigonus Doson, a cousin of Demetrius II, became his regent. Doson always acknowledged Philip as king, but he made sure he held the reins of power and from 229 to 221 ruled as Antigonus III.[58] He ended the threat from the Dardanians and even recovered towns in Greece. Just as it seemed Macedonia was on the rise, he was killed fighting against invading Illyrians. Philip was still too young to rule in his own right, but Doson had tasked a group of guardians to look after him. Their internal bickering, however, led Philip to engineer their demise once he came of age two or so years later.

Philip V ruled until 179, another much-needed long reign, though by this point Rome was involved in Illyria and Greece and eventually Macedonia.[59] The king fought hard to protect his kingdom and faced off threats from a hostile Pergamum and discontent among the Greeks. He and Rome went to war twice in his reign—the First Macedonian War (214–205) and the Second Macedonian War (200–197)—and he had the upper hand several times in these wars. But in 197 he was soundly defeated at Cynoscephalae in Thessaly, when the renowned phalanx became disrupted on uneven ground and fell to the onslaught of the Roman legion. Still, he was allowed to retain the throne and spent the rest of his reign introducing economic reforms and rebuilding manpower as well as expanding his kingdom's territory in Thrace despite Rome's concerns.

[56] Antigonus II: Tarn 1921; Gabbert 1997; Hammond and Walbank 1988, pp. 259–316; Waterfield 2020; cf. Waterfield 2011, pp. 197–212.

[57] Alexander II: Kuzmin 2019; Hammond and Walbank 1988, pp. 317–336.

[58] Antigonus III: Hammond and Walbank 1988, pp. 337–364; LeBohec 1993b.

[59] Philip V: Walbank 1940; Hammond and Walbank 1988, pp. 367–487; Errington 1990, pp. 184–212; Hammond 1992a, pp. 330–362; Waterfield 2014, *passim*; King 2018, pp. 246–256; D'Agostini 2019; Worthington 2023, pp. 25–179. Rise of Rome in the Greek east: Gruen 1984; Kallet-Marx 1995; Waterfield 2014, for example.

Macedonia was thus rising again when Philip died in 179 and was succeeded by his son Perseus.[60] During his short reign (179–168) Perseus was able to preserve Macedonian manpower and stimulated its economy, but increasing tensions with Rome and Pergamum, largely due to both powers' aim to dethrone him, brought about the Third Macedonian War of 171–168. Perseus' army was routed at the battle of Pydna in 168, after which the Roman Senate abolished the Antigonid dynasty and divided the former kingdom into four self-governing districts (*merides*), but subject to Roman laws and strict economic, military, and social restrictions.

Rome's stranglehold over Macedonia led to economic pressures and discontent over the years, and in 150 a man named Andriscus declared himself a son of Perseus and gathered enough support to become king; hence he is sometimes called Philip VI.[61] He re-established the single kingdom and conducted a purge of opponents and Roman-backed officials, but unsurprisingly the Romans did not take this lying down. In 149 they declared war on him—the Fourth Macedonian War—and defeated him the following year in the second battle of Pydna, after which they sacked Pella. A year later, in 148, came the final fall for Macedonia when Rome likely turned it into a province under a governor with the capital at Thessalonica.[62]

Argead Macedonia was in many respects like Antigonid Macedonia when it came to rises and falls—until the obvious arrival of the Romans, though then again, they changed every place where they went, from Italy to Syria to Egypt. Argead kings such as Perdiccas II, Archelaus, Alexander II, Ptolemy, and Perdiccas III, as we have seen, found themselves all too often facing hostile, superior forces from Greece and Illyria, not to mention outside interference in domestic matters. Likewise, Philip V, Perseus, and Andriscus had to contend with the ever-present Illyrian threat and Roman presence on their doorstep in Illyria and Greece. And just as several Argead kings were overshadowed by the successes of Philip II and Alexander the Great, so Philip V and Perseus can be lost in the rise of Rome in the east.

When we set these rulers at center stage, it is a different story. As we have seen, all the Argeads, the subjects of this book, were important in their own

[60] Perseus: Hammond and Walbank 1988, pp. 488–558; Errington 1990, pp. 212–221; Hammond 1992a, pp. 362–381; Waterfield 2014, pp. 165–167 and 173–193; Burton 2017, pp. 56–175; King 2018, pp. 256–260; Worthington 2023, pp. 180–245.

[61] Andriscus: Gruen 1984, pp. 431–436; Helliesen 1986; Waterfield 2014, pp. 219–220; Burton 2017, pp. 186–188; Worthington 2023, pp. 245–250.

[62] Vanderspoel 2010; Vanderspoel 2015, especially pp. 201–206; Worthington 2023, pp. 251–254, citing bibliography.

way for what they did for Macedonia, and many of their achievements enabled Philip II to transform Macedonia and bequeath a powerful kingdom, on the cusp of empire, to Alexander III. Likewise, Antigonid kings managed to keep Macedonia stable and even increase its influence in the Greek and Mediterranean worlds, with Philip V and Perseus defiantly playing David to the Goliath that was Rome—and having the upper hand at times.

It is this protection of a kingdom that is the driving force of Macedonia's history from early times to the Hellenistic. All kings rightly fought to secure their lands and promote the well-being of their subjects regardless of the odds facing them. The earlier Argead kings struggled even more, as Macedonia was still developing in the days before Archelaus. They had to battle hostile peoples, play diplomatic games, and even contend with threats to their kingships as they expanded the kingdom, developed its economy, and maintained a formidable and successful army. In this respect, decline should not be associated with the Argead kings; rather, their roles in the rise of Macedonia from traditional "hearth" to imperial power should be lauded.

Macedonia under the Argead Kings: The Rise and Fall of an Ancient Superpower. Ian Worthington, Oxford University Press. © Oxford University Press 2026. DOI: 10.1093/9780197668009.003.0013

Timeline

Mid 7th century (?)	Three brothers from Argos journey to Macedonia (?). Perdiccas I king until later seventh century; foundation of Aegae as capital.
547(?)–498	Amyntas I king; possibly submits to Persian authority; Persian envoys at Macedonian court allegedly murdered and a cover up by future Alexander I.
498–454	Alexander I king; Mardonius to Macedonian court seeking submission (492); battle of Marathon (490); Xerxes' invasion (481); Alexander warns Greeks at Tempe (480); battle of Thermopylae (480); Alexander sent to Athens by Mardonius (winter 480–479); Alexander at Plataea and battle (479); expansion of kingdom, especially after Persian defeat at Plataea; Alexander strikes first coinage (479); Alexander at Olympic Games (476); death (454).
454/435–413	Perdiccas II king; Athenians found Amphipolis (437); first coins to show Perdiccas ruled in his own name (435); he clashes with Athens and city makes alliance with Philip and Derdas of Elimea against him (432); Perdiccas helps found Chalcidian League (432); Athens and Perdiccas come to terms (432, 431); Peloponnesian War breaks out (431–404); Sitalces invades Macedonia (429); Perdiccas aligns with Sparta (424); campaigns against Arrhabaeus of Lyncus (424); makes treaty with Athens (423); breaks with Athens (417); reconciles with Athens (414?); death (413).
413–399	Archelaus king; aligns with Athens; various military, economic, and social reforms plus increased hellenization of court; Peloponnesian War ends with Athens' defeat (404); Archelaus intervenes in Thessaly (400?); foundation of Pella as capital (399?); assassinated (399).
404–371	Spartan hegemony over Greece, which ends with Thebes defeating Sparta at the battle of Leuctra (371).
400/399–397/6	Orestes king; only a toddler, so Aeropus was his regent and probably murdered Orestes (397/6).
397/6–394	Aeropus II king; defiance of Spartans (394); defeats Illyrians (unknown date); death (394).

394/3	Pausanias king and Amyntas II "the Little" king in possible joint rule; Amyntas assassinated (393); Pausanias murdered by Amyntas III (393).
393/2–369/8	Amyntas III king; expelled after Illyrian invasion and returns within three months (393/2); expelled by Argaeus and in exile for two years (387/6–385/4); makes alliances with Chalcidians (380s); declares war on Chalcidians and seeks Spartan help (383); alliance with Athens (375 or 373); invited to Congress of Greeks at Corinth (371); alliance with Jason of Pherae (371); death (369/8).
371–362	Theban hegemony over Greece, which ends with an Athenian-led coalition defeating Thebes at the battle of Mantinea (362).
369/8	Alexander II king; faces Illyrian invasion; opposed by Pausanias the pretender; receives Athenian help to expel Pausanias; campaigns in Thessaly; opposed by Ptolemy the pretender; Thebans expel Ptolemy; Ptolemy returns and may have had Alexander assassinated (368).
368/7–365/4	Ptolemy as regent; forced to do Thebes' bidding; assassinated perhaps at the bidding of the future Perdiccas III (365).
365/4–360/59	Perdiccas III king; supporter of Thebes but submits to Athens' will (364–363); severs contacts with Athens and allies with Chalcidian League (363); begins to reassert control of his coastline at Athens' expense (363–362); faces Illyrian invasion (359); killed along with 4,000 troops in battle (359).
359–336	Philip II king; arranges an armistice (?) with the Illyrians; nullifies threats from Paeonians, Thracians, and Athenians; begins military reforms (359); defeats Illyrians and Paeonians; unites Upper and Lower Macedonia; makes alliance with Thessaly to secure his southern border (358); Philinna (third wife) gives birth to Arrhidaeus (357); Philip allies with Epirus and marries Olympias of Epirus, his fourth wife (357); Athens declares war on Philip over Amphipolis (357); Olympias gives birth to Alexander (356); Third Sacred War (355–346); expands into Chalcidice and Greece; Peace of Philocrates ends war between Philip and Athens (346); breakdown of peace and Philip's campaigns in Illyria, Epirus, Thrace, and Chersonese (345–340); Athens declares war on Philip (340); battle of Chaeronea gives Philip hegemony over Greece (338); League of Corinth and plan to invade Asia (337); assassination (336).
336–323	Alexander III ("the Great") king; Greek revolt against Macedonian hegemony ended by Alexander; resurrects League of Corinth and Philip's plan to invade Asia; campaign in

	Thrace and Illyria (335); invades Asia and topples Persian Empire (334–330); invasion of Bactria and Sogdiana (330–327); invasion of India (327–325); dies in Babylon (323).
323–322	Babylon settlement divides up Alexander's empire among senior staff and dual monarchy of Alexander IV and Philip III Arrhidaeus (323); Greek revolt against Macedonian hegemony known as Lamian War (323–322); Antipater reimposes Macedonian rule over Greece (322); Wars of the Successors begin.
320–319	Triparadeisus settlement; Antipater becomes guardian of Alexander IV and Philip III Arrhidaeus (320); death of Antipater (319); clashes between his nominated successor Polyperchon and his son Cassander for control of Macedonia.
317–310	Death of Philip III Arrhidaeus and his wife (317); Cassander marries Thessalonice (daughter of Philip II and his fifth wife, Nicesipolis of Pherae) and assumes guardianship of Alexander IV; imprisons Alexander IV and his mother Roxane at Amphipolis; continuing clashes between Cassander and other former generals of Alexander.
310	Murders of Alexander IV and Roxane; end of Argead dynasty; some years of upheaval before establishment of Antigonid dynasty.
297	Death of Cassander; his son Philip IV becomes king but dies months later; his young sons Antipater I and Alexander V—half-Argeads—rule jointly with their mother Thessalonice as regent.
295–288	Antipater I murders Thessalonice and expels Alexander V (295); overthrown next year and Alexander V becomes sole king; murdered by the Antigonid Demetrius I Poliorcetes, who becomes king of Macedonia (294); exiled Antipater I killed by Lysimachus (288)—the end of the Argead bloodline.
294–168	Antigonid kings rule Macedonia until defeated by Rome at the battle of Pydna (168); Romans end the dynasty (168); Macedonia under Roman control.
150–148	Revolt of Macedonia led by Andriscus, sometimes called Philip VI (150); defeated by Rome at the second battle of Pydna (148); Macedonia becomes a Roman province (148).

Cast of Principal Characters

Aeropus II

King of Macedonia, 397/6–394. He may have been a Lyncestian prince or even another son of Perdiccas. Little is known of his reign: he was anti-Spartan and, at some point, defeated the Illyrians. He died in 394.

Alexander I

King of Macedonia, 498–454, son of Amyntas I. He likely submitted to Persian rule. He sided with Persia in the Persian Wars but still helped the Greeks with a warning about the Persians at Tempe and before Plataea. He was responsible for a major expansion of his kingdom after the Persians left Greece, introduced the first state coinage in 479, and likely made reforms to the military. He was also the first to claim his family originally came from Argos in Greece and was a competitor in the Olympic Games, probably those of476. He promoted closer contacts with the Greeks, and his love of Greek culture probably earned him the nickname "philhellene."

Alexander II

King of Macedonia, 369/8, son of Amyntas III and Eurydice. He defeated the Illyrians and the attempts of two pretenders—Pausanias and Ptolemy—on the throne but may have been assassinated by the latter in 368.

Alexander III (the Great)

King of Macedonia, 336–323, son of Philip II and his fourth wife, Olympias of Epirus. He invaded Asia in 334, toppling the Achaemenid ruling dynasty and establishing an empire that stretched from Greece to what the Greeks called India (Pakistan and Kashmir). His next campaign, an invasion of Arabia, was abandoned on his death.

Alexander IV

King of Macedonia, 323–310, son of Alexander III and Roxane, born after his father's death in 323. He first shared the throne with his half-brother Philip III Arrhidaeus until the latter's death in 317. He and Roxane were imprisoned in Amphipolis and put to death on Cassander's orders in 310.

Alexander V

King of Macedonia, 297–294, son of Cassander and Thessalonice, hence a half-Argead. He ruled jointly with his brother Antipater I but was expelled by him in 295 and returned as king in 294, but in that year was murdered by Demetrius I Poliorcetes.

Amyntas I

King of Macedonia, c. 547–498. Little is known of his reign except that he increased the territory of Macedonia and may have submitted to Persian authority.

Amyntas II "the Little"

King of Macedonia, 394/3. His parents are unknown. He may have ruled jointly with Pausanias, a son of Archelaus. He was assassinated by Derdas of Elimea in 393.

Amyntas III

King of Macedonia, 393/2–369/8, son of Arrhidaeus and grandson of Perdiccas II's brother Amyntas. He was expelled by the Illyrians soon after coming to power but returned three months later. He was expelled again by a certain Argaeus and in exile for two years (387/6–385/4) before returning to the throne. Amyntas made alliances with Sparta and Athens as needed and went to war against the Chalcidians. He also allied with Jason of Pherae as part of a move to involve himself in Greek affairs but died in 369.

Antipater I

King of Macedonia, 297–295, son of Cassander and Thessalonice, hence a half-Argead. He ruled jointly with his brother Alexander V until he expelled the latter and murdered Thessalonice in 295. He fled into exile and was killed in 288.

Antipater, general

Antipater served as a general under Philip and was the first to proclaim Alexander III king in 336. He was Alexnder's guardian (*epitropos*) of Macedonia and deputy hegemon of the League of Corinth when the king was in Asia. Antipater clashed frequently with Olympias and became guardian of Philip III Arrhidaeus and Alexander IV under the Triparadeisus settlement. He died in 319.

Archelaus

King of Macedonia, 411–399, son of Perdiccas II. He apparently murdered rival claimants to the throne to become king, though this can be doubted. His reign saw various military, economic, and social reforms, and he is particularly known for his philhellenism and for increasing the hellenization of the court, at which Euripides lived and worked. He generally stayed an ally of Athens and is credited with founding a new capital at Pella in 399. He was assassinated in 399.

Argaeus

Ousted Amyntas III from the throne in 387 and rules for two years. Little is known of him, and he could even have been another son of Archelaus. His support base is also unknown: possibly the Olynthians or even the Athenians. He was overthrown by Amyntas in 385 and may have fled to Athens, as that city backed a pretender named Argaeus when Perdiccas III died in 359.

Cassander

Son of Antipater. He expected to assume his father's position in Greece and Macedonia on his death in 319, but Antipater named Polyperchon his successor. Cassander allied with various Successors in his quest for power, eventually became ruler of Macedonia, and married Thessalonice, a daughter of Philip II. He became guardian of Alexander IV and imprisoned him and his mother Roxane in Amphipolis, putting them to death in 310. He died in 297. His sons Philip IV, Alexander V, and Antipater I briefly ruled Macedonia.

Heracles

Bastard son of Alexander III and Barsine, born in 327. He was briefly considered as a successor to Alexander by the generals at Babylon in 323 but rejected. He and his mother were murdered on Polyperchon's order in 309.

Olympias

A princess of Epirus who married Philip II in 357 as part of a diplomatic alliance between Macedonia and Epirus. In 356 Olympias gave birth to Alexander (III). She disliked Philip greatly and may even have had played a role in his assassination. She frequently clashed with Antipater when Alexander was in Asia but withdrew to Epirus from 331 to 317. In that year she returned to Macedonia to champion her grandson Alexander IV but earned the dislike of Cassander for her ruthlessness and was put to death in 316.

Orestes

King of Macedonia, 400/399–397/6, son of Archelaus. He was only a toddler, so Aeropus, about whom little is known, became his regent. Orestes was murdered, perhaps by Aeropus, in 397.

Pausanias, king

King of Macedonia, 394/3, son of Aeropus II. He may have ruled jointly with Amyntas II "the Little." He was murdered by Amyntas (III) in 393.

Pausanias, pretender

A pretender, perhaps Archelaus' grandson, who with possibly Olynthian help challenged Alexander II for the throne before being expelled by an Athenian force.

Perdiccas I

King of Macedonia, c. mid seventh century-later seventh century; one of three brothers supposedly from Argos who journeyed to Macedonia. He became its first king, founding the Argead dynasty and the first capital at Aegae. Nothing else is known of him.

Perdiccas II

King of Macedonia, 454 or 435–413, son of Alexander I. He may have ruled in some joint fashion with his brothers, but from 435 coinage bears his name, showing he was sole king. He survived an invasion of his kingdom by Sitalces of Thrace in 429. He made and broke alliances throughout his reign with other powers such as Athens, Sparta, and the Chalcidian League as it suited his needs, for which he is often criticized for inconsistency. In fact, he was no different from any Greek state's leaders, and his actions were always undertaken to protect his kingship and kingdom.

Perdiccas III

King of Macedonia, 365/4–360/59, son of Amyntas III and Eurydice. His reign saw issues with Athens and an alliance with the Chalcidian League, as well as successful moves to reassert Macedonia's control of its coastline at Athens' expense. He was killed in battle along with 4,000 troops when the Illyrians invaded in 359.

Philip II

King of Macedonia, 359–336, son of Amyntas III and Eurydice. His reign transformed Macedonia from an economically, politically, and militarily weak kingdom on the periphery of Greece into a superpower, in the process conquering the lands adjoining his borders as well as Thrace and Greece. He also made plans to invade Asia, but before doing so he was assassinated in 336.

Philip III Arrhidaeus

Arrhidaeus, son of Philip II and his third wife, Philinna of Thessaly, was born in 357. He suffered some type of mental incapacity, and his younger brother Alexander (the future Alexander III) became heir. Arrhidaeus lived at Pella; on Alexander's death in 323 he was proclaimed king as Philip III Arrhidaeus. However, he shared regnal power with Alexander IV, son of Alexander III and Roxane. Arrhidaeus was a pawn in the wars of Alexander's generals, and he and his wife Eurydice were executed in 317.

Philip IV

Son of Cassander; he succeeded his father as king in 297 but died in the same year.

Polyperchon

Tapped by Antipater to be his successor but thwarted by Antipater's son Cassander Polyperchon, he made several attempts to overcome Cassander and eventually persuaded Olympias to return from Epirus and march on Macedonia to support her grandson Alexander IV over Philip III (317). Polyperchon made peace with Cassander in 309 and became made governor of the Peloponnese. He also ordered the deaths of Heracles and Barsine.

Ptolemy

Regent, 368/7–365/4, perhaps from Alorus. He challenged Alexander II for power but after Theban arbitration left Macedonia. He returned and may have arranged the death of Alexander II (368). As regent, he aligned with Thebes and was murdered, perhaps orchestrated by Perdiccas III.

Bibliography

I have used the original publications and paginations for articles that have been reprinted in collections of scholars' works rather than the page numbers in the latter. I also use the first edition of Borza 1990.

Adams, W.L., "The Other People's Games: the Olympics, Macedonia and Greek Athletics," *Journal of Sport History* 30 (2003a), pp. 205–217

Adams, W.L., "The Episode of Philotas: An Insight," in W. Heckel and L. Tritle (eds.), *Crossroads of History, The Age of Alexander* (Claremont: 2003b), pp. 113–126

Adams, W.L., "The Hellenistic Kingdoms," in G.R. Bugh (ed.), *The Cambridge Companion to the Hellenistic World* (Cambridge: 2007), pp. 28–51

Adams, W.L., "Alexander's Successors to 221 BC," in J. Roisman and Ian Worthington (eds.), *A Companion to Ancient Macedonia* (Malden: 2010), pp. 208–224

Adler, W. and P. Tuffin, *The Chronography of George Synkellos: A Byzantine Chronicle of Universal History from the Creation* (Oxford: 2002)

Akamatis, I.M., "Pella," in R.J. Lane Fox (ed.), *Brill's Companion to Ancient Macedon* (Leiden: 2011), pp. 393–408

Allan, W. and L. Swift, *Euripides: Bacchae* (Cambridge: 2024)

Allen, L., *The Persian Empire* (Chicago: 2005)

Andrewes, A., *The Greek Tyrants* (London: 1956)

Andronikos, M., "The Finds from the Royal Tombs at Vergina," *PBA* 65 (1979), pp. 355–367

Andronikos, M., "The Royal Tombs at Aigai (Vergina)," in M.B. Hatzopoulos and L.D. Loukopoulos (eds.), *Philip of Macedon* (London 1980), pp. 188–231

Andronikos, M., "Some Reflections on the Macedonian Tombs," *BSA* 82 (1987), pp. 1–16

Andronikos, M., *Vergina: The Royal Tombs and the Ancient City* (Athens: 2004)

Anson, E.M., "The Meaning of the Term *Makedones*," *Anc. World* 10 (1984), pp. 67–68

Anson, E.M., "Macedonia's Alleged Consitutionalism," *CJ* 80 (1985a), pp. 303–316

Anson, E.M, "The Hypaspists: Macedonia's Professional Citizen-Soldiers," *Historia* 34 (1985b), pp. 246–248

Anson, E.M., "The Evolution of the Macedonian Army Assembly (330-315)," *Historia* 40 (1991), pp. 230–247

Anson, E.M., "Alexander and Siwah," *Anc. World* 34 (2003), pp. 117–130

Anson, E.M., "Macedonian Judicial Assemblies," *CPh* 103 (2008a), pp. 135–149

Anson, E.M., "Philip II and the Transformation of Macedonia: A Reappraisal," in T. Howe and J. Reames (eds.), *Macedonian Legacies. Studies in Ancient Macedonian History and Culture in Honor of Eugene N. Borza* (Claremont: 2008b), pp. 17–30

Anson, E.M., "Philip II, Amyntas Perdicca, and Macedonian Royal Succession," *Historia* 58 (2009), pp. 276–286

Anson, E.M., "The Introduction of the Sarisa in Macedonian Warfare," *Ancient Society* 40 (2010), pp. 51–68

Anson, E.M., *Alexander the Great. Themes and Issues* (London: 2013)

Anson, E.M, *Alexander's Heirs: The Age of the Successors* (Malden: 2014)

Anson, E.M., *Philip II, the Father of Alexander the Great* (BLM: 2020)

Antela-Bernárdez, B., "Simply the Best. Alexander's Last Words and the Macedonian Kingship," *Eirene* 47 (2011), pp. 118–126

Antela-Bernárdez, B., "Philip and Pausanias: A Deadly Love in Macedonian Politics," *CQ*[2] 62 (2012), pp. 859–861

Antela-Bernárdez, B., "Requiem for a Great King. The Death of Darius III," *Karanos* 6 (2023), pp. 9–16

Antonetti, C. and P. Biagi (eds.), *With Alexander in India and Central Asia. Moving East & Back to West* (Oxford: 2017)

Archibald, Z.H., *The Odrysian Kingdom of Thrace: Orpheus Unmasked* (Oxford: 1998)

Archibald, Z., "Macedonia and Thrace," in J. Roisman and Ian Worthington (eds.), *A Companion to Ancient Macedonia* (Malden: 2010), pp. 326–341

Arnhold, M., Review of M.B. Hatzopoulos, *Ancient Macedonia* (de Gruyter: 2020), *BMCR* 2021.09.40

Asirvatham, S.L., "No Patriotic Fervor for Pella: Aelius Aristides and the Presentation of the Macedonians in the Second Sophistic," *Mnemosyne* 61 (2008), pp. 207–227

Asirvatham, S., "Perspectives on the Macedonians from Greece, Rome, and Beyond," in J. Roisman and Ian Worthington (eds.), *A Companion to Ancient Macedonia* (Malden: 2010a), pp. 99–124

Asirvatham, S.L., "His Son's Father? Philip II in the Second Sophistic," in E.D. Carney and D. Ogden (eds.), *Philip II and Alexander the Great: Lives and Afterlives* (Oxford: 2010b), pp. 193–204

Asirvatham, S.L., "The Argeads and the Second Sophistic," in S. Müller, T. Howe, H. Bowden, and R. Rollinger (eds.), *The History of the Argeads: New Perspectives* (Wiesbaden: 2017), pp. 281–295

Ashley, J.R., *The Macedonian Empire. The Era of Warfare under Philip II and Alexander the Great, 359–323 B.C.* (Jefferson: 1998)

Ashton, N.G., "The Lamian War – stat magni nominis umbra," *JHS* 94 (1984), pp. 152–157

Atkinson, J.E., "Euripides' *Bacchae* in its Historical Context," *Akroterion* 47 (2002), pp. 5–15

Austin, M.M., "Alexander and the Macedonian Invasion of Asia," in J. Rich and G. Shipley (eds.), *War and Society in the Greek World* (London: 1993), pp. 197–223

Aymard, A., "Philippe II de Macedoine otage à Thébes," *REA* 56 (1954), pp. 15–36

Badian, E., "The Death of Parmenio," *TAPhA* 91 (1960), pp. 324–338

Badian, E., "The Death of Philip II," *Phoenix* 17 (1963), pp. 244–250

Badian, E., "Alexander the Great and the Loneliness of Power," in E. Badian (ed.), *Studies in Greek and Roman History* (Oxford: 1964), pp. 192–205

Badian, E., "The Administration of the Empire," *G&R*[2] 12 (1965), pp. 166–182

Badian, E., "Alexander the Great and the Greeks of Asia," in E. Badian (ed.), *Ancient Society and Institutions. Studies Presented to V. Ehrenberg on his 75th Birthday* (Oxford: 1966), pp. 37–69

Badian, E., "A King's Notebooks," *HSCPh* 72 (1967), pp. 183–204

Badian, E., "The Battle of the Granicus: A New Look," *Ancient Macedonia* 2 (Institute for Balkan Studies, Thessaloniki: 1977), pp. 271–293

Badian, E., "The Deification of Alexander the Great," in H.J. Dell (ed.), *Ancient Macedonian Studies in Honor of C.F. Edson* (Thessaloniki: 1981), pp. 27–71

Badian, E., "Greeks and Macedonians," in B. Barr-Sharrar and E.N. Borza (eds.), *Macedonia and Greece in Late Classical and Early Hellenistic Times* (Washington: 1982a), pp. 33–51

Badian, E., "Eurydice," in W.L. Adams and E.N. Borza (eds.), *Philip II, Alexander the Great, and the Macedonian Heritage* (Lanham: 1982b), pp. 99–110

Badian, E., "Philip II and Thrace," *Pulpudeva* 4 (1983), pp. 51–71

Badian, E., "Alexander the Great and the Scientific Exploration of the Oriental Part of his Empire," *Ancient Society* 22 (1991), pp. 127–138

Badian, E., "Thucydides and the *Archê* of Philip," in Badian, E. (ed.), *From Plataea to Potidaea: Studies in the History and Historiography of the Pentacontaetia* (Baltimore: 1993), pp. 171–185 and 239–244 (notes)

Badian, E., "Herodotus on Alexander I of Macedon: A Study in Some Subtle Silence," in S. Hornblower (ed.), *Greek Historiography* (Oxford 1994), pp. 107–130

Badian, E., "The Ghost of Empire: Reflections on Athenian Foreign Policy in the Fourth Century," in W. Eder (ed.), *Die athenische Demokratie im 4. Jahrhundert v. Chr.* (Stuttgart: 1995), pp. 79–106

Badian, E., "Conspiracies," in A.B. Bosworth and E. Baynham (eds.), *Alexander the Great in Fact and Fiction* (Oxford: 1996), pp. 60–92

Badian, E., "Philip II and the Last of the Thessalians," *Ancient Macedonia* 6 (Institute for Balkan Studies, Thessaloniki: 1999), pp. 109–122

Badian, E., "Darius III," *HSCPh* 100 (2000), pp. 241–268

Badian, E., "Once More the Death of Philip," *Ancient Macedonia* 7 (Institute for Balkan Studies, Thessaloniki: 2007), pp. 389–406

Balcer, J.M., "Persian Occupied Thrace," *Historia* 33 (1988), pp. 1–21

Baynham, E., "The Question of Macedonian Divine Honours for Philip II," *Mediterranean Archaeology* 7 (1994a), pp. 35–43

Baynham, E., "Antipater: Manager of Kings," in Ian Worthington (ed.), *Ventures into Greek History. Essays in Honour of N.G.L. Hammond* (Oxford: 1994b), pp. 331–356

Baynham, E., "Why didn't Alexander Marry a Nice Macedonian Girl Before Leaving Home? Observations on Factional Politics at Alexander's Court in 336-334 BC," in T. Hillard (ed.), *Ancient History in a Modern University* 1 (Sydney: 1997), pp. 148–155

Baynham, E., "The Ancient Evidence for Alexander the Great," in J. Roisman (ed.), *Brill's Companion to Alexander the Great* (Leiden: 2003), pp. 3–29

Baynham, E., "Cleomenes of Naucratis, Villain or Victim?," in T. Howe, E.E. Garvan, and G. Wrightson (eds.), *Greece, Macedon and Persia: Studies in Social, Political and Military History in Honour of W. Heckel* (Haverton: 2015), pp. 127–134

Baynham, E. and P. Wheatley (eds.), *East and West in the World of Alexander: Essays in Honour of A.B. Bosworth* (Oxford: 2014)

Bearzot, C., "La tradizione su Parmenione negli storici di Alessandro," *Aevum* 61 (1987), pp. 89–104

Bennett, B. and M. Roberts, *The Wars of Alexander's Successors, 323–281 BC* 1 (Barnsley: 2008) and 2 (Barnsley: 2009)

Bichler, R., "Philip II and the Scythians in the Light of Alexander Historiography," in S. Müller, T. Howe, H. Bowden, and R. Rollinger (eds.), *The History of the Argeads: New Perspectives* (Wiesbaden: 2017), pp. 253–268

Billows, R., *Antigonus the One-Eyed and the Creation of the Hellenistic State* (Berkeley and Los Angeles: 1990)

Billows, R., *Kings and Colonists: Aspects of Macedonian Imperialism* (Leiden 1995)

Blackman, D., "Triremes and Shipsheds," in H.E. Tzalas (ed.), *Tropis II. 2nd International Symposium on Ship Construction in Antiquity* (Delphi: 1990), pp. 35–52

Blackwell, C.W., *In the Absence of Alexander. Harpalus and the Failure of Macedonian Authority* (New York: 1998)

Bloedow, E.F., "The Siege of Tyre in 332 BC: Alexander at the Crossroads in his Career," *La Parola del Passato* 301 (1990), pp. 255–293

Bloedow, E.F., "Alexander the Great and Bactria," *PP* 46 (1991), pp. 44–80

Bloedow, E.F., "The So-called "Scythian Campaign" of Philip II in 339 BC," *La Parola del Passato* 322 (2002), pp. 25–61

Bloedow, E., "Why did Philip and Alexander Launch a War against the Persian Empire?," *L'Ant. Class.* 72 (2003), pp. 261–274

Bloedow, E., "Egypt in Alexander's Scheme of Things," *QUCC* 77 (2004), pp. 75–99

Bloedow, E. and H.M. Loube, "Alexander the Great 'Under Fire' at Persepolis," *Klio* 79 (1997), pp. 341–353

Bolmarcich, S., "The Afterlife of a Treaty," *CQ*² 57 (2007), pp. 477–489

Borza, E.N., "Fire from Heaven: Alexander at Persepolis," *CPh* 67 (1972), pp. 233–245
Borza, E.N., Some Observations on Malaria and the Ecology of Central Macedonia in Antiquity', *AJAH* 4 (1979), pp. 102–124
Borzȧ, E.N., "Anaxagoras and Callisthenes: Academic Intrigue at Alexander's Court," in H.J. Dell (ed.), *Ancient Macedonian Studies in Honour of C.F. Edson* (Thessaloniki: 1981), pp. 73–86
Borza, E.N., "The Natural Resources of Early Macedonia," in W.L. Adams and E.N. Borza (eds.), *Philip II, Alexander the Great, and the Macedonian Heritage* (Lanham: 1982a), pp. 1–20
Borza, E.N., "Athenians, Macedonians, and the Origins of the Macedonian Royal House," in *Studies in Attic Epigraphy, History and Topography Presented to Eugene Vanderpool* (Princeton 1982b), pp. 7–13
Borza, E.N., "Timber and Politics in the Ancient World: Macedon and the Greeks," *Proceedings of the American Philosophical Society* 131 (1987), pp. 32–52
Borza, E.N., *In the Shadow of Olympus: The Emergence of Macedon* (Princeton: 1990)
Borza, E.N., "Ethnicity and Cultural Policy at Alexander's Court," *Anc. World* 22 (1991), pp. 21–25
Borza, E.N., "The Philhellenism of Archelaus," *Ancient Macedonia* 5 (Institute for Balkan Studies, Thessaloniki: 1993), pp. 237–244
Borza, E.N. and O. Palagia, "The Chronology of the Royal Macedonian Tombs at Vergina," *Jahrbuch des Deutsche Archaeologischen Instituts* 122 (2007), pp. 81–125
Bosworth, A.B., "Philip II and Upper Macedonia," *CQ*[2] 21 (1971a), pp. 93–105
Bosworth, A.B., "The Death of Alexander the Great: Rumour and Propaganda," *CQ*[2] 21 (1971b), pp. 112–136
Bosworth A.B. "Alexander and the Iranians," *JHS* 100 (1980), pp. 1–21
Bosworth, A.B., "A Missing Year in the History of Alexander the Great," *JHS* 101 (1981), pp. 17–39
Bosworth, A.B., "The Location of Alexander's Campaign against against the Illyrians in 335 B.C.," in B. Barr-Sharrar and E.N. Borza (eds.), *Macedonia and Greece in Late Classical and Early Hellenistic Times* (Washington: 1982), pp. 74–84
Bosworth, A.B., "The Indian Satrapies under Alexander the Great," *Antichthon* 17 (1983), pp. 37–46
Bosworth, A.B., "Alexander the Great and the Decline of Macedon," *JHS* 106 (1986), pp. 1–12
Bosworth, A.B., *Conquest and Empire. The Reign of Alexander the Great* (Cambridge: 1988)
Bosworth, A.B., "Perdiccas and the Kings" *CQ*[2] 43 (1993), pp. 420–427
Bosworth, A.B., *Alexander and the East. The Tragedy of Triumph* (Oxford: 1996a)
Bosworth, A.B., "The Tumult and the Shouting: Two Interpretations of the Cleitus Episode," *AHB* 10 (1996b), pp. 19–30
Bosworth, A.B., "Alexander, Euripides and Dionysos: The Motivation for Apotheosis," in R.W. Wallace and E.M. Harris (eds.), *Transitions to Empire. Essays in Honor of E. Badian* (Norman: 1996c), pp. 140–166
Bosworth, A.B., "Calanus and the Brahman Opposition," in W. Will (ed.), *Alexander der Grosse: Eine Welteroberung und ihr Hintergrund* (Bonn: 1998), pp. 173–203
Bosworth, A.B., *The Legacy of Alexander. Politics, Warfare and Propaganda under the Successors* (Oxford: 2002)
Bosworth, A.B,. "The Indian Campaigns, 327–325 BC," in J. Roisman (ed.), *Brill's Companion to Alexander the Great* (Leiden: 2003), pp. 59–68
Bosworth, A.B., "Alexander the Great and the Creation of the Hellenistic Age," in G.R. Bugh (ed.), *The Cambridge Companion to the Hellenistic World* (Cambridge: 2007), pp. 9–27
Bosworth, A.B. and E.J. Baynham (eds.), *Alexander the Great in Fact and Fiction* (Oxford: 2000)

Boufalis, A., "The Role of Methone in the Macedonian Timber Trade," in S.P. Morris and J.K. Papadopoulos (eds.), *Ancient Methone 2003–2013* 2 (Los Angeles: 2022), pp. 735–769

Bowden, H., "On Kissing and Making Up: Court Protocol and Historiography in Alexander the Great's 'Experiment with Proskynesis,'" *BICS* 56 (2013), pp. 55–77

Bowden, H., "Alexander in Egypt: Considering the Egyptian Evidence," in P. Bosman (ed.), *Alexander in Africa* (Pretoria: 2014), pp. 38–55

Bousquet, J., "La stèle des Kyténiens àu Létôon de *Xanthos*," *REG* 101 (1988), pp. 12–53

Bouzek, J., "Macedonia and Thrace in the Early Iron Age," *Ancient Macedonia* 4 (Institute for Balkan Studies, Thessaloniki: 1986), pp. 123–132

Braund, D., "After Alexander: The Emergence of the Hellenistic World, 323-281," in A. Erskine (ed.), *The Blackwell Companion to the Hellenistic World* (Malden: 2003), pp. 19–34

Brecoulaki, H., *La peinture funéraire de Macédoine. Emplois et fonctions de la couleur. IVe—IIe s. av. J.-C.* (Athens: 2006)

Briant, P., *From Cyrus to Alexander: A History of the Persian Empire*, trans. P.T. Daniels (Winona Lake: 2002)

Briant, P., *Alexander the Great and his Empire*, trans. A. Kuhrt (Princeton: 2010)

Briant, P., *Darius in the Shadow of Alexander*, trans. J.M. Todd (Cambridge: 2015)

Brosius, M., "Alexander and the Persians," in J. Roisman (ed.), *Brill's Companion to Alexander the Great* (Leiden: 2003), pp. 169–193

Brosius, M., *A History of Ancient Persia: The Achaemenid Empire* (Malden: 2020)

Brown, T.S., "Callisthenes and Alexander," *AJPh* 70 (1949), pp. 225–234

Brun, P., "Demosthenes, between Fake News and Alternative Facts," in A. Kapellos (ed.), *The Orators and Their Treatment of the Recent Past* (Berlin: 2022), pp. 307–321

Brunt, P.A., "The Aims of Alexander," *G&R*[2] 12 (1965), pp. 205–215

Brunt, P.A., "Alexander, Barsine, and Heracles," *Rivista di Filologia* 103 (1975), pp. 22–34

Brunt, P.A., "Anaximenes and King Alexander I of Macedon," *JHS* 96 (1976), pp. 151–153

Buckler, J., *The Theban Hegemony 371–362 BC* (Cambridge: 1980)

Buckler, J., *Philip II and the Sacred War* (Leiden: 1989)

Buckler, J., "Philip II, the Greeks, and the King, 346–336 B.C.," *ICS* 19 (1994), pp. 99–122

Buckler, J., "Philip II's Designs on Greece," in W.R. Wallace and E.M. Harris (eds.), *Transitions to Empire. Essays in Honor of E. Badian* (Norman: 1996), pp. 77–97

Buckler, J., "Demosthenes and Aeschines," in Ian Worthington (ed.), *Demosthenes: Statesman and Orator* (London: 2000), pp. 114–158

Bugh, G.R. (ed.), *The Cambridge Companion to the Hellenistic World* (Cambridge: 2007)

Burn, A.R., "The Generalship of Alexander," *G&R*[2] 12 (1965), pp. 140–154

Burstein, S.M., "IG II[2] 561 and the Court of Alexander IV," *ZPE* 24 (1977), pp. 223–225

Burstein, S.M., "Pharaoh Alexander: A Scholarly Myth," *Ancient Society* 22 (1991), pp. 139–145

Burstein, S.M., "Alexander in Egypt: Continuity and Change," *Ach. Hist.* 8 (1994), pp. 381–387

Burstein, S.M., "Alexander's Organization of Egypt: A Note on the Career of Cleomenes of Naucratis," in T. Howe and J. Reams (eds.), *Macedonian Legacies: Studies in Ancient Macedonian History and Culture in Honor of E.N. Borza* (Claremont: 2008), pp. 183–194

Burton, P.J., *Rome and the Third Macedonian War* (Cambridge: 2017)

Cabanes, P., "Histoire Comparée de la Macédoine, de l'Épire et de l'Illyrie Méridionale (IVe-IIe s. a.C.)," *Ancient Macedonia* 5 (Institute for Balkan Studies, Thessaloniki: 1993), pp. 293–311

Caccamo Caltabiano, M., "The Identity of the Two Horsemen on Philip II's Coinage," *Ancient Macedonia* 6 (Institute for Balkan Studies, Thessaloniki: 1999), pp. 197–207

Caccamo Caltabiano, M., "The 'Knights' on the Coins of Alexander I: From 'Adventus' to Dynastic Succession," *Ancient Macedonia* 7 (Institute for Balkan Studies, Thessaloniki: 2007), pp. 759–772

Cahill, N., "The Treasury at Persepolis: Gift-Giving at the City of the Persians," *AJA* 89 (1985), pp. 373–389

Cargill, J., *The Second Athenian League* (Berkeley: 1981)

Carney, E.D., "Alexander the Lyncestian: The Disloyal Opposition," *GRBS* 21 (1980a), pp. 23–33

Carney, E.D., "The Conspiracy of Hermolaus," *CJ* 76 (1980b), pp. 223–231

Carney, E.D., "The Death of Clitus," *GRBS* 22 (1981), pp. 149–160

Carney, E.D., "Regicide in Macedonia," *La Parola del Passato* 211 (1983), pp. 260–272

Carney, E.D., "The Politics of Polygamy: Olympias, Alexander and the Murder of Philip II," *Historia* 41 (1992), pp. 169–189

Carney, E.D., "Women and *Basileia*: Legitinacy and Female Political Action in Macedonia," *CJ* 90 (1995), pp. 367–391

Carney, E.D., "Macedonians and Mutiny: Discipline and Indiscipline in the Army of Philip and Alexander," *CPh* 91 (1996), pp. 19–44

Carney, E.D., *Women and Monarchy in Macedonia* (Norman: 2000)

Carney, E.D., "Hunting and the Macedonian Elite: Sharing the Rivalry of the Chase (Arrian 4.13.1)," in D. Ogden (ed.), *The Hellenistic World: New Perspectives* (London: 2002), pp. 59–80

Carney, E.D., "Elite Education and High Culture in Macedonia," in W. Heckel and L.A. Tritle (eds.), *Crossroads of History. The Age of Alexander* (Claremont: 2003), pp. 47–63.

Carney, E.D., "Women in Alexander's Court," in J. Roisman (ed.), *Brill's Companion to Alexander the Great* (Leiden: 2003), pp. 239–252

Carney, E.D., *Olympias, Mother of Alexander the Great* (London: 2006)

Carney, E.D., "The Role of the Basilikoi Paides at the Argead Court," in T. Howe and J. Reames (eds.) *Macedonian Legacies: Studies in Ancient Macedonian in Honour of E.N. Borza* (Claremont: 2008), pp. 145–164

Carney, E.D., "Macedonian Women," in J. Roisman and Ian Worthington (eds.), *A Companion to Ancient Macedonia* (Malden: 2010), pp. 409–427

Carney, E.D., "Women and Symposia in Macedonia," in T. Howe, E.E. Garvin, and G. Wrightson (eds.), *Greece, Macedon, and Persia. Studies in Social, Political, and Military History in Honour of Waldemar Heckel* (Philadelphia: 2015), pp. 33–40

Carney, E.D., "Argead Marriage Policy," in S. Müller, T. Howe, H. Bowden, and R. Rollinger (eds.), *The History of the Argeads: New Perspectives* (Wiesbaden: 2017), pp. 139–150

Carney, E.D., "Royal Women as Succession Advocates," in T. Howe and F. Pownall (eds.), *Ancient Macedonians in the Greek and Roman Sources. From History to Historiography* (Swansea: 2018), pp. 29–40

Carney, E.D., *Eurydice and the Birth of Macedonian Power* (New York: 2019)

Carney, E.D., "The End of the Argead Dynasty: Causes and Commemoration," *Ancient Macedonia* 8 (Institute for Balkan Studies, Thessaloniki: 2021), pp. 437–450

Carney, E.D. and D. Ogden (eds.), *Philip II and Alexander the Great: Lives and Afterlives* (Oxford: 2010)

Carter, J.M., "Athens, Euboea and Olynthus," *Historia* 20 (1971), pp. 418–429

Cartledge, P., *Alexander the Great: The Hunt for a New Past* (London: 2003)

Casson, S., *Macedonia, Thrace and Illyria* (Oxford 1926)

Castritius, H., "Die Okkupation Thrakiens durch die Perser und der Sturz des athenischen Tyrannen Hippias," *Chiron* 2 (1972), pp. 1–15

Cawkwell, G.L., "Aeschines and the Peace of Philocrates," *REG* 73 (1960), pp. 416–438

Cawkwell, G.L., "Notes on the Social War," *Cl.& Med.* 23 (1962a), pp. 34–40

Cawkwell, G.L., "The Defence of Olynthus," *CQ*[2] 12 (1962b), pp. 122–140

Cawkwell, G.L., "Demosthenes' Policy after the Peace of Philocrates I and II," *CQ*[2] 13 (1963), pp. 120–138 and 200–213

Cawkwell, G.L., "The Crowning of Demosthenes," *CQ*² 19 (1969), pp. 163–180
Cawkwell, G.L., *Philip of Macedon* (London: 1978a)
Cawkwell, G.L., "The Peace of Philocrates Again," *CQ*² 28 (1978b), pp. 93–104
Cawkwell, G.L., "Philip and Athens," in M.B. Hatzopoulos and L.D. Loukopoulos (eds.), *Philip of Macedon* (Athens: 1980), pp. 100–110
Cawkell, G.L., "Athenian Naval Power in the Fourth Century," *CQ*² 34 (1984), pp. 334–345
Cawkwell, G.L., "The End of Greek Liberty," in W.R. Wallace and E.M. Harris (eds.), *Transitions to Empire: Essays in Honor of E. Badian* (Norman: 1996), pp. 98–121
Cawkwell, G.L., *The Greek Wars. The Failure of Persia* (Oxford: 2005)
Chambers, J.T., "Perdiccas, Thucydides, and the Greek City-States," *Ancient Macedonia* 4 (Institute for Balkan Studies, Thessaloniki: 1986), pp. 139–145
Chambers, J.T., "Macedonia and the Peace of Nicias," *Ancient Macedonia* 5 (Institute for Balkan Studies, Thessaloniki: 1993), pp. 325–335
Chambers, J.T., "Perdiccas, Sitalces, and Athens," *Ancient Macedonia* 6 (Institute for Balkan Studies, Thessaloniki: 1999), pp. 217–224
Champion, J., *Antigonus the One-Eyed: Greatest of the Successors* (Barnsley: 2014)
Chaniotis, A., "The Divinity of Hellenistic Rulers," in A. Erskine (ed.), *Blackwell Companion to the Hellenistic World* (Oxford: 2003), pp. 431–445
Chapinal-Heras, D., "Archelaos I and the Development of Macedon," *Karanos* 5 (2022), pp. 11–29
Christesen, P. and S.C. Murray, "Macedonian Religion," in J. Roisman and Ian Worthington (eds.), *A Companion to Ancient Macedonia* (Malden: 2010), pp. 428–445
Chrysostomou, P., "*Οι Μακεδόνες του Αρχοντικού Πέλλας*," in E.B. Tsigarida and S. Nanoglou (eds.), *Before the Great Capital* (Pella 2018), pp. 83–110
Chugg, A., *Alexander's Lovers* (Bristol: 2006)
Chugg, A., "The Identity of the Occupant of the Amphipolis Tomb Beneath the Kasta Mound," *Macedonian Studies Journal* 2 (2021), pp. 42–94
Cloché, P., *Un Fondateur d'Empire.Philippe II, Roi de Macédoine* (Paris: 1955)
Cloché, P., *Histoire de la Macedoine jusqu' à l'avènement d'Alexandre le Grande* (Paris: 1960)
Cohen, A., *The Alexander Mosaic. Stories of Victory and Defeat* (Cambridge: 1997)
Cole, J.W., "Perdiccas and Athens," *Phoenix* 28 (1974), pp. 55–72
Cole, J.W., "Not Alexander but Perdikkas (Dem. 20 and 13.14)," *GRBS* 18 (1977), pp. 25–32
Cole, J.W., "Alexander Philhellene and Themistocles," *L'Antiquité Classique* 47 (1978), pp. 37–49
Collins, A., "Alexander's Visit to Siwah: A New Analysis," *Phoenix* 68 (2014), pp. 62–77
Consolo Langher, S.N., "La Macedonia da Aminta III a Filippo II (La Formazione del Grande Stato Territoriale Macedone)," *Ancient Macedonia* 7 (Institute for Balkan Studies, Thessaloniki: 2007), pp. 229–233
Cook, B.L., "The Essential Philip of Macedon," *GRBS* 45 (2005), pp. 189–211
Costanzi, V., "Le Vicende Di Aniinta III Nel Primo Decennio Del Siio Regno," *Klio* 1 (1901), pp. 297–303
Crick, N., "The Rhetoric of Deflection: Demosthenes" Funeral Oration as Propaganda," in A. Kapellos (ed.), *The Orators and Their Treatment of the Recent Past* (Berlin: 2022), pp. 291–306
Crowther, N.B., "Resolving an Impasse: Draws, Dead Heats, and Similar Decisions in Greek Athletics," *Nikephoros* 13 (2000), pp. 125–140
Csapo, E., *Actors and Icons of the Ancient Theater* (Oxford 2010)
D'Agostini, M., *The Rise of Philip V. Kingship and Rule in the Hellenistic World* (Edizioni dell'Orso: 2019)
Dahmen, K., *The Legend of Alexander the Great on Greek and Roman Coins* (London: 2007)
Dahmen, K., "The Numismatic Evidence," in J. Roisman and Ian Worthington (eds.), *A Blackwell Companion to Ancient Macedonia* (Malden: 2010), pp. 41–62

Dandamaev, M., *A Political History of the Achaemenid Empire* (Leiden 1989)
Dascalakis, A., *The Hellenism of the Ancient Macedonians* (Thessaloniki: 1965)
Dascalakis, A., "L'origine de la maison royale de Macédoine et les légendes relatives de l'antiquité," *Ancient Macedonia* 1 (Institute for Balkan Studies, Thessaloniki: 1970), pp. 155–161
Davies, J.K., "The Tradition about the First Sacred War," in S. Hornblower (ed.), *Greek Historiography* (Oxford: 1994), pp. 193–212
Davison, J.A., "Peisistratus and Homer," *TAPA* 86 (1975), pp. 1–22
Degen, J., "Alexander III., Dareios I., und das speererworbere Land (Diod. 17,17,2)," *Journal of Ancient Near Eastern History* 6 (2019), pp. 53–95
Delev, P., "Stratifying Herodotus: Local Tribes between the Lower Axios and the Nestos," *Thracia* 16 (2005), pp. 1–22
Delev, P., "The Edonians," *Thracia* 17 (2007), pp. 85–106
Dell, H.J., "The Western Frontier of the Macedonian Monarchy," *Ancient Macedonia* 1 (Institute for Balkan Studies, Thessaloniki: 1970), pp. 115–126
Despoini, A., et al., *Σίνδος. Το νεκροταφείο, ανασκαφικές έρευνες 1980–1982*, 1–3 (Athens: 2016)
Depuydt, L., "The Time of Death of Alexander the Great: 11 June 323 B.C., ca. 4:00-5:00 p.m.," *Die Welt des Orients* 28 (1997), pp. 117–135
de Ste. Croix, G.E.M., "The Alleged Secret Pact between Athens and Philip II Concerning Amphipolis and Pydna," *CQ*[2] 13 (1963), pp. 110–119
Develin, R., "The Murder of Philip II," *Antichthon* 15 (1981), pp. 86–99
Devine, A.M., "Grand Tactics at Gaugamela," *Phoenix* 29 (1975), 374–385
Devine, A.M., "The Strategies of Alexander the Great and Darius III in the Issus Campaign (333 BC)," *Anc. World* 12 (1985a), pp. 25–38
Devine, A.M., "Grand Tactics at the Battle of Issus," *Anc. World* 12 (1985b), pp. 39–59
Devine, A.M., "Demythologizing the Battle of the Granicus," *Phoenix* 40 (1986a), pp. 265–278
Devine, A.M., "The Battle of Gaugamela: A Tactical and Source-Critical Study," *Anc. World* 13 (1986b), pp. 87–115
Devine, A.M. "The Battle of Hydaspes; A Tactical and Source-Critical Study," *Anc. World* 16 (1987), pp. 91–113
Devine, A.M., "A Pawn-Sacrifice at the Battle of the Granicus: The Origins of a Favorite Stratagem of Alexander the Great," *Anc. World* 18 (1988), pp. 3–20
Devine, A.M., "Alexander the Great," in J. Hackett (ed.), *Warfare in the Ancient World* (New York: 1989a), pp. 104–129
Devine, A.M., "The Macedonian Army at Gaugamela: Its Strength and the Length of Its Battle-Line," *Anc. World* 19 (1989b), pp. 77–80
Diels, H. and W. Kranz, *Fragmente der Vorsokratiker*[2] (Berlin 1952)
Di Giuseppe, L., "Euripide e la grecitá dei Macedoni: Archelao presso cisseo," *Prometheus* 30 (2004), pp. 125–128
Dmitriev, S., "Alexander's Exile's Decree," *Klio* 86 (2004), pp. 348–381
Dmitriev, S., *The Greek Slogan of Freedom and Early Roman Politics in Greece* (Oxford: 2011)
Dmitriev, S., "From the Cadmea to Chaeronea: The Second League as A Form of Athenian Imperialism," in D. Prichard and Ian Worthington (eds.), *Waging War in Fourth Century Athens: New Appraisals* (London: 2025), pp. 213–238
Dobbins, K.M., "Alexander's Eastern Satrapies," *Persica* 11 (1984), pp. 74–108
Dreyer, B., "Heroes, Cults, and Divinity," in W. Heckel, and L. Tritle (eds.), *Alexander the Great: A New History* (Malden: 2009), pp. 218–234
Drougou, S., "Vergina – The Ancient City of Aegae," in R.J. Lane Fox (ed.), *Brill's Companion to Ancient Macedon* (Leiden: 2011), pp. 243–256
Drougou S. and C. Saatsoglou-Paliadeli, *Vergina. Wandering through the Archaeological Site* (Athens: 2004)

Ducoeur, G. and C. Muckensturm-Poulle (eds.), *Mondes grec et indien, d'Alexandre le Grand à Kaniska* (Besançon: 2023)
Dusanic, S., "Plato's Academy and Timotheus' Policy, 365–359 BC," *Chiron* 10 (1980), pp. 111–121
Edson, C.F., "Early Macedonia," *Ancient Macedonia* 1 (Institute for Balkan Studies, Thessaloniki: 1970), pp. 17–44
Efstathiou, A., "The 'Peace of Philocrates': The Assembles of 18th and 19th Elaphebolion," *Historia* 53 (2004), pp. 385–407
Ehrhardt, C., "Two Notes on Philip of Macedon's First Interventions in Thessaly," *CQ*² 17 (1967), pp. 296–301
Ellis, J.R., "Amyntas III, Illyria and Olynthos, 393/2-380/79," *Makedonika* 9 (1969a), pp. 1–8
Ellis, J.R., "Population-transplants by Philip II," *Makedonika* 9 (1969b), pp. 9–17
Ellis, J.R., "The Security of the Macedonian Throne Under Philip II," *Ancient Macedonia* 1 (Institute for Balkan Studies, Thessaloniki: 1970), pp. 68–75
Ellis, J.R., "Amyntas Perdikka, Philip II and Alexander the Great," *JHS* 91 (1971), pp. 15–24
Ellis, J.R., "The Stepbrothers of Philip II," *Historia* 22 (1973), pp. 350–354
Ellis, J.R., *Philip II and Macedonian Imperialism* (London: 1976)
Ellis, J.R., "The Dynamics of Fourth-Century Macedonian Imperialism," *Ancient Macedonia* 2 (Institute for Balkan Studies, Thessaloniki: 1977), pp. 103–114
Ellis, J.R., "The Unification of Macedonia," in M.B. Hatzopoulos and L.D. Loukopoulos (eds.), *Philip of Macedon* (Athens: 1980), pp. 36–47
Ellis, J.R., "The Assassination of Philip II," in H.J. Dell (ed.), *Ancient Macedonian Studies in Honour of C.F. Edson* (Thessaloniki: 1981), pp. 99–137
Ellis, J.R., "Philip and the Peace of Philokrates," in W.L. Adams and E.N. Borza (eds.), *Philip II, Alexander the Great, and the Macedonian Heritage* (Lanham: 1982a), pp. 43–59
Ellis, J.R., "The First Months of Alexander's Reign," in B. Barr-Sharrar and E.N. Borza (eds.), *Macedonia and Greece in Late Classical and Early Hellenistic Times* (Washington: 1982b), pp. 69–73
Engels, D., *Alexander the Great and the Logistics of the Macedonian Army* (Berkeley and Los Angeles: 1978)
Engels, J., "Macedonians and Greeks," in J. Roisman and Ian Worthington (eds.), *A Companion to Ancient Macedonia* (Malden: 2010), pp. 81–98
English, S., *The Army of Alexander the Great* (Barnsley: 2009a)
English, S., *The Sieges of Alexander the Great* (Barnsley: 2009b)
English, S., *The Field Campaigns of Alexander the Great* (Barnsley: 2011)
Errington, R.M., "From Babylon to Triparadeisos," *JHS* 90 (1970), pp. 49–77
Errington, R.M., "Macedonian Royal Style and Its Historical Significance," *JHS* 90 (1974), pp. 20–38
Errington, R.M., "Arybbas the Molossian," *GRBS* 16 (1975), pp. 41–50
Errington, R.M., "The Nature of the Macedonian State under the Monarchy," *Chiron* 8 (1978), pp. 77–133
Errington, R.M., "Alexander the Philhellene and Persia," in H.J. Dell (ed.), *Ancient Macedonian Studies in Honour of C.F. Edson* (Thessaloniki: 1981), pp. 139–143
Errington, R.M., "The Historiographical Origins of Macedonian Staatsrecht," *Ancient Macedonia* 3 (Institute for Balkan Studies, Thessaloniki: 1983), pp. 89–101
Errington, R.M., *A History of Macedonia*, transl. C. Errington (Berkeley and Los Angeles: 1990)
Erskine, A., "Culture and Power in Ptolemaic Egypt: The Museum and Library of Alexandria," *G&R*² 42 (1995), pp. 38–48
Erskine, A., "Life after Death: Alexandria and the Body of Alexander," *G&R* 49 (2002), pp. 167–179
Erskine, A. (ed.), *A Companion to the Hellenistic World* (Malden: 2003)

Faklaris, P.B., "Aegae: Determining the Site of the First Capital of the Macedonians," *AJA* 98 (1994), pp. 609–616

Faraguna, M., "Alexander and the Greeks," in J. Roisman (ed.), *Alexander the Great* (Leiden: 2003), pp. 99–130

Fearn, D., "Herodotos 5.17-22. Narrating Ambiguity: Murder and Macedonian Allegiance," in E. Irwin and E. Greenwood (eds.), *Reading Herodotus: A Study of the logoi of Book 5 of Herodotus' Histories* (Cambridge: 2007a), pp. 98–127

Fearn, D., *Bacchylides: Politics, Performance, Poetic Tradition* (New York: 2007b)

Fears, J.R., "Pausanias, the Assassin of Philip," *Athenaeum* 53 (1975), pp. 111–135

Feil, F.D., "Perdikkas und seine Brüder. Politik und Mythos im Makedonien des 5. Jahrhunderts," *Historia* 317 (2023), pp. 541–571

Ferguson, M.P. and Ian Worthington, *The Military Legacy of Alexander the Great: Lessons for the Information Age* (London: 2024)

Ferrari, M.F., "Un simbolo persiano sui tetroboli di Alessandro I? Considerazioni di tipologia monetale," *Historika* V.12 (2022), pp. 53–77

Finn, J., "Alexander's Return of the Tyrannicide Statues to Athens," *Historia* 63 (2014), pp. 385–403

Flensted-Jensen, P., "The Bottiaians and their Poleis," in M.H. Hansen and K. Rauflaub (eds.), *Studies in the Ancient Greek Polis* (Stuttgart: 1995), pp. 103–132

Flower, M., *Theopompus of Chios: History and Rhetoric in the Fourth Century* BC (Oxford 1994)

Fol, A., "Thrace and Macedonia in the 6th-4th Century BC in Euripides' Bacchae," *Ancient Macedonia* 5 (Institute for Balkan Studies, Thessaloniki: 1993), pp. 433–441

Forrest, W.G.G., *The Emergence of Greek Democracy* (London: 1966)

Fowler, R.L., "AI*Γ* – in Early Greek Language and Myth," *Phoenix* 42 (1988), pp. 99–102

Fraser, P., *Ptolemaic Alexandria*, 3 vols. (Oxford: 1972)

Fraser, P., *Cities of Alexander the Great* (Oxford: 1996)

Fredricksmeyer, E.A., "Alexander, Midas, and the Oracle at Gordium," *CPh* 56 (1961), pp. 160–168

Fredricksmeyer, E.A., "Divine Honors for Philip II," *TAPA* 109 (1979), pp. 39–61

Fredricksmeyer, E.A., "On The Background of the Ruler Cult," in H.J. Dell (ed.), *Ancient Macedonian Studies in Honor of C.F. Edson* (Thessaloniki: 1981), pp. 145–156

Fredricksmeyer, E.A., "On the Final Aims of Philip II," in W.L. Adams and E.N. Borza (eds.), *Philip II, Alexander the Great, and the Macedonian Heritage* (Lanham: 1982), pp. 85–98

Fredricksmeyer, E.A., "Alexander and Philip: Emulation and Resentment," *CJ* 85 (1990), pp. 300–315

Fredricksmeyer, E.A., "Alexander the Great and the Kingship of Asia," in A.B. Bosworth and E.J. Baynham (eds.), *Alexander the Great in Fact and Fiction* (Oxford: 2000), pp. 136–166

Fredricksmeyer, E.A., "Alexander's Religion and Divinity," in J. Roisman, (ed.), *Brill's Companion to Alexander the Great* (Leiden: 2003), pp. 253–278

Frei, P., "Der Wagen von Gordion," *Museum Helveticum* 29 (1972), pp. 110–123

French, V. and P. Dixon, "The Pixodarus Affair: Another View," *Anc. World* 13 (1986), pp. 73–86.

Fuller, J.F.C., *The Generalship of Alexander the Great* (repr. New Brunswick: 1960)

Gabbert, J.J., *Antigonus II Gonatas. A Political Biography* (London: 1997)

Gabriel, R.A., *Philip II of Macedon: Greater than Alexander* (Washington: 2010)

Garlan, Y., *Recherches de poliorcétique grecque* (Paris: 1974)

Georges, P., "Persian Ionia under Darius: The Revolt Reconsidered," *Historia* 49 (2000), pp. 1–39

Gerolymatos, A., "The *proxenia* of Alexandros I of Makedonia," *LCM* 11 (1986), pp. 75–76

Gill, D.W.J., "Inscribed Silver Plate from Tomb II at Vergina. Chronological Implications," *Hesperia* 77 (2008), pp. 335–358

Gilley, D. and Ian Worthington, "Alexander the Great, Macedonia and Asia," in J. Roisman and Ian Worthington (eds.), *A Companion to Ancient Macedonia* (Malden: 2010), pp. 186–207

Gimatzidis, S., *Die Stadt Sindos* (Rahden: 2010)

Golan, D., "The Fate of a Court Historian: Callisthenes," *Athenaeum* 66 (1988), pp. 99–120

Goukowsky, P., *Essai sur les origines du mythe d'Alexandre*, 2 vols. (Nancy: 1978)yy

Goukowsky, P., "Un aspect de l'administration d'Alexandre dans les Hautes-Satrapies: la première revolt des colons grecs de Bactriane en 325," in *La géographie administrative et politique d'Alexandre à Mahomet*. Actes de Colloque de Strasbourg, 14–16 Juin 1979 (Leiden: 1981), pp. 7–17

Goukowsky, P., "Les maisons princières de Macédoine de Perdiccas II à Philippe II," in P. Goukowsky and C. Brixhe (eds.), *Hellenika Symmikta, histoire, archéologie, épigraphie* (Nancy: 1991), pp. 43–66

Graf, D., "Medism: The Origins and Significance of the Term," *JHS* 104 (1984), pp. 15–30

Grainger, J., *Alexander the Great Failure: The Collapse of the Macedonian Empire* (London: 2007)

Graninger, D., "Macedonia and Thessaly," in J. Roisman and Ian Worthington (eds.), *A Companion to Ancient Macedonia* (Malden: 2010), pp. 306–325

Green, P., *Alexander of Macedon* (Harmondsworth: 1974)

Green, P., *Alexander to Actium. The Historical Evolution of the Hellenistic Age* (Berkeley and Los Angeles: 1990)

Green, P., *The Greco-Persian Wars*, 2nd ed. (Berkeley and Los Angeles: 1998)

Greenwalt, W.S., "The Introduction of Caranus into the Argead King List," *GRBS* 26 (1985a), pp. 43–49

Greenwalt, W.S., "The Search for Arrhidaeus," *Anc. World* 10 (1985), pp. 69–77

Greenwalt, W.S., "Herodotus and the Foundation of Argead Macedonia," *Anc.* World 13 (1986), pp. 117–122

Greenwalt, W.S., "Amyntas III and the Political Stability of Argfead Macedonia," *Anc. World* 18 (1988), pp. 35–44

Greenwalt, W.S., "Polygamy and Succession in Argead Macedonia," *Arethusa* 22 (1989), pp. 19–45

Greenwalt, W.S., "The Iconographical Significance of Amyntas III's Mounted Hunter Stater," *Ancient Macedonia* 5 (Institute for Balkan Studies, Thessaloniki: 1993), pp. 509–519

Greenwalt, W.S., "A Solar Dionysus and Argead Legitimacy," *Anc. World* 25 (1994a), pp. 3–8

Greenwalt, W.S., "The Production of Coinage from Archelaus to Perdiccas III and the Evolution of Argead Macedonia," in Ian Worthington (ed.), *Ventures into Greek History. Essays in Honour of N.G.L. Hammond* (Oxford: 1994b), pp. 105–134

Greenwalt, W.S., "Thracian Influence on the Ideology of Argead Kingship," *Actes 2e Symposium International Des Etudes Thraciennes* 1 (Komotini: 1997), pp. 121–133

Greenwalt, W.S., "Why Pella?," *Historia* 48 (1999), pp. 158–183

Greenwalt, W.S., "Archelaus the Philhellene," *Anc. World* 34 (2003), pp. 131–153

Greenwalt, W.S., "The Development of a Middle Class in Macedonia," *Ancient Macedonia* 7 (Institute for Balkan Studies, Thessaloniki 2007), pp. 87–96

Greenwalt, W.S., "Philip and Olympias on Samothrace: A Clue to Macedonian Politics During the 360s," in T. Howe and J. Reames (eds.), *Macedonian Legacies. Studies in Ancient Macedonian History and Culture in Honor of Eugene N. Borza* (Claremont: 2008), pp. 79–106

Greenwalt, W.S., "Macedonia, Illyria, and Epirus," in J. Roisman and Ian Worthington (eds.), *A Companion to Ancient Macedonia* (Malden: 2010), pp. 279–305

Greenwalt, W.S., "Alexander II of Macedon," in T. Howe, S. Müller, and R. Stoneman (eds.), *Ancient Historiography on War and Empire* (Oxford: 2017), pp. 80–91

Greenwalt, W.S., "The Assassination of Archelaus and the Significance of the Macedonian Royal Hunt," *Karanos* 2 (2019), pp. 11–17

Griffith, G.T., "Alexander's Generalship at Gaugamela," *JHS* 67 (1947), pp. 77–89
Griffith, G.T. (ed.), *Alexander the Great: The Main Problems* (Cambridge: 1966)
Griffith, G.T., "Philip of Macedon's Early Intervention in Thessaly (358-352 B.C.)," *CQ*² 20 (1970), pp. 67–80
Griffith, G.T., "Philip as a General and the Macedonian Army," in M.B. Hatzopoulos and L.D. Loukopoulos (eds.), *Philip of Macedon* (Athens: 1980), pp. 48–57
Grimm, G., *Alexandria, Die erste Königsstadt der hellenistichen Welt* (Mainz: 1998)
Gruen, E., *The Hellenistic World and the Coming of Rome* (Berkeley and Los Angeles: 1984)
Guth, D., "Rhetoric and Historical Narrative: The Theban-Athenian Alliance of 339 BCE," *Historia* 63 (2014), pp. 151–165
Habicht, C., *Gottmenschentum und griechische Städte* (Munich: 1970)
Hall, J.M., "Contested Ethnicities: Perceptions of Macedonia within Evolving Definitions of Greek Identity," in I. Malkin (ed.), *Ancient Perceptions of Greek Ethnicity* (Cambridge: 2001), pp. 159–186
Hamilton, C.D., "Philip II and Archidamus," in W.L. Adams and E.N. Borza (eds.), *Philip II, Alexander the Great, and the Macedonian Heritage* (Lanham: 1982), pp. 61–77
Hamilton, C.D., "Amyntas III and Agesilaus: Macedon and Sparta in the Fourth Century," *Ancient Macedonia* 4 (Institute for Balkan Studies, Thessaloniki: 1986), pp. 239–245
Hamilton, J.R., "Alexander and his 'So-called' Father," *CQ*² 3 (1953), pp. 151–157
Hammond, N.G.L., "The Kingdoms in Illyria circa 400-167 BC," *BSA* 61 (1966), pp. 239–253
Hammond, N.G.L., *Epirus* (Oxford 1967)
Hammond, N.G.L., *A History of Macedonia* 1 (Oxford: 1972a)
Hammond, N.G.L., "The Archaeological Background to the Macedonian Kingdom," *Ancient Macedonia* 1 (Institute for Balkan Studies, Thessaloniki: 1972b), pp. 53–67
Hammond, N.G.L., "The Victory of Macedon at Chaeronea," in N.G.L. Hammond, *Studies in Greek History* (Oxford: 1973), pp. 534–557
Hammond, N.G.L., "Alexander's Campaign in Illyria," *JHS* 94 (1974), pp. 67–87
Hammond, N.G.L., "The Campaign of Alexander against Cleitus and Glaucias," *Ancient Macedonia* 2 (Institute for Balkan Studies, Thessaloniki: 1977), pp. 503–509
Hammond, N.G.L., "Philip's Tomb in Historical Context," *GRBS* 19 (1978), pp. 331–350
Hammond, N.G.L., "The Extent of Persian Occupation in Thrace," *Chiron* 10 (1980a), pp. 53–61
Hammond, N.G.L., "Training in the Use of the Sarissa and its Effect in Battle 359-333 BC," *Antichthon* 14 (1980b), pp. 53–63
Hammond, N.G.L., "The End of Philip," in M.B. Hatzopoulos and L.D. Loukopoulos (eds.), *Philip of Macedon* (London: 1980c), pp. 166–175
Hammond, N.G.L., "The Battle of the Granicus River," *JHS* 100 (1980d), pp. 73–88
Hammond, N.G.L., "The Western Frontier in the Reign of Philip II," in H.J. Dell (ed.), *Ancient Macedonian Studies in Honour of C.F. Edson* (Institute for Balkan Studies, Thessaloniki: 1981), pp. 199–217
Hammond, N.G.L., "The King and the Land in the Macedonian Kingdom," *CQ*² 38 (1988), pp. 383–391
Hammond, N.G.L., "The Battle between Philip and Bardylis," *Antichthon* 23 (1989a), pp. 1–9
Hammond, N.G.L., *Alexander the Great: King, Commander and Statesman*² (Bristol: 1989b)
Hammond, N.G.L., "Casualties and Reinforcements of Citizen Soldiers in Greece and Macedonia," *JHS* 109 (1989c), pp. 56–68
Hammond, N.G.L., "Royal Pages, Personal Pages, and Boys Trained in the Macedonian Manner during the Period of the Temenid Monarchy," *Historia* 39 (1990), pp. 261–290
Hammond, N.G.L., "The Koina of Epirus and Macedonia," *ICS* 16 (1991), pp. 183–192
Hammond, N.G.L., *The Macedonian State: Origins, Institutions, and History* (Oxford: 1992a)

Hammond, N.G.L., "Alexander's Charge at the Battle of Issus in 333 B.C," *Historia* 41 (1992b), pp. 395–406
Hammond, N.G.L., "The Archaeological and Literary Evidence for the Burning of the Persepolis Palace," *CQ*² 42 (1992c), pp. 358–364
Hammond, N.G.L., *Philip of Macedon* (London: 1994)
Hammond, N.G.L., 'Connotations of "Macedonia" and of "Macedones," *CQ*² 45 (1995a), pp. 120–128
Hammond, N.G.L., "Philip's Innovations in Macedonian Economy," *SO* 70 (1995b), pp. 22–29
Hammond, N.G.L., "The Location of Aegae," *JHS* 117 (1997a), pp. 177–179
Hammond, N.G.L., "What may Philip have Learnt as a Hostage in Thebes," *GRBS* 38 (1997b), pp. 355–372
Hammond, N.G.L., *The Genius of Alexander the Great* (London: 1997c)
Hammond, N.G.L. and G.T. Griffith, *A History of Macedonia* 2 (Oxford: 1979)
Hammond, N.G.L. and F.W. Walbank *A History of Macedonia* 3 (Oxford: 1988)
Hanson, V.D., *The Western Way of War. Infantry Battle in Classical Greece* (New York: 1989)
Harder, A., *Euripides' Kresphontes and Archelaos: Introduction, Text and Commentary* (Leiden: 1985)
Hardiman, C.L., "Classical Art to 221 BC," in J. Roisman and Ian Worthington (eds.), *A Companion to Ancient Macedonia* (Malden: 2010), pp. 505–521
Harding, P.E., *From the End of the Peloponnesian War to the Battle of Ipsus* (Cambridge: 1985)
Harding, P.E., "Athenian Foreign Policy in the Fourth Century," *Klio* 77 (1995), pp. 105–125
Harris, E.M., *Aeschines and Athenian Politics* (Oxford: 1995)
Hatzopoulos, M.B., "The Oleveni Inscription and the Dates of Philip II's Reign," in W.L. Adams and E.N. Borza (eds.), *Philip II, Alexander the Great, and the Macedonian Heritage* (Lanham: 1982a), pp. 21–42
Hatzopoulos, M.B., "A Reconsideration of the Pixodaros Affair," in B. Barr-Sharrar and E.N. Borza (eds.), *Macedonia and Greece in Late Classical and Early Hellenistic Times. Studies in the History of Art* 10 (Washington: 1982b), pp. 59–66
Hatzopoulos, M.B., "La Béotie et la Macédoine à l'époque de l'hégémonie thebaine; le point de vue macédonien," in G. Argoud and P. Roesch (eds.), *La Béotie antique* (Paris: 1985), pp. 247–256
Hatzopoulos, M.B., "Succession and Regency in Classical Macedonia," *Ancient Macedonia* 4 (Institute for Balkan Studies, Thessaloniki: 1986), pp. 279–292
Hatzopoulos, M.B., "Strepsa: A Reconsideration, or New Evidence on the Road System of Lower Macedonia," in M.B. Htazopoulos and L.D. Loukopoulou, *Two Studies in Ancient Macedonian Topography* (Athens 1987), pp. 21–60
Hatzopoulos, M.B., *Cultes et rites de passage en Macédoine* (Athens: 1994a)
Hatzopoulos, M.B. (ed.), *Macedonia from Philip II to the Roman Conquest* (Princeton: 1994b)
Hatzopoulos, M.B., "Apollonia Ellenis," in Ian Worthington (ed.), *Ventures into Greek History. Essays in Honour of N.G.L. Hammond* (Oxford: 1994c), pp. 159–183
Hatzopoulos, M.B., "La letter royale d'Oleveni," *Chiron* 25 (1995), pp. 163–185
Hatzopoulos, M.B., *Macedonian Institutions under the Kings. A Historical and Epigraphical Study*, 2 vols. (Athens: 1996)
Hatzopoulos, M.B., "L'histoire par les noms in Macedonia," in S. Hornblower and E. Matthews (eds.), *Greek Personal Names: Their Value as Evidence* (Oxford 2000), pp. 99–117
Hatzopoulos, M.B., *L'organisation de l'armée macédonienne sous les Antigonides. Problèmes anciens et documents nouveaux* (Athens 2001)
Hatzopoulos, M.B., "Herodotus (8.137-8), the Manumissions from Leukopetra, and the Topography of the Middle Haliakmon Valley," in P. Derow and R. Parker (eds.), *Herodotus and his World. Essays from a Conference in Memory of George Forrest* (Oxford: 2003), pp. 203–218

Hatzopoulos, M.B., "De vie à trépas: rites de passage, lamelles dionysiaques et tombes macédoniennes," in A.M. Guimier-Sorbets, M.B. Hatzopoulos, and Y. Morizot (eds.), *Rois, Cités, Nécropoles. Institutions, Rites et Monuments en Macédoine* (Athens: 2006), pp. 131–141

Hatzopoulos, M.B., "Macedonia and Macedonians," in R. Lane Fox (ed.), *Brill's Companion to Ancient Macedon* (Leiden: 2011a), pp. 43–50

Hatzopoulos, M.B., "Macedonians and Other Greeks," in R. Lane Fox (ed.), *Brill's Companion to Ancient Macedon* (Leiden: 2011b), pp. 51–78

Hatzopoulos, M.B., "Federal Makedonia," in H. Beck and P. Funke (eds.), *Federalism in Greek Antiquity* (Cambridge: 2015), pp. 319–340

Hatzopoulos, M.B., "Recent Research in the Ancient Macedonian Dialect: Consolidation and New Perspectives," in G.K. Gianakis, E. Crespo, and F. Panagiotis (eds.), *Studies in Ancient Greek Dialects. From Central Greece to the Black Sea* (Berlin: 2017), pp. 299–328

Hatzopoulos, M.B., *Ancient Macedonia* (Berlin: 2020)

Hatzopoulos, M.B., "Facts Among Rumours: The Case of Alexander's Accession," *Ancient Macedonia* 8 (Institute for Balkan Studies, Thessaloniki: 2021), pp. 519–526

Hauben, H. and A. Meeus (eds.), *The Age of the Successors and the Creation of the Hellenistic Kingdoms (323–276 B.C.)* (Louvain: 2014)

Hecht, C., *Zwischen Athen und Alexandria: Dichter und Künstler beim makedonischen König Archelaos* (Wiesbaden: 2017)

Heckel, W., "The Conspiracy *against* Philotas," *Phoenix* 31 (1977), pp. 9–21

Heckel, W., "Cleopatra or Eurydice?," *Phoenix* 32 (1978), pp. 155–158

Heckel, W., "Alexander at the Persian Gates," *Athenaeum* 58 (1980a), pp. 168–174

Heckel, W., "IG II2 561 and the Status of Alexander IV," *ZPE* 40 (1980b), pp. 249–250

Heckel, W., "Polyxena, the Mother of Alexander the Great," *Chiron* 11 (1981a), pp. 79–86

Heckel, W., "Philip and Olympias (337/6 BC)," in G.S. Shrimpton and D.J. McCargar (eds.), *Classical Contributions: Studies in Honor of M.F. McGregor* (Locust Valley: 1981b), pp. 51–57

Heckel, W., *The Last Days and Testament of Alexander the Great: A Prosopographical Study* (Stuttgart: 1988)

Heckel, W., "The Politics of Distrust: Alexander and his Successors," in D. Ogden (ed.), *The Hellenistic World: New Perspectives* (London: 2000), pp. 81–95.

Heckel, W., "King and 'Companions': Observations on the Nature of Power in the Reign of Alexander," in J. Roisman (ed.), *Brill's Companion to Alexander the Great* (Leiden: 2003a), pp. 197–225

Heckel, W., "Alexander the Great and the 'Limits of Civilised World'," in W. Heckel and L. Tritle (eds.), *Crossroads of History, The Age of Alexander* (Claremont: 2003b), pp. 147–174

Heckel, W., *Who's Who in the Age of Alexander the Great* (Malden: 2006)

Heckel, W., *The Conquests of Alexander the Great* (Cambridge: 2008)

Heckel, W., "A King and His Army," in W. Heckel and L. Tritle (eds.), *Alexander the Great: A New History* (Malden: 2009), pp. 69–82

Heckel, W., "Geography and Politics in Argead Macedonia," in S. Müller, T. Howe, H. Bowden, and R. Rollinger (eds.), *The History of the Argeads: New Perspectives* (Wiesbaden: 2017), pp. 67–78

Heckel, W. and L. Tritle (eds.), *Alexander the Great: A New History* (Oxford: 2009)

Heckel, W., T. Howe, and S. Müller, "The Giver of the Bride, the Bridegroom, and the Bride: A Study of the Murder of Philip II and its Aftermath," in T. Howe, S. Müller, and R. Stoneman (eds.), *Ancient Historiography on War and Empire* (Oxford: 2017), pp. 92–124

Heinrichs, J., "Münzen als Krisensymptome? Zur makedonischen Silberprägung under Amyntas III, und Perdikkas III. (ca. 393-359)," *ZPE* 181 (2012), pp. 117–139

Heinrichs, J., "Coins and Constructions: The Origins of Argead Coinage under Alexander I," in S. Müller, T. Howe, H. Bowden, and R. Rollinger (eds.), *The History of the Argeads: New Perspectives* (Wiesbaden: 2017), pp. 79–98

Heinrichs, J. and S. Müller, "Ein persisches Statussymbol auf Münzen Alexanders I. von Makedonien," *ZPE* 167 (2008), pp. 283–309

Helliesen, J., "Andriscus and the Revolt of the Macedonians, 149-148 B.C.," *Ancient Macedonia* 4 (Institute for Balkan Studies, Thessaloniki: 1986), pp. 307–314
Helly, B., "Une liste des cités de Perrhébie dans la premiere moitié du IVe siecle avant J.-C.," in B. Helly (ed.), *La Thessalie* (Paris 1975), pp. 165–200
Heskel, J., "Philip II and Argaios: A Pretender's Story," in R.W. Wallace and E.M. Harris (eds.), *Transitions to Empire, Essays in Honor of E. Badian* (Norman: 1996), pp. 37–56
Heskel, J., "Macedonia and the North, 400-336," in L. Tritle (ed.), *The Greek World in the Fourth Century BC* (London: 1997a), pp. 167–188
Heskel, J., *The North Aegean Wars, 371–360 BC* (Stuttgart: 1997b)
Higgins, W.E., "Aspects of Alexander's Imperial Administration: Some Modern Methods and Views Reviewed," *Athenaeum* 58 (1980), pp. 129–152
Hoddinott, R.F., *The Thracians* (London: 1981)
Hoffman, R., "Perdikkas and the Outbreak of the Peloponnesian War," *GRBS* 16 (1975), pp. 359–377
Holt, F.L., "The Hyphasis Mutiny: A Source Study," *Anc. World* 5 (1982), pp. 33–59
Holt, F.L., "Alexander's Settlements in Central Asia," *Ancient Macedonia* 4 (Institute for Balkan Studies, Thessaloniki: 1985), pp. 315–323
Holt, F.L., *Alexander the Great and Bactria: The Formation of a Greek Frontier in Central Asia* (Leiden: 1989)
Holt, F.L., "The Death of Coenus," *AHB* 14 (2000), pp. 49–55
Holt, F.L., *Alexander the Great and the Mystery of the Elephant Medallions* (Berkeley and Los Angeles: 2003)
Holt, F.L., *Into the Land of Bones: Alexander the Great in Afghanistan* (Berkeley and Los Angeles: 2005)
Holt, F.L., *The Treasures of Alexander the Great* (New York: 2016)
Howe, T., "Alexander in India: Ptolemy as Near Eastern Historiographer," in T. Howe and J. Reams (eds.), *Macedonian Legacies: Studies in Ancient Macedonian History and Culture in Honor of E.N. Borza* (Claremont: 2008), pp. 215–234
Howe, T., "Founding Alexandria: Alexander the Great and the Politics of Memory," in P. Bosman (ed.), *Alexander in Africa* (Pretoria: 2014), pp. 72–91
Howe, T., "Introducing Ptolemy: Alexander and the Persian Gates," in W. Heckel, S. Müller, and G. Wrightson (eds.), *The Many Faces of War in Antiquity* (Cambridge: 2015a), pp. 166–195
Howe, T., "Alexander and 'Afghan' Insurgency: A Reassessment," in T. Howe and L.L. Brice (eds.), *Brill's Companion to Insurgency and Terrorism in the Ancient Mediterranean* (Leiden: 2015b), pp. 151–182
Howe, T., "Plain Tales from the Hills: Illyrian Influences on Argead Military Development," in S. Müller, T. Howe, H. Bowden, and R. Rollinger (eds.), *The History of the Argeads: New Perspectives* (Wiesbaden: 2017), pp. 99–111
Howe, T., "A Founding Mother? Eurydike I, Pilip II and Macedonian Royal Mythology," in T. Howe and F. Pownall (eds.), *Ancient Macedonians in the Greek and Roman Sources. From History to Historiography* (Swansea: 2018), pp. 1–28
Howe, T. and S. Müller, "Mission Accomplished: Alexander at the Hyphasis," *AHB* 26 (2012), pp. 21–38
Iliakis, M., "Greek Mercenary Revolts in Bactria: A Re-appraisal," *Historia* 62 (2013), pp. 182–195
Instinsky, H., "Herodot und der Erste zug es Mardonios gegen Griechenland," *Hermes* 84 (1956), pp. 477–494
Isserlin, B.S.J., M. Arvantis, R. Jones, and V. Karastathis, "The Canal of Xerxes in Northern Greece: Fact or Fiction? Recent Geophysical and Geoarchaeological Investigations," in Y. Facorellis, N. Zacharias, and K. Polikreti (eds.), *Proceedings of the Fourth Symposium of the Hellenic Society for Archaeometry* (Oxford: 2008), pp. 59–64
Jähne, A., "Alexander der Grosse. Persönlichkeit, Politik, Ökonomie," *Jahrbuch für Wirtschaftgeschichte* (1978), pp. 245–264

Jehne, M., "Die Anerkennung der athenischen Besitzansprüche auf Amphipolis und die Chersones: Zu den Implikationen der Territorialklausel *echein tên eautôn (chôran)* in Verträgen des 4. Jahrhunderts v. Chr.," *Historia* 41 (1992), pp. 272–282

Jehne, M., *Koine Eirene* (Stuttgart:1994)

Juhel. P.O., *Armes, armement et contexte funéraire dans la Macédoine hellénistique. Avec un appendice sur les trouvailles d'armes relatives à l'archaïsme et aux débuts de l'époque classique en Macédoine et sur ses confins* (Gdańsk: 2017)

Kagan, D., *The Outbreak of the Peloponnesian War* (Ithaca: 1969)

Kagan, D., *The Archidamian War* (Ithaca: 1974)

Kagan, D., *The Peace of Nicias and the Sicilian Expedition* (Ithaca: 1981)

Kagan, D., *The Fall of the Athenian Empire* (Ithaca: 1987)

Kagan, D., *The Peloponnesian War* (London: 2005)

Kahrstedt, U., "Städte in Makedonien," *Hermes* 81 (1953), pp. 85–111

Kalléris, J.N., "L'armee macedoine sous Alexandre I, Le Philhellene," in J. Servais, T. Hackens, and B. Servais-Soyez (eds.), *Stemmata: Melanges de philologie, d'histoire et d'archeologie grecques offerts Jules Labarbe* (Liege 1987), pp. 317–331

Kalléris, J.N., *Les anciens Macédoniens. Etude linguistique et historique*, 2 vols. (Athens: 1988)

Kallet-Marx, R.M., *Hegemony to Empire: The Development of the Roman Imperium in the East from 148 to 62 B.C.* (Berkeley and Los Angeles: 1995)

Kanatsoulis, D., *'O 'Archélaos kaì ai metarruthmíseis tou* (Thessaloniki: 1948)

Kapetanopoulos, E., "Sirras," *Anc. World* 25 (1994), pp. 9–14

Karamitrou-Mentessidi, G., "Aiani – Historical and Geographical Context," in R.J. Lane Fox (ed.), *Brill's Companion to Ancient Macedon* (Leiden: 2011), pp. 93–112

Karunanithy D., *The Macedonian War Machine. Neglected Aspects of the Armies of Philip, Alexander and the Successors 359–281 BC* (Barnsley: 2013)

Karathanasis, K., "A Game of Timber Monopoly: Atheno-Macedonian Relations on the Eve of the Peloponnesian War," *Hesperia* 88 (2019), pp. 707–726

Karavites, P., "Macedonian Pragmatism and the Persian Wars," *Anc. World* 28 (1997), pp. 119–126

Kassel, R. and C. Austin, *Poetae Comici Graeci* 5 (Berlin: 1986)

Keegan, J., *The Mask of Command* (London: 1987).

Kertész, I., "When did Alexander I visit Olympia?," *Nikephoros* 18 (2005), pp. 115–126

Keyser, P.T., "The Use of Artillery by Philip II and Alexander the Great," *Anc. World* 15 (1994), pp. 27–49

Kholod, M.M., "The Garrisons of Alexander the Great in the Greek Cities of Asia Minor," *Eos* 97 (2010), pp. 249–258

Kholod, M.M., "On the Financial Relations of Alexander the Great and the Greek Cities in Asia Minor: The Case of *Syntaxis*," in A. Mehl, A.V. Makhlayuk, and O. Gabelko (eds.), *Ruthenia Classica Aetatis Novae. A Collection of Works by Russian Scholars in Ancient Greek and Roman History* (Stuttgart: 2013), pp. 83–92

King, C.J., "Kingship and Other Political Institutions," in J. Roisman and Ian Worthington (eds.), *A Companion to Ancient Macedonia* (Malden: 2010), pp. 374–391

King, C.J., *Ancient Macedonia* (London: 2018)

Koiv, M., "The Dating of Pheidon in Antiquity," *Klio* 83 (2001), pp. 327–347

Kosmidou, E., "Macedonian and Thracian Relations in Northern Greece after the Persian Wars with Particular Reference to the Coinage and Politics of Alexander I," in J. Rotaru et al., (eds.), *Travaux de symposium international: Le Livre. La Roumanie. L'Europe* 4 (Bucharest: 2011), pp. 439–452

Kosmidou, E., "Further Thoughts on the Coinage and Politics of Alexander I," in A. Rufin Solas et al. (eds.), *Armées grecques et romaines dans le nord des Balkans* (Gdańsk: 2013), pp. 15–27

Kottaridi, A., "Discovering Aigai, the Old Macedonian Capital," in M. Stamatopoulou and M. Yeroulanou (eds.), *Excavating Classical Culture* (Oxford: 2002), pp. 75–81

Kottaridi, A., "Queens, Princesses, and High Priestesses: The Role of Women at the Macedonian Court," in A. Kottaridi and S. Walker (eds.), *Heracles to Alexander the Great: Treasures from the Royal Capital of Macedonia, A Hellenic Kingdom in the Age of Democracy* (Oxford: 2011a), pp. 93–126

Kottaridi, A., "The Palace of Aegae," in R.J. Lane Fox (ed.), *Brill's Companion to Ancient Macedon* (Leiden: 2011b), pp. 297–333

Kottaridi, A., *Macedonian Fragments*, trans. N. Wardle (Athens: 2020)

Koukouli-Chrysanthaki, C., "Amphipolis," in R.J. Lane Fox (ed.), *Brill's Companion to Ancient Macedon* (Leiden: 2011), pp. 409–436

Kousser, R., "Hellenistic and Roman Art, 221 BC–AD 337," in J. Roisman and Ian Worthington (eds.), *A Companion to Ancient Macedonia* (Malden: 2010), pp. 522–542

Kraay, C.M., *Archaic and Classical Greek Coins* (Berkeley and Los Angeles: 1976)

Kremydi, S., "Coinage and Finance" in R.J. Lane Fox (ed.), *Brill's Companion to Ancient Macedon* (Leiden: 2011), pp. 159–178

Krentz, P., *The Thirty at Athens* (Ithaca: 1982)

Kuhrt, A., "Earth and Water," *Ach. Hist.* 3 (1988), pp. 87–90

Kuzmin, Y.N., "King Demetrius II of Macedon: In the Shadow of Father and Son," *Ziva Antika* 69 (2019), pp. 59–84

Kuzmin, Y.N., "Was Arrhidaeus a Rival of Alexander? Some Notes on the Pixodarus Affair," *Ziva Antika* 74 (2024), pp. 147–162

Kyriakou, A., "The Sanctuary of Eukleia at Vergina/Aegae: Aspects of the Development of a Cult Place in the Heart of the Macedonian Kingdom," in F.M. Ferrara and P. Vannicelli (eds.), *La Macedonia antica e la nascita dell'Ellenismo alle origini dell'Europa, Scienze dell'Antichità* 26 (2020a), pp. 85–98

Kyriakou, A., "Investigating Interregional Influences and Lifecycles of Two Metal Vessels Used as Funerary Urns in a 4th Century BCE *Intra Muros* Burial at Vergina/Aegae," in M. Gavranović et al. (eds.), *Spheres of Interaction. Perspectives on Balkan Archaeology* 1 (Rahden: 2020b), pp. 295–315

Landucci Gattinoni, F., "Cassander and the Legacy of Philip II and Alexander III in Diodorus' Library", in E. Carney and D. Ogden (eds.), *Philip II and Alexander the Great: Lives and Afterlives* (New York: 2010), pp. 113–121

Lane Fox, R.J., *Alexander the Great* (London: 1973)

Lane Fox, R.J., "Aeschines and Athenian Politics," in R. Osborne and S. Hornblower (eds.), *Ritual, Finance Politics* (Oxford: 1994), pp. 135–155

Lane Fox, R.J. (ed.), *Brill's Companion to Ancient Macedon* (Leiden: 2011a)

Lane Fox, R.J., "The 360s," in R.J. Lane Fox (ed.), *Brill's Companion to Ancient Macedon* (Leiden: 2011b), pp. 257–269

Lane Fox, R.J., "Dating the Royal Tombs at Vergina," in R.J. Lane Fox (ed.), *Brill's Companion to Ancient Macedon* (Leiden: 2011c), pp. 1–34

Lane Fox, R.J., "399-369 BC," in R.J. Lane Fox (ed.), *Brill's Companion to Ancient Macedon* (Leiden: 2011d), pp. 209–234

Lane Fox, R.J., "Philip of Macedonia: Accession, Ambitions, and Self-Presentation," in R.J. Lane Fox (ed.), *Brill's Companion to Ancient Macedon* (Leiden: 2011e), pp. 335–366

Lane Fox, R.J., "Philip's and Alexander's Macedon," in R.J. Lane Fox (ed.), *Brill's Companion to Ancient Macedon* (Leiden: 2011f), pp. 367–391

Lazaridis, D., *Amphipolis*[2] (Athens: 1997)

LeBohec, S., "Remarques sur l'Âge de la Majorité chez les Rois de Macédoine," *Ancient Macedonia* 5 (Institute for Balkan Studies, Thessaloniki: 1993a), pp. 779–788

LeBohec, S., *Antigone Dôsôn roi de Macédoine* (Nancy: 1993b)

Le Bohec, S., "Réflexions sur la place de la femme dans la Macédoine antique," in A.M. Guimier-Sorbets, M.B. Hatzopoulos, and Y. Morizot (eds.), *Rois, Cités, Nécropoles. Institutions, Rites et Monuments en Macédoine* (Athens: 2006), pp. 187–198

Lehmann, G.A., "Der 'lamische Krieg' und die 'Freiheit der hellenen'. Überlegungen zur hieronymianischen Tradition," *ZPE* 73 (1988), pp. 121–149

Le Rider, G., *Le monnayage d'argent et d'or de Philippe II frappé en Macédoine de 359 à 294* (Paris: 1977)

Le Rider, G., "The Coinage of Philip and the Pangaion Mines," in M.B. Hatzopoulos and L.D. Loukopoulos (eds.), *Philip of Macedon* (Athens: 1980), pp. 48–57

Lerner, J.D., "Persia, Thrake, and Skudra," in S. Müller, T. Howe, H. Bowden, and R. Rollinger (eds.), *The History of the Argeads: New Perspectives* (Wiesbaden: 2017), pp. 7–25

Liampi, K., "The Coinage of King Derdas and the History of the Elimiote Dynasty," in A. Burnett, U. Wartenberg, and R. Witschonke (eds.), *Coins of Macedonia and Rome: Essays in Honour of Charles Hersh* (London: 1998), pp. 5–11

Liddel, P., *Decrees of Fourth-Century Athens (403/2–322/1 BC)*, 2 vols. (Cambridge: 2020)

Lilimbaki-Akamati, M. and I. Akamatis, *Pella and its Environs* (Athens: 2004)

Lindholmer, M.O., "The Assassination of Philip II: An Elusive Mastermind," *Palmades* 11 (2016), pp. 77–111

Lloyd, A.B., "Philip II and Alexander the Great: The Moulding of Macedon's Army," in A.B. Lloyd (ed.), *Battle in Antiquity* (London: 1996), pp. 169–198

Londey, P.D., "The Outbreak of the Fourth Sacred War," *Chiron* 20 (1990), pp. 239–260

Lonsdale, D.J., *Alexander the Great: Lessons in Strategy* (London: 2007)

Lorber, C.C., "The Goats of Aigai," in S. Mani Hurter and C. Arnold Biucchi (eds.), *Pour Denyse. Divertissements Numismatiques* (Bern: 2000), pp. 113–134

Lucas, G., *Les cités antiques de la haute vallée du Titarèse: étude de topographie et de géographie historique* (Lyon 1997)

Ma, J., "Chaironeia 338: Topographies of Commemoration," *JHS* 128 (2008), pp. 172–191

MacLeod, R. (ed.), *The Library of Alexandria. Centre of Learning in the Ancient World* (London: 2000)

Mallios, G., "*Μύθος και ιστορία. Η περίπτωση της αρχαίας Μακεδονίας*," PhD Thesis (Thessaloniki: 2011)

March, D., "The Kings of Makedon: 399-369 B.C," *Historia* 44 (1995), pp. 257–282

Markle, M.M., "Support of Athenian Intellectuals for Philip: A Study of Isocrates' *Philippus* and Speusippus' *Letter to Philip*," *JHS* 96 (1976), pp. 80–99

Mari, M., "Le Olympie macedoni di Dion tra Archelao e l' èta romana," *RIFC* 126 (1998), pp. 137–169

Mari, M., *Al di là dell'Olimpo. Macedoni e grandi santuari della Grecia dall'età arcaica al primo ellenismo* (Athens: 2002)

Mari, M., "The Ruler Cult in Macedonia," *Studi Ellenistici* 20 (2008), pp. 219–268

Mari, M., "Traditional Cults and Beliefs," in R.J. Lane Fox (ed.), *Brill's Companion to Ancient Macedon* (Leiden: 2011a), pp. 453–465

Mari, M., "Archaic and Early Classical Macedonia," in R.J. Lane Fox (ed.), *Brill's Companion to Ancient Macedon* (Leiden: 2011b), pp. 79–92

Marsden, E.W., *The Campaign of Gaugamela* (Liverpool: 1964)

Marsden, E.W., "Macedonian Military Machinery and its Designers under Philip and Alexander," *Ancient Macedonia* 2 (Institute for Balkan Studies, Thessaloniki: 1977), pp. 211–223

Martinez, J-L., N. Mathleux, and M. Tonkova (eds.), *L'épopée des rois thraces: Des Guerres Médiques Aux Invasions Celtes 479–278 Avant J. C.* (Paris: 2015)

Masson, O., "Quelques noms macédoniens dans le traité IG 1^2 71 = IG I^3 89," *ZPE* 123 (1998), pp. 117–120

Matarese, C., "Proskynesis and the Gesture of the Kiss at Alexander's Court: The Creation of a New Elite," *Palamedes* 8 (2013), pp. 75–85

Matthews, R., *Alexander at the Battle of the Granicus: A Campaign in Context* (Stroud: 2008)

Mattingly, H.B., "The Methone Decrees," CQ^2 11 (1961), pp. 154–165

Mattingly, H.B., "Athenian Finance in the Peloponnesian War," *BCH* 92 (1968), pp. 450–485
Meeus, A., "The Power Struggle of the Diadochoi in Babylonia, 323 BC," *Anc. Society* 38 (2008), pp. 39–82
Meeus, A., "Alexander's Image in the Age of the Successors," in W. Heckel and L. Tritle (eds.), *Alexander the Great: A New History* (Malden: 2009), pp. 235–250
Meiggs, R., *The Athenian Empire* (Oxford: 1972)
Meiggs, R., *Trees and Timber in the Ancient Mediterranean World* (Oxford: 1982)
Meritt, B.D., "Archelaos and the Decelean War," in *Classical Studies Presented to Edward Capps on his Seventieth Birthday* (Princeton: 1936), pp. 246–252
Merker, I.L., "The Ancient Kingdom of Paionia," *Balkan Studies* 6 (1965), pp. 35–54
Mihailov, G., "Sitalcès et la Macédoine, Athènes et la Guerre du Peloponnèse: Histoire et Poésie," *Ancient Macedonia* 2 (Institute for Balkan Studies, Thessaloniki 1977), pp. 237–250
Mihajlovic, V.D., "Tracing Ethnicity Backwards: The Case of the 'Central Balkan Tribes,'" in C.N. Popa and S. Stoddart (eds.), *Fingerprinting the Iron Age. Approaches to Identity in the European Iron Age. Integrating South-Eastern Europe into the Debate* (Oxford: 2014), pp. 97–107
Mikalson, J., *Ancient Greek Religion* (Oxford 2005)
Mikrogiannakês, E., "*Archélaos*," *Ancient Macedonia* 7 (Institute for Balkan Studies, Thessaloniki: 2007), pp. 221–227
Miller, M.C.J., "The Macedonian Pretender Pausanias and His Coinage," *Anc. World* 13 (1968), pp. 23–27
Miller, M.C. J., "The 'Porus' Decadrachm of Alexander and the Founding of Bucephala," *Anc. World* 25 (1994), pp. 109–120
Miller, S.G., "The Philippeion and Macedonian Hellenistic Architecture," *Athenische Mitteilungen* 88 (1973), pp. 189–218
Millett, P., "The Political Economy of Macedonia," in J. Roisman and Ian Worthington (eds.), *A Companion to Ancient Macedonia* (Malden: 2010), pp. 472–504
Milns, R.D., "The Army of Alexander the Great," in E. Badian (ed.), *Alexandre le Grand. Image et réalité* (Geneva 1976), pp. 87–136
Mirón Pérez, D., "Transmitters and Representatives of Power: Royal Women in Ancient Macedonia," *Ancient Society* 30 (2000), pp. 35–52
Mladenovska-Ristovska, K., "The Macedonian King Caranos: Among the Myth, History and Tradition," *Glasnik* 1 (2017), pp. 29–40
Molinero, C.G., "Los tres mitos fundacionales de la monarquía Macedonia," in J. García, J. Marin, J. Vidal, and V. Gallar (eds), *Un paseo por la historia antigua* (Murcia: 2024), pp. 93–116
Moloney, E.P., "The Paradox of Allegiances: Alexander I of Macedon and Persian Power," *Hermathena* 204/205 (2018), pp. 137–208
Momigliano, A., *Filippo il Macedone* (Florence: 1934)
Montgomery, H., "The Economic Revolution of Philip II - Myth or Reality," *SO* 60 (1985), pp. 37–47
Moretti, L., *Olympionikai. i vincitori negli antichi agoni olimpici* (Rome: 1957)
Morison, W., Theopompus *BNJ* 115 (Leiden)
Morrison, G., "Alexander, Combat Psychology, and Persepolis," *Antichthon* 35 (2001), pp. 30–44
Mortensen, C., "The Career of Bardylis," *Anc. World* 22 (1991), pp. 49–59
Mortensen, K., "Eurydice: Demonic or Devoted Mother?," *AHB* 6 (1992), pp. 156–171
Mortensen, K., "Harmony or Hatred? The Inter-Relationship of Philip's Wives," *Ancient Macedonia* 6 (Institute for Balkan Studies, Thessaloniki: 1999), pp. 797–805
Mosley, D.J., "Crossing Greek Frontiers Under Arms," *RIDA* 20 (1973), pp. 161–169
Müller, S., "Philip II," in J. Roisman and Ian Worthington (eds.), *A Companion to Ancient Macedonia* (Malden: 2010), pp. 166–185

Müller, S., "The Career of Hephaestion – A Reassessment," in T. Howe and F. Pownall (eds.), *Power, Kingship and Memory in Ancient Mediterranean History: A Study in Method and Context* (Swansea: 2015), pp. 77–102

Müller, S., *Die Argeaden. Geschichte Makedoniens bis zum Zeitalter Alexanders des Grossen* (Paderborn: 2016)

Müller, S., "The Symbolic Capital of the Argeads," in S. Müller, T. Howe, H. Bowden, and R. Rollinger (eds.), *The History of the Argeads: New Perspectives* (Wiesbaden: 2017a), pp. 183–198

Müller, S., *Perdikkas II—Retter Makedoniens* (Berlin: 2017b)

Müller, S., "Hephaestion – A Reassessment of his Career," in T. Howe and F. Pownall (eds.), *Ancient Macedonians in the Greek and Roman Sources. From History to Historiography* (Swansea: 2018), pp. 77–102

Müller, S., T. Howe, H. Bowden, and R. Rollinger (eds.), *The History of the Argeads: New Perspectives* (Wiesbaden: 2017)

Murison, C.L., "Darius III and the Battle of Issus," *Historia* 21 (1972), pp. 399–423

Murray, O., "Hellenistic Royal Symposia," in P. Bilde, T. Engberg-Pedersen, L. Hannestad, and J. Zahle (eds.), *Aspects of Hellenistic Kingship* (Aarhus: 1996), pp. 1–21

Musgrave, J.H., R.A.H Neave, and A.J.N.W. Prag, "The Skull from Tomb II at Vergina: King Philip II of Macedon," *JHS* 104 (1984), pp. 60–78

Narain, A.K., "Alexander and India," *G&R*^{2} 12 (1965), pp. 155–165

Natoli, A.F., *The Letter of Speusippus to Philip II* (Stuttgart 2004)

Nawotka, K., "Freedom of Greek Cities in Asia Minor in the Age of Alexander the Great," *Klio* 85 (2003), pp. 15–41

Nawotka, K., *Alexander the Great* (Newcastle: 2010)

Németh, G., *Kritias und die Dreißig Tyrannen: Untersuchungen zur Politik und Prosopographie der Führungselite in Athen 404/403 v.Chr.* (Stuttgart: 2006)

Noguera Borel, A., "L'evolution de la Phalange Macédonienne: Le Cas de la Sarisse," *Ancient Macedonia* 6 (Thessaloniki 1999), pp. 839–850

Noguera Borel, A., "L'armée macédonienne avant Philippi II," *Ancient Macedonia* 7 (Institute for Balkan Studies, Thessaloniki 2007), pp. 97–111

Nylander, C., "Darius III – The Coward King. Point and Counterpoint," in J. Carlsen (ed.), *Alexander the Great. Reality and Myth* (Rome: 1993), pp. 145–159

Oikonomedes, A.N., "The Epigram on the Tomb of Olympias at Pydna," *Anc. World* 5 (1982), pp. 9–16

Oikonomides, A.N., "A New Inscription from Vergina and Eurydice the Mother of Philip II," *Anc.* World 7 (1983), pp. 62–64

Oikonomides, A., "The Decree of the Athenian Orator Hyperides honoring the Macedonians Iolaos and Medios," *Praktika B'* (Athens: 1987), pp. 169–182

Olbrycht, M.J., "Curtius Rufus, the Macedonian Mutiny at Opis and Alexander's Iranian Policy," in J. Pigon (ed.), *The Children of Herodotus* (Newcastle: 2008), pp. 231–252

Olbrycht, M.J., "Macedonia and Persia," in J. Roisman and Ian Worthington (eds.), *A Companion to Ancient Macedonia* (Malden: 2010), pp. 342–369

Ogden, D., *Polygamy, Prostitues and Death: The Hellenistic Dynasties* (London: 1999)

Ogden, D., *Alexander the Great. Myth, Genesis and Sexuality* (Exeter: 2011)

Ogden, D. (ed.), *The Cambridge Companion to Alexander the Great* (Cambridge: 2024)

Pafford, I., "Amyntas son of Perdikkas, King of the Macedonians, at the Sanctuary of Trophonius, Lebadeia," *Anc. World* 42 (2011), pp. 211–222

Palagia, O., "Hellenistic Art," in R. Lane Fox (ed.), *Brill's Companion to Ancient Macedon* (Leiden: 2011), pp. 477–493

Palagia, O., "The Argeads: Archaeological Evidence," in S. Müller, T. Howe, H. Bowden, and R. Rollinger (eds.), *The History of the Argeads: New Perspectives* (Wiesbaden: 2017), pp. 151–161

Paliadeli, C., "The Alexander Mosaic and its Lost Original. A Working Hypothesis," in G. Adornato, E. Falaschi, and A. Poggio eds.), *Περί γραφικής. Pittori, techniche, trattati, contesti. Tra testimonianze e ricezione* (Milan: 2019), pp. 151–172

Pandermalis, D., *Dion, The Archaeological Site and Museum* (Athens: 1997)

Papastravrou, I., *Makedonikê politikê katà tòn 5on p.Ch. aiôna. Aléxandros I. Teûchos Aon.* (Thessaloniki: 1936)

Papastavrou, I., "The Foreign Policy of Perdiccas II," *Hellenika* 15 (1957), pp. 256–265

Papazoglou, F., "Les origines et la destinée de l'état illyrien: Illyrii Proprie Dicti," *Historia* 14 (1965), pp. 143–179

Papazoglou, F., *The Central Balkan Tribes in Pre-Roman Times*, trans. M. Stansfield-Popovic (Amsterdam: 1978)

Papazoglou, F., *Villes de Macédoine à l'époque romaine* (Paris: 1988)

Parke, H.W. and J. Boardman, "The Struggle for the Tripod and the First Sacred War," *JHS* 77 (1957), pp. 276–282

Parker, V., "Sparta, Amyntas, and the Olynthians in 383 B.C.," *RhM* 146 (2003), pp. 113–137

Paspalas, S.A., "Classical Art," in R.J. Lane Fox (ed.), *Brill's Companion to Ancient Macedon* (Leiden: 2011), pp. 179–207

Perlman, S., "Greek Diplomatic Tradition and the Corinthian League of Philip of Macedon," *Historia* 34 (1985), pp. 153–174

Perlman, S., "Fourth Century Treaties and the League of Corinth of Philip of Macedon," *Ancient Macedonia* 4 (Institute for Balkan Studies, Thessaloniki: 1986), pp. 437–442

Petsas, P., *Pella, Alexander the Great's Capital* (Thessaloniki: 1978)

Picard, O., "Mines, Monnaies et Impérialisme: Conflits autour du Pangee (478-413 av. J. -C)," in A.M. Guimier-Sorbets, M.B. Hatzopoulos, and Y. Morizot (eds.), *Rois, Cités, Nécropoles. Institutions, Rites et Monuments en Macédoine* (Athens: 2006), pp. 269–283

Pjakowski, W., "Einige Bemerkungen zur Lokalisierung der persischen Provinz (Satrapie) Skudra," *Eos* 71 (1983), pp. 243–255

Poulios, V., "Macedonian Coinage from the 6th Century to 148 BC," in J. Vokotopoulou (ed.), *Greek Civilization: Macedonia, Kingdom of Alexander the Great* (Athens: 1993), pp. 83–103

Pownall, F., "The Role of Greek Literature at the Argead Court," in S. Müller, T. Howe, H. Bowden, and R. Rollinger (eds.), *The History of the Argeads: New Perspectives* (Wiesbaden: 2017), pp. 215–229

Prag, A.J.N.W., "Reconstructing the Skull of Philip of Macedon," in E.C. Danien (ed.), *The World of Philip and Alexander* (Philadelphia: 1990a), pp. 17–37

Prag, A.J.N.W., "Reconstructing King Philip II: The 'Nice' Version," *AJA* 94 (1990b), pp. 237–247

Prestianni Giallombardo, A.M. and E. Tripodi, "Iconografia monetale e ideologia reale macedone: il tipo del cavaliere sulle emissioni di Alessandro I e di Filippo II," *REA* 98 (1996), pp. 311–355

Price, M.J., *Coins of the Macedonians* (London 1974)

Price, M., "The Coinage of Philip II," *NC* 139 (1979), pp. 230–241

Psoma, S., "Monnaies de poids réduit d'Alexandre I et de Perdiccas II de Macédoine," *ZPE* 128 (1999), pp. 273–282

Psoma, S., *Olynthe et les Chalcidiens de Thrace: études de numismatique et d'histoire* (Stuttgart: 2001)

Psoma, S., "Thucydide I.61.4: Béroia, la nouvelle localisation de Bréa et les *Potidaeatika*," *REG* 122 (2009), pp. 263–280

Psoma, S., "The Kingdom of Macedonia and the Chalcidic League," in R. Lane Fox (ed.), *Brill's Companion to Ancient Macedon* (Leiden: 2011), pp. 113–135

Rahe, P.A., "The Annihilation of the Sacred Band at Chaeronea," *AJA* 85 (1981), pp. 84–87

Rathmann, M., *Perdikkas zwischen 322 und 320: Nachlassverwalter des Alexanderreiches oder Autokrat*? (Vienna: 2005)

Raymond, D., *Macedonian Regal Coinage to 413 B.C.* (New York: 1953)

Rawlings, L., *The Ancient Greeks at War* (Manchester: 2007)

Reames-Zimmerman, J., "An Atypical Affair? Alexander the Great, Hephaistion Amyntoros and the Nature of their Relationship," *AHB* 13 (1999), pp. 81–96

Renard, M. and J. Servais, "A propos du mariage d'Alexandre et de Roxane," *L'Ant. Class.* 24 (1955), pp. 29–50

Riginos, A.S., "The Wounding of Philip II of Macedon: Fact and Fabrication," *JHS* 114 (1994), pp. 103–119

Robertson, N., "The Thessalian Expedition of 480 B.C.," *JHS* 96 (1976), pp. 100–120

Robinson, C.A., *The History of Alexander the Great* 1 (Providence: 1953)

Roebuck, C., "The Settlement of Philip II with the Greek States in 338 B.C.," *CP* 43 (1948), pp. 73–92

Roesch, P., "Un décret inédit de la ligue Thébaine," *REG* 97 (1984), pp. 45–60

Roisman, J. (ed.), *Brill's Companion to Alexander the Great* (Leiden: 2003a)

Roisman, J., "Honor in Alexander's Campaign," in J. Roisman (ed.), *Brill's Companion to Alexander the Great* (Leiden: 2003b), pp. 279–321

Roisman, J., "Classical Macedonia to Perdiccas III," in J. Roisman and Ian Worthington (eds.), *A Companion to Ancient Macedonia* (Malden: 2010), pp. 145–165

Roisman, J., "Royal Power, Law and Justice in Ancient Macedonia," *AHB* 26 (2012a), pp. 131–148

Roisman, J., *Alexander's Veterans and the Early Wars of the Successors* (Austin: 2012b)

Roisman, J. and Ian Worthington (eds.), *A Companion to Ancient Macedonia* (Malden: 2010)

Roller, L.E., "The Legend of Midas," *Class. Antiquity* 2 (1983), pp. 299–313

Roller, L.E., "Midas and the Gordian Knot," *Class. Antiquity* 3 (1984), pp. 256–271

Romane, P., "Alexander's Siege of Tyre," *Anc. World* 16 (1987), pp. 79–90

Romane, P., "Alexander's Siege of Gaza," *Anc. World* 18 (1988), pp. 21–30

Roos, P., "Alexander I in Olympia," *Eranos* 83 (1985), pp. 162–168

Rosen, K., "Die Gründung der makedonischen Herrschaft," *Chiron* 8 (1978), pp. 1–27

Rosen, K., "Alexander I., Herodot und die makedonische Basileia," in W. Will and J. Heinrichs (eds.), *Zu Alexander d. Gr., Festschrift G. Wirth* (Hakkert 1987), pp. 25–51

Rosenberg, A., "Amyntas, der Vater Philipps II," *Hermes* 51 (1916), pp. 499–509

Rtveladze, E.V., "Alessandro in Battriana e Sogdiana," *Parthica* 9 (2007), pp. 153–204

Rubinsohn, W.Z., "The 'Philotas Affair' – A Reconsideration," *Ancient Macedonia* 2 (Institute for Balkan Studies, Thessaloniki: 1977), pp. 409–420

Ruffing, K., "The Macedonian Economy under the Argeads," in S. Müller, T. Howe, H. Bowden, and R. Rollinger (eds.), *The History of the Argeads: New Perspectives* (Wiesbaden: 2017), pp. 125–135

Rung, E., "The Language of the Achaemenid Imperial Diplomacy towards the Greeks: The Meaning of Earth and Water," *Klio* 97 (2015), pp. 503–515

Ruzicka, S., "The Pixodarus Affair Reconsidered Again," in E. Carney and D. Ogden (eds.), *Philip II and Alexander the Great: Lives and Afterlives* (New York: 2010), pp. 3–11

Ryder, T.T.B., *Koine Eirene* (Oxford: 1965)

Ryder, T.T.B., "The Diplomatic Skills of Philip II," in Ian Worthington (ed.), *Ventures into Greek History. Essays in Honour of N.G.L. Hammond* (Oxford: 1994), pp. 228–257

Ryder, T.T.B., "Demosthenes and Philip II," in Ian Worthington (ed.), *Demosthenes: Statesman and Orator* (London: 2000), pp. 45–89

Saatsoglou-Paliadeli, C., "In the Shadow of History: The Emergence of Archaeology," *BSA* 94 (1999), pp. 353–367

Saatsoglou-Paliadeli, C., "Queenly Appearances at Vergina-Aegae: Old and New Epigraphic and Literary Evidence," *Archäologischer Anzeiger* 3 (2000), pp. 392–403

Saatsoglou-Paliadeli, C., "Arts and Politics in the Macedonian Court before Alexander," *Ancient Macedonia* 7 (2007), pp. 345–356

Saatsoglou- Paliadeli, C., "The Arts at Vergina-Aegae, The Cradle of the Macedonian Kingdom," in R.J. Lane Fox (ed.), *Brill's Companion to Ancient Macedon* (Leiden: 2011), pp. 271–295

Salminen, E.M., *Age, Gender and Status in Macedonian Society,550–300 BCE: Intersectional Approaches to Mortuary Archaeology* (Edinburgh: 2023)

Sancisi-Weerdenburg, H., "Alexander and Persepolis," in J. Carlsen (ed.), *Alexander the Great. Reality and Myth* (Rome: 1993), pp. 177–188

San José Campos, C., "Alexander the Great in Persepolis," *Karanos* 4 (2021), pp. 13–33

Sarakinski, V. and S. Panovski, "*Αργεάδα από Τημένου*. The Temenidae/Argeadae Dichotomy Revisited," *Ziva Antika* 73 (2023), pp. 97–124

Saripanidi, V., "Constructing Continuities with a 'Heroic' Past: Death, Feasting and Political Ideology in the Archaic Macedonian Kingdom," in A. Tsingarida and I.S. Lemos (eds.), *Constructing Social Identities in Early Iron Age and Archaic Greece* (Brussels: 2017), pp. 73–135

Saripanidi, V., "Vases, Funerary Practices, and Political Power in the Macedonian Kingdom During the Classical Period Before the Rise of Philip II," *AJA* 123 (2019a), pp. 381–410

Saripanidi, V., "Macedonian Necropoleis in the Archaic Period: Shifting Practices and Emerging Identities," in H. Frielinghaus, J. Stroszeck, and P. Valavanis (eds.), *Griechische Nekropolen. Neue Forschungen und Funde* (Möhnesee: 2019b), pp. 185–191

Saripanidi, V., "Genre, statut social et pouvoir dans la Macédoine archaïque," in I. Algrain (ed.), *Archéologie du genre. Construction sociale des identités et culture matérielle* (Brussels: 2020), pp. 73–109

Sawada, N., "A Reconsideration of the Peace of Philocrates," *Kodai* 4 (1993), pp. 21–50

Sawada, N., "Athenian Politics in the Age of Alexander the Great: A Reconsideration of the Trial of Ctesiphon," *Chiron* 26 (1996), pp. 57–84

Sawada, N., "Macedonian Social Customs," in J. Roisman and Ian Worthington (eds.), *A Companion to Ancient Macedonia* (Malden: 2010), pp. 392–408

Sawada, N., 古代マケドニア王国史研究: フィリッポス二世のギリシア征服 (*The Ancient Macedonian Kingdom*) (Tokyo: 2022)

Scaife, R., "Alexander I in the *Histories* of Herodotus," *Hermes* 117 (1989), pp. 129–137

Schmitt, O., *Der Lamische Krieg* (Bonn: 1992)

Schmitthenner, W., "Über eine Formveränderung der Monarchie set Alexander d. Gr.," *Saeculum* 19 (1968), pp. 31–46

Schultz, P., "Leochares" Argead Portraits in the Philippeion," in P. Schultz and R. von den Hoff (eds.), *Early Hellenistic Portraiture: Image, Style, Context* (Cambridge: 2007), pp. 205–233

Scullion, S., "Euripides and Macedon, or the Silence of the *Frogs*," *CQ*² 53 (2003), pp. 389–400

Seibert, J., *Das Zeitalter der Diadochen* (Darmstadt: 1983)

Sears, M.A. and C. Willekes, "Alexander's Cavalry Charge at Chaeronea, 338 BCE," *Journal of Military History* 80 (2016), pp. 1017–1035

Seibert, J., *Alexander der Grosse* (Darmstadt: 1972)

Seibert, J., "Alexander der Grosse in Persepolis," *Iranistik* 364 (2004/05), pp. 5–105

Sekunda, N.V., "The Sarissa," *Acta Universitatis Lodziensis, Folia Archaeologica* 23 (2001) pp. 13–41

Sekunda, N.V., "The Macedonian Army," in J. Roisman and Ian Worthington (eds.), *A Companion to Ancient Macedonia* (Malden: 2010), pp. 446–471

Sekunda, N.V., *The Antigonid Army* (Gdansk: 2013)

Sekunda, N.V. and A. McBride, *The Army of Alexander the Great* (London 1984)

Sekunda, N.V. and J. Warry, *Alexander the Great: His Armies and Campaigns, 334–323 BC.* (Oxford: 1998)

Sekunda, N.V. and P. Dennis, *The Macedonian Army after Alexander 323–168 BC* (Oxford: 2012)

Shrimpton, G., "Theopompos' Treatment of Philip in the *Philippica*," *Phoenix* 31 (1977), pp. 123–144

Sickinger, J., *Marmor Parium*, *BNJ* 239 (Leiden)

Sidky, K., *The Greek Kingdom of Bactria* (Lanham: 2000)

Siganidou, M., "Urban Centres in Macedonia," in J. Vokotopoulou (ed.), *Greek Civilization: Macedonia, Kingdom of Alexander the Great* (Athens: 1993), pp. 29–31

Smart, J.D., "Kimon's capture of Eion," *JHS* 87 (1967), pp. 136–138

Sordi, M., *La Lega Thessala fino ad Alessandro* (Rome: 1958)

Sordi, M., "Larissa e la dinastia Alevade," *Aevum* 70 (1996), pp. 37–45

Speck, H., "Alexander at the Persian Gates: A Study in Historiography and Topography," *AJAH*² 1 (2002), pp. 15–23

Sprawski, S., *Jason of Pherae. A Study on History of Thessaly in Years 431–370 BC* (Krakow: 1999)

Sprawski, S., "Philip II and the Freedom of the Thessalians," *Electrum* 9 (2003), pp. 55–66

Sprawski, S., "Were Lycophron and Jason Tyrants of Pherae? Xenophon on the History of Thessaly," in C. Tuplin (ed.), *Xenophon and His World* (Stuttgart: 2004), pp. 437–452

Sprawski, S., "All the King's Men. Thessalians and Philip II's Designs on Greece," in D. Musial (ed.), *Society and Religions. Studies in Greek and Roman History* (Torun: 2005), pp. 31–49

Sprawski, S., "From the Bronze Age to Alexander I," in J. Roisman and Ian Worthington (eds.), *A Companion to Ancient Macedonia* (Malden: 2010), pp. 127–144

Sprawski, S., "When did Alexander I of Macedon get his cognomen 'Philhellene'?," *Przeglad Humanistyczny* 2 (2013), pp. 45–58

Sprawski, S. and T. Mojsik, Nicomedes, *BNJ* 2 no. 772 (Leiden)

Stewart, A., *Faces of Power. Alexander's Image and Hellenistic Politics* (Berkeley: 1993)

Stewart, A., "Tragedy and Tyranny: Euripides, Archelaus of Macedon and Popular Patronage," in S. Lewis (ed.), *Tyranny: New Contexts* (Besancon: 2021), pp. 81–101

Strauss, B.S., "Alexander: The Military Campaign," in J. Roisman (ed.), *Brill's Companion to Alexander the Great* (Leiden: 2003), pp. 133–156

Stronk, J., "Crossing the Straits: The Persians in Thrace," *Talanta* 30–31 (1998–1999), pp. 55–72

Stylianou, P.J., *A Historical Commentary on Diodorus Siculus Book 15* (Oxford: 1998)

Squillace, G., *Filippo il Macedone* (Bari: 2009)

Squillace, G., "Consensus Strategies under Philip and Alexander: The Revenge Theme," in E. Carney and D. Ogden (eds.), *Philip II and Alexander the Great: Lives and Afterlives* (New York: 2010), pp. 69–80

Squillace, S., "The Comparison between Alexander and Philip. Use and Metamorphosis of an Ideological Theme," in T. Howe, E.E. Garvan, and G. Wrightson (eds.), *Greece, Macedon and Persia: Studies in Social, Political and Military History in Honour of W. Heckel* (Haverton: 2015), pp. 107–113

Taceva, M., "On the Problems of the Coinage of Alexander I, Sparadokos and the So-Called Thracian-Macedonian Tribes," *Historia* 41 (1992), pp. 58–74

Tarn, W.W., "Heracles, Son of Barsine," *JHS* 41 (1921), pp. 18–28

Tarn, W.W. and G.T. Griffith, *Hellenistic Civilisation*³ (London: 1952)

Taylor, R., *The Macedonian Phalanx: Equipment, Organization and Tactics from Philip and Alexander to the Roman Conquest* (Barnsley: 2020)

Thomas, C.G., *Alexander the Great in his World* (Malden: 2006)

Thomas, C.G., "The Physical Kingdom," in J. Roisman and Ian Worthington (eds.), *A Companion to Ancient Macedonia* (Malden: 2010), pp. 65–80

Tiverios, M., "*Κάρανος, ο γενάρχης της μακεδονικής βασιλικής δυναστίας. Η νομισματική μαρτυρία*," *Archaeologike Ephemeris* 158 (2019), pp. 195–212

Tomlinson, R.A., "Ancient Macedonian Symposia," *Ancient Macedonia* 1 (Institute for Balkan Studies, Thessaloniki: 1970), pp. 308–315

Touratsoglou, J., "Art in the Hellenistic Period," in M.B. Sakellariou (ed.), *Macedonia, 4000 Years of Greek History and Civilization* (Athens: 1983), pp. 170–191

Touratsoglou, I., "A la recherche du monnayage de bronze de Philippe II de Macédoine. Note préliminaire," *BSFN* 58 (2003), pp. 97–101

Townsend, R.F., "The Philippeion and Fourth-Century Athenian Architecture," in O. Palagia and S.V. Tracy (eds.), *The Macedonians in Athens, 322–229 BC* (Oxford 2003), pp. 93–101

Trevett, J., "Demosthenes and Thebes," *Historia* 48 (1999), pp. 184–202

Tripodi, B., "Sulla morte di Alessandro I di Macedonia," *AnnPisa* 14 (1984), pp. 1263–1268

Tripodi, B., "Aminta I, Alessandro I e gli hyparchoi in Erodoto," *Ancient Macedonia* 7 (Institute for Balkan Studies, Thessaloniki: 2007), pp. 67–85

Tritle, L., "Alexander and the Killing of Cleitus the Black," in W. Heckel and L. Tritle (eds.), *Crossroads of History, The Age of Alexander* (Claremont: 2003), pp. 127–146

Tritle, L., *A New History of the Peloponnesian War* (Westport: 2004)

Tritle, L., "Alexander and the Greeks. Artists and Soldiers, Friends and Enemies," in W. Heckel and L. Tritle (eds.), *Alexander the Great: A New History* (Malden: 2009), pp. 121–140

Tronson, A.D., "Satyrus the Peripatetic and the Marriages of Philip II," *JHS* 104 (1984), pp. 116–126

Tsigarida, B., "Chalcidice," in R.J. Lane Fox (ed.), *Brill's Companion to Ancient Macedon* (Leiden: 2011), pp. 137–158

Tsimboukides, D., *Philip II the Macedonian* (Athens: 1985)

Vacanta, S., "Alexander the Great and the 'Defeat' of the Sogdianian Revolt," *AHB* 26 (2012), pp. 87–130

Vanderspoel, J., "Provincia Macedonia" in J. Roisman and Ian Worthington (eds.), *A Companion to Ancient Macedonia* (Malden: 2010), pp. 251–275

Vanderspoel, J., "Rome's Apparent Disinterest in Macedonia 168-148 BCE," in T. Howe, E.E. Garvin, and G. Wrightson (eds.), *Greece, Macedon, and Persia. Studies in Social, Political, and Military History in Honour of Waldemar Heckel* (Philadelphia: 2015), pp. 198–206

Van Wees, H. (ed.), *War and Violence in Ancient Greece* (Swansea: 2000)

Van Wees, H., *Greek Warfare: Myths and Realities* (London: 2004)

Vasilev, M.I., "Thucydides II.99 and the Early Expansion of the Argeadae," *Eirene* 47 (2011a), pp. 93–105

Vasilev, M.I., "The Military-Political Campaign of Sitalces against Perdiccas II and the Chalcidians (431-429 BC)," *Ziva Antika* 61 (2011b), pp. 15–38

Vasilev, M.I., "Herodotus VIII.137-139 and the Foundation of Argead Macedonia," *Ziva Antika* 62 (2012), pp. 37–47

Vasilev, M.I., *The Policy of Darius and Xerxes Towards Thrace and Macedonia* (Leiden: 2015)

Vasilev, M.I., "The Date of Herodotus' Visit to Macedonia," *Ancient West and East* 15 (2016), pp. 31–51

Vassileva, M., "King Midas and the Early History of Macedonia," *Ancient Macedonia* 7 (Institute for Balkan Studies, Thessaloniki: 2007), pp. 773–779

Vlassopoulos, K., *Greeks and Barbarians* (Cambridge: 2013)

Vogt, J., "Kleomenes von Naukratis – Herr von Aegypten," *Chiron* 1 (1971), pp. 153–157

Voller, P., "*IG* i^3 89 and the Argead Family Tree," *Klio* 107 (2025), pp. 94–125

Voutiras, E., "Le culte de Zeus en Macédoine avant la conquête romaine," in A.M. Guimier-Sorbets, M.B. Hatzopoulos, and Y. Morizot (eds.), *Rois, Cités, Nécropoles. Institutions, Rites et Monuments en Macédoine* (Athens: 2006), pp. 333–346

Voutiras, E. and K. Sismanides, "Dikaiopolitôn Summachia. Mia Nea Epigraphê Apo Tê Dikaia Apoikia Tês Eretrias," *Ancient Macedonia* 7 (Institute for Balkan Studies, Thessaloniki: 2007), pp. 253–274

Wace, A.J.B. and M.S. Thompson, "A Latin Inscription from Perrhaebia," BSA 17 (1910–1911), pp. 193–204

Walbank, M.B., *Athenian Proxenies of the Fifth Century BC* (Toronto: 1978)

Walbank, F.W., *Philip V of Macedon* (Cambridge: 1940)

Wallace, M.B., "Early Greek 'Proxenoi'," *Phoenix* 24 (1970), pp. 189–208

Wartenberg, U., "A Small Group of Tetradrachms of Alexander I of Macedon (CH 9.9)," *Coin Hoards* 9 (2002), pp. 85–86

Waterfield, R., *Dividing the Spoils. The War for Alexander the Great's Empire* (Oxford: 2011)

Waterfield, R., *Taken at the Flood: The Roman Conquest of Greece* (New York: 2014)

Waterfield, R., *A Time of Transition: Antigonus Gonatas and the Greeks* (Chicago: 2020)

Waters, M., *Ancient Persia. A Concise History of the Achaemenid Empire, 550–330 BCE* (Cambridge: 2014)

Weber, G., "The Court of Alexander the Great as Social System," in W. Heckel and L. Tritle (eds.), *Alexander the Great: A New History* (Malden: 2009), pp. 83–98

Werner, O., *Pindar: Siegesgesänge und Fragmente* (Munich: 1967)

West, A.B., *The History of the Chalcidic League* (Madison: 1918)

Westlake, H.D., *Thessaly in the Fourth Century B.C.* (repr. Chicago: 1993)

Wheatley, P and C. Dunn, *Demetrius the Besieger* (New York: 2020)

Wiesehöfer, J., "The Persian Impact on Macedonia: Three Case Studs," in S. Müller, T. Howe, H. Bowden, and R. Rollinger (eds.), *The History of the Argeads: New Perspectives* (Wiesbaden: 2017), pp. 57–64

Wilkes, J., *The Illyrians* (Oxford: 1995)

Will, W., *Die Perserkriege* (Munich: 2010)

Williams, M.F., Anaximenes, *BNJ* 74 (Leiden)

Wirth, G., "Alexander zwischen Gaugamela und Persepolis," *Historia* 20 (1971), pp. 617–632

Wirth, G., "Vermutungen zum frühen Alexander (I-II)," in G. Wirth (ed.), *Studien zur Alexandergeschichte* (Darmstadt: 1985a), pp. 168–203

Wirth, G., *Philipp II* (Stuttgart: 1985b)

Wirth, G., *Der Brand von Persepolis. Folgerungen zur Geschichte Alexanders des Grossen* (Amsterdam: 1993)

Worthington, Ian, "The Date of the Tegea decree (Tod ii 202): A Response to the *Diagramma* of Alexander III or of Polyperchon?," *AHB* 7 (1993), pp. 59–64

Worthington, Ian, "The Harpalus Affair and the Greek Response to the Macedonian Hegemony," in Ian Worthington (ed.), *Ventures Into Greek History. Essays in Honour of N.G.L. Hammond* (Oxford 1994), pp. 307–330

Worthington, Ian, "Alexander the Great and the 'Interests of Historical Accuracy': A Reply," *AHB* 13 (1999), pp. 136–140

Worthington, Ian (ed.), *Demosthenes: Statesman and Orator* (London: 2000)

Worthington, Ian, "Alexander, Philip, and the Macedonian Background," in J. Roisman (ed.), *Brill's Companion to Alexander the Great* (Leiden: 2003a), pp. 69–98

Worthington, Ian, "Alexander's Destruction of Thebes," in W. Heckel and L.A. Tritle (eds.), *Crossroads of History. The Age of Alexander the Great* (Claremont: 2003b), pp. 65–86

Worthington, Ian, *Philip II of Macedonia* (New Haven: 2008a)

Worthington, Ian, "*IG* ii^2 236 and Philip's Common Peace of 337," in L.G. Mitchell (ed.), *Greek Epigraphy and History: Essays in Honour of P J. Rhodes* (Swansea: 2008b), pp. 213–223

Worthington, Ian, "Worldwide Empire vs Glorious Enterprise: Diodorus and Justin on Philip II and Alexander the Great," in E. Carney and D. Ogden (eds.), *Philip II and Alexander the Great: Lives and Afterlives* (New York: 2010a), pp. 165–174

Worthington, Ian, "Alexander the Great, Nation-building, and the Creation and Maintenance of Empire," in V.D. Hanson (ed.), *Makers of Ancient Strategy: From the Persian Wars to the Fall of Rome* (Princeton: 2010b), pp. 118–137

Worthington, Ian (ed.), *Alexander the Great: A Reader*^{2} (London: 2011)

Worthington, Ian, *Demosthenes of Athens and the Fall of Classical Greece* (New York: 2013)

Worthington, Ian, *By the Spear. Philip II, Alexander the Great, and the Rise and Fall of the Macedonian Empire* (New York: 2014a)

Worthington, Ian, "From East to West: Alexander and the Exiles Decree," in E. Baynham and P. Wheatley (eds.), *East and West in the World of Alexander: Essays in Honour of A.B. Bosworth* (Oxford: 2014b), pp. 93–106

Worthington, Ian, *Ptolemy I: King and Pharaoh of Egypt* (New York: 2016)

Worthington, Ian, "Campaigns of Alexander the Great, 336-323 BC," in H. Sidebottom and M. Whitby (eds.), *Blackwell Encyclopaedia of Ancient Battles* (Malden: 2017), pp. 1–71

Worthington, Ian, *Athens after Empire: A History from Alexander the Great to the Emperor Hadrian* (New York: 2021)

Worthington, Ian, "Dinarchus, the 'Recent' and the 'Very Recent' Past: Lessons from Aeschines, Demosthenes and Lycurgus?," in A. Kapellos (ed.), *The Orators and Their Treatment of the Recent Past* (Berlin: 2022a), pp. 431–445

Worthington, Ian, "Why Arrian Favoured Ptolemy in the Preface of his *Anabasis*: A Simple Solution," in R. Rollinger and J. Degen (eds.), *Contextualizing Arrian: The World of Alexander in Perspective* (Wiesbaden: 2022b), pp. 231–241

Worthington, Ian, *The Last Kings of Macedonia and the Triumph of Rome* (New York: 2023)

Wüst, F.R., *Philipp II von Makedonien und Griechenland in den Jahren 346 bis 339* (Munich: 1938)

Xanthakis-Karamanos, G., "The *Archelaus* of Euripides: Reconstruction and Motifs," in D. Rosenbloom and J. Davidson (eds.), *Greek Drama IV: Texts, Contexts, Performances* (Oxford: 2012), pp. 108–126

Xydopoulos, I.K., *Κοινωνικές και πολιτιστικές σχέσεις των Μακεδόνων και των άλλων Ελλήνων* (Thessaloniki: 2006)

Xydopoulos, I.K., "Upper Macedonia," in M. Tiverios, P. Nigdelis, and P. Adam-Veleni (eds.), *Threpteria. Studies on Ancient Macedonia* (Thessaloniki: 2012a), pp. 520–539

Xydopoulos, I.K., "Anthemus and Hippias: The Policy of Amyntas I," *ICS* 37 (2012b), pp. 21–37

Xydopoulos, I.K., "*Τα ανατολικά σύνορα της Μακεδονίας επί Αλεξάνδρου Α*," in M. Giannopoulou and C. Kallini (eds.), *Ηχάδιν ΙΙ. Τιμητικός τόμος για τη Στέλλα Δρούγου* (Athens: 2016), pp. 246–264

Yeon, Jae-hoon, "Korean Dialects: A General Survey," in N. Tranter (ed.), *The Languages of Japan and Korea* (London: 2012), pp. 168–185

Zahrnt, M., *Olynth und die Chalkidier. Untersuchungen zur Staatenbildung auf der Chalkidischen Halbinsel im 5. und 4. Jahrhundert v. Chr.* (Munich: 1971)

Zahrnt, M., "Die Entwicklung des makedonischen Reiches bis zu den Perserkriegen," *Chiron* 14 (1984), pp. 325–368

Zahrnt, M., "Der Mardonioszug des Jahres 492 v.Chr. und seine historische Einordnung," *Chiron* 22 (1992), pp. 237–279

Zahrnt, M., "Alexanders Übergang über den Hellespont," *Chiron* 26 (1996), pp. 129–147

Zahrnt, M., "Versöhnen oder Spalten? Überlegungen zu Alexanders Verbanntendekret," *Hermes* 131 (2003), pp. 407–432

Zahrnt, M., "Macedonia and Thrace in Thucydides," in A. Rengakos and A. Tsakmakis (eds.), *Brill's Companion to Thucydides* (Leiden: 2006a), pp. 589–614

Zahrnt, M., "Amyntas III: Fall und Aufstieg eines Makedonenkönigs," *Hermes* 134 (2006b), pp. 127–141

Zahrnt, M., "Amyntas III. und die griechischen Mächte," *Ancient Macedonia* 7 (Institute for Balkan Studies, Thessaloniki: 2007), pp. 239–251

Zahrnt, M., "The Macedonian Background," in W. Heckel and L. Tritle (eds.), *Alexander the Great: A New History* (Malden: 2009), pp. 7–25

Zahrnt, M., "Herodot und die Makedonenkönige," in R. Rollinger, B. Truschnegg, and R. Bichler (eds.), *Herodot und das Persische Weltreich* (Wiesbaden: 2011), pp. 761–777

Zambrini, A., "The Historians of Alexander the Great," in J. Marincola (ed.), *A Companion to Greek and Roman Historiography* (Malden: 2007), pp. 193–202

Index